# RICHARD T. GRIFFITHS

# CONFIGURING THE WORLD

A CRITICAL POLITICAL ECONOMY APPROACH

ISBN: 978-9-4924-3900-0 (sc)
ISBN: 978-9-4924-3901-7 (e)

Library of Congress Control Number: 2016905229

Publisher information:
Name: HIPE Publications
Address:
PO Box 1075
2302 BB Leiden
The Netherlands
Legal Name: HIPE Publications
Registered with Netherlands Chamber of Commerce reg. nr. 64752461

Because of the dynamic nature of the Internet, any web addresses or links contained in
this book may have changed since publication and may no longer be valid. The views
expressed in this work are solely those of the author and do not necessarily reflect the
views of the publisher, and the publisher hereby disclaims any responsibility for them.

Lulu Publishing Services rev. date: 04/15/2016

# Contents

# List of Figures

# Abbreviations

BBC: British Broadcasting Corporation

BEA: Bureau of Economic Analysis

CIA: Central Intelligence Agency (USA)

Cif: Carriage, insurance and freight

CNN: Cable News Network (USA)

CPB: Central Planning Bureau (Netherlands)

DAC: Development Aid Committee (OECD)

ECLAC: UN Economic Commission for Latin America and the Caribbean

ECSC: European Coal and Steel Community

EEC: European Economic Community

ERT: European Round Table

ESA: European System of Accounts (EU)

EU: European Union

EVI: Economic Vulnerability Index

FDI: Foreign Direct Investment

Fob: Free-on-board

FRBNY: Federal Reserve Bank of New York

FSI: Failed State Index (since 2014 Fragile State Index)

GATT: General Agreement on Tariffs and Trade

GDP: Gross Domestic Product

GII: Gender Inequality Index

GNI: Gross National Income

HDI; Human Development Index

HIV: Human Immunodeficiency Virus

IBRD: International Bank for Reconstruction and Development

ICP: International Comparisons Project

IMF: International Monetary Fund

IPE: International Political Economy

IR: International Relations

ITO: International Trade Organisation

KOF: Konjunkturforschungsstelle of the Eidgenössische Technische Hochschule, Zürich

OECD: Organisation for Economic Cooperation and Development

ONS: Office of National Statistics (UK)

OPEC: Organization of the Petroleum Exporting Countries

NGO: Non-governmental Organisation

NGO: Non-governmental Organisation

MNC: Multinational corporations

MPI: Multidimensional Poverty Index

NI: National Income

PAC: Political Action Committee (USA)

PPP: Purchasing Power Parities

PWT: Penn World Tables

R&D: Research and Development

SIDS: Small island developing states

SME: Small and Medium Sized Enterprise

SNA: System of National Accounts (UN)

UAE: United Arab Emirates

UN: United Nations

UNCTAD: United Nations Committee for Trade and Development

UNDP: United Nations Development Program

UNICEF: United Nations International Children's Emergency Fund

USA: United States of America

WBI: World Bank Institute

WGI: World Bank Governance Indicator

WTO: World Trade Organization

WVS: World Values Survey

# Preface

This is a book I am proud to have written even though it was not the one that I had initially set out to write. Let me explain. I am an economic historian, which means that I try to explain the drivers of economic change and the causes and consequences of economic policies. I love data but working with the past data made me ever aware that data is fragmentary and often untrustworthy. For many areas of economics data does not exist at all, partly because the concepts themselves did not exist, and historians are left attempting to reconstruct data from other sources. Nowadays reliable data for population, national income, employment, inflation and trade all seem to be a mouse-click away. Economic historians could work for weeks to produce just one such number for a single year. Not only that, but social scientists have constructed numbers for such topics as trust, democracy and governance. And when these data were linked together with refined statistical techniques, scholars turned out a veritable cornucopia of scientific research. When starting to write this book I felt as though I had belatedly been invited to join the feast. This is where it all started to go wrong.

Perhaps because of my training, or perhaps because it took so much sweat and effort to produce the data, I started to look at what the numbers represented. Historical numbers are recognised as approximations surrounded by qualifications and used with due caution. Modern numbers were collected, collated and hearded into databases and processed by statistical formulae without many questions raised about their accuracy. Some social scientists would agonise about their own constructs, but then throw them together with others that they hardly worry about at all, even though they too may have been published with cautionary labels. Data is not homogeneous. It varies in quality according to when it was produced and the care and attention devoted to its production. This means that it is not always suited to comparisons over time (which are implicit when explaining differences in rates of growth or the nature of change) and over space (which are implicit explanations dependeing upon differences in wealth or relative size). Thus a large part of the book's focus is on deconstructing the information upon which much of our view of the world is based. Only by examining what lies behind the fancy-sounding labels attatched to data categories can we judge the veracity of claims made upon the basis of their analysis. In an increasingly complex and interdependent society, it is the duty of an informed citizenship to know when the wool is being pulled over their eyes.

This book is a tool-box that allows you to take apart the world as you know it, examine its component parts and then to reassemble it in a more meaningful form. In other words, it allows you to configure the world. It introduces you to differences between countries, regions and continents and it encourages you to explore the underlying data that purported to represent, and ultimately to explain, those differences. The elements that have been chosen all lie at the intersection between politics and economics, or between states and markets. They all have profound societal consequences.

Figure 0.1: Support Structure for Configuring the World

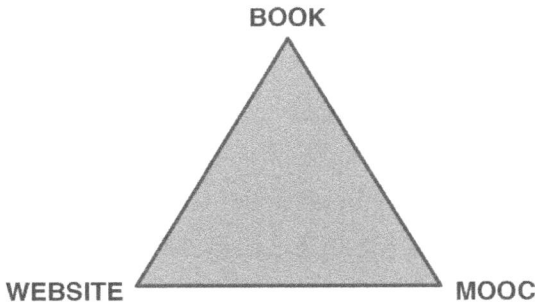

BOOK

WEBSITE          MOOC

The book does not stand alone. While I was writing it, I was also teaching a MOOC of the same title. A MOOC is a 'massive, open online course' offered by a renowned university and participation is free to anyone who wants to join. In the first year in which we ran the course some 27,000 people watched one or more of the video lectures. The MOOC has now been redesigned and the book covers the materials for the first two courses: 'Comparative Political Economy' and the 'Political Economy of Globalisation'. There will be a third course 'The Political Economy of Finite Resources' and, for those who complete all three courses there is an opportunity to engage in a 'capstone' project, where they write a more extended piece of their own research. The MOOC platform does not only support the lectures, it also allows me to offer commentary on and visualisations of some of the maps. In addition there is a forum where participants can ask questions and discuss topics of interest as well as a portal to electronic publications and access to the databases employed in the course. The MOOC run on the platform offered by Coursera (https://www.coursera.org/).

The book is also supported by its own website. This will provide more detailed commentary on individual indices, as well as any changes that have taken place in their construction. It will also offer an opportunity for educators to exchange experiences on how to employ the book in classroom settings. The site is located at http://www.configuringtheworld.com

If there is a motto to this book it lies in a paraphrase of something (wrongly) attributed to Albert Einstein. Not everything that counts can be counted and not everything that can be counted counts. For those for whom English is not their native language this means that not everything that is important can be expressed as numbers and that not all numbers are necessarily important. I hope that you enjoy the book.

There are several people I must thank in the creation of this work. First, I would like to thank all the students in the BA International Studies at Leiden University for acting as guinea pigs as we developed the course upon which the book is based and to the thousands of students in Coursera who in 2014/15 followed this course as a MOOC (Massive Open Online Course). I must also thank Dr. Jeff Fynn-Paul with whom I have shared the teaching of the Leiden course these past few years. A particular thanks also goes to Grace Atkinson who conconstructed the original databases and to Juan Leandro Costa who constructed the website. In addition I would like to thank the team from Worldmapper who made the beautiful morphed maps that you will find in this volume. Finally I owe a special word of thanks to Einat Shitrit who has been my teaching assistant throughout the various runs of the Configuring the World MOOC and Clémence Overeem who has been responsible for making of the maps employed in this volume.

# Introduction

This textbook aims to provide a critical guide to key concepts and perspectives that are widely used in academic analysis to make sense of the world economy. It also analyses within a comparative international framework the differences in the world distribution of growth and prosperity and the various explanations offered at the intersection between economics and politics. It asks questions about the changes in the structure of the world economy, about the policies recommended or adopted to deal with these changes, and the power balances that lie behind the system. In this respect it resembles the aims and ambitions of many books in the field of International Political Economy (IPE) or development studies. Where it differs from most of these is in its rigorous scrutiny of the data and methods employed by social scientists to demonstrate the relationships between economics, politics and society. All too often the data used in statistical exercises is simply not sufficiently accurate to justify any conclusions based on them. Statistical data is not a homogeneous commodity. Its quality varies according to the time and place of its creation, and the ambition of its creator. Were the consequences confined to arcane academic debates among scholars this might all have been of little consequence. However, the pseudo-sophistication of these exercises and the pseudo-exactness of their conclusions have served to underpin our understanding of the world and determine the policies adopted to control it. Understanding how this all occurs is the first step in reclaiming our world and wresting back control. An informed citizenship stands at the centre of our democracy and our individual responsibility should not be abandoned because the information is difficult to find, or packaged in a mass of impenetrable statistical jargon. Appreciating the nature of the data explaining our world should be the first step in reconfiguring it. This is where the book breaks new ground.

The book covers the main fields of an (international) political economy textbook but in a less formal way. It surveys the main arguments and causal relationships proposed in the field, and it critically examines the use of quantification to establish these. That is the small 'c' in the title. Academics are often critical of their own self-constructed indices, but blissfully indifferent to glaring flaws in the other series they employ. This is especially true when key questions of global wealth and poverty are involved. This book therefore critically reviews many of the main datasets underpinning IPE analysis whilst not denying (some of) the underlying logic.

The first chapter explains the intentions behind the book's title before tracing the development of IPE as a discipline and as a subject for investigation. The two are not the same and this has contributed to the emergence of an exciting area for investigation, but one where the researchers, bound in their own self-defined (sub-)disciplinary approaches, scarcely engage each other in debate. The chapter then moves to discuss the nature of statistical data and the quantification of socio-political phenomena that economists and social scientists begin to create as 'facts'. The chapter ends with a review of basic statistical analyses and the problems in drawing conclusions from these.

There follow three chapters that configure some of the main dimensions in wealth and poverty that exist in the world (see Figure 0.2). They examine population because it is a basic determinant of the world's needs and resources and they examine national income because that is the standard expression of the size and distribution of the world's output. When national income is divided by population we obtain measures of per capita output, which are often used as indicators of the relative wealth and poverty of states. Some critics argue that converting output at nominal values does not properly reflect the lives of citizens and they adjust national income figures to compensate for differences in the prices of goods people consume. Still others contend that using average per capita data fails to capture the full extent of poverty. The World Bank responds to this by using a per capita income threshold to identify the numbers of poor. The United Nations Development Programme, however, argues that national income figures alone cannot adequately capture the phenomenon of poverty. It has constructed a new measure that also incorporates indicators for health and education. In defining the Millennium Development Goals (and their successor, the Sustainable Development Goals) the United Nations has employed a variety of indicators but treated them separately. These measures all determine the way we configure wealth and poverty in the world and how we use this data when trying to explain the differences that have arisen and still persist. The chapters compare these indicators across states and over time. If any of these measures do not capture reality, it must undermine the confidence we place in any explanation that rests on the numerical values they express, regardless of the empirical techniques employed. The explanation may still be valid, but the statistical underpinning will not.

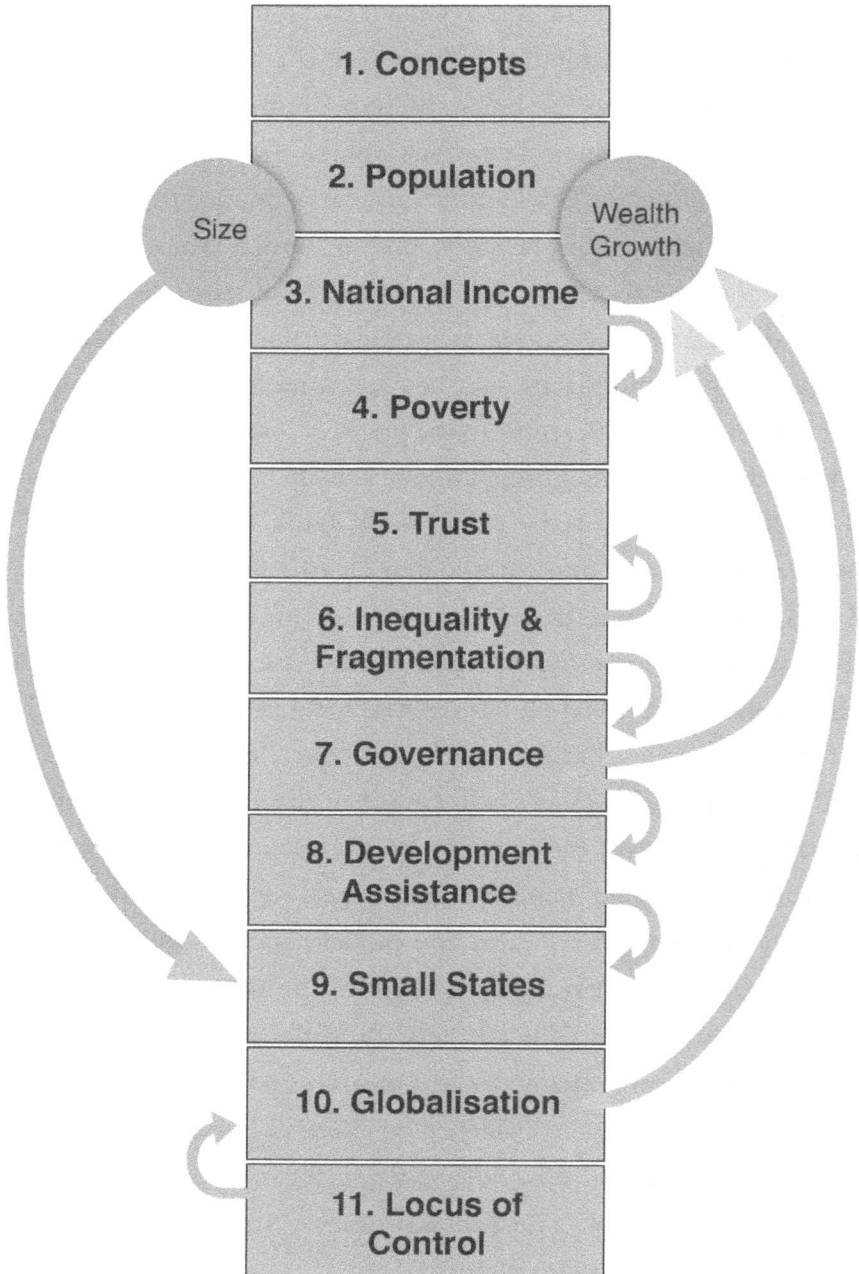

Figure 0.2: Outline of the Book

1. Concepts

2. Population

Size

Wealth Growth

3. National Income

4. Poverty

5. Trust

6. Inequality & Fragmentation

7. Governance

8. Development Assistance

9. Small States

10. Globalisation

11. Locus of Control

Chapter two looks at the growth of population over the past century, the shifts in its distribution and the dynamics of population change. It introduces population pyramids to view the impact of population change in creating challenges to which societies try to adjust and it assesses the accuracy of national population counts. If these are inaccurate, then so is everything expressed in per capita terms. The chapter ends with a case study on China's one-child policy. It employs population pyramids to demonstrate the impact on the country's demographic structure and the challenge it poses for the future.

Chapter three explains the different stages in calculating national income and the dynamics of economic growth. It looks at the balance of economic power, compared with the balance in terms of population size. It also explores some of the sources of error in compiling national statistics and the massive changes produced by so-called 'rebasing exercises' and definitional changes. Finally, it examines the attempts to correct national income statistics to take account of differences in living costs, and the errors that have influenced the results. It shows the problems of compiling reliable national income statistics by using Nigeria as a case study. In 2014 this country almost doubled its national income overnight as a result of 'redoing' the national accounts – a record, for now.

Chapter four looks critically at various attempts to measure poverty among poor nations, whether by establishing a monetary benchmark, as advocated by the World Bank, by constructing composite indices, such as the Human Development Index constructed by the UN's Development Programme, or by adopting a dash-board method, as had been done for the UN's Millennium Development Goals. The chapter also examines the definition and measurement of poverty in the richer countries in the West. The case study on Nepal looks behind the composite development indices. The case study shows that reducing complex phenomena to a single number does nothing to help identify problems, let alone find solutions. It looks at the experience of Nepal and the remarkable reduction it achieved in maternal mortality rates.

Chapter five examines the concept of 'trust'. This is the first of three chapters examining the interrelationship between trust, societal fragmentation, governance and economic prosperity and growth. Chapter five itself introduces the explanations why different levels of trust exist between societies and it examines the difficulties in measuring the concept, whether by experiments or opinion surveys. It then proceeds to explore the (causal) links between trust and inequality and fragmentation in society and between trust and governance. The case study looks at the institutionalisation of trust-building measures in The Netherlands and explores how, and to what extent, the consensual nature of governance contributed to resolving the country's economic difficulties in the early 1980s.

Chapter six deals with the inequality and fragmentation that exist in societies. It starts by examining the analysis of income and wealth inequality made by the famous economist Thomas Piketty before exploring more comprehensive analyses compiled by the OECD and the World Bank. It investigates the difficulties encountered in measuring societal fragmentation in terms of ethnicity, language and religion, let alone explaining its causal relationship to trust. The case study looks at a unique, locally-based study in the USA that seemed to establish a direct relationship between ethnicity (race) and the nature of trust in society.

Subsequently, chapter seven explores the origins of concerns with 'good governance' as a policy goal and examines the efforts of the World Bank to define its components and to measure them. It then looks at the casual links between good governance and economic growth. The case study examines the phenomenon of corruption in Latin America. It looks at the corruption scandal engulfing Petrobras in and also the effect of corruption on the day-to-day lives of the citizens.

Having examined the pattern of wealth and poverty and explored the mutual interrelationships implications of differences in trust, inequality, ethnic, linguistic and religious diversity and practices of governance, chapter eight then focuses on whether richer countries can help poorer countries to grow and lift them out of poverty. It starts by examining the engagement and strategies of the international community with development aid and the determinants of donor generosity. It then turns to the issue of aid effectiveness especially in conditionality and efforts to improve governance. It ends by looking at the question of state failure, and efforts to measure and predict it. The case study looks at the development of the micro-credit movement, which is often cited as of the few effective policies capable of lifting large swathes of villagers out of poverty. To test these claims, it returns to the birthplace of the movement in Bangladesh.

Chapter nine examines whether small states confront special development challenges. This is because the UN has defined 'small island developing states' and has suggested that their specific problems merit special attention. The chapter explores the various attempts to measure the vulnerability that accompanies size but it suggests that separating small developing states from the rest has helped create a culture of pessimism around their development potential. The case study explores the governance problems confronting small states by focusing on the history of two of the smallest (semi-)autonomous districts in the world – Pitcairn and Norfolk Island.

The final two chapters focus on globalisation. So much of the current literature describes the success of economic liberalisation and its challenge to effective government, or even the need for it, that we cannot leave the analysis of wealth and poverty without examining the phenomenon in greater depth. Chapter ten starts by looking at the globalisation debate before turning to the measurement of national exposure to the global economy. It looks at the factors behind the increased openness of trade, investment and financial services before combining the most recent estimates to gauge the size and nature of the global economy. Especially for international finance the results are quite spectacular, which poses challenges for the management of the global system. The case study explores the nature of the common and lucrative margin trading in the context of how one 'rogue trader' brought about the collapse of the oldest bank in Asia.

The final chapter asks who 'controls' the system. It starts by looking at the UN bodies established to manage global trade and finance and examines the theories whether they can manage or modify behaviour. It then asks whether cities are not becoming more autonomous and posing a challenge for both domestic and international control. The discussion then shifts to organised business, examines their lobby activities and their interlocking board and ownership structures. The chapter concludes by looking at (relative) power and organisation of transnational advocacy groups. The case study looks at the cosy nature of control of large financial institutions by US federal agencies employing the secret tape recordings of 'whistle-blower' employed by Goldman Sachs

# Chapter One

# Configuring the World

This chapter will begin by explaining what the book is about, starting with the title. It will explore the meanings behind the words 'configuring the world', and it will then untangle the subtitle. It will explain how the (sub-) discipline of *Political Economy* has evolved and where it stands today. This part of the chapter is very important because it will show that the various strands of scholarship that make up political economy are so narrowly focused that they act almost as if they are unaware of each other. The different 'schools' rarely engage each other in academic discourse. So, although there is a self-proclaimed branch of *Critical Political Economy*, there is very little critical Political Economy, with a lower-case 'c'. This book tries to bridge this gap, by examining some of the fundamental data employed by social scientists and by seeing whether the data can support the hypotheses and conclusions drawn from their use. Since the answer is that usually they cannot, an understanding of this section is important for appreciating the rest of the volume.

## Why this title?

The titles of most academic books tends to reflect their content, and this one is no exception. '*Configuring the World*' is a large claim. The word 'to configure' implies assembling components in such a way as to make a comprehensible whole. For example, an electrical engineer may take some components and arrange them on a circuit board to form part of a computer. On the other hand, many of those same components could be configured another way and the final result could have a different function. So, 'to configure' something implies to have a goal in mind. Alternatively, one could simply experiment with different components to see what the results might be before settling on the desired construction. The components could always be disassembled to see whether they can be configured in a more satisfactory way.

The problem is that a world already exists. It is a world which we can see and a world of which we, ourselves, are a part. Therefore, if we want to configure it, we first have to disassemble it into its component parts. Throughout this volume the world has been deconstructed into nation states, which constitute the main element of analysis. There are several reasons for this choice. The first reason is that, since the 19th century, nation states have increasingly concentrated upon themselves formal decision-making powers over the territories within the borders that define and delineate them. These powers are not absolute, and states have always been confronted by constraints to their effective exercise, but nonetheless the pretense still remains. The second reason is that states are a major source in the collection and compilation of data, especially of statistical data. They employ officials whose express task it is to count things. They have tax-and-spend functions that also generate statistics. Finally, they employ more officials to put all these numbers together on a monthly, quarterly or annual basis within a standardised format, often one that has been internationally agreed. The final reason is that many social scientists also use the state as the unit of their own analyses. They too construct data at a national level and use these for the purposes of international comparisons to test their hypotheses and, basically, to configure the world... but on a template that they have already created. That template lies at an intersection of the world commonly known as 'political economy', which forms the second part of the title '*a critical Political Economy approach*'.

## Why this Sub-title?

In 1975, in what would become one of the standard textbooks in the field, Robert Gilpin defined (International) Political Economy as "the reciprocal and dynamic interaction.... of the pursuit of wealth and the pursuit of power" (Gilpin 1975, 43). Possibly because it blurred the distinction between economics and politics he later amended the definition to "the field of study that analyzes the problems and questions that arise from the parallel existence and dynamic interaction of 'state' and 'markets'" (Gilpin 1987, 13). In many ways the original definition is preferable since it goes to the core of power, and it is power that defines the context, and the outcome, of many of the choices confronted in society. Whatever definition one chooses, Political Economy is not so much a social science discipline as a series of overlapping questions that lie at the intersection between economics, sociology and politics. We have shown this in Figure 1.1. Before progressing further, I want to show how ideas that were once seen as an interdependent whole developed into separate disciplines. These disciplines have each developed and cultivated their own distinct approaches and specialist vocabularies, and in the process they have lost any sense that they are all investigating different facets on one and the same problem.

The result is that they rarely engage in mutual discourse. One of the objects of this volume is to ignore these self-imposed restrictions and to reopen the field. If you want to reconfigure the world, therefore you also need to know how the view of the world became so framgmented in the first place. The following paragraphs, therefore, will trace the evolution of political economy from its roots in the eighteenth century to the present day.

Figure 1.1: The Geometry of Political Economy

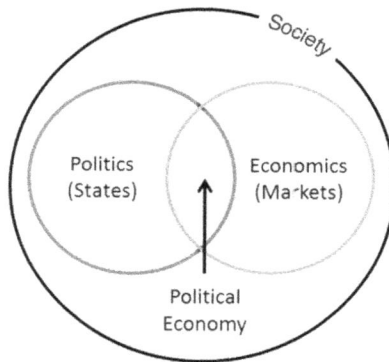

Source: Inspired by Balaam and Veseth 1996, 7.

The term 'political economy' was first coined in 1671 by an English administrator, William Petty. His task was to measure 'national wealth' in order to determine the levels of taxation the economy could sustain, and therefore the size of the military it could afford. If, however, we date the 'modern' approach to political economy from its earliest distinguished practitioner, someone whose ideas are still in common use today, the concept can probably be dated back to Adam Smith. His book, *The Wealth of Nations* (1776/2014) first articulated the idea of the 'division of labour', whereby allowing workers to concentrate on one task would increase productivity and, with it, the size of the country's output. More quoted today, however, is his demonstration that the pursuit of personal gain could also enhance the common good that laid the foundation of the faith in the self-regulating mechanisms of free market capitalism (Pettman, 1996, 10-11). Smith's economics were firmly anchored in a real world of societal choices and political mechanisms. It would never have occurred to him, or to the social scientists that followed him, to disentangle economy and society into separate areas of contemplation and analysis. The same holds true of Smith's counter-pole at the other end of the spectrum of political economy thought. This is formed by Karl Marx's publication *Das Kapital* (1867/2010) which contended that market capitalism was a device by which the capital-owning class maintained their exploitative power over the industrial working class. Indeed it was not until Alfred Marshall's *Principles of Economics* (1890/2009) that economics started to define itself as a discipline on its own, as something separate from politics. Marshall's work signaled the start of the increasing professionalisation of economics and its emergence as a separate (sub-) discipline. The developments after that can be followed in Figure 1.2, and its contents will be discussed in the following paragraphs.

Figure 1.2: Evolution towards a new 'critical' Political Economy

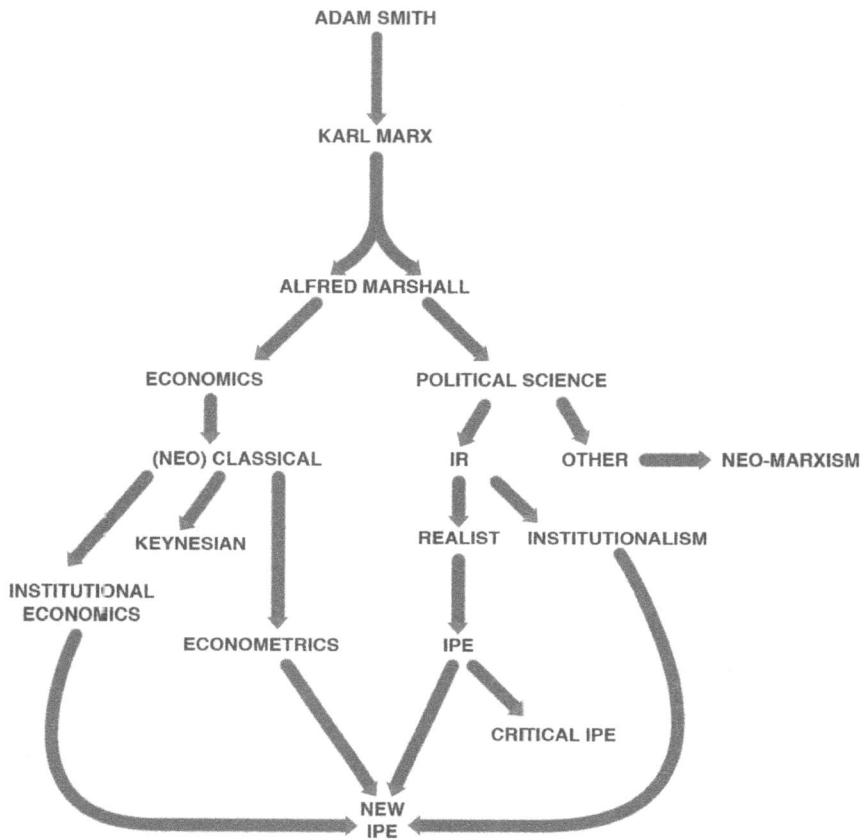

Let us begin by following first the evolution of the field of economics. Its major initial thrust was in the direction of what has become known as classical and neo-classical economics. These theories assumed that the economy is governed almost exclusively by markets and market forces. As a result, the state quickly lost its central position in economic analysis and became instead an economic actor; one among others – consumers, enterprises, government. At the core of the analysis was the assumption of a 'rational actor model', which held that all actors in the economy operated on the principles of perfect rationality, with enterprises aiming to maximise profits and consumers aiming at maximising satisfaction.

Economics experienced a major split in the 1930s when a supposedly self-regulating world economy refused to emerge by itself from the Great Depression but seemed to settle at a new, sub-optimal equilibrium. A group of economists, most noticeably John Maynard Keynes (1936/2013), argued that the government should intervene by increasing its own spending to compensate for the slump in demand. This new approach had several consequences. It brought the state, and its preferences, more centrally into economic analysis. It also led to the search for, and construction of, more tools for tracking economic progress, including measures of national accounts. Finally, it contributed to the construction of economic models and statistical techniques to assist economic forecasting. Although the early postwar experiments with economic modelling and forecasting had fallen short of original expectations, economists reverted to less ambitious model specifications and started employing simpler, neo-classical assumptions. This new field of research became known as *econometrics* (Louçã 2007). For example, throughout the 1960s economists had been using comparative international statistics to test assumptions on the relationship between growth, inflation and unemployment or to that between government deficits, the money supply and inflation. Econometrics also entered the field of economic history (where the field was defined as *cliometrics*) to question the contribution of the railways to economic growth in the 19th century (Fogel, 1964) or to explain the economic rationality of slavery in the USA before the Civil War (Fogel and Engerman, 1974).

There is one final divide within the field of economics that deserves mentioning and that was the reassertion that institutions, and the way that institutions were organised, mattered. These ideas had been around at the end of the 19th century but had never coalesced into a coherent body of thought. In 1937 Richard Coase launched what could be called the *new institutional economics*. He articulated the role that organisations could play in reducing costs and promoting economic activity. These ideas were further refined, largely in the context of American economic history, to provide an intellectual reconnection of politics with the rarified world of econometrics (North, 1989, 1990). We will leave the economics strand of developments at this juncture, at the beginning of the 1970s and turn our attention to the development of political science since the 1890s.

Political science, relieved now of the burden of contributing to (or even incorporating) economic analysis became a discipline in its own right, as too did sociology. The techniques of neglect were simple. 'Black-boxes', the name given to areas not requiring further investigation, began to accumulate wherever an unfamiliar field of knowledge threatened to intrude on some newly espoused theoretical purity. One area of study that made an early attempt to achieve academic autonomy was made by International Relations (IR). Relations between states were considered sufficiently important to be studied in their own right and IR was considered sufficiently different to evolve its own tools and perspectives for analysis. By the 1930s some British and American universities even established separate departments devoted to its study. It was at this stage that IR began its first(?) 'great debate' – the question mark has been included because there is some arguement whether there was a second 'great debate'; or whether it had been part of the first, and even whether the description 'debate' actually occurred; but that is political science for you. Basically, the debate involved the 'realists' who considered that states were motivated primarily by national interests and the 'institutionalists' who held onto the belief that international cooperation could modify state behaviour. Neither side disputed that the state was the central 'unitary actor' for analysis. The growing strength of militaristic dictatorships in the 1930s seemed to tilt the debate in favour of the 'realists' and to justify labelling those maintaining a faith in international organisations as mere 'idealists'.

Following the Second World War, the failure of the United Nations to deliver on its early promise and the start of the Cold War helped establish 'realism' as the dominant paradigm for much of the following decades (Quirk and Vigneswaran, 2005). By this time, the United States had become the only Western superpower. Realism became IR's dominant paradigm and American scholars became its chief interlocutors. 'American' themes, especially relating to security and the cold war, tended to dominate the academic agenda. One thing that characterised US scholarship, as opposed to that being developed in Europe, was an increasing theorisation of the discipline. IR was somewhat in awe of the status and prestige achieved by economics and sought to emulate its intellectual rigour, and later its empirical approach. The 'gate-keepers' of the main academic journals and the heads of the main university departments made sure that 'theory' remained entry-track into the academia. The result was endless recurring debates on theories, definitions, approaches and verifications. In parallel with this theorisation of the discipline, came an increasing need to make the discipline more 'scientific', in much the same way as economics had done (Waever, 1998). Throughout this period, IR remained attached to a state-centric approach that implied an 'objective' national interest. The effect was to isolate the discipline from all the other important cross-currents in political science. It removed any need to identify the domestic processes by which decisions emerged (if you are a realist, why bother and if you are interested, park it in another 'black box'). It also marginalised the role of non-state actors and international organisations (Milner, 1998: 767).

At the beginning of the 1970s international economic events imposed themselves on the discipline. The breakup of the Bretton Woods system (1971-73) and the first oil crisis (1972-73) brought the international economy to the forefront of analysis. American scholars, such as Robert Keohane and Joseph Nye penetrated the editorial Board of the established journal *'International Organization'* and turned it into the main outlet for the new genre. However, although American IPE publications had succeeded in shifting the focus of study away from traditional IR, they were still characterised by an excessive attachment to conceptualisation and theorisation. American IPE soon embraced the trend towards increasing quantification and statistical analysis already apparant in political science. In addition it moved beyond the traditional analysis that placed great importance on voter behavior, attitudinal surveys and census data (Murphy and Nelson, 2001). In the fight to establish IPE as a 'hard science', the reductionist theory and methodology employed by Economics became the standard for professionalism in American IPE circles (Cohen, 2007).

American IR influenced much of the work being conducted elsewhere in the World. Its concepts and theories were often simply transposed onto more local settings and contexts. However, European IR scholarship had always been more broadly based than that in the US. There were several reasons for this. First, European scholars had to confront their own colonial (and post-colonial) experience, and the decline in European power and influence. All these factors contributed to a more global analysis than the polarised, confrontational mind-map of American scholarship. The study of IR was also more deeply rooted in disciplines such as history, sociology and law (Cohen, 2007: 211-13). Moreover, Europe was the setting for many far-reaching efforts at international cooperation, which made the realist/institutionalist divide less logical as a framework for analysis. These efforts had resulted in the 1950s culminating in the creation of the European Coal and Steel Community (ECSC) and the European Economic Communities (EEC), although it is ironic that early theoretical work had been advanced by American scholars (Haas, 1958; Lindberg, 1963). Finally, the entire spectrum of political discourse in Western Europe was generally to the left of that in the USA (and still is). The existence of the welfare state and the attachment to Keynesian policies of demand management, both presumed a greater role for the state than in the United States. Moreover, with Europe finding itself literally in the middle of the super-power stand-off between the USA and Russia, there was a greater search for accommodation. In the 1960s this emerged as 'convergence theory'. This suggested that Western experiments with indicative planning and Communist experiments with market mechanisms implied that the two systems – capitalism and communism – were growing together. This was reinforced by the emergence of 'Eurocommunist' parties, committed to democracy and seemingly free from Moscow's influence. All of these influences, therefore, offered a wider range of concerns for social scientists in Europe to analyses and debate. But it was analysed in a 'softer' way, with more descriptive and normative approaches than the IR discipline being practiced in the USA.

Thus, when in the 1970s, the international monetary system began to collapse and the 'oil crises' signaled a shift in global economic power, political scientists in Europe reacted differently from their colleagues in the USA. The prime-mover in reestablishing IPE in Europe was the British scholar Susan Strange. She had already been working on a study on international economic relations when, in 1970, she pointed to the failure of IR scholarship to connect international economics. This failure, she argued, would ultimately destroy the relevance of IR as an academic discipline (Strange, 1970). She went on to create an IPE study group to bring interested scholars together. Since this conscious self-definition of IPE as a sub-discipline predates similar efforts in the USA, Strange could properly be credited with being its founder. However, from the start, this 'British school' of IPE was highly critical. It was skeptical over American leadership and American economic policy, with its accent on liberalisation, and it demanded a more fundamental analysis of the international system that US hegemony had bequeathed (Murphy and Nelson, 2001). Susan Strange, herself, also openly dismissive of the empiricism embodied in much American IPE analysis. But this was all 'critical' with a small 'c'.

The credit for creating Critical PE, with a capital 'C' lies with another British scholar Robert Cox. In an article published in 1981 he condemned those political scientists who analysed societal problems from 'within' the system, whilst ignoring the fact that the system itself might be the cause of the problems. The system in question, of course, was the exploitative capitalist system. Cox, therefore staked out a space for a neo-Marxist reply to the dominant liberal ideology (Cox, 1981), though this ideological position limited his influence on scholarship on both sides of the Atlantic (Ravenhill, 2007: 20-23).

The eclectic group of scholars that gathered under the banner of CPE now also embraced leftist thinkers, as well as swathe of emancipatory scholars, working to promote the causes of issues marginalised by the dominant IPE paradigm.

Let us take stock of where we are now. We have a self-defined 'American school' of IPE, wedded to solid theory and empirical verification, and a self-defined 'British school' that is not, but that claims to analyse at a more fundamental level. Incidentally, both 'schools' celebrated themselves with special journal editions in 2009 (the British in *International Political Economy* 14, 3, 2009 and the Americans in *Review of International Political Economy*, 16, 1, 2009). We also have a school of Critical Political Economy that embraces Marxist and other non-main stream approaches to the subject. Unfortunately these 'schools' rarely engage in scientific discourse other than to disparage each others' work. The Americans consider the British as descriptive and normative. The British consider the Americans pretentious and over-theorised. Both have adopted different methodologies and they publish mostly in different journals. Both are dismissive of Marxist and alternative approaches, basically because they know what will be said before reading it. It is no exaggeration to describe the situation as a dialogue of the deaf (Cohen, 2007).

But where, you may ask, are the economists? Their world, too, was altered by the collapse of the international monetary system and by subsequent events. They too have worked on alternative policy responses to recessions, on the causes of exchange rate volatility, on the nature of the debt and the causes of prosperity and the persistence of poverty. Increasingly, they are adopting and testing concepts framed by institutional economics as well as those long employed by political science Their work is central in the debates on the interconnection of trust governance and growth, which lie at the core of this volume. The sad answer is that they are ignored. They are not even seen as constituting part of the IPE genre (Cohen 2007, 205-6). To me it is quite frightening that a university researcher can pretend to survey the state of IPE by looking at only twelve journals, all of which specialise in international relations (Maliniak and Tierney, 2009) while ignoring publications in whole swathes of economic journals and working papers and monographs (McNamara, 2009). Today we stand at a stage where we have a field of interest (IPE) that poses essential questions of great societal importance, which is blessed by a rich variety of methodological approaches but whose practitioners are bounded within their self-imposed, self-restricting disciplinary fortresses. It is enough to make anyone critical!

At the core of Political Economy is a (not unreasonable) belief that economy and politics are inextricably interlinked. In the context of this book, we could formulate in two statements. First, economic growth and prosperity cannot be achieved or maintained in conditions of political anarchy. Second, stable and effective institutions are a necessary (but not sufficient) foundation for growth and prosperity. However, there is a second direct link between the two and that is that rich countries can afford good institutions and poor countries cannot. It is at this juncture, that political economy offers another layer of analysis, in terms of economic and political power. It asks what determines the distribution of resources and rewards in a society, and how this impacts institutional quality. It looks at whether institutions simply reflect power balances in society or whether institutions can modify behaviour in groups and classes. It can move a level deeper still, and ask the extent to which the present day performance simply reflects current realities or whether it still (even partly) bears the imprint of the past. This is often referred to by social scientists as 'path dependency', but basically it ascribes an important role in explanations of current reality to history and culture. These relationships are shown in Figure 1.3.

Figure 1.3: The World of Political Economy

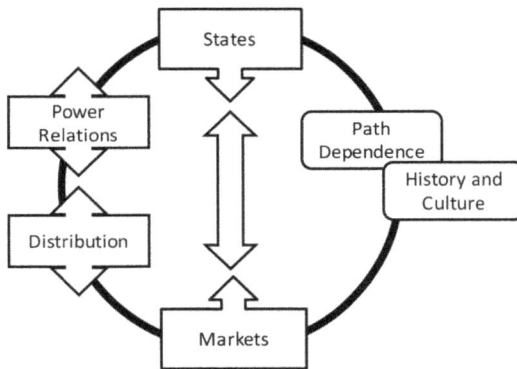

Source: Inspired by Strange, 1998.

## Data: how and when to use it

For much of the world's history we have very few accurate comparative statistics. To fill the gap economic hsitorians have laboured long and hard to reconstruct national income accounts from fractured and fragmentary pieces of evidence ranging from trade and shipping data, land and harvest information to early tax and inheritance records. All of their results, however, come with a warning of wide margins of error. That error margin does not disappear when these national statistics are unified under an equally fallible common price and currency label. One interesting study showed how difficult it was to compare British and French growth in the 19th expressing each country's national income statistics in their own prices and that of the other (O'Brien and Keyder, 1978). The pioneer in historical national accounting was the former OECD economist and later professor of Economic History at Groningen University, Angus Maddison. His early work tracked back centuries of national accounts all expressed in contemporary '1990 US dollars', adjusted for inflation (Maddison, 1995). Rather more speculatively he took the figures further back to the year 1000AD and even to 1AD. It was a mistake. What he had done was to assume a minimum per capita figure in current dollars and adjust it by whether a region was considered advanced or not. By then multiplying these figures by the (dubious) population estimates, he was able to calculate world gross domestic product (GDP) at $105.4 billion (at current 1990 prices) (Maddison, 2001). The Maddison project, which continues his work, now only ventures a GDP estimate for the entire world in 1820, 1870 and 1913 and then the rest of the twentieth century, all still expressed in 'real 1990 ppp dollars'. The project now explicitly highlights the degree of probable error contained in these estimates. It considers the most trustworthy to be the official statistics, made by national or international agencies, based on a common methodology. Next in terms of trustworthiness are the historical reconstructions, using the same methods and employing a wide range of data sources. After that come the reconstructions using indirect proxy variables. Finally there are guestimates, or conjectures, to cover the gaps between years where estimates exist. In this explanation, the project team suggests that the first category statistics are always reliable, but they acknowledge and that weak 'official' estimates (e.g from Africa) might be no better than those in the second category (Bolt and van Zanden, 2013: 3-4). In a more recent version they assess the data quality for different World regions, and they add a qualitative label to each data source, starting with 'high' for the official data. However they now omit the nuance about the fallibility of modern statistics, suggesting that all statistics published by official international bodies after 1950 are of the same high, and reliable, standard (van Zanden e.a., 2014: 29, 61-62). As will become evident in this book, this is simply not true[1].

At least the Maddison project warns its users about the quality of the data it presents. That is not often the case. So, when you see some clever visualisation taking you seamlessly through the centuries with a bubble chart, showing the relationship between per capita income and something like family size (with the bubble showing the size of the country) it is worth always remembering that the quality of data is not constant. This applies to almost anything that you can actually count – the number of people, boats, trains, workers and the unemployed. Matters deteriorate further when the objects of attention are expressed in terms of money and then converted to a common currency, possibly adjusted to take account of (differential) levels of inflation. This applies to things like earnings, prices, taxes and trade.

Let us now move onto the infinitely murkier terrain of 'composite indices'. These indices combine the different data-series together into one number (or index) in order to construct a new 'reality'. The results for different countries are usually lined up along-side each other to form a 'ranking', to judge which is doing better or worse. One classic example of a composite index is 'national income', of which GDP represents a part. National income combines calculations for incomes,

---

[1]  Curiously, the team breaches its own convention of automatically labelling official data as being of high standard by conceding that population data for some regions between 1950 and 1973 might not be of the same quality (Van Zanden, e.a., 2014, 40).

expenditures, imports, exports, investment and depreciation in order to determine the (annual) size of the economy. As we will see in Chapter Three, it was only in the 1930s that governments started doing this regularly, and it was only in the 1950s that it became general practice. Most people accept the construction of national accounts because it is useful to know how an economy is performing and because the composition makes sense. This does not necessarily hold true for other composite indices.

Composite indices purport to measure such matters as the state of human development, levels of democracy, the rule of law, different aspects of governance, degrees of corruption and so on. All of these indices will be examined critically later in this volume. There are many others including the ease of doing business, the competitiveness of an economy, the liveability of cities, and the fragility of states. In order to judge their usefulness we need to ask ourselves three questions. What is in these numbers? Are they likely to reflect reality? How are they being used?

A good starting point for assessing composite indices would be to ask whether the concept is one for which one would expect a single number if it were not on offer. Can a question as complex as democracy or the rule of law be condenced into a single number? The next question is whether the various components employed in the construction of the index combine to produce a credible answer. In other words, are they all indeed different aspects of the same phenomenon and do they constitute something approaching a rounded picture of the phenomenon being represented? If that condition is satisfied, as it was with the construction of national accounts, there is probably some value to be gained in combining them into a single number. If, on the other hand, the elements offer only a partial pricture or mix the context and the substance, it is worth questioning whether anything is gained by pulling them together, and whether the components could not better be grouped differently, or not at all.

The next step is to look at the components themselves, and ask what is there to measure or count. If it is some hard, quantifyable evidence, then simply establishing the accuracy of the source should be sufficient. All too often, however, the basis is provided by opinion surveys, expert panels or counting laws and procedures. At this point there are two further questions that need to be asked. The first question is whether the sources cover what they are supposed to cover. Many sub-indices are, in fact, proxies where some partial indicator is pressed into service to represent the whole phenomenon. The labelling of many (sub-)indices are prone to what can best be described as definitional slippage as the nuance exhibited by the authors in constructing the initial index is abandoned once they are used. The second question requires us to look at the proportions, or weights, assigned to each component in the final index and to decide whether the balance is satisfactory (Ravallion, 2010). These are all important issues, and we will be examining many composite indices against these criteria in the following chapters.

Once we have an index, it is necessary to establish whether it is accurate. Practically any index, and almost any component within it, contains what statisticians call a 'margin of error'. There are approved, tried-and tested methods for calculating such error margins. Unfortunately, very few sources publish information on these error margins, and even fewer 'headline' articles refer to it. One should always start by assuming that both the individual components of an index and the final index itself will contain error margins, and we need, therefore, to ask ourselves whether they are likely to be small or large (Høyland e.a., 2012). One also needs to ask whether the error is likely to be constant or whether it varies over time and space. One should not be fobbed off by statisticians who assert that there is a 'central tendency', meaning basically that errors tend to cancel each other out. A good rule-of-thumb is that the fewer resources a society can dedicate to collecting and collating information, the less accurate the results will probably be. Data for richer societies will also be better than for poorer, more recent data will be better than older data. Finally, data that has to be reconstructed for periods before the question was even asked, or before the concept was known, will be worst of all. Figure 1.4 provides a scheme against which statistical series can be tested and which suggest the care that should be taken in their use.

Figure 1.4: Five Questions to ask with Statistical Data

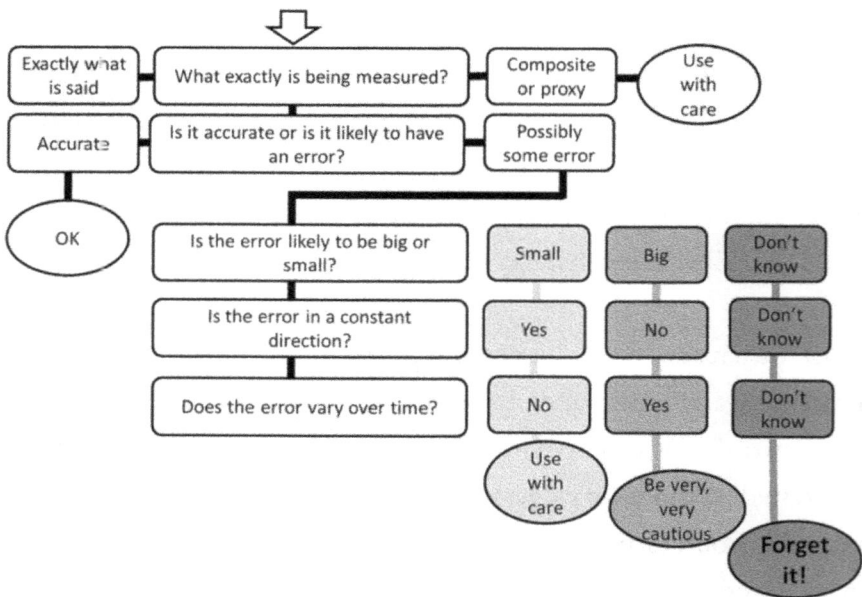

Now we come to the last set of questions. Who uses the data, and how? Many of the important measures we will be using throughout this volume are compiled either by governments, by powerful international bodies (often under the umbrella of the United Nations) or by academic and private think-tanks and institutes. Some of the data, such as national income figures, is indeed fed into the policy-making process, but is usually employed alongside other data. However, many other indices are too cluttered and too ambiguous to be of much use for assisting in indicating the direction of policy change. Despite all the effort of the World Bank Institute to construct 'governance indicators', or the UN Development Programme to construct 'development indices', one can rest assured that both organisations employ far more nuanced and specific data to help them make policy choices, and so too do national governments. These institutions are much more likely to use these indices as 'headline' numbers – designed to highlight policy issues and spotlight the good, the bad and the ugly. They help focus the public debate and garner legitimacy for action. After all, these indices are constructed by political (or politicised) agents and one should not be surprised that they are used for political purposes.

This brings us to our second main question – what is the cause and what is effect in the relationship between these constructed 'realities'? How does the world hang together? It is to address these issues that many social scientists, working either in academia or in the institutions responsible for producing the data in the first place, employ international rankings. For this purpose they use approved, tried-and-tested statistical techniques. The basis of most analysis lies in what is called correlation and regression. At a basic level, correlation plots two variables on a graph (usually a scatter diagram) and determines the statistical 'closeness' of the results to each other. In a regression analysis one decides which is the caual variable and which is the result and calculates a 'best fit' line through the observations. Having done this, it is possible to determine the probablility that the relationship is statistically 'significant' and the degree of confidence one can have in the result. In fact, it is not necessary to draw a graph at all and it is also possible to undertake the exercise with as many variables as one likes (in which case it is known as 'multivariate regression'). In this case one can imagine the graph as a three-dimensional space traversed by intersecting lines. These statistical exercises, therefore, should establish whether there is a statistical relationship between the variables, the reliability or trustworthiness of that relationship and, finally, its strength (does a change in one variable alter the other a lot or a little?). Note, by the way, that question of cause and effect is framed as a 'testable hypothesis' by the researcher. This leaves the reader to consider whether it is possible that the causation is the reverse of that suggested or even that the behaviour of one or both variables is influenced by a factor that has not been included in the exercise.

Correlation and regression analyses are usually employed to show inter-relationships between these indices and important issues of economic growth (the difference between recent national income data and older national income data) and of relative wealth and poverty. Most social scientists carefully follow these procedures, but not all. Therefore it is important to be alert.

There are established tests to determine the confidence that one can have in a statistical relationship. These tests rely on the closeness of the scatter of observations and their number, and they can tell the degree of confidence that one can have in the results. Most social scientists would fix this at 95 per cent or above, and they would report or highlight that outcome. Some, however, do not. They may show a graph with a line drawn through the scattered plotted results and make a statement to the effect that there is clearly a 'strong' relationship between the two variables. They may even skip this and tell you that the graph shows that X causes Y. They may even offer a calculation of the degree of the line (how much X changes when Y changes) but the one thing they do not tell you is whether it is statistically significant. While we are on the subject of testing, there is one other observation worth making. Many publications when reporting negative results draw the conclusion that the hypothesis should therefore be rejected. But this is not true. It only shows that that particular sample of data did not conclusively statistically support the hypothesis at the level chosen. One survey of the economics literature demonstrated that fully 20 per cent of the papers tested used the failure of the significance test as evidence to reject the hypothesis. In political science literature that error was even higher, between 40 and 50 per cent (Mayer, 2012: 273-4).

There is another problem that is almost the reverse of the one that we have been discussing. This concerns publications that do give the results of significance testing, but fail to indicate the degree of the relationship. Let us compare two cases. In one case a 20 percent change in X leads to a 20 per cent change in Y, every year and the significance is 99.9 per cent. In the second case a 20 per cent change in X leads to a 0.001 per cent change in Y, every year with the same significance level. The latter is also statistically significant, but not economically significant or significant for policy makers. It lacks what Deirde McCloskey, who has been tenaciously tracking this phenomenon for the last thirty years or more (McClosky, 1985), calls the 'policy oomph' factor. From an examination of articles published in the *American Economic Review*, she and her colleagues claimed that in the 1980s, 70 per cent of publications made no distinction between the two, a figure rising to almost 80 per cent in the 1990s (Ziliak and McCloskey, 2004. For criticism see Hoover and Siegler, 2008; Engsted, 2009). A survey of political science publications from the same period also suggests that many publications confuse statistical and substantive significance and place over much reliance on the mechanical application of confidence thresholds. It goes on to blame journals editors for demanding rigorous, empirical work and the fear of rejection if there are insufficient 'stars' in the Tables (Gill, 1999). The stars refer to the ★★ and ★★★ placed in Tables, usually near the end of the article, next to 95 and 99 percent confidence levels to 'help' the reader. A recent survey of sociology bemoaned the way that statistical significance testing had permeated the discipline, with little consideration of either the initial conditions or of interpreting the end results. It suggested that the consequence of misinterpreting the outcomes might even outweigh the benefits of using such procedures in the first place (Engman, 2013).

If we sum up the discussion in this section so far, we have looked at the problems involved in compiling quantitative data and the even larger problems involved in constructing composite indices. I have also suggested that many social scientists use statistics to demonstrate relationships, but fail to comment properly either on the reliability of the statistical relationship or the importance of that relationship. However, there is one last problem. All too often social scientists ignore the possibility that the inputs into their statistical models may themselves be seriously flawed or biased in the first place. They want to test their hypotheses and they grab the 'best available data'. If previous researchers have used it, so much the better. It is an illusion that the sophistication of an econometric model can compensate for unreliable evidence (Mayer, 2006).

# Chapter Two

# Population

The size and distribution of the World's population are important. Population size provides the base line of human beings requiring food and shelter and other basic needs. It also determines the human resources available for providing these necessities and more besides. Harnessed to the appropriate capital and technology, it offers the potential for (and the constraint on) the provision of even more goods and services. If we reverse the picture, it determines the level of consumer demand. The satisfaction of those needs also influences the rate at which the Earth's non-renewable resources are depleted. Moreover, population size determines the scale of government in individual states – the range of peoples and interests it has to satisfy, but also the human resources to do so.

However, population is not homogeneous. It varies according to both gender and age. Left to nature, the gender distribution at birth will tend to favour boys but by later life, it will have swung decisively in favour of women. The age distribution, however, varies, and that modifies both the productive capacity and the nature of consumption. The most productive segment of the population lies in the middle of the age distribution but even there not all the populations are economically active. This is because human reproduction and social custom restrict female participation, ill-health may render people unfit or unsuited for work and work opportunities may not be sufficiently available to satisfy demand. The very young require food, shelter, healthcare and schooling until ready to enter the labour market The very old do not need schooling, but the physical care and medical costs are disproportionally high. For societies with many young, the challenge is meeting their aspirations for work and the enhanced living standards that go with it. For ageing societies, the challenge is finding the human resources and the money for advanced healthcare. Migration can help solve both problems but often at the cost of societal friction for both the sending and the host society.

## Configuring the World's Population

If you have heard that the most reliable statistics that we have are those relating to population, then this story should make you change your mind. On 31st October 2011, the UN announced that the seven billionth citizen of this planet had been born. This is quite a feat because they announced this date six months in advance, and if you think about it for a moment, it was going to be even more difficult to specify exactly to whom that honour should fall. Many souls enter and leave the world during a day. No less than 250 babies are born every minute and those souls arriving on Earth pass the 105 that depart this life during that self-same sixty seconds. Nevertheless, on the appointed day, UN officials duly arrived at a Manila hospital with the gift of a pair of shoes and a chocolate cake. The local authorities were a little more forthcoming, promised the parents some cash to start up a shop. In the event, baby Danica May Camacho had been in such a hurry to be the seven billionth that she was actually born two minutes before midnight on the 30th (*Guardian*, 31.10.2011). The same day a children's rights group called Plan International announced that the seven billionth citizen had been born in Uttar Pradesh; a baby girl called Nigris. The organisation had favoured a girl in order to draw attention to the common practice of female infanticide in that part of India (*BBC News. South Asia* 31.10.2011). Not to be outdone, the newspaper Ottawa Citizen claimed the seven billionth citizen for their city – a baby boy named Caiden Lewis McCrindle. The father reflected "It's amazing. It really is. To think there are seven billion people in the world, and we have our mark in history is quite surreal" (*Ottawa Citizen*, 1.11.2011).

Meanwhile, a second UN delegation arrived in Kaliningrad to welcome Petya Nikolayev into the world as the seven billionth citizen. So pleased was the regional governor that he granted the family a plot of land on which to build a new house. For some reason, the Association of South African orange growers promised to send him seventy boxes of oranges, equivalent to one ton in weight (*South African Embassy in Moscow* News 13.12.2011). In the middle of the chaos, the UN Secretary-General Ban Ki-Moon admitted that the chosen baby, and even the pre-chosen date, were both meant to be symbolic. He confessed that he did not have a clue who the seven billionth citizen had been (*UN News Centre*, 31.10.2011). At the same time, the head of the population division of the UN's Department of Economic and Social Affairs, Hania Zlotnik, was delivering a decidedly downbeat welcoming speech. Her long discourse dwelt on the need for family planning, and she reflected that if every country had limited their number of children as well as Bangladesh had done, there would have been 22 per cent fewer children under fifteen years old in the world today (*UN DESA*, 31.10.2011) – presumably including Danica, Nigris, Caiden and Petya.

It is true that we cannot count the World's population with pin-point accuracy, but aside from data on surface area population statistics are probably the most reliable data we have, whether comparing current data across countries or tracking population numbers back in time. For recent history, the national statistics should be considered pretty accurate but this confidence should not extend to sub-national data. Broadly speaking, therefore, we can state that the World's population has grown since 1900 from approximately 1.6 billion to over 7 billion today. The pace of increase has been declining from an annual rate of over 2 per cent between 1960 and 1974 (when population grew from three billion to four billion) to slightly under 1.3 per cent in the current century (UN, DESA, Population Division database). Not only has the world's population been increasing, there have been major shifts in its geographical distribution. The best way to configure change is to employ what is known as a 'cartogram', whereby the size of countries are morphed to reflect their relative size (according to the indicator adopted) while retaining something approximating their shape.

Figure 2.1: World Map of Population 1900 and 2011

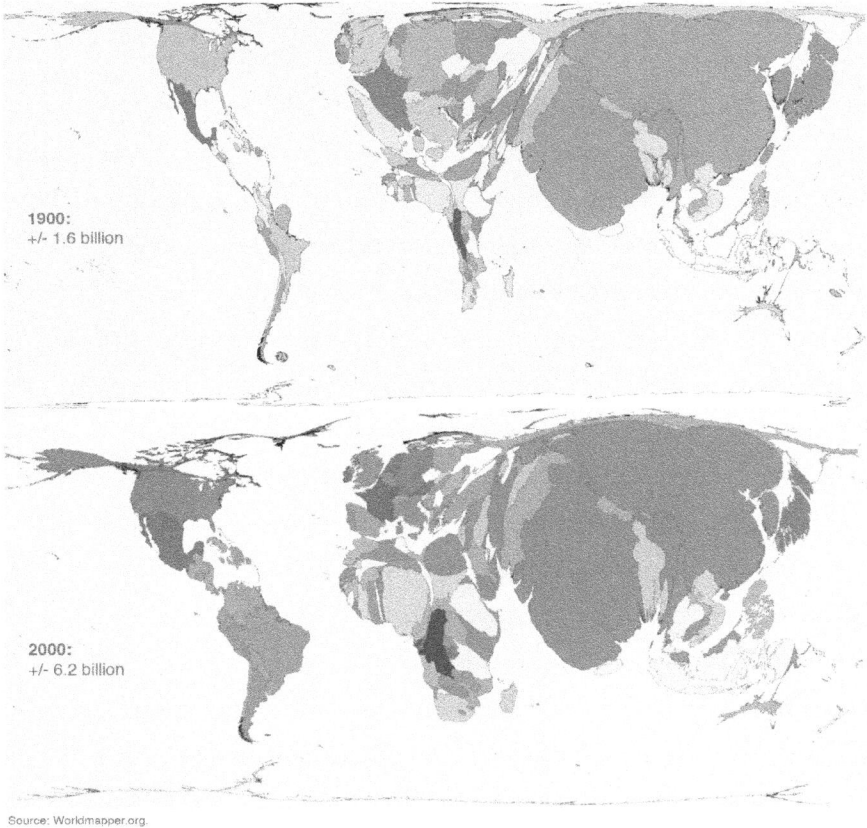

Figure 2.1 shows the distribution of the world population in 1900 and in 2011. The most obvious change over this period is the enormous shrinkage in the share of Europe in the world's total, and the contraction in Japan. By contrast both Africa and South America show considerable increases in their share of the world's population, as too do the countries of South East Asia and the Indian sub-continent. The drawback with the cartogram is that it is difficult to see the relative positions of individual countries; and states do matter. They do have specific functions. To start with, someone has

to do the counting and collate the results. As a result, many of our statistics come pre-wrapped, as it were, in a country-sized package. However, countries do more than simply deliver statistics – they provide the framework for law and regulation; they impose duties and confer rights on their citizens; they protect the borders and so on. In exercising all of these functions, population size actually matters. Larger populations may offer opportunities for a broader scale of activities, but they may also be more diffuse and are therefore more difficult to fit into a single set of regulations and more difficult to satisfy with a single package of policies. Smaller countries, on the other hand, may have difficulties in supplying labour for a wide range of activities and although they may be more homogenous, they may be vulnerable to 'state capture' and the absence of any countervailing power. Thus, countries do matter and so does the size and development of their populations.

If we move away from the visually strong (but amorphous) analysis by areas and turn to individual countries, the largest countries in 2011 by some considerable margin were China (1.4 billion) and India (1.3 billion). Next in order come the United States with 312 million, Indonesia with 245 million and Brazil with 201 million. There are six countries with a population between 100 and 200 million (in descending order Pakistan, Nigeria, Bangladesh, Russia, Japan and Mexico). There are fourteen countries with a population between 100 and 50 million and a further twenty-five between 50 and 25 million, and thirty-eight between 25 and 10 million. Finally, there are sixty-six countries in the population range 10-1.5 million (UN, DESA, Population Division, Database). Leaving aside the smaller countries (those with populations less than 1.5 million), half the countries in the world have populations above 11 million and half below. This measure of the half-way point in a series of observations is known in statistics as the 'median'. If we add the smaller states to the picture, we slide down to around 4.5 million.

Throughout the analysis here, and in the rest of the book, we will omit countries with a population below 1.5 million. The choice is somewhat arbitrary, but a cut-off point had to be made somewhere because the smaller countries tend not to have the full range of statistics. As a result, their presence or absence in statistical series would tend to distort comparisons. One reason for choosing 1.5 million as the threshold for analysis stems from the fact that the UN also uses this population number for the start of their treatment of 'small island developing states', using the argument that states of this size face special problems. These states will receive separate treatment in Chapter Nine.

Let us move away from the relative size of countries to the tempo of change and its nature over time. Since the end of World War Two, the fastest rates of population growth have been concentrated in the poorer countries of the world, led by Africa (and Sub-Saharan Africa, in particular) and by Latin America and the Caribbean. These areas all have growth rates well over double the world average. Were we to focus on the top-fifteen fastest growing countries between 1980 and 2010, four of the states are in the Arab peninsula, two from the Middle East, and the remainder are all in Sub-Saharan Africa. These countries fall into two distinct groups, which we will explore more fully later in this chapter. The Sub-Saharan African group comprises countries with high birth rates that could be considered relatively poor and underdeveloped (Malmberg 2008). Jordan and the Palestinian territories also fall into this group (Gilbar 1997). On the

31

other hand, the oil-rich Arab states have been fueling their population growth with imported labour (Forstenlechner and Rutledge 2011). By contrast, the slowest growth rates have been located in Europe with many countries in the former Soviet Union and in Eastern Europe. Some have even been registering small declines, caused by the impact on the already very low birth rates of the social and economic disruption that followed the disintegration of the Soviet bloc (Rodin 2011). In the case of the Russian Federation, this has been compounded by a decline in life expectancy, particularly among the male population (Anderson 2002).

## Dynamics of Population Growth

Population growth is explained by what is called the 'natural rate' of change. This is a sum total of the number of births minus the number of deaths plus net migration (immigration minus emigration). If we divide the number of births by the population number for a country, we obtain a *'crude' birth rate*, and we can do the same with the number of deaths to calculate a *'crude' death rate*. Just to complicate matters, whilst growth rates are expressed in terms of percentages, birth and death rates are expressed in the numbers per thousand. Birth and death rates can be applied to the existing population, as a first step in estimating future population growth.

The birth rate measures the number of live births relative to the total population, but that is a pretty crude indicator. Evidently, not everyone can have babies. That biological role is (still) a preserve of females, and, moreover, females of childbearing age. Thus it is important to know both the gender balance and the age distribution within a society. For this reason, demographers tend to prefer to think of a 'general fertility rate', which is the number of births relative to the number of women of childbearing age. This is usually defined as women's ages between 15 and 49, but this measure, too, varies from country to country (and between regions or groups within a country) and through historical time (Guengant 2002). In most societies these days, women rarely conceive throughout their reproductive lives. If they did, they would give birth at the rate of one child every 15-18 months. For many of us, looking back to our great-grandparents, we might find them with families of ten or twelve children, having had a couple of stillbirths or child deaths. It is interesting in the literature that nobody seems to comment on male fertility. However, there is a debate raging over whether male fertility is declining, whether it is declining among groups exposed to certain pollutants or stress, or whether the delay in child-bearing means that men are trying to reproduce at a later stage of their (natural) fertility decline (Cocuzza and Esteves, 2013).

One important factor in determining the fertility rate is the age of marriage, or the age at the birth of the first child, since this determines the length of the period of fertility. Today, only in a few societies is the age of marriage extremely early, occasionally before pubescence, and childbearing starts with puberty. In others cohabitation or marriage occurs when the couple are able to establish an independent household, with a corresponding delay in the age at which the first child is conceived (Caldwell and Schindlmayr 2003). In traditional societies, another important factor is the periods of fecundity (infertility). Women tend to be infertile during periods of breast-feeding, and in some African cultures the custom of breast feeding children until they are two or three years old is used to spread child bearing (van Ginneken 1974). The social norms and cultures influencing childbearing and marriage are not fixed or even stable, but most observers agree their impact is most pervasive in small-scale (often rural) societies. Elsewhere, more individual patterns emerge, though that is not to say that these too are immune to social conventions (Kulu 2013).

A major factor in determining the birth rate today is the ability of women, or couples, to limit the number of children they have. This option has always been available to societies, whether through the use of contraceptive devices, through abortion or through deliberate neglect or infanticide. The last was often applied to (unwanted) female babies, but this function has now been taken over by (selective) abortion (Arnold e.a., 2002; Zhu, Lu and Hesketh, 2009). Family limitation may be part of official policy, either on the part of development agencies or NGO's or of government policy, as in the case of India and China. In fact, in China it was forbidden to have more than one child, although recently the policy has been relaxed. This question will be dealt with in the case study at the end of this Chapter. In other societies, the availability of contraception has allowed sexual activity to be decoupled from child bearing and child rearing. In India, publicity campaigns and the availability of contraception have helped to reduce the birthrate, but the three quarters of contraception users in India have chosen the extreme, but effective, route of sterilisation (Pathak e.a., 1998). The use of contraception to enable later and smaller families may also be explained by the wider employment opportunities available to women, and their decision, for economic reasons or for reasons of personal development, to exploit them (Brewster and Rindfuss 2000). Moreover, once the decision had been taken to start a family, the situation where children's income was less important in old age, accompanied by a cultural shift towards investing more time and resources in child-rearing, has contributed to limiting family size (Preston, 1986).

We cannot just keep adding people to the Earth. If no one had ever left, we would be stuck with over 106 billion – most of them very, very old (Haub, 2002)! Thus we should be thankful that there is a death rate, the number of deaths per thousand of the population. One of the main determinants is the age structure of the population, since generally the older the people tend to die more often (males earlier than females). This is not always the case since epidemics seem to fall hardest on the very young as well as the old, and wars always rip the young (usually males) out of the heart of the population. Generally, however, a population with a high birth rate will tend have a lower death rate than one with a low birth rate, assuming that the life expectancy is the same.

But then, life expectancy never is the same, whether through space or through time. One basic determinant of life expectancy is poverty; badly housed, poorly fed, susceptible to disease, deprived of medical care, ignorant of hygiene and nutrition – the poor die early. Poverty, in turn, depends on levels of development, returns to labour and the regularity of work, and the distribution of the income that a society generates. Back in 1975, the demographer Samuel Preston demonstrated a relationship suggesting that the higher the level of per capita income, the higher would be life expectancy at birth. This was interesting not only as a piece of scholarship but, because it helped reinforce the prevailing idea that the best way to reach development policy goals was to raise income levels (Preston, 1975). Since then, the idea of one-way causation has been called into question and so too the emphasis on income as the instrumental variable, rather than access to health care or general environmental factors (Georgiadis e.a., 2010). The grim geography of death has been laid bare recently by a group of scientists and was published in the medical magazine, *The Lancet*. They analysed the death statistics for 187 countries and divided them by cause and by region. They also calculated the lost years of life by computing the standardised life expectancy (i.e. for the whole world) at a given age (with an upper limit of 80 years, because of lack of data at older age) and comparing that to the age at death from each cause. Among the poorer countries, the category of diarrhea is significantly present (typical among the causes of death among young children) as well as HIV/Aids and tuberculosis, tropical diseases and malaria. In richer societies, many of these problems are prevented by immunisation, limited by good public health care arrangements or cured by drugs. But then, as life expectancy increases, so a new set of tumours and cancers attack a deteriorating immune system. Health expenditures and health care (and health insurance) may help delay the impact of these for some but ultimately some bits of the body simply stop working. Among the richer countries, therefore, it is cancers and cardiovascular diseases that slash years off our lives. Many living in poorer countries are long dead before these diseases can carry them off. Moreover, in North Africa and the Middle East, the bony finger of violent death reaches down to claim more than half the total of the lost years of lives (Lozano e.a., 2012).

So far, we have listed factors determining birth and death rates, without employing any overarching pattern. Thomas Malthus, writing in 1798, produced one of the most enduring set of ideas on population growth and it consequences for society. He argued that population growth, without voluntary checks, would tend to hit constraints of food production. Similar ideas were articulate by the so-called 'Club of Rome' whose reports in the 1970s warned that economic growth (and population growth) would eventually exhaust the Earth's resources. Without entering the recent debates, however, it is still possible to see that Malthusian ideas have only a limited explanatory power – the historical experience is too varied and the explanatory variables too few (Kreager, 2014).

A more nuanced approach, admittedly with specific conditions, is offered by so-called 'transition theory' which, in its classic form, envisages a four-stage model of population growth. In the first stage death rates were high and life expectancy low as societies struggled to maintain themselves in the face of harsh living conditions. High birth rates were encouraged (associated with status and virility), but they were also necessary to compensate for the attrition of hunger, war and disease. The second stage is marked by a fall in the death rates, probably because of improved nutrition and health and because women were healthier and lived longer, birth rates might have increased as well. It was for this second stage that in 1945 the demographer Kingsley Davis coined the phrase "the population explosion". In this stage population surges ahead until it either places pressures on resources or until the imperatives towards large families diminish. At this point, the third stage is reached, and the birth rate falls until it approaches the levels reached by the death rate, and population growth slows down appreciably. From then onwards, in the fourth stage, falling death rates and falling birth rates serve to maintain, at best, a low population growth or (in its more modern version) to allow the population to slides into a decline. Many advanced Western countries are considered to have passed through all four stages. The beauty of transition theory is that the process is not seen as one single monolithic change but rather as a set of interrelated transitions. For example, the staggered impact of medical advances may change the pattern of death rates. The move from countryside to town may loosen social controls on birth rates. The impact of increasing living standards may percolate through social classes, with middle classes limiting family size before working classes. And the arrival of migrant groups at an earlier stage of the process (i.e. with higher birth rates) may even help neutralise the effects of change among the indigenous population (Caldwell, 2006; Kirk, 1996).

## Population Pyramids

The rates of population change have a great impact on a country's age and sex distribution, which can be conveniently configured in a form of visualisation known as a 'population pyramid'. The pyramid begins by dividing the horizontal axis in the middle into male and female, and by dividing the vertical axis into equal segments according to age. With natural growth, the population in each category will decline over time, more typically faster for men than for women.

This process of change in the distribution of the population is not neutral. It is also the case that population changes, in conjunction with other factors, it may itself be the instigator of social and political change. One typical example is the chain of events known as the Arab Spring The trigger was provided in December 2010 when Mohamed Bouazizi, a young market trader, frustrated by the bureaucracy, set light to himself outside the local Governor's office and subsequently died of his injuries. This sparked massive street protests throughout the country and, less than a month later, the government resigned, paving the way for the first free elections in more than fifty years. Meanwhile, in January 2011 young protestors occupied Tahrir square in the middle of Cairo and within a month, they had forced the resignation of President Hosni Mubarak. Shortly after that, protestors gained control of Benghazi, precipitating Libya into a civil war that would lead by the end of the year to the removal of Muammar Gaddafi's regime. In Yemen, street-protests also broke out in the spring of 2011 and, despite heavy-handed repression, eventually achieved the resignation of the 33-year long dictator Ali Abdullah Saleh (Anderson, 2011). Finally, in March/April 2011 popular street protests spread through many of the provinces of Syria, sparking an increasingly vicious (and confused) civil war which, at time of writing, is still decimating the country (Lynch e.a., 2014).

Figure 2.2: Age and Sex Distribution of Tunisia (thousands) 2011

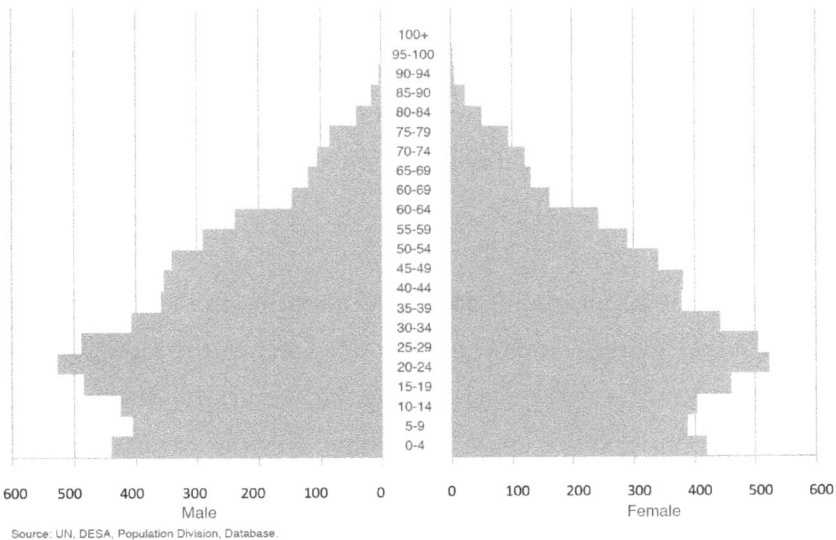

Source: UN, DESA, Population Division, Database.

One of the elements binding these uprisings together was the youthfulness of the protestors. Figure 2.2 shows the population pyramid for Tunisia, where it all started. Quite clearly visible is a concentration of the population in the lower age groups, with a bulge in the age-group 20-24, or more generally 15-30. All the countries involved in the Arab Spring experienced rapid population growth, which is generally characterised by a wide base of the population pyramid. In each of the cases of the Arab countries described there was the same preponderance of youth. Having a large young population, however, is not by itself a sufficient precondition for protest and revolt. In February 2011, *The Economist* ran a light-hearted article in which it took for the Arab League member-states some of the existing composite indices (democracy, corruption and press freedom) added a few other factors (length in power, level of GDP and the size of the youth cohort) and constructed a 'shoe-throwers index'. In that Index, it ascribed the greatest weight (35 per cent) to the proportion of the population aged under 25, and a further 5 per cent to the absolute size of that age cohort. It ranked the Yemen, Libya, Egypt, Syria and Iraq as the most unstable countries. Tunisia came in eleventh place, sandwiched between Jordan and Morocco. The oil-rich states anchored places for the 'most stable regimes (*Economist* 9.2.2011).

This was all too simple, but it does draw attention to the demographic drivers of the chain of revolutions that swept across the region and are collectively known as the Arab Spring. However, the demographics of the region were not new, and some commentators drew the distinction that earlier generations had accepted the repressive regimes because they were accompanied by stability and increased welfare (Shahine, 2011). Others emphasised the role of the internet in giving access to global discussions on citizenship and facilitating the development of a new discourse within which the youth could formulate their aspirations (Al-Momani, 2011). Still others have pointed to the steep rise in the price of staple foods and another factor contributing to the unrest (Harrigan, 2011; Johnstone and Mazo, 2011). Some studies applied regression techniques to establish links between possible causal variables. One study suggested that the issue lay not so much with the weight of the youthful cohort as with their higher levels of education, coupled with the lack of employment opportunities, especially in the 15-25 and 26-35 age cohort (Campante and Char 2012). As for the motivation, a survey of opinion suggested that the youth was relatively conservative and that the protest was less one against the status-quota as one in favour of greater opportunities (Hoffman and Jamal, 2012).

If there is a consensus among demographers it is that the world would benefit from a slower rate of population growth or, better still, none at all. However, countries that contribute to this goal by un-growing their populations face unique problems of their own. These may also require 'revolutionary' solutions.

Figure 2.3: Age and Sex Distribution of Japan (millions) 2011

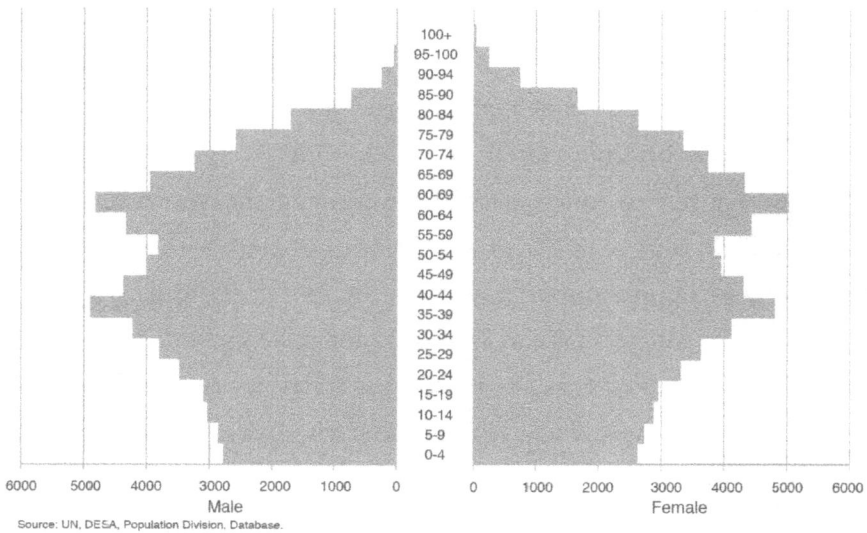

Source: UN, DESA, Population Division, Database.

Japan's population has declined every year for the last five years and, in the absence of migration, it is likely to do so for much of the foreseeable future. Japan's population pyramid is shown in Figure 2.3. The base of the pyramid has been becoming progressively smaller for the past fourty years, as a result of a large fall in the birth rate. This would already have had a negative impact on population growth, but it Japan's case, it is aggravated by a spectacular rise in life expectancy. Japan has one of the highest life-expectancies in the world, with the result that this reduced working-age population is supporting an ever larger, and ever older, non-productive cohort of elderly. On the other hand, the working population is no longer supporting and educating such a large cohort of children and young adults. In fact, the dependency ratio today is similar to what it was in the 1950s and early 60s (Ogawa and Matsukura, 2007: 200-202). However, there are important differences. First, as a population ages, the medical and care costs rise disproportionately with each decade of extra life, and especially in the last year of life (Muramatsu and Akiyama, 2011). The costs also rise because the burden of care is shifting from the home and the family, where the real costs are hidden, to institutions where the costs are not only more transparent, but are also passed on to public expenditure. This is true throughout the richer societies, including Japan where the proportion of elderly living with children has fallen dramatically from 87 per cent in 1960 to less than 50 per cent today (WHO, 2011: 23).

The shift in the age distribution also has impacts on the financial system. In Japan, the young tend to borrow, and the elderly tends to save, though later in life, the old start to liquidate their assets. Unfortunatly, the two flows are not synchronous. Thus the banks find themselves receiving more cash than they can lend, with the result that potential returns on investment are decreasing. This pushes the banks into riskier lending strategies, introducing an extra destabilising element into the financial system (Imam, 2013). As the dimensions of the problem grow in Japan and elsewhere, aggravated by further advances in medical science, so one can expect generational conflicts over scarce resources to increase. Attitudes towards familial responsibilities in caring for the elderly have already altered dramatically over the years, and it is to be expected that opinion towards voluntary euthanasia will as well. One policy option in every case is to import people in the working-age range to augment the middle band of the population.

This brings our discussion conveniently to the impact of migration. Migration refers to the re-location of peoples. For this analysis, we will not make a strict division between emigration and immigration, treating them as the reverse sides of the same coin. We may lose some nuances, but it makes matters simpler and less boring. Migration may happen internally, within a country, or internationally. It may be through regular channels (i.e. those recognised by the authorities of the receiving location), or it may be irregular (i.e. where the passage or the stay is against local regulations). The latter is often (in my opinion, wrongly) referred to as illegal migration. Finally, the relocation may be because migrants fear extreme danger to life and are granted exemption from existing regulations for the duration of the threat. These migrants are called refugees, and their rights and movement in the recipient country are usually restricted (van Hear e.a., 2012). The most-recent estimates suggest a total of 15.1 million international refugees in the world, with a further 35 million displaced within their own country (UNHCR, 2015). Although these international refugees (rightly) claim much press attention, they represent only seven per cent of the world's total international migration (DESA Population Facts, September 2013).

Escape from hunger or violence has often been a force for international migration in the past – the millions of Irish fleeing the famine of the 1840s and the millions of Jews fleeing the pogroms in Russia and Eastern Europe constituted an important element in US immigration in the 19th century and were assimilated into the nation's society. This migration still exists in the regions of Darfur or on the borders of Syria, but it is bottled up there by legislation in receiving countries, and by the international conventions that underpin them. However, most migrations are driven by less extreme considerations. Although one of the main considerations still remains a desire on the part of migrants to better their lives, it is too simple to suggest that differences in living standards are the only driver of migration movements. Migration, at least initially, has costs. Migrants lose their friends, families and support networks, and they have to adapt to unfamiliar surroundings and, sometimes, languages. It is not the absolute levels of wages but the prospect of improvement that is the driver. Thus, if there is a prospect of betterment by remaining in the place of origin, it can considerably mute the urge for drastic change that relocation involves. Note, once one has moved away from the push of desperate necessity, everything else depends on perception. One way that costs are reduced, and perceptions changed, is the presence of one's local population in the target destination. Initially, the presence of a group from one's village or church in the target destination may help reduce uncertainties (by providing information, housing and work) and defray part of the costs (making gifts or loans to cover the travel). Since the early migrants are usually young and of working age, as they settle down they may bring over immediate family and even prospective brides or grooms. In these ways, migration may continue long after the original impulse has disappeared. This phenomenon is often known a 'chain migration' (Faist, 2012).

A final factor influencing migration is the simple fact of getting from one location to the other. Distance and cost are two obvious considerations, but these are not as absolute as might seem at first sight. In many cases, migrants are deliberately sought and recruited by authorities (or businesses) in the recipient nation. In the 19th century, Indian workers were recruited by the British for plantation work or the construction of railways in East Africa and South-East Asia. Industrialists there sometimes subsidised the passage of migrants to the USA, often in return for labour-service until the debt was paid. Immediately after the Second World War, emigration from the UK and The Netherlands to Australia and Canada was fostered by assisted passages. London Transport deliberately recruited staff from the West Indies just as in the 1960's German automobile factories recruited workers from Turkey and Yugoslavia.

Figure 2.4: Age and Sex Distribution of Qatar (thousands) 2011

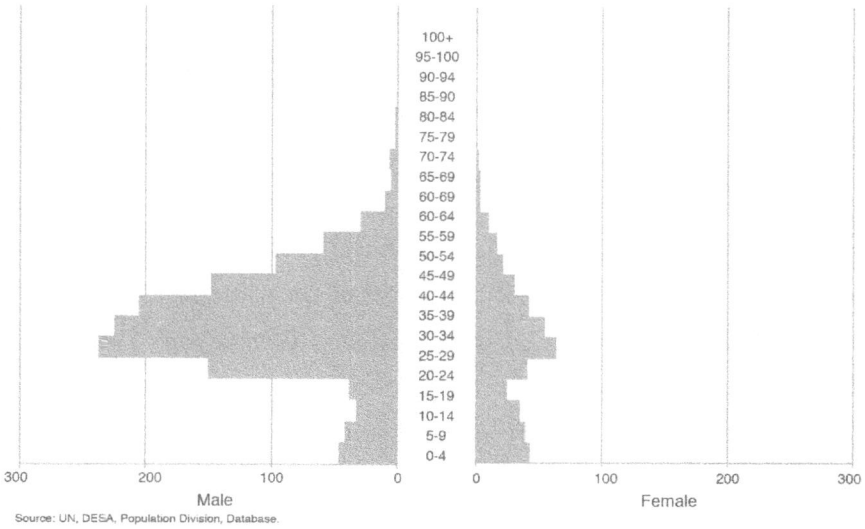

The age categories shown (top to bottom): 100+, 95-100, 90-94, 85-90, 80-84, 75-79, 70-74, 65-69, 60-69, 60-64, 55-59, 50-54, 45-49, 40-44, 35-39, 30-34, 25-29, 20-24, 15-19, 10-14, 5-9, 0-4

Male axis: 300, 200, 100, 0
Female axis: 0, 100, 200, 300

Male      Female

Source: UN, DESA, Population Division, Database.

The impact of migration is dramatically apparent in the Gulf States, none more so than in Qatar whose population growth of slightly over 7 per cent a year since 1985 has primarily been fuelled by the immigration of mainly young, male workers and, to a far lesser extent, by female maids, from the Indian sub-continent. This is clearly visible in its population pyramid, shown in Figure 2.4. Back in 1950, Qatar was a small desert state with just over 20,000 citizens. Since then it has grown to above 1.5 million inhabitants and has become one of the richest countries on the planet. In the process, the foreign population outnumbers the host population by a ratio of more than 10:1. In order to keep this population under control, and to contain the socio-cultural consequences, most of the labour is recruited ('sponsored') directly by the employer and the labour permits are strictly temporary. This system leaves the migrants, almost all of whom are employed in the private sector, vulnerable to systematic exploitation and abuse. Nonetheless, migrants continue to be attracted by relatively higher wages but also by an illusion that conditions are better than they are, an image fostered not only by intermediaries but by the migrants themselves, who tend to hide the shame of their situations from friends and relatives at home (Breeding, 2012; Gardner, 2012).

There is one group of migrants for whom the passage is far more difficult; those who have to avoid the authorities to enter the country and to keep avoiding them once they have arrived. Some of these, it is true, arrive with legitimate visas (for tourism or study) and the fail to return once they expire. For others, it involves a long and uncertain journey in the hands of criminal gangs whose own safely takes precedence over the migrants under their care. The lowest estimate for unauthorised immigrants in the USA is 11.3 million, but the actual number could be much higher (Pew Research Center, Press Release 3.9.2014). A ten-year old report by the South African government seemed content to leave estimates of irregular migrants living in South Africa, which has a considerably smaller population, at anywhere between 2.5 and 7 million (Waller, 2006). Within the European Union, in 2008 the numbers are estimated to lie between 2 million and 4 million (Morehouse and Blomfield, 2011) a number which, by now, must be considerably larger. In the twelve months to mid-2015 a total of almost 750,000 refugees sought asylum in the European Union (Eurostat 2015, Asylum quarterly report).

## Assessing Data Accuracy

Since the second half of the previous century the census has been the benchmark of population statistics – a deliberate count of the population held at regular intervals (usually every ten years). Its accuracy, however, depends on the resources devoted to the exercise and the breadth of coverage. In this respect, poorer countries tend to produce fewer reliable results but lack of resources is not the only factor that plays a role. Even worse is the situation in countries with political unrest, rebellion, revolution or civil war, or their aftermath. In these cases, it is almost impossible to conduct a census, and even if one is held, there is a strong probability that census results on religion or ethnicity would be deliberately distorted. Another factor playing a role is the political environment within which the census takes place. In Nigeria, for example, the 1953 census took place when the country was under British colonial rule. Since it was feared that it would be used as the basis for tax assessment, there was a significant degree of under-counting. The 1962 census, by contrast took place after independence, and since this it was thought that the results would be used to helpdetermine the distribution of government expenditure, it probably led to an overestimate. Since both the North and the South had helped inflate the figures, the census results were politically contentious, and have remained so ever since. In any event, the census outcomes have generated implausible growth rates, with those between 1953 and 1962/3 being overestimated and those between the widely rejected census of 1973 and disputed census of 1991 being underestimated. The results generated from Nigeria are still considered unreliable and, for much of the period, the UN has simply assumed a growth rate, and extrapolated the population numbers from there (Jerven, 2013: 56-61). Errors in the Nigerian census are not an isolated incident. The most-recent census in Kenya has shown how politically charged the simple act of counting people can be. In 2007, the country was emerging from a convulsive burst of blood-letting across its tribal lines, which had killed one thousand people and displaced another

600,000 or more (Mueller, 2011). It was known that the new census would be used to define electoral boundaries and distribute development funds. The authorities cancelled the results in eight districts in the North East for producing unrealistically high growth rates. The local authorities' response suggested that the problem lay elsewhere, in the under-recording of the nomadic livestock herders in the previous count, though the census question was the same in both cases (Jerven 2013: 73-74).

Census errors also occur in the absence of political or tribal differences. A failure by the authorities to identify the dwellings, to list the household correctly, to send out the questionnaires to everyone and the failure of the informant to understand the scope of inquiry can all lead to undercounting. The degree of error is usually individual visits to a sample of addresses to check the accuracy of the reported results. These results are often wide of the mark. The 2011 census in South Africa eventually reported an undercount of 14.6 per cent, or 6.3 million in a (revised) total of 51.7 million, ranging from 18.6 per cent in Western Cape province to 10 per cent in Limpopo (Statistics South Africa, 2012). Western countries are also capable of generating unreliable census data. The Australian authorities, for example, estimated that its 2011 census had failed to record 374,500 of its (re-estimated) 20.5 million inhabitants; an undercount of 1.7 per cent (with an error of 0.2 per cent either way). The undercount rates were particularly striking among males in the age cohort 20-30, which were undercounted by over 7 per cent. There was also a high underrecording of the 'indigenous' population, but this was as much due to misreporting of ethnic status as to being absent from the census altogether (Australian Bureau of Statistics, 2012).

Many countries no longer hold a regular census and rely instead on data routinely collected in the process of registering births and deaths and residence, supplemented for control purposes by sample data. Most countries anyway employ this kind of material to estimate the size of population between census dates and extrapolate forwards from the census data itself. For example, the last full census conducted in The Netherlands was in 1971. The 1981 census was postponed and eventually cancelled and the 1991 census ran onto such a storm of protest against the infringement of privacy that it was abandoned. Since then, no further efforts have been made. Germany conducted its last full census in 1987 and Sweden in 1990.

If one leaves aside the obvious trouble-spots, then one can be reasonably confident with (corrected) national population estimates, but a little less certain when one moves to a disaggregate level of provinces or cities. For example, the *China Peoples' Daily* in February 2010 confidently estimated the population of Shanghai in mid-2009 at 19.21 million (13.79 million permanent inhabitants and 5.42 million temporary residents). The 2010 census recorded a population of 23.02 million (14.10 million permanent and 8.92 million temporary). In both cases, a temporary resident had to be in the city for at least six months, most of them being internal migrants from the country-side (National Bureau of Statistics, China). To some extent, the error may be the result of underestimating the length of stay of these migrant workers, but to overlook 3.5 million (mostly workers) is not a minor glitch – it is like overlooking the equivalent of the entire labour force of Bulgaria or Hong Kong.

At least for Shanghai the census offers some reference point. In the case of Kibera, characterised as the largest slum in Africa, it does not.

Kibera lies just outside Nairobi, the capital of Kenya. The official 2009 census recorded the population at 170,000, which is wildly at odds with UN Habitat whose most recent estimate places the number between 500,000 and 700,000. UN Habitat has its Head Quarters in Nairobi and has several projects in the area. The larger the problem, the more resources it requires and thus the greater the incentive it has to inflate the population size. Its estimates are based on an assumed density of population in the slums. In 2008 a Map-Kibera project started actually counting the population house-by-house, street-by-street. Having mapped a small corner (of 5000 houses) and extrapolating to the whole area, its estimates lie between 235,000 and 270,000 people; closer to the census data than the UN estimates (Robbins, 2012). Most of the migrants in these two examples are internal migrants, legally resident in the area; they have simply not been counted properly.

The 2012 Olympics were located in the London Borough of Newham. It is in the East End of London, which, since the disappearance of the London docks, has been an area of great deprivation. To help its regeneration, decades ago the government reduced planning restrictions and all around the borough the shiny new tower blocks of the Docklands have risen. It was the lack of planning restrictions that also made possible the reallocation of land to allow the stadiums and other facilities for the Olympic Games to be built there, and a huge shopping mall. One function that has not changed is Newham's role as a magnet for new immigrants. It was assumed that, once they have some income, they would move out of the area. Newham, however, remains a sump for poor, usually unemployed, migrants. With low taxation potential and large social problems, it depends heavily on central government funding to run its social services, and that in turn, depends on the number of inhabitants. The Office of National Statistics (ONS), on which funding depends, estimated for 2009 that the borough housed 245,800 residents, whereas the Greater London Council (GLC) put the number at 281,948 – difference of 13 per cent. Unfortunately for the local council, the ONS figures provided the basis for government funding (Newham Council, 2010). The council put the population in 2011 at 295,772 whereas the ONS suggested that the numbers were falling. In July 2012 the annual census seemed to resolve the debate. It gave a figure for March 2011 of 308,000 (ONS, 16.7.2012). The reason for the difference was that the ONS relied on projections based on past migration trends and on out-dated information on household size. The relaxed planning regime did not just benefit business high-rise, it also allowed the proliferation of extensions and sheds, in back gardens, many crammed with new migrants. The London police, by the way, put the figure nearer 320,000 (Hurley, 2013).

## Summary

Let us summarise the discussion. This chapter has focused on the nature of population change and its impact on population distribution. It has suggested that the tempo of world population growth has been slowing since the 1970s but that there has been a shift in its relative distribution towards Africa and, to a lesser extent, South America. Population change in countries results from changes in birth and death rates and in net migration. The 'Preston Curve' has suggested that increases in life expectancy are linked to increases in per capita income, but that the relationship flattens at higher income levels. 'Transition theory' offers a more nuanced model whereby population change follows a pattern in which falls in the death rate precede declines in the birth rates, until both stabilise at a lower level.

Population pyramids are used to show the age and gender distribution of the population. Fast-growing populations tend to have relatively young populations, which may have been a driver in the protests that characterised the 'Arab Spring'. By contrast, slow-growing or declining populations tend to have a disproportionally older population which imposes extra health-care challenges and costs. Countries' populations can also change through migration, which is a reflection of push- and pull- factors and, later, of the phenomenon of 'chain migration'.

Errors in recent national census data are still possible through over and undercounting, but these results are adjusted accordingly. On the other hand, resistance to disclosure of ethnic, religious, social or economic information have led many countries to abandoning censuses altogether and relying on large-scale sampling. Finally, even if the national data looks reliable, local data may still have a large margin of error, especially if the area has experienced large-scale migrations.

Richard T. Griffiths

# Case Study: China's One Child Policy

In the immediate post-war years the world faced a rapid acceleration in population, particularly among countries least able to sustain it. It was described as a population time-bomb and, although the tempo of growth has diminished, it sometimes still is. One country in particular – China – has long maintained a highly restrictive policy towards family planning by restricting most families in the country to only one child. This policy has been credited with having reduced China's population by preventing the birth of 400 million children (not even counting the children that they would have had in their turn). However, these figures have been questioned, and so too have the severity and the duration of the policy.

Before looking at what happened in China, it is worth examining the global context. As we have already observed, in the 1950s policy-makers showed increasing concern at the pace of demographic change, particularly at the increase in the numbers of poor people. In response there emerged a global movement in favour of (voluntary) birth control, though there were doubts about its effectiveness under the prevailing social attitudes and means of education. By the mid-1970s these doubts had hardened and the mood swung in favour of compulsory measures. In 1975-76 India conducted a forced sterilisation campaign that resulted in eight million sterilisations. Similar policies were followed in Indonesia and Bangladesh. Gradually there reverberated a backlash against the policy, and national governments and Western aid agencies began a policy reappraisal. By the end of the 1980s most governments relied instead on propaganda, education, tax incentives and free hand-out of contraceptives. Thus, when we look at China's policy we have to take into account both the concern with population growth and the earlier consensus that government policy could be effective in controlling it (Feng, Cai and Gu, 2012).

In the 1970s, as population numbers were recovering from the famine following the so-called 'Great Leap Forward' (1958-1962), China relied on voluntary measures (delayed marriage, birth spacing and contraception and abortion) to influence population size. At the same time, however, the country was creating the bureaucracy (propaganda offices, information centres, clinics) of population control. Then, in 1979 the one-child policy was slotted into place, and it is still there, more or less, today. Basically every family was limited to one child with some exceptions:

- If the first child had a disability;
- If the parents worked in a dangerous profession;
- If both parents were themselves single children (in some areas only);
- If the first child was a girl (after 1984-88, in some areas only).

Note that these exceptions were limited to certain areas and although these look vast on a map, they are sparsely populated. In the crowded eastern provinces of China, no exemptions were allowed. The policy was enforced by punative fines, loss of employment (especially if in a government job or a party member), forced contraception (fitting of an IUD, relaxed after 1995) and forced abortion.

One feature of China's demographic development has indeed been a marked decline in the so-called total fertility rate, which measures the number of children a woman could be expected to bear in a life-time. The beginning of Communist rule was accompanied by a 'traditional' high rate. It plunged sharply during the famine that accompanied the 'Great Leap Forward' but, after briefly bouncing back to a new 'peak' in 1964, it continued to decline until it dropped below the replacement rate in the late 1980s (Gu, nd: 13). This is what is held to be the 'success' of the policy and the claim that we mentioned in the introduction, that the birth of 400 million children had been averted. It is interesting to pause at how this was originally calculated. The state took the rate of decline in the birth rate between 1950 and 1970 and projected it forwards to 1998 to see how many children would have been born. It then looked at how the actual situation had evolved and came with a shortfall of 388 million children. Pulling the calculations through one more decade and the figure became 400 million. The question, of course, is whether this can be ascribed to the one-child policy. Remember, the policy was only introduced in 1979. However, already in the 1970s the total fertility rate had already dropped to close to replacement levels (Whyte, Feng and Cai, 2015). This fall in fertility rates has also appeared elsewhere in East Asia, most notably in Japan. It is therefore possible that a voluntary policy may have had the same effect in China.

Figure 2.5: Age and Sex Distribution of China (millions) 2011 and 2050

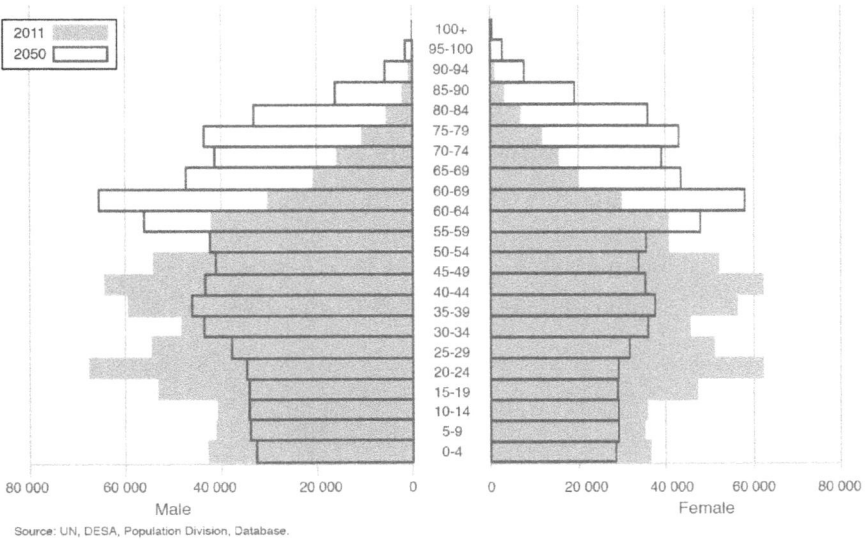

Source: UN, DESA, Population Division, Database.

China's population pyramid for 2011 and the latest projection for 2050 is shown in Figure 2.5. One result of this transformation is that China's population after 2050 will begin to decline. This decline will not only involve smaller numbers, it will also alter the composition of the population. And this has led commentators in both China and the West to argue that the controls have been too severe and maintained for too long. One effect is that the population will age rapidly, especially above the age of sixty but also among the very old. Because males die earlier than females, this will be an ageing population of old women. A further complication concerns the cities. These have expanded rapidly in the last twenty years, with an influx of young workers from the countryside, which had produced a typical 'migrant bulge' in their population pyramid. Although the 'official' line is that most of these are temporary workers, it is highly unlikely that many of these will return to the countryside. The result is that the projection forward of Shanghai's population pyramid, shown in

Figure 2.6, takes on an uncanny similarity to the mushroom cloud following a nuclear explosion. Repeat this throughout the cities in the East and China is facing a population bomb of an entirely different order…a massive overhang of older people, consisting of parents with only one child, probably already near retirement age, to help care for them.

Figure 2.6: Age and Sex Distribution of
Shanghai (000,000s) 2010 and 2050

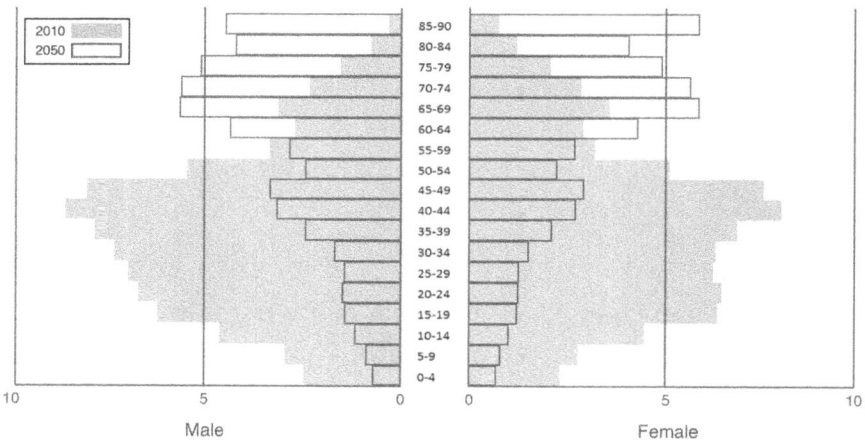

Since 2013 the policy has been relaxed. Whereas previously if both parents had been single children themselves they were allowed a second child, the concession was now extended to couples where one parent has been a single child. The expectation was that this would create a 'mini baby-boom' of an extra one million children a year, but the early results have been disappointing. This might yet be only temporary, because of the bureaucracy involved or because potential parents want to space their children. However it is also probably that expectations have changed and that smaller family-size has become accepted; that families have become used to higher standards of living and are reluctant to incur the higher costs of child-rearing. It is also possible that they choose for an investment in depth for their one child (in terms of schooling and earning potential) rather than having more, but lower earning, off-spring. In October 2015 a further amendment was suggested allowing any family to have a second child. This still has now been approved by the Party Congress. Hopefully, some of the bureaucratic pre-conception hassle involved in having a child will also be abolished. Otherwise it is difficult to envisage it having much impact.

# Chapter Three

# National Income

National Income is the means by which we measure the output of an economy at a specific point in time, and changes in that output over time. Most of us normally never look at the numbers, but almost subliminally we are constantly exposed to messages than are underpinned by national income calculations. We talk about economies being large or small (we compare national incomes). We talk about being rich or poor (we divide national incomes by population size and compare them). We talk about growth and stagnation and overtaking countries (we compare national incomes over periods of time). We are appalled by recessions (we calculate two consecutive quarters of decline). We read about debt crises (we divide the total sum borrowed by government by one year's national income). We are impressed by economic growth and depressed when we get too little and yet, in the back of our minds, we worry about the impact of the economy on the climate and the environment. We all enter this discourse, almost regularly. After population, national income is probably the most common way in which we configure the world. However, most of us never refer to the data itself, let alone reflect on how it is constructed. We share an almost pre-Copernican faith in the numbers, especially when results are presented as calculated to one or two decimal points of accuracy.

Modern national income data begins to emerge only at the end of the 19th century. Of course, before then people knew if the economy was performing well or badly. Usually, they saw it through cycles of plenty or scarcity and they experienced it, most often, through fluctuations in prices. When times were good tax revenues increased, farms were improved, houses repaired and upgraded and large civic or religious projects were undertaken. Equally, economic difficulties manifested themselves in straitened circumstances for governments, beggars on the streets, houses abandoned or in disrepair, urban depopulation and the reduction, or cessation, of grand public work's schemes. Golden Ages came and went, and everyone knew about them. However, rarely did they express all of this as a single measureable concept, or try to measure it. Individual officials and scholars made occasional estimates for isolated years. However, the first official series was for the eight Australian colonies and dated from 1890 to 1904. The oldest continuous series, starting in 1925, is that of Canada (Studenski, 1958).

It was the onset of the 'Great Depression' of the 1930s that forced the pace of national income accounting. The 'crash' of the stock market in 1929 signalled the start of a prolonged and serious economic downturn. In the United States, President Hoover and his advisors stood by powerless, and clueless, as economic conditions worsened. His successor, President Roosevelt was determined to do something, anything, to intervene. However, it was difficult to construct a policy when the picture of what was happening to the economy was made up of disparate fragments of data like the volume of freight on railways or of imports and exports. As a result, he commissioned a team led by Simon Kuznets, from the National Bureau for Economic Research, to rectify the situation. In 1934, he presented to the US Senate the first national income calculations, covering the period 1929-1932

(Fioramonti, 2013: 23-33). When I was working in the archives of
the Central Bureau of Statistics (CBS) in The Netherlands, I stumbled
across a committee discussion from this same period on the impact
of the economic downturn. Everyone present knew the wealth of
the rich had been eroded by the fall in share prices while the real
spending power of those in work had been boosted by falling prices.
On balance, the members of the committee felt that the economy
had shrunk, but had it fallen by 5 per cent or by 20 per cent? They
did not have a clue. Under the leadership of Jan Tinbergen and Jan
Derksen, the CBS began work on constructing national income
estimates. In 1933, the CBS published its first results, for 1929, and
in 1939 it produced a more refined and longer-run series covering
the period 1921-1936 (Bakker, 1992; Bos, 2008). Other countries
followed suit. After 1945, national accounts became an important
adjunct to the execution of governments' domestic macro-economic
policies and in framing foreign aid and development policies. They
were also incorporated into the vocabulary of the 'Cold War' as the
Soviets and Americans pronounced on the benefits and defects of
each other's economic system.

## Measuring National Income

In the title of this chapter we have referred to the concept of what
are generally known as 'national income' accounts. More precisely,
however, this usually refers to one of two composite indices, known
respectively as Gross Domestic Product (GDP) and Gross National
Income (GNI). It is important that you should not confuse the
two. Curiously enough, neither measure has much to do with
production or with income. In fact, both measures provide data on
(cash) transactions. That is not quite the same thing. For example,

if you go out to a café and have a cup of coffee, it is a transaction. You will pay for it, and it will register on GDP figures. If you stay at home, and you make yourself a cup of coffee, the effect is the same; you have a cup of coffee, but there is no transaction involved in making the coffee or providing you with a seat while you consume it. Only the original purchase of the coffee will appear on GDP figures. Similarly, if you put your grandmother in a nice comfortable retirement home to be looked after, it will appear on GDP figures. If, on the other hand, you look after her at home, and it costs nothing, or you make no transactions, it will not appear on GDP figures. In the same way, GDP only records income in terms of cash, and not in goods, services and other favours. Thus, if no cash changes hands, the data will not enter the calculations. For example, if you manage to find a plumber to fix a leaking tap and pay him, it will appear in GDP figures. If, one the other hand, a neighbour does it in exchange for a cup of tea and a piece of cake, it will make no difference to the GDP calculations. Equally, if the cash transaction remains unrecorded, and our plumber does not declare this payment to the tax authorities, it will not enter the calculations either.

There are various ways in which these indices can be calculated, depending on the sources employed. These are shown in Figure 3.1. Each broadly comes to the same total result, but the breakdowns within these totals will differ. Since basically everything earned in a society is equal to everything consumed (or saved) in that society and since everything consumed in a society must be equal to everything produced, it stands to reason that Income = Expenditure = Production.

Figure 3.1: Three Routes to calculating National Income

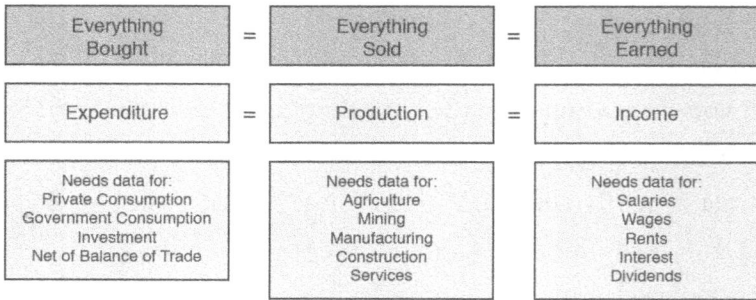

| Everything Bought | = | Everything Sold | = | Everything Earned |
|---|---|---|---|---|
| Expenditure | = | Production | = | Income |
| Needs data for:<br>Private Consumption<br>Government Consumption<br>Investment<br>Net of Balance of Trade | | Needs data for:<br>Agriculture<br>Mining<br>Manufacturing<br>Construction<br>Services | | Needs data for:<br>Salaries<br>Wages<br>Rents<br>Interest<br>Dividends |

Within a given period (usually a year, but quarterly and monthly as well) GDP measures the accumulated 'value added' of all goods and services inside a country, regardless of whether the production unit is nationally owned or owned by foreigners. The sum is often broken down into three categories, namely consumption + investment + government expenditure. After that, exports of goods and services are added to the outcome and imports are deducted.

GNI measures the accumulated 'value-added' of goods and services by all citizens of a country, regardless of where the production unit is located. It therefore excludes the value added (dividend, interest and profits) earned by foreign-owned companies in the country and adds the value added (dividend, interest and profits) of national owned companies abroad. It is calculated as GDP plus or minus net income from foreign assets. (Net) National Income (NI) is calculated by deducting capital depreciation from GNI. In the course of a year, businesses invest in buildings and machines for the future, and these sums enter the calculations, but equally in the course of a year the value of existing assets declines, and an allowance made in company accounts. This is called capital depreciation, and in NI calculations it is set against the new capital that has been purchased. These steps are all shown in Figure 3.2.

Figure 3.2: National Income and its Components

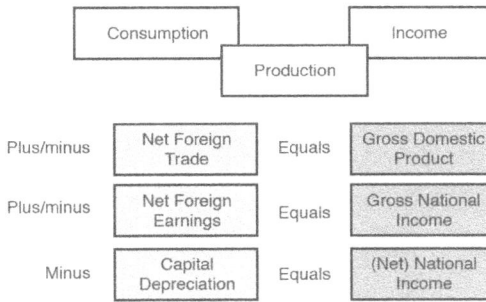

| | | | | | |
|---|---|---|---|---|---|
| | Consumption | | | Income | |
| | | Production | | | |
| Plus/minus | Net Foreign Trade | Equals | | Gross Domestic Product | |
| Plus/minus | Net Foreign Earnings | Equals | | Gross National Income | |
| Minus | Capital Depreciation | Equals | | (Net) National Income | |

It is very important always to hold on to the same definition to make sure that any time series you may make and any comparisons will be valid and consistent. However, you should always be aware that there can be serious differences between GDP and GNI. For example, Luxembourg is a small country with an extremely large financial sector, much of it foreign owned. In 2011 Luxembourg's GDP (converted into current US dollars) was $59,201 million (making its citizens among the richest in the world), but its GNI was almost a third less, standing at $40,109 million (still keeping its citizens among the richest in the world, but by a more modest margin). The opposite can be seen in the case of The Netherlands, a medium-sized country with a relatively large concentration of multinationals and a great foreign investment portfolio. Its GNI, at $892,013 million is 6.6 per cent higher than its GDP figure of $836,074 million (World Bank Database). Most countries nowadays prefer to use GDP data as the main measure because it is easier to collect, is available earlier and is less susceptible to subsequent revisions.

# Explaining Growth

It is worth reflecting that most of the growth in the world economy is the product of the last century. For long swathes of history empires have risen and declined, leaving the ruins of their shimmering existence buried in jungles or deserts or beneath modern cities. The tempo of innovation gathered pace as we passed through the 'scientific revolutions' in Southern Europe and the Ottoman Empire and through the 'commercial revolution' in Italy and the Low Countries (Broadberry, 2013). Even so, in the 18th century, when the UK became the centre of the first industrial revolution, which was based on mass production of textiles and the application of steam power, British growth probably did not exceed one per cent per annum (Calculated from Crafts and Harley, 1992: 725-727). From that point economic growth in the UK, the USA and other industrialising areas of Europe began to accelerate. By the 1830s and 40s, the mechanisation of textiles was complete and the railways and steam shipping began to make an impact in the UK. In the 1850s, the free-trade movement gathered pace, and Britain lauded itself as 'the workshop of the world'. By the 1860s and 70s, the start of the 'second industrial revolution' began to manifest itself, based on electricity and chemical processes and by the 1890s, the leadership of the world economy had definitely passed to the United States of America (USA). New mechanical processes appeared, modern forms of business organisation and many of the consumer goods that we now take for granted all derive from this cluster of innovations, which continued to drive the world economy through two world wars and the turbulent decades between them, into the 1960s and 70s and through to the present (Mokyr, 1998). These technological revolutions do not start and stop conveniently at key dates, but rather they overlap and coexist, often for many decades. So, slowly, the outlines of the 'third industrial revolution' began to make itself felt with computer-led innovations in industrial production, services and communications and which have still to have their full impact in fields, for example, like genetic modification and human health. From the 1970s and 80s, however, the pattern of growth has changed. Growth in the advanced, developed countries has slowed appreciably while that of the developing world (though by no means all of it) has accelerated.

Let us now look in a more abstract way at how an economy actually grows. Basically, the output of an economy reflects the volume of resources used in production, and the ingenuity employed in their utilisation. This is expressed in a formula whereby the output of an economy (Y) is the sum of Labour (L) Capital (K) and Productivity (P). Growth in the economy may be the result of any of the three. Capital nowadays combines both land and physical capital; in less sophisticated economies the two may be separated.

$$Y=L+K+P$$

Labour within an economy is in limited supply. It is determined by the birth rates, the lower and upper bounds of accepted working age and by the participation rate. The participation rates are the proportion of the population within an age group or within a gender group that are engaged in work. However, this demographic bottleneck may be broken by immigration. Likewise, within an economy, capital is in limited supply. It is limited by the degree to which the population is willing to sacrifice current consumption and the ability of the financial system to create money. This potential bottleneck, too, can be relieved by foreigners choosing to invest their assets in the country. That leaves productivity.

An increase in productivity can be defined as either adding relatively more value with the same amount of resources, or by adding the same value with fewer resources. There are various routes to productivity growth, all of which are shown in Figure 3.3. One way the productivity of an economy may be improved is by reallocating resources so that they are engaged in producing higher value-added goods and services, and possibly importing the output sacrificed. Indeed, the advantages of specialisation and trade underpin much of today's rhetoric on free markets and globalisation. Historically, the main shift observed has been the transfer of labour from agriculture and into industry and services. However significant it may be in the long run, by itself the structural shift in resources can only make a one-off contribution to growth. Long-term growth requires innovation. This can take three forms. First, one may distinguish technological innovation in which the production process itself is improved. The second form is product innovation, in which new products are introduced, or existing products redesigned, to add a higher price. Finally, one can distinguish organisational innovation, which involves improvement in management structures and the overall organisation of the enterprise.

Figure 3.3: Sources of Economic Growth

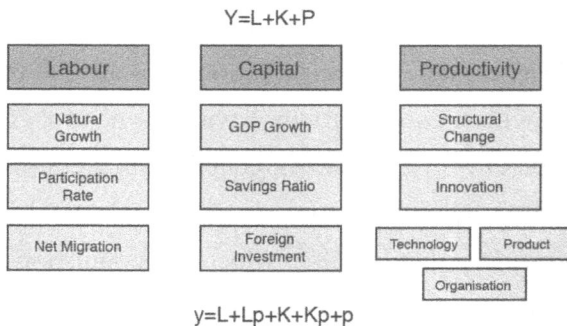

$$Y=L+K+P$$

| Labour | Capital | Productivity |
|---|---|---|
| Natural Growth | GDP Growth | Structural Change |
| Participation Rate | Savings Ratio | Innovation |
| Net Migration | Foreign Investment | Technology / Product |
| | | Organisation |

$$y=L+Lp+K+Kp+p$$

When, in the 1950s, studies were made using long-run (reconstructed) national income series, it was discovered that labour and capital, by themselves accounted for very little of the observed economic growth. Most of the change came from productivity, so much as almost to make the whole exercise futile (Griliches, 1995). Scholars decided that it was wrong to treat productivity as though it was some sort of external variable. Innovation is not a pool available to all. Economies have to invest in new buildings or machines, or in new designers or managers, in order to benefit from productivity change. Thus the calculations were redesigned, this time 'embodying' some of the productivity improvement in labour (through more education) and in capital (through better machines and a younger machine park). The formula now made the output of the economy (Y) dependent on Labour (L) plus the embodied productivity (lp) plus capital (K) and its embodied productivity (kp) plus the residual productivity (p):

$$Y = L + lp + K + kp + p$$

This may all have enhanced the conceptual strength of the exercise, but it did little to make the calculations any easier. And it still left open what actually triggered higher investment or greater innovation in the first place. However, that discussion would provide sufficient material for a whole course by itself, and falls outside the confines of this chapter.

Now that we have established that economies grow, it is evident that changes in GDP are an appropriate way of capturing those developments. Every year countries are engaged in compiling their national accounts, so all that is required is a way of linking them together. The problem is that between one year and the next two things have happened concurrently – the size of the economy has changed and so too have prices. Thus, to compile numbers for GDP growth, statistical offices have to compile an index for inflation. Most of us are familiar with a 'consumer price index' or a 'retail price index', which are often used to measure changes in the so-called 'cost-of-living'. A similar price index has to be constructed for national income purposes. It is known as a 'GDP–deflator' and is much wider in scope, since it has to capture changes not only in end-use consumption articles, but also intermediary inputs and investment goods as well as a wider range of services. Thus, when we have adjusted the nominal GDP calculations to take account of price fluctuations, we have a figure for 'real' GDP which we can express either as an index number (where the base year is 100 and the intermediary data shows the percentage difference) or in terms of national currency (also of a particular year).

There is one major difficulty in the construction of a GDP deflator. In order to construct a composite price index, the 'weight' of each component should reflect the importance of that item in the outcome to which it is linked. Thus in the same way that the price components in a cost-of-living index will be linked to the importance of each in the final pattern of consumption, so the items in a GDP-deflator will be linked to the importance in the overall structure of the economy. This composition is then fixed for a 'base year' and the calculations are made using that distribution. The problem arises that as the economy develops, shifts will occur in the pattern of production as some sectors will grow faster than others, and these expanding areas will become increasingly underrepresented in the index. For this reason, the UN recommends changing the base year of the calculations every five to ten years (UNSD, nd). This does not remove the problem, but it diminishes its impact. Some statisticians use these base years to calculate the index (known as a Laspeyres Index) whereas others prefer to project backwards from a final base calculation (known as a Paasche Index) and still others employ an average of the two (known as a Fischer Index) (Stuval, 1989).[2] Basically, if a country is capable of assembling the necessary information (and one can imagine the difficulties in meeting even this simple criterion in poorer countries) and as long as the base year is changed regularly, major distortions are unlikely to arise. If that is not the case, we have a problem.

## Assessing Results

Compiling national income accounts is not the same as counting people. It involves collating data from many different sources and integrating them into one consistent number. They are often reported monthly or quarterly, but most attention focuses on the twelve-month picture (usually coinciding with the calendar year).

The first and most obvious problem occurs when a country categorically denies the existence of the market and rejects western concepts of GDP. The Soviet Union is the most obvious case of this happening. For most of its history (1928-1992) it had a centrally planned economy, run on an accounting principle of 'material balances', the result of which was measured in prices that were bureaucratically determined. The Soviet Union did provide an all-round number of the size of its economy. However it discounted the service sector, it

---

[2] Statistically, the Laspeyres Index tends to overstate inflation whereas the Paasche Index tends to underestimate it. The Fischer Index, therefore reduces the margin or 'error', but loses the control over the direction on the residual error.

contained a large degree of double-counting and it was expressed in prices that had little relationship to those prevailing in the world market (though this last point did improve in the 1960s) (Pockney, 1991). Since the Soviet Union, at the time, was locked in a military and ideological struggle with the USA, military planners considered it important to be able to make the data comparable with that of Western countries. That involved imposing Western definitions on the Soviet data, making some adjustments for differences in quality and converting the result into Western prices. This task devolved to the US Central Intelligence Agency (CIA). However, with all its resources the CIA consistently overestimated Soviet growth, not by much but small differences accumulate into a large gap. As a result, it overestimated the size of the Soviet economy, and therefore also its economic and military capacity. In the late 1980s, the CIA estimated the size of the Soviet economy as 52 per cent that of the USA, whilst critics at the time suggested 33 per cent might be closer to the mark. After the event Igor Birman suggested that even 25 per cent might have been too optimistic (Bekker, 1994: Maddison, 1998). One interesting consequence of these new insights, of course, lies in our interpretation of the collapse of the Soviet Union. As the USA accelerated the arms' race in the 1980s and as the Soviet Union became embroiled in its intervention in Afghanistan, so its military expenditure increased (Firth and Noren, 1998). This diversion of resources imposed a greater burden on the remainder of the economy (now estimated as being much smaller) than had been realised, and may well have precipitated in the final collapse of the Soviet system.

This same problem afflicted the estimates for other communist countries, including those in Eastern Europe and in South-East Asia. This is equally true for China where differences in the definition of the 'economy' and the nature of prices were compounded by systemic misreporting from all levels of the administration, leading to extreme skepticism, to say the least, of the very high growth rates reported in the 1980s and 1990s (Wu, 2000).

If we leave such instances of fundamental differences in definition aside, a second problem in national accounting is simply poverty. Earlier in this chapter, we stated that expenditure equalled production and that they together equalled income. This was not just an exercise in semantics. Ideally national income should be calculated independently through all three methods, producing the same result. We showed this already Figure 3.1. The range of evidence required for calculating national income through one method, let alone all three simultaneously, already gives an indication why and where things can go wrong. Just look at the categories and think about all the small farms, shops, truckers and day labourers from which to gather information on output, sales, wages and profits, not to mention the large national firms and multinationals from which one hopes to extract accurate and honest information. Then set that against the small, understaffed and underequipped agencies charged with assembling all this data and transforming it into a national income statistic that meets all the international standards, then you get an idea of the mismatch between the ideal and the reality in many poorer countries. Since most UN agencies insist on GDP figures to underpin their policy analyses and since most African statistical agencies are in no state to provide them, the result has been described by one observer as little better than random numbers (Jerven, 2012).

There are two ways in which to acquire the data, either as the by-product of statistics routinely collected by government agencies (known as administrative data) or by specifically collecting answers from those bodies responsible for producing the data in the first place (known as survey data). Obviously, there may be an overlap. The tax authorities may get data from firms' reported profits from businesses themselves, or they may try to elicit the information through statistical surveys. Whether either answer is remotely correct is often a matter of conjecture. Equally, the surveys may not even be comprehensive and the authorities may themselves employ proxy indicators. For example, a sector of economic activity may be estimated by obtaining information on the numbers engaged in an activity, whether employment or crop acreage, and estimating (or guessing) the output or yield on that basis (Jerven, 2013: 13-14). Crop yields anyway are difficult. In the West, the harvest usually takes place in one campaign, but in Africa, many crops can be left in the ground until ready for consumption. In such circumstances, some estimates use rainfall to gauge output or 'eye estimates' by experts. Interestingly, when Ugandans were asked to record their daily harvesting in diaries, the totals were up to 60 per cent higher than those reported to the national household survey, which was used in the compilation of national accounts (Jerven, 2013: 78-79, 88).

The political context within which data is collected may also influence outcomes. For example, Malawi estimated maize production in 2006 at 3.4 million tonnes. This was based on the crop area as recorded fifteen years earlier and the estimated yields. The figure was way too high. Either maize was piling-up in hidden granaries, or the Malawi's were stuffing themselves with maize to an unhealthy degree (4000 calories daily). The 2006 census showed an output for maize of 2.1 million tonnes. The census also suggested that there were one million fewer farmers than had been estimated. The reason for the discrepancy was not hard to find. The government has been issuing subsidy vouchers to poor farmers, which explains the existence of the 'ghost farmers', and officials were anxious to show that the scheme was working, which explains the inflated statistics (Jerven, 2013: 75-77).

A further complication lies in the existence of a large informal, non-monetary, unrecorded economy. We can illustrate this from two examples from Tanzania. Before 1967, its accounts made no estimate for the unrecorded economy, but in 1967 it decided to enter data for construction and rents in the informal sector. The effect was to increase national income by 25 per cent. It repeated the exercise in the 1990s. Guesses varied from 30 per cent to 200 per cent. In the end, the authorities decided to increase GDP by 62 per cent, explained as an ad-hoc adjustment that lay outside the accounting procedures. Usually the outcome is a compromise decided in a meeting with officials of international organisations, like the World Bank. Little wonder that, with some exceptions, one scholar suggested that entire Sub-Saharan Africa should be treated as one poor economy, and that statistical analyses trying to suggest some nuanced relationship between individual GDP data and other variables be abandoned (Jerven, 2012).

Another problem in poorer countries lies in the long time intervals between serious attempts to gauge the size of the economy. As a result, the base of the calculations rapidly becomes outdated. Let us take a theoretical example. One way in which a country may count the impact of the telecommunication sector is through the number of telephones connected to land lines. These land lines are very expensive and this influences the 'value added' to the GDP totals. The authorities then count the new registrations every year and adjusts the 'value added' accordingly. They continue doing this for ten to fifteen years, but in the meantime mobile phones have entered the market and have found an enthusiastic demand. No one bothers with land lines anymore, so that it appears as though the telecommunications sector is stagnating whereas the opposite might be true.

The example of Ghana is fairly typical. Before the most recent change, the national income statistics were calculated on a price index base established in 1993. When, in 2006 a new price-index was constructed, the estimated GDP increased by no less than 62 per cent. The World Bank immediately upgraded Ghana's status from a 'poor' to a 'lower-middle income' country (Jerven, 2013: 26-27). However the prize for GDP gains from such rebasing exercises lies with Nigeria, whose experience we will examine in the Case Study section at the end of this chapter. Figure 3.4 shows the results of other rebasing exercises in African and South American countries. It is evident that the results of rebasing have led to major revisions in GDP estimates. Moreover, very often there is no data to revise the figures for the previous years. The doubts over current estimates, therefore, should also translate to doubts over earlier years, and therefore also to the estimates of economic growth. which does no more than tie together estimates made for different points of time.

Figure 3.4: The Impact of Rebasing Exercises in Africa
and South America (percentage change in GDP)

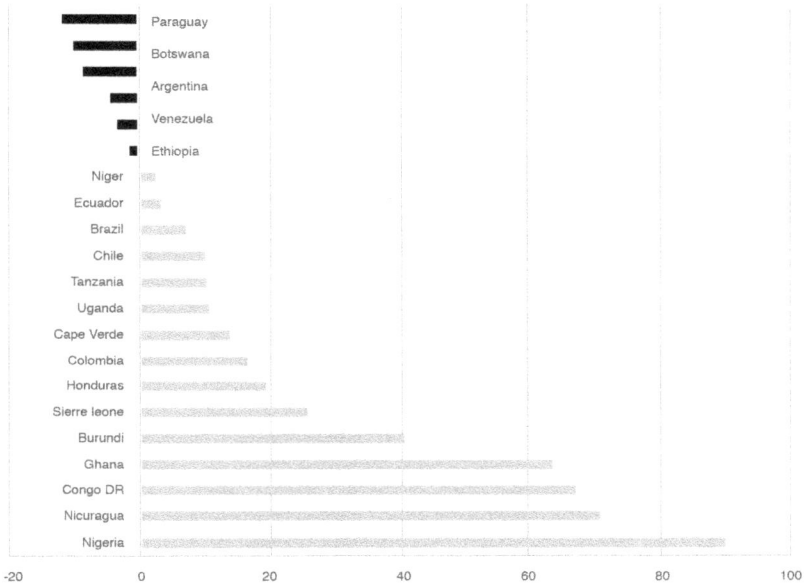

Source: Kale, 2014, 12-13.

The informal economy is not confined to poorer countries but is a feature of all national economies. The problem, of course, lies in measuring something that citizens wish to remain concealed, either because it is illegal or because declaring it will involve some sanction (either in the form of taxation or enforced compliance to some law or regulation). There are several approaches to solving this problem. The first is by enquiring whether people engage in the informal economy as a supplier or as a consumer, and asking the sums involved. Not surprisingly, most social scientists think that the results of such exercises vastly underestimate the size of the informal economy. The second approach is to measure an indicator whose size is related to the size of the economy, seeing how far this diverges from what is expected and relating this to the official recorded GDP.

One favoured indicator is the size of electricity consumption (on the assumption that this will vary with economic activity). Another is the amount of cash (coins and notes) in circulation relative to the total money supply (assuming that those wishing to avoid detection would prefer cash payment). A third method lies in seeing whether there is a discrepancy between national income calculated by the expenditure method and that calculated by the income method (the informal economy being revealed by less being earned than is being spent). However, the problem with is approach is that statisticians do everything in their power to prevent such discrepancies occurring, and they declare the rest as 'errors and omissions' (Schneider and Enste, 2000; Feld and Schneider, 2010).

One man who has made almost a life work in measuring the 'shadow' economy is Francis Schneider from the Johannes Kepler University in Linz, Austria. His first venture into the field was in 1985 when he wrote on the shadow economy in the USA during the 1980s, and he has been active in the field ever since. His estimates have been used in official publications of the World Bank, the OECD and the European Union, and so have almost received 'official' status. However, although they may be the best we have, that does not make them right. The method he employs he describes as the MIMIC method – multiple indicator, multiple causes. This combines supposed indictors for the size of the 'real economy', such as employment rates, working hours and cash in circulation, with proxy indicators for probable causes of non–declaration, such as the weight of taxes and social insurance contributions in the economy and proxy indicators for the efficiency of state institutions and tax morale. These results are collected for many countries and for several years, and are then run against national income data to establish a 'best fit' relationship. Any deviation from this is assumed to represent the shadow economy. Before we examine this, it is worth noting that the method makes no distinction between legal and illegal activities (the result covers both) and he is not interested in capturing income declared in tax havens or other countries for the purposes of tax avoidance. The results are shown in the Figure 3.5. Schneider's estimates suggest that the world average size of the shadow economy in 2005 was 17.1 per cent. This ranged from 13.4 among the high income OECD countries to 37.6 per cent in Sub-Saharan Africa. The USA performs best with only 8.6 per cent with Bolivia, Georgia, Panama and Zimbabwe anchoring the bottom of the range with results of over 60 per cent (Schneider and Williams, 2013).

There are several problems with this approach. Let us with the quantifiable indicators. It is perfectly possible to be legitimately employed and, at the same time, to be engaged in the shadow economy and there is no reason to assume that one type of work is more productive than the other. Therefore the relationship between recorded employment and total economic activity is tendentious. Similarly there are other factors that can explain the preference for cash, other than for shadow payments. These range from the state of development of the banking system to the prospect of being ejected from a currency union. If we turn to the proxy indicators, the burden of state regulation is represented by a *Heritage Foundation* index of six factors (weighted equally) and the quality of state institutions is represented by the World Bank composite index for the ' rule of law'. As we will see in Chapter Seven, the World Bank itself warns against using its indicators for strict international comparison. The tax morale indicator is taken from a question in the *World Value Survey*, which we will be criticising in Chapter Five. Not only are there criticisms of what is put into the model used to construct the

Figure 3.5: World Map of the Shadow Economy (percentage GDP) 1999–2007 av.

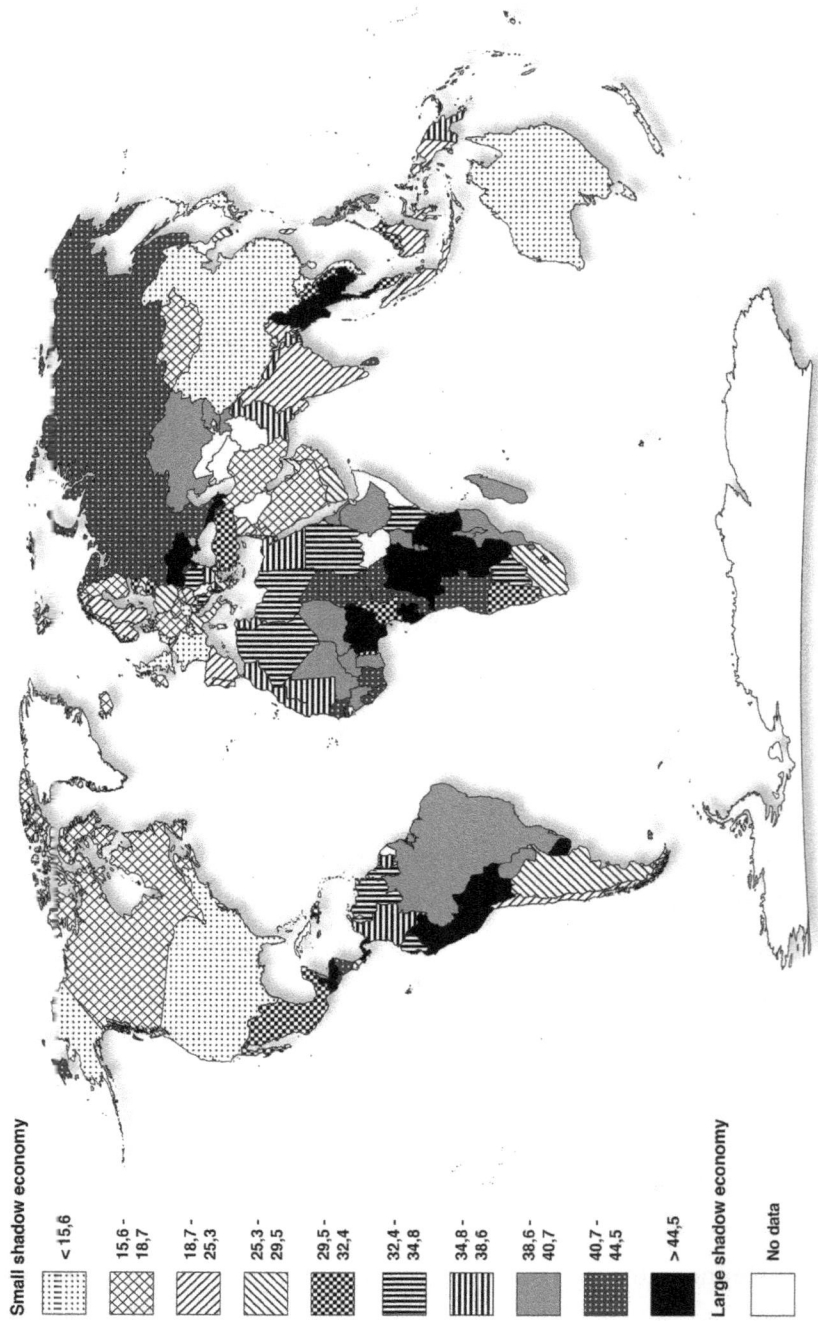

Small shadow economy

< 15,6

15,6 - 18,7

18,7 - 25,3

25,3 - 29,5

29,5 - 32,4

32,4 - 34,8

34,8 - 38,6

38,6 - 40,7

40,7 - 44,5

> 44,5

Large shadow economy

No data

Source: Schnieder and Williams, 2013.

'real' economy, the basis data used for the exercise are the GDP data, adjusted for structural differences in prices, using the base of 2005. As discuss elsewhere in this Chapter, these estimates are highly dubious and had the effect of exaggerating real differences between highly developed and other economies. The final problem is that the results do not convince. For example, it is difficult to believe that the relative size of the shadow economy in Finland is twice as large as that of the USA.

Another phenomenon we need to discuss is the impact of changes in the definition of what to include in national income calculations and, more importantly, where. This usually implies shifting items from single-use goods (where they appear once) and durable goods or assets (where they can earn income later). In 2008 the UN published recommended changes in the structure of national accounts, known as SNA 2008. By applying these in July 2013, the USA increased its GDP estimates by fully three per cent, which had the effect of adding an output equivalent to the GDP of Belgium to the world economy. The new element in the statistics is 'intangible assets'. These have two components. The biggest (two per cent) is formed by the reservoir of research and development (R&D) created and held in the American economy. Before the revision, R&D was seen as costs in the production process, an input into every single i-pad or smart phone, but having no further intrinsic value. Now it gets its very own entry into the calculations, affecting not only GDP but also the share of the investment and government spending elements, and substantially altering its regional distribution. New Mexico and Maryland both obtained a huge lift, growing by ten per cent and six per cent respectively. Another element in the revision (one per cent) will be accounted for by the inherent value stored in movies, television series and books and music, etc. The head of the US Bureau for Economic Analysis claims great things for the fresh insights obtained and boasts that the new series will be back projected to 1929 (*Financial Times*, 21.4.2013).

The European Union (EU) followed suit in September 2014 when the new system ESA2010 came into force, incorporating some, but not all, of the elements in SNA2008. When the calculations appeared based on the new system, the EU's statistical services were quite sanguine about the effect. The changes served to add 0.1 percentage points to growth rates between 1997 and 2013. The overall result was to raise the EU's GDP for 2010 by 2.3 per cent, of which 1.9 per cent resulted from changes in the way R&D expenditures were included in the data and 0.2 per cent for the fact that weapons systems expenditures were counted as investment. At the press briefing, Eurostat's Director of National Accounts had concluded "no revolution, no rewriting of economic history" (Eurostat Press briefing 17.10.2014), words he might yet come to regret. No sooner were the revisions announced than a row blew up in the UK when the new estimates were applied to each country's contribution to the EU's common budget (this is a balancing item that is capped of each country at 1.24 per cent of its GNI). The demand from the UK to contribute an extra €2.1 billion to cover the effect of these changes when applied to the budget for 2010–2013 led to headlines of outrage across the British press. These were followed a few days later by a very public declaration by the Prime-Minister not to pay, a position from which he was forced to retreat. The new calculations and their financial consequence have helped fuel the growing disaffection within the UK towards the EU which may yet result in a decision to leave the Union. Eurostat might not be rewriting economic history, but it is helping reconfigure British attitudes towards the EU. If we want to understand what had happened there are three things to consider – the extent of the UK's upward revision of its GDP, the extent of the changes in the other member states (and the combination of the two determining whether one gained or lost in the renewed budget calculations) and, finally, the contribution of the new accounting system to the problem. The UK's GDP in 2010 had indeed gained more than the rest of the EU (4.9 per cent, against the EU's average increase of 3.7 per cent) but over half of that increase had been the result of statistical improvements in the UK's own national statistical office (Eurostat News Release 17.10.2014), primarily the inclusion of 'not-for-profit' institutions providing household services and receiving voluntary donations (charities) (ONS News Release 9.7.2014).

With the explosion of interest around the UK few noticed that The Netherlands had itself become 7.6 per cent richer than previously thought. This is, indeed, a massive increase, and all the more interesting since only 1.7 per cent of the change came from the implementation of ESA2010. Statistical improvements accounted for the rest (Eurostat News Release 17.10.2014). The Netherlands is a rich country (and now even richer) with a sophisticated statistical office. In theory, it should not be having such large readjustments. It resulted from of the Statistical Office's investment in automatic computer linkages to new and better databases, including those of the taxation authorities and chambers of commerce. These provided more complete data than the previous estimates from sample data. New estimates were made for the burgeoning category of self-employed and small businesses, for salaries paid to employees, for the growing ICT industry and for financial payments to and from abroad (TKSW, 21 501-03Begrotingsraad, 11.11.2014). Undoubtedly the Dutch statistics have improved but two questions remain  How can this extra income be back-projected into revised economic growth data, and how comparable are the Dutch statistics now with other countries that have (yet) to introduce the same improvements?

So far, we have been dealing with annual data, but the purpose of these national accounting exercises is not only to allow governments to reconstruct the recent past. They also want access to timely and accurate statistics to help them choose and implement appropriate policy measures. In Western Europe, for example, many observers claimed that the marriage of economic statistics with improved economic insights had allowed post-war governments to 'conquer the trade cycle' and to hold their economies on optimal growth trajectories, a claim that was revealed for its hollowness by the advent of the oil crises of the 1970s. However, let us take a more recent example. In September 2008, the bankruptcy of the Lehmann Brothers bank in the USA precipitated what was to become the greatest economic slump since the Great Depression of the 1930s. The information upon which the American government relied for its analysis was provided by the Bureau for Economic Analysis (BEA). The BEA did pick up on the fact that the economy was sliding into a recession, but utterly underestimated its impact. In January 2009, it reported that in the 4th quarter of 2008 the economy had contracted at an annualised rate of 3.8 per cent. One month later, it had revised its estimate to a decline of 6.2 percent (BEA Press Release, 27.2.2009). In the following months it edged the figure higher still, to 6.8 per cent (BEA Press Release, 26.3.2009). But then, in its latest estimate (BEA Press Release, 29.7.2011) it altered the figure to a staggering 8.9 per cent. What had gone wrong? First, the earliest estimates are, indeed, just that. The early statistics are estimates and they arrive with a delay, sometimes of two or even three months. Thus the first hikes, from January to February/March, stemmed from the ability to include the real data from the last month (i.e. December) of the quarter. Second, in the absence of any data, the estimates are based on projections from previous trends. This practice assumes basically that the near future will resemble the recent past – a reasonable assumption in most circumstances but not when a sea change, from growth to decline, is taking place. These are called 'turning point errors' and they bedevil all attempts at economic forecasting. Finally, the original data itself is revised and reworked. The data may come in a year or more after the events, and then they have to be complied and collated and, by this route, we arrive at the final revisions of July 2011 (BEA FAQ 1003, 5.8.2011). Incidentally, the 2013 switch in the System of Accounts also had the effect of making the impact of the financial crash a little less than estimated at the time, and the recovery marginally faster (BEA Press Release, 31.7.2013).

Deliberate cheating is another source of error. In February 2013, Argentina became the first country ever to be censured by the International Monetary Fund (IMF) for defects in its inflation and economic growth data (IMF Press Release, 1.2.2013). Since 2007 the government had been replacing expert staff in the statistical office with its own nominees and had started manipulating the official statistics. The inflation statistics were one area of interest, since the reported statistics would be expected to impact on wage demands and on funding its international debt (Economist, Don't lie to me Argentina, 25.2.2012). The deliberate understatement of inflation rebounded onto the GDP-deflator and from there onto the GDP figures. The IMF in its bi-annual World Economic Surveys for 2013, made it very clear in the presentation of GDP statistics that it was using its own GDP estimates and not those supplied by the Argentine government.

Finally, one last source of error is exactly what it says, an error. On 23rd May 2013, the Thai Commerce Ministry announced that exports for April showed an increase of 10.5 per cent on the year before. Exports data is important for Thailand since they constitute 70 per cent of GDP. One week later, they revised the growth downwards to 2.89 per cent. The reason? The spokesperson "admitted there was an error in the entry for export items that resulted in an unusually high figure for April. One transaction for electronics worth 300,000 baht was wrongly entered by an employee as 30 billion, causing a huge error" (Bangkok Post. 1.6.2013). Whoops.

## Comparing GDP

In the previous chapter, we configured the world in terms of population and we traced the changes in its distribution over the course of the 20th century. We return to the world's population in 2011 in Figure 3.6, but this time we compare it not with population from an earlier period but with an indication of the world's output in the same year. The differences are striking. In the year 2011 world output, measured by its gross domestic product expressed in current dollars, is dominated by North America, Europe and Japan, but four of the five BRICSs are also in the top decile (top ten percent) in terms of size. The missing country, South Africa, would have ranked 29th. Since the distortions in the cartogram make a detailed country-by-country comparison difficult, it is worth commenting on the larger ones. The largest economy in the world is the USA, which is still twice as large as that of its nearest competitor, China. In third place is Japan, with a total GDP that is one third the size of that of the USA, followed by Germany, France, and Brazil. The United Kingdom (UK), Italy, Russia and India make up the remainder of the ten largest economies.

Figure 3.6: World Map of Population and GDP 2011

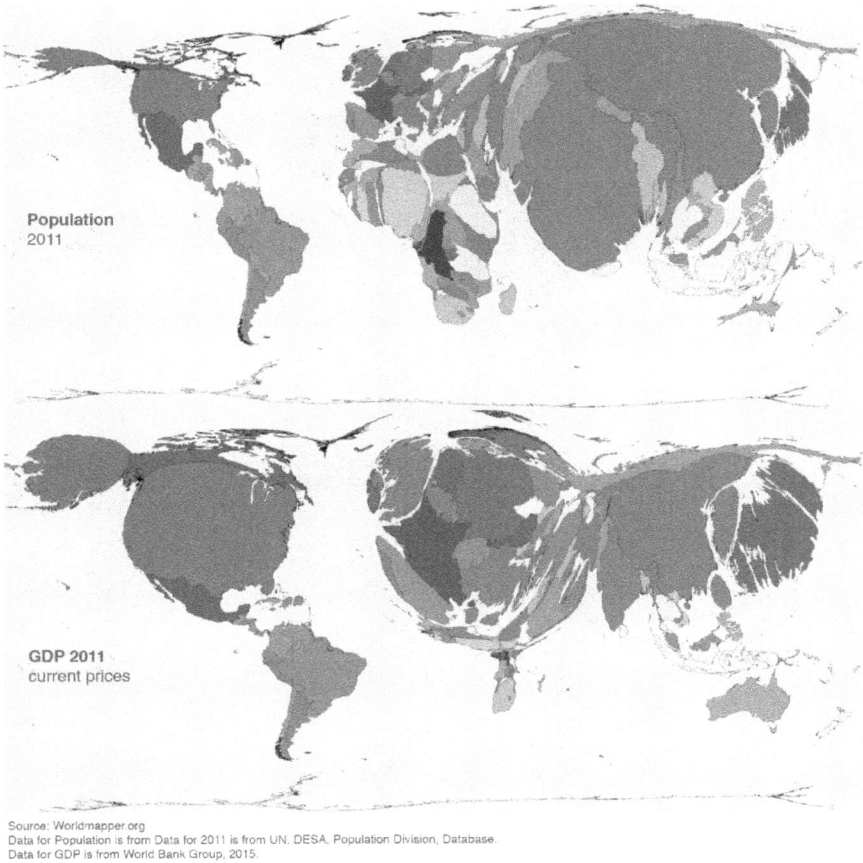

Figure 3.7: World Map of per capita GDP 2011 (current dollars)

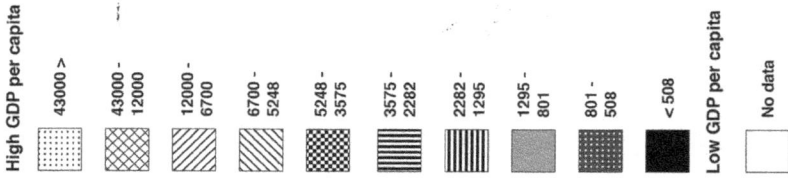

**High GDP per capita**

- 43000 >
- 43000 - 12000
- 12000 - 6700
- 6700 - 5248
- 5248 - 3575
- 3575 - 2282
- 2282 - 1295
- 1295 - 801
- 801 - 508
- < 508

**Low GDP per capita**

- No data

Source: World Bank Group, 2015.

The size of a country's economy is obviously important since what happens there spills over into the rest of the world economy. This occurs through the rise or fall in the demand for imports, through its willingness to invest abroad and, in a more abstract way, through the effect on 'investor confidence' in the immediate future of the world economy as a whole. Now, large economies are a function of both the population size and their productive capacity. If we divide the GDP figures by population size, we obtain a picture of the command, on average, that each person in that economy has over world resources. These resources are paid for in real dollars, or currencies that can be transferred into real dollars. They provide a preliminary assessment of the income that an economy can offer its citizens in a given year. We have deliberately taken the data for 2011 because we will want to compare it with an alternative set of data adjusted for structural differences in prices later in this chapter. The results for countries with populations over 1.5 million are shown in Figure 3.7.

The data is arranged in deciles so that each shading is equivalent to ten per cent of the total number of countries. What is interesting is that not one of the top-ten countries in terms of total GDP makes it into the top-ten when measured in per capita terms – the closest is the USA which is in eleventh place. In 2011 Norway was the richest country in the world, followed by Qatar. It would be easy to explain this by reference to their energy output, which would also help explain Kuwait's position as seventh. Australia's fourth place, too, owes a great deal to its mineral wealth. However, that does not really explain the other countries which include Switzerland in third place, Denmark and Sweden in fifth and sixth place respectively, and Canada, Singapore and The Netherlands which follow Kuwait to make up the top-ten. If we then pass the USA, the next countries are Austria, Ireland, Finland and Belgium. This list, then covers the top decile. The one feature that binds the non-resource-rich states is that they would all be considered among the 'smaller' economies or, as the group identified itself in the 1970s and 80s, as 'middle powers'. The second decile rescues some of the more familiar developed economies – Japan, Germany, France, the UK, Italy and South Korea – and includes two more oil-states – the United Arab Emirates and Saudi Arabia.

If we move to the opposite end of the spectrum, the lowest decile is entirely occupied by states from Sub-Saharan Africa, and they are also over-represented in the next decile, with nine of the fifteen places. The remaining countries are Haiti, Nepal, Tajikistan, Bangladesh, Myanmar and Cambodia. For reasons we explain elsewhere in this chapter it is not wise to put too much store on the exact rankings of these poorer countries. At this level, any country could easily slip across a decile or two, but not much more than that. The numbers may not be exact, but that does not mean that they are completely useless.

Until now, we have been dealing with national income statistics that are expressed as a value or as a percentage of the nominal sum in a given year (the effect is the same). The obvious way to compare countries is to convert them to a common currency, at the exchange rates prevailing in that year. That currency is usually the US dollar, although the European Union uses the euro. If the currency conversion takes place in the same year as the GDP figure, then we refer to the data as being expressed in "current" dollars or euros and if we are taking historical data and anchoring it on a specific year we express the data as "constant dollars" and we quote the year (e.g. constant 2010 dollars). We will see later in this section that there is an alternative way of comparing national income data, one which tries to take account of the purchasing power of currencies in different countries. In this case the data will be expressed in purchasing power parity dollars or "PPP dollars" of that year. Now, we must appreciate that we do not get paid in PPP dollars; we do not earn PPP dollars, and we do not spend PPP dollars. They are all statistical constructions. Thus, for a world of actual payments and real transactions we should always deal in real dollars. If they buy more in one country and less in another, tough luck, that is life. Whether we are looking at the size of economies in a globalised world, at the size of trade and investment flows, of international payments and debts or the size of economies to support it all, we should be using current dollars. There should be no 'debate' on this issue.

As we have seen, the first step towards an international comparison is to convert all the data to a single currency. However, while this solves one problem, it creates others. Firstly, the exchange rates at which the dollar is converted into other currencies fluctuate over time. If, for example, the euro drops ten per cent against the dollar, it does not mean that the European countries have become relatively ten per cent poorer (they will be a little poorer to the extent that dollar imports will cost more, but nowhere near that magnitude). Thus we have to find a way to compensate for the impact of fluctuating exchange rates because that will alter relative price levels, when they are expressed in the chosen currency. That brings us to the second problem. It is not only (changing) exchange rates that affect prices. As any tourist knows, some countries (usually poorer ones) have structurally lower prices than others. This is because local prices are determined by local supply and demand factors, and important elements in that process such as rents, wages and even some raw materials differ between countries (and even within countries). Usually, but not automatically, prices are lower in poorer countries (Deaton and Heston 2009). Thus, if we are to compare countries, we have to eliminate the effect of both fluctuating exchange rates and these structural differences in price levels. In other words we have to calculate the 'purchasing power parities' of the common currency so that the purchasing power of a currency will buy is equal in each country.

This is an enormous undertaking since it involves collecting and comparing prices across a wide range of products in over 190 countries, and often also within countries (to reflect urban/rural price differences and regional variations). It all started in 1968 when a group of economists working at the University of Pennsylvania, the UN and the World Bank together formed a joint venture named 'The International Comparisons Project (ICP)'. The Pennsylvania team later left the group but has continued producing its own estimates in various versions of Penn World Tables (PWT) and extended these back to 1950. Many economists use the PWT for their cross-country empirical work, partly because these also disaggregates the national accounting data into consumption, investment, government expenditure etc., but there have been damning condemnations of the impacts of revisions of its methodology on comparisons, especially over small-time intervals (Johnson e.a. 2009). If it is the national income data only that is required, it is best to stick with the original source for the time being.

The first ICP studies were to see whether an international comparison of prices was possible at all. The very first study covered only 16 countries, and the number slowly rose to 34 for 1975, 60 for 1980 and

65 for 1985. The increase was largely the result of the EU and the OECD beginning their own price comparisons in parallel with the ICP project, which meant that the increased coverage was confined mainly to richer, developed Western economies. At this point the project introduced a ten-year gap to allow it to tighten procedures and to train officials in other (usually poorer) countries. This pause was an implicit recognition of the shortcomings in the quality of the results (Deaton and Heston 2009; Johnson ea. 2009). After the ICP resumed, the country coverage increased to 115 in 1996, 146 in 2005 and no less than 199 for 2011 (though data was provided for only 177), whose results were released in 2014. However, the increase in the country-coverage complicated price comparison. For the 1996 exercise, the world was divided into six regions, each with its own responsibilities for collecting the price data. The idea was that countries in a region should share similar economic structures, but this consideration was somewhat undone by the definition of the regions – Africa, Asia-Pacific, Russia and the CIS, South America, West Asia and Europe/OECD. Each region would construct its own list of goods and establish price comparisons. The idea was that these regions would then be linked to each other, using 'bridging countries' that shared characteristics of more than one region. However, since each region had chosen a different selection of goods, this was not a very elegant performance. Still, the results determined the PPP results until the next round, almost a decade later. The way GDP was updated between the surveys was to take the reported national 'real' growth rates (changes in nominal GDP divided by changes in prices) and adjust the base year accordingly – but note, the prices used in the ICP exercise are not the same as those used to construct the consumer price index for individual countries (Deaton and Heston, 2009: 27-28).

In 2005 the number of countries partaking in the exercise had risen to 146, the first time we can suggest that there was near comprehensive coverage of the world's economies. The idea of starting with a regional base remained unchanged (and so did the regions themselves). In addition a 'ring' of eighteen countries, spread over the regions, was selected that would compile price data for a smaller common list of goods and services. In this way, it was hoped to link the eighteen countries in a multilateral price comparison and apply the results to the regional comparisons. Even at the time, there were doubts about the methodology of separate lists. Moreover, it proved difficult to select products that were consumed in all the countries involved. Cameroon, Kenya Senegal, Zambia and Sri Lanka had to price a vintage bottle of Bordeaux, a front-loaded washing machine with a pre-specified spin speed and a Peugot 407 with air conditioning and climate control. In addition, the selection of countries was a little bizarre since not all countries were willing to take part in a second separate exercise. There were six countries for Africa but only two (the UK and Japan) from the OECD (Deaton and Aten 2014). Up to this moment, the tendency in each ICP round had, in retrospect, been to overstate price levels in poorer countries and therefore, to understate their levels of PPP-adjusted GDP. It came as some surprise, therefore, when the ICP exercise for 2005 showed them to be almost 40 per cent poorer (and some 30 per cent smaller) than had previously been accepted. Basing itself on extrapolations from the 1996 ICP exercise, the World Bank had in 2007 recorded China's per capita income as $6757 and that of India as $3452. The first results of the 2005 ICP exercise (published in 2007) suggested that the figures should be $4091 and $2162 respectively (all in constant 2005 US dollars PPP). In China's case, several explanations were offered. First, the original data was suspect. China's extrapolation had been made from 1985, since it had not participated in the 1996 exercise, and so there was more time for discrepancies in relative prices to emerge. Second, there were deficiencies in the 2005 exercise itself. Only eleven cities were included in the Chinese survey. These may have been regionally suspect, and may have left the countryside underrepresented. Moreover, in an effort to make the products for which prices were collected more comparable, they may have become less representative. Comparable products (like Starbucks or McDonalds) tended to be at the 'high end' of the market and may not even be consumed by most of the population, who prefer lower price (and possibly lower quality) alternatives. A third element lay in changes in GDP calculation itself, especially in the treatment of government activities that may have led to their overvaluation (Hill and Syed, 2011).

Although doubts were raised almost immediately about the 2005 comparison, the figures stood uncorrected, and formed the basis of new sets of PPP-adjusted data for economists and social scientists to play with, until the publication of the next round in 2014. This most recent exercise led to banner headlines of China catching up, and threatening to overtake, the USA and India overtaking Japan. Most of the poorer countries also recorded upward GDP revisions compared with the extrapolations from the previous round. Figure 3.8 portrays cartograms showing the difference between world GDP measured in current dollars and in PPP dollars. Basically the switch to PPP data makes most OECD countries lose ground when compared with the USA and the rest of the world, including the head-line grabbing big-economies like China and India, to gain.

Figure 3.8: World Map of GDP in current
dollars and in ppp dollars 2011

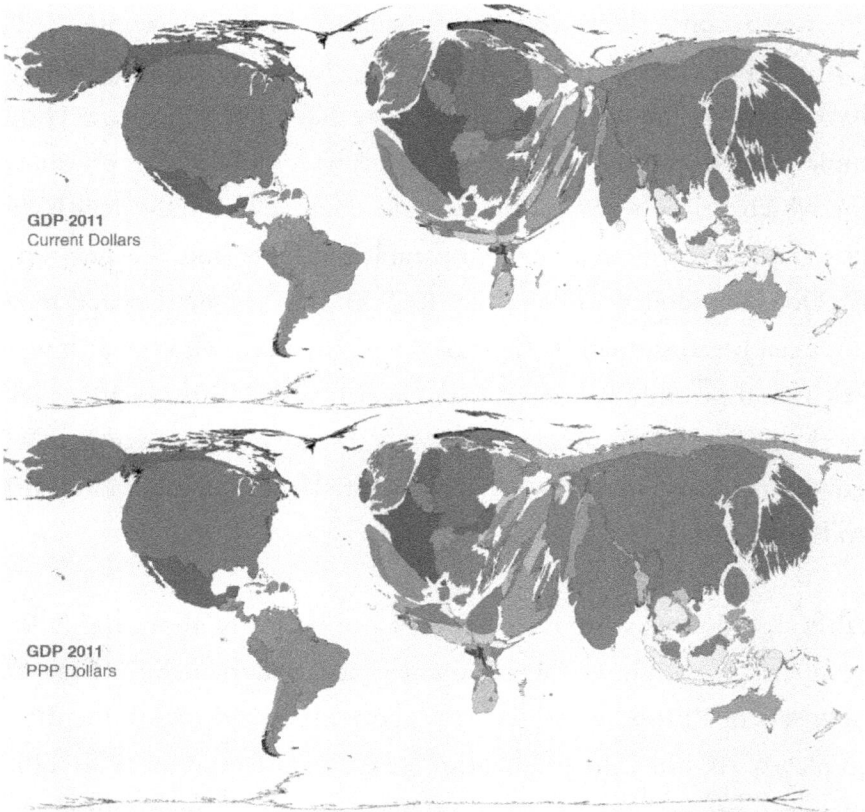

GDP 2011
Current Dollars

GDP 2011
PPP Dollars

Source: Worldmapper.org
Data for Population is from Data for 2011 is from UN, DESA, Population Division, Database.
Data for GDP is from World Bank Group, 2015.

The effect of ICP 2011 was a huge upward revision for poorer countries
compared with the estimates based on forward projections from the
ICP 2005 exercise. To some extent, the size of the discrepancy
compensated for the (mistaken) downward revisions caused by ICP
2005. Moreover, since the differences within regions were far less
than the differences between them, it seems that much of the change
came from how the different regions were linked. In ICP 2005,
the link was made through a 'ring' of eighteen countries. For ICP

2011 all the countries were compared based on a (shorter) common list of goods. A comparison of the two methods has suggested that measurement errors were large for the poorer ring members, but less so for the richer (Deaton and Aten, 2014; Inklaar and Prasada Rao, 2014; Ravallion, 2014).

The ICP 2011 results may be the best we have ever had, with wider coverage and a more credible methodology, but that does not make them accurate. The project advises users to assume measurement errors of up to five per cent on all data. It also warns that comparisons between larger economies with diverse domestic structures, such as the USA, China, India and Brazil, could have error margins approaching 15 per cent. Even higher error margins could be anticipated for Africa. In addition, the project specifically warns that the ICP exercise was only intended to measure differences at the specific points of comparison (i.e. 2011) and not at points between them (World Bank Group 2015).

This brings us to some final reflections. "Over the last thirty years, more and better data have fundamentally changed the practice of both microeconomics and macroeconomics. No new data have been more important and more influential than those of the International Price Comparison" (Deaton and Heston, 2009: 1). So trumpets the opening of a paper criticising the 2005 ICP, but being broadly in favour of such an exercise being undertaken. It is difficult not to agree. Policy-makers and academics need to compare countries across space and across time, and this need does not stop in 1980, or 1950. Economic historians working to reconstruct national income data from the fragmentary surviving records of the past, must be able to make statements about the cause and timing of relative advance and decline. On the other hand this kind of data should not be entered into sophisticated statistical analysis. The ICP 2011 exercise may be accurate (at the time and within limits) but what about previous exercises? Those of 2005 and 1996 were flawed in their methodologies and all the exercises that preceded them, whatever their methodological weaknesses, also suffered from a lack of geographical coverage. Nevertheless, thousands of academic articles have used this data for cross-country comparisons at single points in time (and not always the survey years) or translated into economic growth, between points of time.

Our doubts over the quality of national income data become even more acute when we bear in mind that the ICP exercises do nothing more than convert the 'official' GDP data into PPP-comparable measures. However, we have also seen that for less-developed countries, these are often founded on inadequate procedures and out-of-date base years. Even now, over half of the Sub-Saharan African countries are in the process of GDP rebasing exercises that can change their estimates anything up to 90 per cent, and once these exercises have been completed we still have no accurate idea of how, over time, they reached these new levels. We have also seen that even among developed countries the timing of statistical improvements can open up gaps of four, five, six per cent between countries (although here we may obtain reliable back projections).

Global comparison of GDP data is not 100 per cent reliable even today. It was less so a year ago. Yet all this time social scientists have seized on GDP data as though the quality was all the same, as though it portrayed what the text books said it should portray. Their label seems to shield the data from closer scrutiny and, should ever a doubt arise, their use is legitimised by the legions of scientists that have used them previously. It was interesting that in reading all the literature commenting on and criticising the ICP data, almost all expended pages on different measures of constructing price indices; none questioned the validity of the official GDP figures themselves.

## Summary

Lets us summarise what we have learned. This chapter started by examining the drivers of growth of the world's economies. It noted that the systematic compilation of national accounts began slightly over a century ago and only became common after the second half of the previous century. It warned that there are important differences between gross domestic product (GDP), gross national income (GNI) and net national income (NNI).

It showed wide discrepancies among countries between the size of their populations and the size of their economies. These are the result of differences in the supply of labour and capital and in productivity. National income measured over time is obtained by converting nominal national income to constant prices using a GDP-deflator and this measure is used to describe economic growth.

It demonstrated that the national income data collected is not always reliable. Many poorer countries lack the resources to collect the required data and they often leave the base-year for calculations remains unchanged for too long. In addition, all countries have an informal sector or shadow economy which is difficult to measure.

Finally, changes in the definition of GDP can lead to significant changes also in developed economies.

The chapter then reviewed the attempts since 1968 to construct another basis for comparing national incomes that took account of structural differences in prices. These were expressed in 'PPP dollars'. It showed that the early attempts at PPP-adjustment suffered from a restricted geographical coverage whilst the quality of more recent adjustments have suffered from methodological problems in linking regional comparisons with each other. It cautioned that PPP-adjusted data does contain error margins and should only be employed for the year of construction and not for growth over time.

Finally, this chapter suggested that none of the PPP-data pays any attention to deficiencies in the original national accounts. Hoever, this does not seem to have stopped social scientists using either the original national income estimates or their PPP-adjusted counterparts as indicators for relative wealth or poverty or for economic growth in their sophisticated statistical or econometric analyses. Do not forget this, since we will come across GDP data throughout this book, either by itself, or incorporated into so-called composite indices. This starts with the next chapter on poverty.

# Case Study: Nigeria's GDP

On 6th April 2014 the Statistician-General of the National Bureau of Statistics, Dr Yemi Kale (2014), announced that Nigeria's GDP had increased from $264 billion to $510 billion, an increase of fully 89 per cent. This, he observed, allowed the country to overtake South Africa and made Nigeria the largest economy on the African continent, and the 26th largest in the world. Of course, on the ground, nothing else had changed – people earned the same, spent the same and the poor remained as poor as they had been before. So, what had been going on?

Nigeria's previous calculations of its GDP had been based on 1990. Changes since then had been a combination of changes in volume of output and changes in prices. To determine growth, statisticians had first to eliminate the effect of price changes and then to express the volume changes in terms of 1990 prices. They tend not to do this for every single product, but instead calculate a 'price deflator' for the economy as a whole, and this is expressed in terms of the relative importance of each sector in 1990. Since economies tend to change structure over time, the base year gradually becomes less and less relevant, which is why most governments change it every five years or so. Nigeria had not changed its base year for almost a quarter of a century.

These things do not always happen by accident and it has been suggested that the fact that the Obasanjo administration (1999-2007) was negotiating with international creditors for a debt rescheduling may have contributed to not wanting Nigeria to emerge (officially at least) as being more prosperous that it appeared. In the event, the government pulled off a write-off of $20 billion and a payments reschedule for the rest – a deal so (over-)generous that the debt had finally been paid (Mudasiru and Adabonyon, 2011). Under such circumstances it is not surprising that updating the GDP statistics was not a priority. Besides, there were no new numbers available. The statistical services that calculate GDP statistics very rarely collect the data themselves. They rely on inputs from other parts of the administration such as tax data, customs revenues, business accounts, agricultural estimates, labour statistics and so on. If these numbers are not collected, there is not much that the central office can do about it. They do the best with what they have and the quality of the results depends on the numbers of staff, their training and the computer facilities available to them – and the latter is usually far behind what is available in the West. Basically, national accounts were not a priority. There were often no numbers and too little resources.

Since 1990 there have been three areas of change in the international definitions of national income (Kale, 2014). The first lay in the way government services were calculated. The second was a change in the calculations for the entertainment industry and for R&D. The final one, and the one most likely to impact on Nigeria was an attempt to capture more of the informal economy. However, the most important factor influencing Nigeria's statistics was the number of enterprises included in the exercise. Officials cannot survey all businesses every year and so they take a representative sample, assuming that changes there will reflect changes in the sector as a whole. The 1990 census had 83,733 units; the latest estimates surveyed 851,628. In other words, the sample size had increased by a factor 10.2. The biggest changes were in real estate (up from 610 to 11,721), professional services (from 4593 to 125,482), construction (from 551 to 53,507) and trade and vehicle repair (from 16,583 to 502,085). The effect has not only been to raise Nigeria's GDP estimates, but to reveal a far more complex economy than had been captured in the statistics previously.

Although the weight of agriculture declines only slightly, the figures reveal a wider diversity of crops and a marked decrease in the importance of forestry. By constrast the industrial sector declines dramatically and the share of oil in the economy is reduced from from 42.5 to 15.5 per cent. Within the industrial sector, manufacturing expands from 1.9 to 6.6 per cent. The most noticeable change is the major shift in the importance of the service sector whose share in the economy had grown from 26 per cent to 50 per cent, with the most dramatic increase being shown by telecommunications and ICT, whose share of GDP has grown from 0.7 to 9.1 per cent. More importantly, perhaps, it records a service sector considerably more diverse and more dynamic than had previously been revealed.

So, Nigeria has new and better statistics. For the government this will allow overall for better planning and for the formulation of more targeted sectoral policy. For example it could target more support towards the emerging film industry which in 2013 is estimated to have contributed 1.2 per cent to GDP. The new statistics also shows that there is room for more government involvement in the economy. The level of government debt is only 11 per cent of GDP rather than the 19 per cent previously estimated, and the government's tax income is only 12 per cent of GDP instead of 20 per cent, though is it still reliant on oil for over half of that income. It also gives the government some 'bragging rights'.... it is the largest African economy and perhaps the BRIC countries had been too fast to add the 'S' of South Africa to their club.

However, we should pause for a moment and consider what this does for all the analyses conducted by international organisations, NGO's and academics who have all used current GDP data or data for economic growth (raw or corrected for PPP) in their statistical analyses Nigeria is the largest of the recent rebasing exercises in Africa, but it is not the only one (Sy, 2015). Previous exercises have also resulted in greater or smaller corrections in GDP estimates, although none as large as recorded by Nigeria. More than half of the African countries are still overdue for revision. At the start of 2014, seven African countries still employed base years dating from 1990 or earlier, and a further ten used base years between 1990 and 2000. All of these will hopefully emerge with national accounts that more accurately reflect reality. But what should we do now of all the exercises that tried to link socio-political data to rankings of relative prosperity, poverty or human development? And if we do not know what the situation is now, what should we do with those studies that employ changes in relative prosperity, poverty or human development that start in years where we know even less?

# Chapter Four

# Poverty

In the previous chapter, we examined the way in which the comparability of GDP between nations was established by correcting the nominal data for differences in the purchasing power of the currency. Of course, PPP dollars do not exist, and citizens of poorer countries would soon realise that real dollars buy less in wealthier countries than they do at home. Nevertheless, 'home' is where the locally earned currency is usually spent – on food, housing, clothing and the like. Thus the PPP calculation gives a first indication of how much each inhabitant produces (and indirectly a link to the productivity of an economy) or how much each inhabitant spends (either directly in consumption, or through investment). Since national population estimates are readily available (and reasonably accurate) and so too are GDP statistics (with a greater margin of error, but no so much as to make poor countries rich and rich countries poor), we can divide the latter by the former and obtain per capita GDP data. Figure 4.1 shows the decile breakdown for world per capita GDP in 2011 (expressed in 2011 PPP dollars) for countries with populations above 1.5 million. The reason why the price base is 2011 is because that was the last available bench mark year for the International Comparisons Project.

Figure 4.1: World Map of per capita GDP 2011 (2011 ppp dollars)

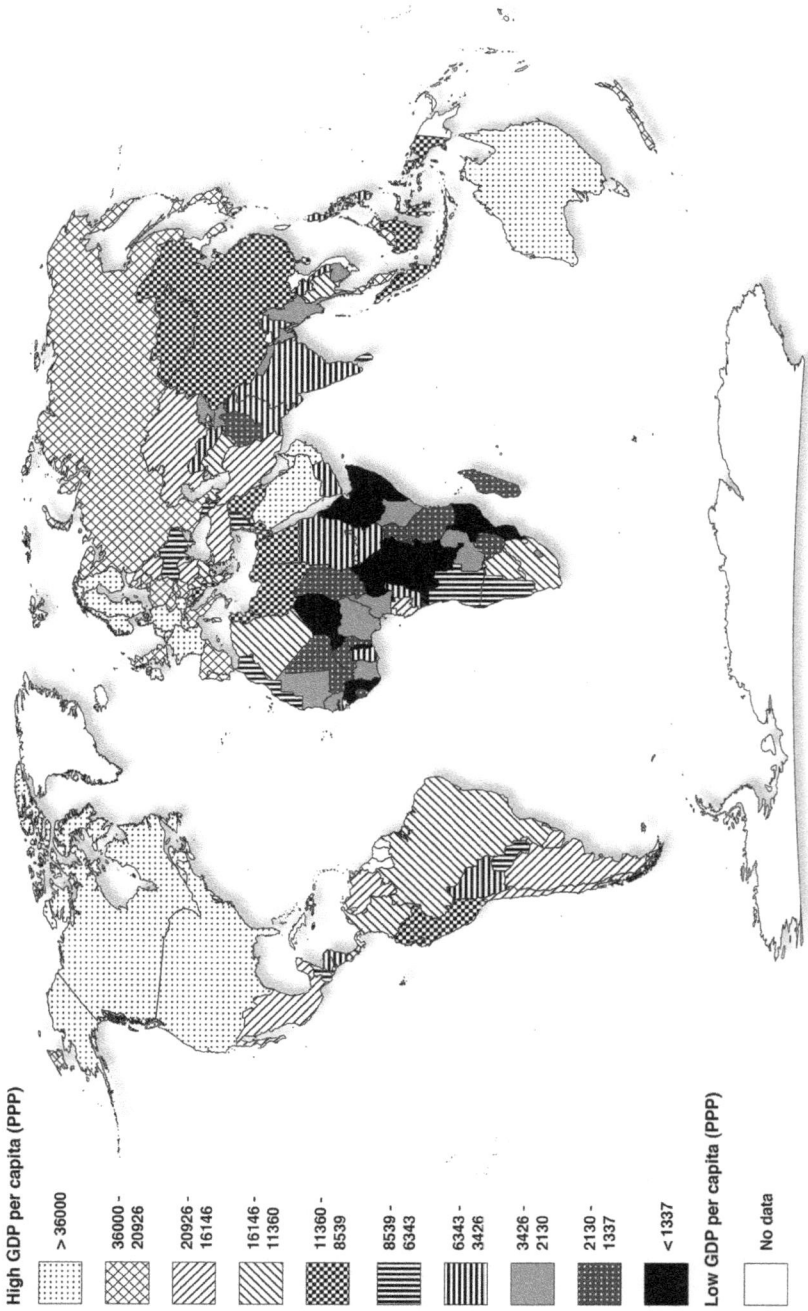

**High GDP per capita (PPP)**

| | |
|---|---|
| | > 36000 |
| | 36000 - 20926 |
| | 20926 - 16146 |
| | 16146 - 11360 |
| | 11360 - 8539 |
| | 8539 - 6343 |
| | 6343 - 3426 |
| | 3426 - 2130 |
| | 2130 - 1337 |
| | < 1337 |

**Low GDP per capita (PPP)**

| | |
|---|---|
| | No data |

Source: World Bank Group, 2015.

The main effect of the ICP was to lower the incomes of many of the rich (European) nations relative to the USA and to raise the incomes of less developed countries. However the effects were not such as to produce dramatic changes in the rankings. These are shown in the decile map in Figure 4.1. Four of the top-ten countries (Qatar, Kuwait, UAE and Saudi Arabia) are oil producing countries, five if one includes Norway. The USA makes it into the list in seventh place. Singapore, Switzerland, Hong Kong and The Netherlands complete the top-ten. To complete the first decile is one more oil producer (Oman) and more of the 'middle powers' that occupied the top positions in the nominal dollar analysis (pp 88-89), namely Austria, Ireland, Australia and Denmark. At the other end of the spectrum, the bottom two deciles are dominated by Sub-Saharan African states with only Haiti, Tajikistan and Cambodia breaking the pattern. Although the PPP-based GDP calculations reduce the inequality between the richest and poorest states, what is still noticeable is the gulf separating the top from the bottom. The incomes in the second decile from the top range from $30,000 to $42,000 PPP, whereas those in the second decile from the bottom range from $1,400-$2,300 PPP.

## Monetising Poverty

It was against this background of differences in income and wealth that the World Bank tried to reorient its programmes towards the extreme poor in the world. Although a country may seem poor, it does not necessarily follow that everyone in that country is poor, or that poor people do not live in slightly more prosperous countries. In its annual World Development Report (1990) the Bank announced the definition for measuring global poverty of $1 a day. One should note that this is a figure for private consumption, and not for GDP (which includes investment and government expenditures). The figure was deliberately pitched at the consumption level considered adequate for the poor in the very poorest countries. The Bank studiously avoided setting a mark for those that could be considered 'relatively poor' since their researchers noticed that the 'official' poverty line tended to drift upwards with overall levels of income. Thus having surveyed poverty lines in different countries, it converted these to a common currency and expressed this in 1985 PPP prices (employing the work being pioneered at the time by the University of Pennsylvania). At the bottom end of the scale it found poverty lines clustering at monthly consumption levels of $23 for the dozen poorest countries, and of $31 for the next six in line. The Bank settled on this second figure to produce the 'dollar a day' slogan, since it was catchier and easier to measure. (Ravallion e.a., 1991). By this definition, half of the persons living in developing countries (between 960 and 1348 million people) were deemed to be living in 'poverty'. By 1990 the proportion had fallen to 42 per cent. Recently the World Bank has repeated the whole exercise, over a wider range of countries and now using the 2005 international price surveys. It established a new poverty-line at $1.25 dollars a day, measured at 2005 PPP prices. Using this definition, the World Bank judged a quarter of the population in developing countries still to be living below the poverty-line (Ravallion e.a., 2009). The highest proportions living under $1.25 a day were to be found in Sub-Saharan Africa and South Asia.

Before turning to the criticism of the 'dollar a day' exercise, we should emphasise that the World Bank employs many other measures and indicators in its work and that the definition of a poverty-line, especially at the level chosen, was intended to focus public attention to one of the most burning humanitarian issues of the day. Nevertheless, because it was such a 'head-line figure' and because the data generated was employed in subsequent policy analysis and empirical exercises, it did come under fire for several reasons.

One argument was that a global poverty line should be more than an average of the national poverty lines of very poor countries. Moreover, since the price-base for the conversion has also been altered, it is impossible to state with certainty the degree to which the line has risen or fallen. If, instead, the original poverty line had simply been adjusted for domestic inflation in each country, the discrepancy would range from an understatement of 30 per cent to an overstatement of 157 per cent. This would have the effect of creating violently different scales of poverty; raising the numbers in Sub-Saharan Africa and reducing those in Latin America. Furthermore, overlooking for now the questions over the PPP exercise that we have examined in Chapter Three, the fact remains that price data and weightings for PPP conversions were compiled for comparing GDP data and therefore include many items that will not appear in the consumption 'basket' of the very poor. If, for example, a price comparison were limited to food items only, or even 'bread and cereals', it was argued that in most cases the 'poverty-line' would have had to have been drawn higher. This would have the effect, therefore, of raising the estimates of the numbers of poor falling below it (Reddy and Pogge, 2010). The World Bank's reply was that using the poverty lines employed by poor countries themselves would at least not overstate the scale of the problem. Moreover, any exercise aimed at establishing a single basket of consumption goods would lead to new estimation discrepancies and problems (Ravillion, 2010). Whilst these criticisms remained within the frame of 'monetising' the definition of poverty, there were critics who went further still and who argued for a completely new approach.

## Human Development

The Pakistani economist, Mahbub ul Haq was employed in the World Bank from 1970 to 1982. Whilst in its employ, he had published *The Poverty Curtain* (1976) in which he decried the prominence given by international organisations to economic and monetary targets at the expense of the needs of common people. He argued that the happiness and welfare they deserved were being denied to them because they were being deprived of the opportunity for personal development. After a brief period during which he served as his country's finance minister, he joined the United Nations Development Programme (UNDP) in 1988 as head of a team to create a human development index (HDI) that would provide a new measure of deprivation. One of his staff was the Indian economist, and later Nobel Prize winner, Amartya Sen. Sen's idea was that human advance should be measured not by 'top down' by such indicators as per capita GDP. It was true that richer nations may have a better protection of human rights, but that was a consequence of exercising certain 'capabilities', which a surfeit of macro-economic wealth may or may not provide. Access to education and access to health allowed a citizen to exercise his/ her rights, regardless of whether more wealth slushed around the circles of the elites or not. He did not deny that income should be one indicator of development; it should not be the only indicator (Sen, 1970, 1980).

In 1990, the year the World Bank announced its 'dollar a day' poverty-line, the UNDP started publishing its annual *Human Development Report*. Each issue highlighted a different dimension of the development problem. The Report rapidly became the most successful statistics-based publication of its kind that the UN had produced. To correct for the distortion created by the exclusive attention focused on national income figures, the Report started the publication of a new series that would give a more representative portrait of mankind's condition – the Human Development Index (HDI). The number of countries surveyed has steadily risen from 160 in 1991 to 186 today (Morse, 2014: 246). At the core of the Index lay three measures – health, knowledge and living standards. Health was measured by data on life expectancy at birth. Knowledge was measured by data on schooling – the average years of schooling and the 'expected' years of schooling. The latter was an immediate 'reward' for countries introducing educational reforms without having to wait for years before they started impacting the 'average'for the population as a whole. The standard of living was measured by per capita GNI in PPP dollars.

From the beginning of the HDI's publication, the three measures in the index have been weighted equally, with each, therefore, accounting for one-third of the total. However, this is about the only factor that has remained constant throughout the history of the index, where definitions and measurement criteria chopped and changed with annoying regularity. The last major change was made in 2011 and since then it has been relatively stable except for some minor alterations in range of GNI observations incorporated into the index (Morse 2014, 248-249). Within each measure, it is obviously necessary to standardise the results to an equal scale. At the moment, the practice is to place each observation between a minimum and a maximum and to express the results as a percentage within that range. The minimum for life expectancy is 20 years and the minimum per capita GNI is $100 (PPP). The minimums for education are zero. The upper ends of the scale are supplied by the most recent result for the best-performing country in each case. GNI is standardised on a log scale (which compresses differences within the range) while the other two employ the nominal values. What goes into each measure has also changed over time.

The 2011 report changed the measure used for 'living standards' from GDP to GNI. The difference is an important one. Countries with large foreign interests, such as foreign investment portfolios or multinational companies, tend to have a higher GNI (which includes earnings from such activities) than GDP. Since less-developed countries rarely engage in such activities and developed countries do, the effect is to widen the range of experience within that category and to change the rank-order among countries. A second change was to average individual series using the geometric mean rather than the arithmetic mean. This had the effect of producing lower index values for all countries and reduced the scope for compensating a low achievement in one dimension with a higher one another. The 2011 report also changed the weighting within the knowledge category. Whereas previously the (backward looking) mean (average) years of teaching received one third, and the (forward looking) expected years of schooling two-thirds, they were now treated equally (UNDP 2011, Technical Note). This means that it is vitally important, when making comparisons backwards over time, to be consistent in the version employed.

Figure 4.2: Word Map of Human Development (HDI Index) 2014

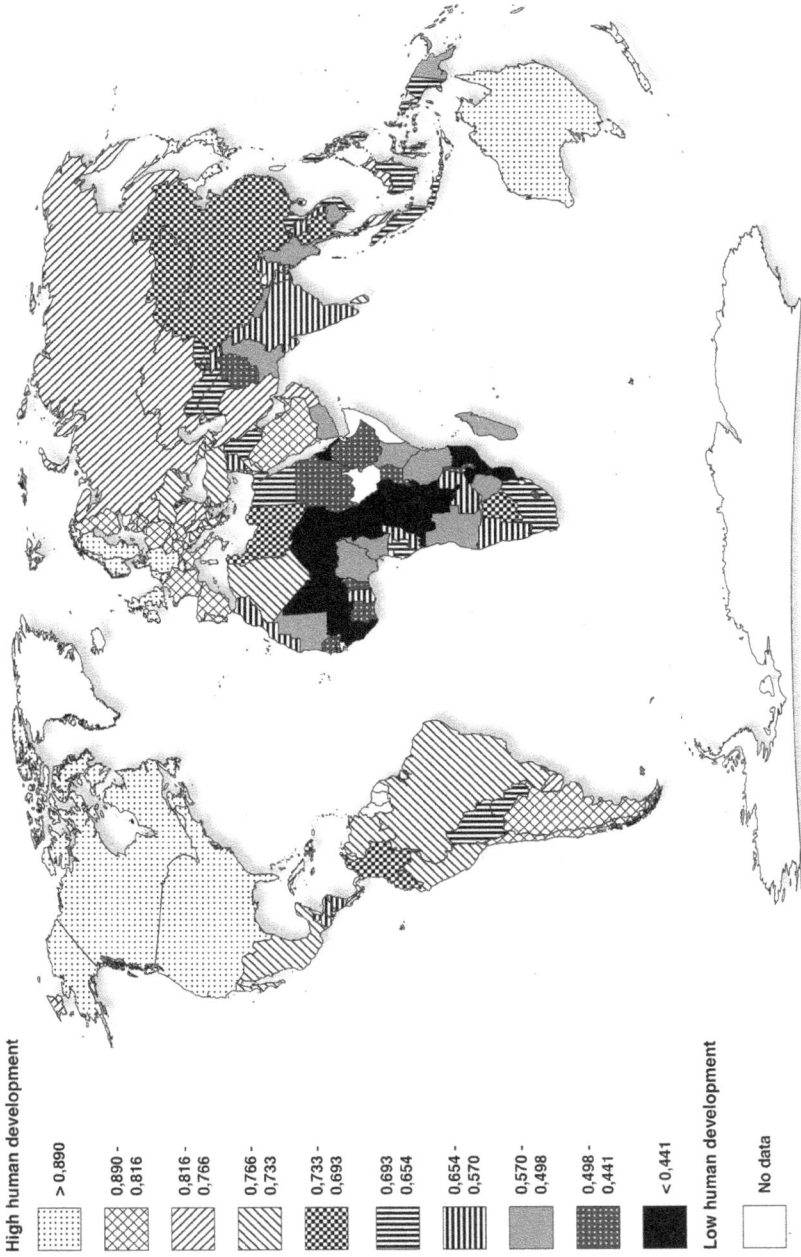

High human development

- > 0,890
- 0,890 - 0,816
- 0,816 - 0,766
- 0,766 - 0,733
- 0,733 - 0,693
- 0,693 - 0,654
- 0,654 - 0,570
- 0,570 - 0,498
- 0,498 - 0,441
- < 0,441

Low human development

- No data

Source: UNDP. Human Development Report. Database.

If we examine a decile map of the global distribution of the HDI, presented in Figure 4.2, it is not surprising that the highest levels of development generally are to be found among the higher income countries and that the lower end of the spectrum is filled with poorer countries. After all, income not only represents one third of the index, but is also a factor, though not the only one, influencing expenditure on education and healthcare. However, beyond this general observation, there are other interesting differences at the top end of the spectrum. If we compare these results with the top countries in terms of PPP-adjusted GDP, which we showed at the start of this chapter, it is interesting that all the Middle-East oil-rich states have disappeared. Qatar, previously the most prosperous country has dropped to 32nd place and Kuwait, that was the second most prosperous has slithered to 48th position. On the other hand, a country like New Zeeland which did not figure in the top decile in terms of prosperity has climbed into the top decile in ninth place. At the bottom end of the scale, it scarcely seems worth differentiating between the degrees of deprivation. African countries occupy all the fifteen places. The only consolation is that, with the exception of the Democratic Republic of the Congo, all countries for which earlier data was available have all substantially improved their absolute HDI scores, even if they have remained anchored at the bottom of the spectrum.

## Assessing Data Accuracy

In assessing the accuracy of the HDI, we will start by examining the criticisms of the three dimensions individually, before moving to more general criticism of the construction, balance and interpretation of the Index.

At the start of this section, we observed that the UNDP was critical of the World Bank's approach of expressing poverty as a dollar sum. It is surprising, therefore, to find that fully one-third of the HDI is still determined by per capita national income (GNI) expressed in PPP and that this is now also supposed to represent the standard of living. This has been updated in the 2013 Report to incorporate the 2011 PPP-adjusted data. There are several observations that spring to mind. In the first place, the per capita measure is an average and it does not reflect the proportion of the population that may be below that number, even far below it. It takes no account of the inequality in income distribution (Harttgen and Klasen, 2012). Secondly, per capita national income is not the same as per capita consumption, and it is even further removed from the standard of living. Part of national income will be diverted into investment needs and other forms of expenditure, such as defence, that have little to do with disposable income. In this respect the World Bank did better by defining a global poverty line in terms of consumption. The World Bank definition may be deficient, but it does at least focus on the poor. This is something that the per capita GNI figure quite demonstrably does not do. One could also question whether it tells much more about the potential for 'capacities' enhancement (Ravallion, 2010). The final observation, of course, derives from our discussion in the previous chapter, namely that the GDP data for poorer countries is highly suspect and that the method for converting them to PPP-values was riddled with measurement problems until the publication of the latest data.

There were criticisms of the contents of the other two indicators as well, although less vehement. The education dimension contains two elements – the years of education experienced by adults over the age of 25 and the expected years of education of a child. This second measure was intended to reward educational reform before it could fully take effect. Equating the question of knowledge with years of education circumvented the very telling question of educational quality in general, and of its relevance, in particular. Every year the OECD compiles scores for pupils' achievements in mathematics, reading and science. In 2012, a total of 64 countries participated either with national surveys of surveys of individual cities. The top seven places were all occupied by Asian schools, with Shanghai at the top. Of the larger countries, Switzerland and The Netherlands came next in line. Among the poorer countries, Vietnam did very well by coming in at 16th and beating countries like Australia, France, the UK and the USA; the last two ranked 24th and 34th respectfully. At the opposite end of the scale were Peru, Indonesia and Qatar. None of the African states were included in the survey (OECD, PISA 2012). There was also the question whether access to all years of education should be treated equally, or whether secondary and higher education should not be more heavily weighted than primary education. In more developed economies, post-secondary education is a better predictor for income growth than the education in earlier years both because of the skills learned during higher education and the extent that students can benefit from further training later in their careers (Blundell e.a., 1999). Similarly, critics raised questions over whether health could really be equated with longevity. As we mentioned briefly in Chapter Two, in many poorer countries a significant part of life expectancy is influenced by extremely high child mortality rates. Some of the literature has suggested therefore treating child mortality separately (Hou e.a., 2014). It is after all possible to live longer but in ill health, and in many poorer, tropical countries diseases were prevalent that would not kill but could leave people permanently physically or mentally damaged. An improvement in mortality need not necessarily be accompanied by any improvement in morbidity. Sen himself questioned the coupling of the longevity with the quality of life (Sen, 1985: 30).

The reply to all these types of criticism was twofold. First, there were inevitably large gaps in the geographical coverage of the data required for these kinds of exercise, especially twenty-five years ago when the HDI started. Second, the index was designed to be both simple and transparent. Perhaps too simple, might be the response. National income data was an item in its own right, but money also provides the means to fund improvements in education and health, so it was more dominant than even its one-third weighting suggests. And if it is supposed to be neat and simple, albeit (slightly) imperfect, then one should not endow it with too much importance. Yet this is exactly what the UNDP was accused of doing.

One of the features of a composite index is the relative importance given to different dimensions. In the HDI the components are weighted equally, but there is no theoretical basis for this, or even for the idea that they should be combined at all. It is what one commentator has called a 'mashup index' in which the analyst is free to select and combine the components in any way seen fit. Moreover, it is difficult to see why Sen's rather abstract discussion on capabilities should be reduced to these particular dimensions in the first place (Ravallion, 2010).

Until 2011, once it had calculated the index, the UNDP selected arbitrary cut-off points and grouped countries into one of the following categories of human development - very high, high, medium and low. The very high category was introduced in 2008. Before then there were three categories – low (below 0.5) medium (between 0.5 and 0.8) and high (above 0.8). The problem was that at the fringes of each category, the differences were always much smaller than the differences within the whole category. Thus the labelling exercise imparted to the analysis a pseudo-refinement that the data did not warrant. The UNDP must have taken this criticism to heart because from 2011, after twenty years, it divided the data series into four equal parts (or quadrilles, which is the statistical term) in the same way that this book divides its maps into deciles (which allows a greater degree of differentiation). Having met the original criticism, one would have expected the UNDP to leave matters there, but instead it has labelled the quadrilles - very high, high, medium and low! This exact categorisation stands at odds with the questionable nature of the results. Apart from the two ends of the spectrum, what stands out is the closeness of the results rather than their distance and the middle sixty percent of the range being virtually covered by the same blanket of error margins (Høyland e.a., 2012).

One final group of criticisms centred on the distortions that were produced by the statistical manipulation of the individual components. These would also have occurred if raw data had been used, but then they would have been different distortions. Nevertheless, it is important to be aware of them; the UNDP is quite open about them in its annual reports. However, accepting these does not mean that there is no effect, nor does it mean that these effects do not contain unstated moral assumptions. Without getting lost in detail, by compressing income differentials and changing the boundaries for longevity, the UNDP has effectively reduced the importance of increases in life-expectancy and given extra importance to changes in schooling compared with the previous method of calculation. "A shorter but better schooled life is preferred by designers of the HDI. One is left wondering how many of the world's poor -many living short lives by rich-country standards - would agree" (Ravillion, 2012: 206).

This discussion on the potential policy trade-offs implicit in the HDI implies that the index is of some practical use in policy-making. However, the indicators used in its construction only suggest in the crudest terms those areas where policy adjustment might be required, but they give absolutely no clue where the cause of the problems might lie or the measures that could be taken for their relief. To start answering these questions one needs recourse to the collection of international statistics that are contained in the extensive databases of the UNDP and the World Bank and that underpin their excellent and informative reports. So, if the HDI is useless as a policy tool, who does use it? The first answer is the press, who love international rankings to frame their stories on the world's best city, the most productive economy and the most desperate place in the world to realise human potential. The second answer is even more depressing – it is academics who want to show their sophistication in eschewing national income measures and who seize instead on the HDI as a more balanced and more relevant indicator to throw into their statistical models.

## Human Development and Gender

One of the constant complaints against the HDI was that it did nothing to capture the distinct life experiences of men and women in society. It was argued that it was meaningless to give a global number, when it was well-known that half the human race might actually have been following a different developmental path. The response was that even though it was known that in some societies men clearly commanded the lions' share of resources, the data for an accurate international comparison was simply not available. In 2010, the UNDP embarked on an attempt to remedy this problem. It calculated inequality indicators separately for men and women and then juxtaposed these to assess the differences in inequality that could be attributed to gender. For the female calculation, the UNDP incorporated three components intended to reflect health, empowerment and labour market experience, whereas for men the health component was omitted (we will return to this later) (UNDP 2011).

The standard of living dimension in the HDI is replaced by a labour force participation index measuring separately the participation rates for males and females and then combining the differences. However, it is only a very partial indicator. It says nothing about the hours of work, nor about the remuneration received. It is almost a truism that throughout the world, women tend to be in lower paid employment categories than men, and even when they do the same work, they are often paid less. It also ignores the work that women perform in the informal sector and within households (Folbre, 2006). This last criticism holds for data on incomes as well, but it is curious that the UNDP omits this aspect altogether, especially since its own report for 2009 contains statistics for the gender pay gap for 154 countries (UNDP Human Development Report, 2009, Table K 186-189).

The education dimension has been replaced by empowerment, although it still incorporates the same education indicator that was earlier employed in the original HDI, but in a cruder form (i.e. using simple participation in secondary education rather than the number of years of education). As we have already mentioned, this totally ignores the important issue of access to higher education, which in many societies offers a real path to emancipation and empowerment. It is true that the UNDP has added a new dimension to the component in the form of the relative number of women representatives in national parliaments (in line with the Millennium Development Goals – see below), but this is a bizarre indicator. Of all the legal and social biases against women, the number of women in parliament can hardly be seen as the most telling. The only justification is that data is easily available.

The UNDP also included a third dimension to cover health. However, unlike the original HDI, it does not use the life expectancy data even though it does have data for male and female life expectancy. Had these been used, it would have shown that in every country in the world for which it had data, with the single exception of Swaziland, women outlived men. Instead, it has chosen to construct an index for female reproductive health, using adolescent pregnancy rates and maternal fatality rates (again, probably in line with the Millennium Development Goals). Leave aside the question whether these components for the health index are the most appropriate, the simple fact is that these cannot be used for men (Permanyer, 2013).

Yet, when the female inequality index is calculated it uses all three components, weighted equally, while the male inequality index only employs two. This is a statistical absurdity. Until the index is constructed in a more satisfactory way, it is not deserving of detailed discussion. Note, however, that this does not apply to the data underpinning the full reports which continues to show the greatest gender differences exist in the poorer countries (UNDP, 2013).

## Absolute Poverty

While the UNDP was trying to capture more elements into its concept of development, another set of questions arose. Researchers sympathetic to the human development concept were trying to find a measure that would indicate not only the numbers of poor but also the degree of their poverty. From the 1990s onwards, various teams of social scientists experimented with various ways of satisfying this demand where they not only wrestled with different methods of calculation but were also forced to recognise that the data they ideally required was simply not available (Bresson and Duclos, 2014; Deutsch and Silber, 2005). In 2010 the UNDP adopted an index being developed by a team at Oxford University (Alkire and Santos, 2010). As part of the 20th anniversary celebrations of the publication of the *Human Development Report*, the UNDP announced a new Multi-dimensional Poverty Index which was designed to focus on the extreme poor. Not one to be shy about their own achievements, their press release trumpeted that "the Multi-Dimensional Poverty Index (MPI) is like a high resolution lens which displays a vivid spectrum of challenges facing the poorest households" (Guardian 13.7.2010). No sooner had the UNDP published its new index then, one year later it changed the method of calculation (something it does with infuriating regularity, but never quite so fast). Like the other indices produced by the UNDP, this is another composite index and as with the main HDI, this index rests on three dimensions (health, education and living standards) all weighted equally (Ferreira and Lugo, 2013).

We have already criticised this choice of equal weighting for the three dimensions, so we will refrain from repeating the criticism here. However, the components have been altered. For health, the compilers have taken nutrition, and child mortality. If there is one under-nourished person in the household, the whole household is counted as poor on that indicator. A similar issue rises with the child mortality indicator. If there has ever been a child's death in the family, regardless of the cause or the number of years that have passed since the tragedy, it too counts towards the absolute poverty level. The education dimension also rests on two components. The years of schooling means that every member of the household above school age, without exception, has to have received a minimum of five years of schooling. School attendance means that if a household should have one child of eight years old not at school, it counts towards the poverty calculation. Finally, living standards are defined by six components, and we will go through them briefly. It will count towards poverty if a household does not cook with gas, electricity or paraffin, if they have to share a toilet, if drinking water is more than 30 minutes away, if it has no access to electricity, if it has an earthern floor and it owns no more than one of the following – a radio, TV, telephone, fridge or motorbike. Note that this last measurement of poverty dispenses with income altogether, and replaces it with indicators of material wealth. This comes from a perception that poverty is more than a simple question of consumption. The new indicators were chosen to reflect the deadening grind of daily life that is more important in the perception of poverty by the poor themselves (Ferreira and Lugo, 2013).

The way that the index is calculated is so that if you are defined as poor in one third of the index, the household is counted as 'poor'.

For good measure, if you score between 20 and 33 per cent, you are considered 'vulnerable to poverty'. Finally, if you count as poor in components adding to 50 per cent, you are classified as living in 'severe poverty'. In this way the UNDP claims to be able not only to identify whether a household is poor, but it can also measure the degree of poverty. The final MPI calculates the percentage of the population who are poor (scoring 33 per cent or higher) and then adjusts that for the depth of poverty experienced by the poor.

The 2013 Report calculated the multidimensional poverty index for 91 countries, and calculated that poverty headcount was 1.5 billion, somewhat higher than the 1.2 billion counted as poor using the $1.25 a day threshold. A further 0.7 billion lived in 'near poverty', a term into which the 'vulnerable to poverty' measure seems to have mutated (HDR 2013, 41). The highest scores (remember, a mixture of the reach of poverty and the depth of deprivation) clearly lie in Africa and, to a lesser extent, in the Indian sub-continent.

It seems a little churlish to attack a database on poverty. The problem lies with whether this particular index is either sensitive or useful. Is it worth reducing all the information gathered into one single index number? The first point to note is that the data required for the index is provided from household surveys conducted in the individual countries, but not all the elements are available for all the countries, and the way the percentages for the index are calculated is adjusted accordingly. Little wonder that a footnote in the statistical appendix (!) warned that the data should be used with caution when making cross-country comparisons – something that does not seem to apply to the authors in the main body of their report. But nor does that data come from the same year. For over half of the original version of the

Figure 4.3: World Map of Multidimensional Poverty (Index) Latest year

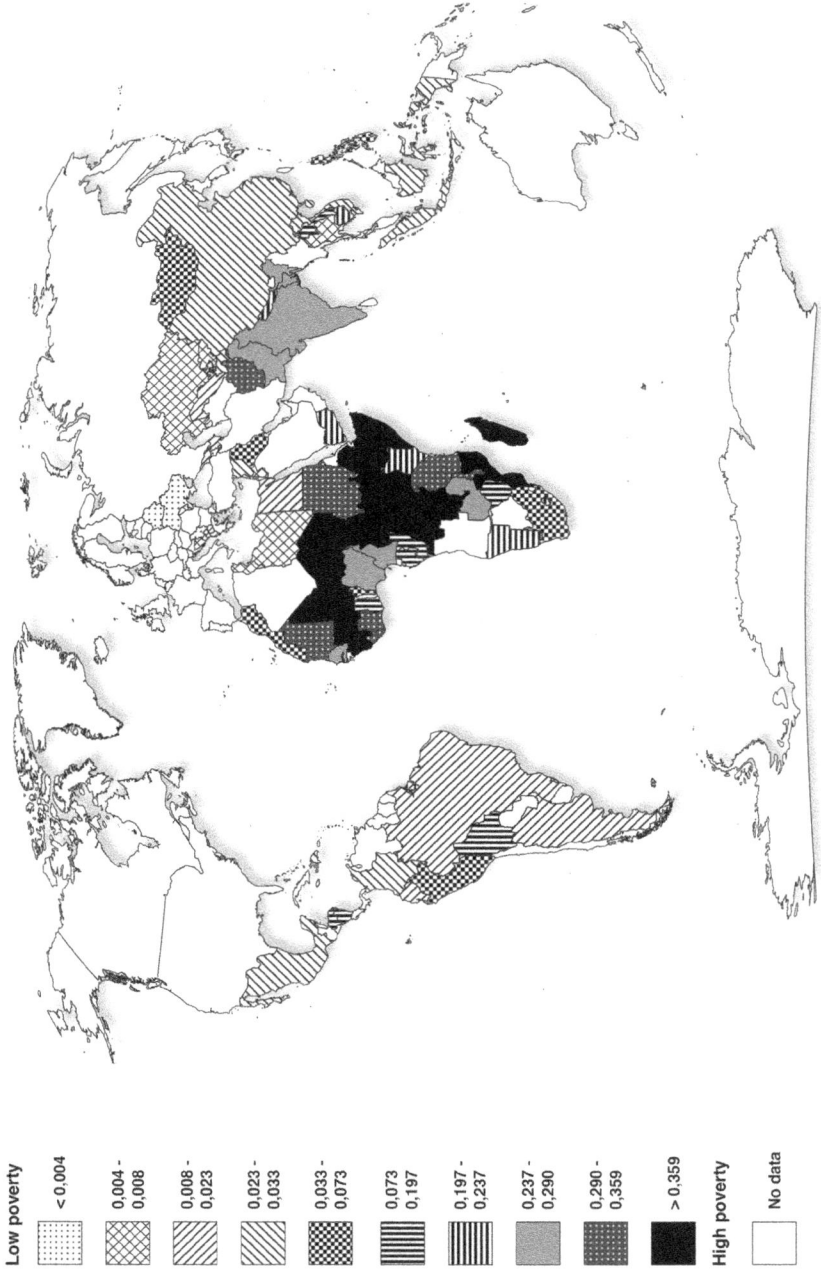

**Low poverty**

< 0,004

0,004 - 0,008

0,008 - 0,023

0,023 - 0,033

0,033 - 0,073

0,073 - 0,197

0,197 - 0,237

0,237 - 0,290

0,290 - 0,359

> 0,359

**High poverty**

No data

Source : UNDP, Human Development Report, Database.

index, the data stemmed from 2006 or earlier - the data for China, for example, dated from 2002 and that for Russia, Sri Lanka, Tunisia and Turkey from 2003. Much has changed in these countries in the intervening years, and yet they are here frozen under one, supposedly "high resolution lens." The results are shown in Figure 4.3.

One of the most persistent criticisms of the index, and of all composite indices, is the trade-off implicit in the weighting. For example, it implies that the life of a child is worth a mobile phone, a small gas cooker and a separate (outside) toilet (Ravallion, 2012). I would add a second criticism to the effect that two of the components, the death of a child and the lack of education of an adult member of a household are not obviously relevant to a current assessment of poverty. A child could have died in the past from an illness or an accident even in a wealthy family, and a now prosperous trader could be married to a poorly educated girl from the same village. In both cases, the household could live in the lap of luxury. Should they choose to educate their child at home, they will already have ratcheted a score of 45, and enter the database as living in extreme poverty.

Perhaps a more telling criticism is whether the Index is any use at all. Is it really so multi-faceted that policy-makers are likely to use it, since that presumably is its primary function? The problem is that once one gets behind the numbers, there is very little substance in the data, and even fewer indicators of the causal variables that need to be changed in order to improve the situation. One does not need an index like the MPI to know that the situation is good or bad. However, the Index will allow journalists and commentators to play the ranking game; it will give social scientists a new statistical series to play with but, as a development tool, it is a complete waste of time.

# Millennium Development Goals Dashboard

Possibly a better approach is the 'dashboard method' where the problem areas are measured separately, targeted separately and controlled separately. In the 1990s, as we have seen, both the World Bank and the UNDP began to highlight the issue of global poverty. At about the same time, the UN reactivated its practice of convening ad-hoc summits on special issues – including the least-developed countries, food, population control, female emancipation and a UNICEF summit on the plight of children. In 1995 the main aid donors, convened in the Development Aid Committee of the OECD, formulated a series of narrow economic, social and environmental targets to guide the aid effort, in contrast to grandiose schemes or blanket slogans. In the midst of these activities, the UN was planning a grand Millennium Assembly in the year 2000. This was designed basically to celebrate itself, since its 50th anniversary celebration in 1997 had been largely unsuccessful.

At the Development Summit in New York in September 2000, the world's leaders agreed to an ambitious programme that aimed at the eradication of extreme poverty by 2015. These fell under two headings – those that would go forward as priorities for implementation and those that were recognised as desirable but would not be a priority, often because of opposition from part of the UN membership. It is interesting that women's rights were in the non-priority zone (it would be rescued in a later stage) and that family planning had dropped out of the programme altogether. Throughout the following year, these goals were reformulated into eight targets with twenty-one sub-targets and sixty measurable indicators, and they began to enter the public discourse. However it was not until 2005 that the US

Republican Administration dropped its opposition that the Millennium Development Goals formally came into effect (Hulme, 2009). These indicators have each been tracked separately and have been applied individually to the member states. Seven of the eight goals, as initially formulated, have been shown in Figure 4.4 (with two additions made later to the original list). The eighth goal referred to the formation of a global coalition. All these goals were to be attained by 2015. Figure 4.4 shows their popularised presentation by the UN itself.

Figure 4.4: Millennium Development Goals

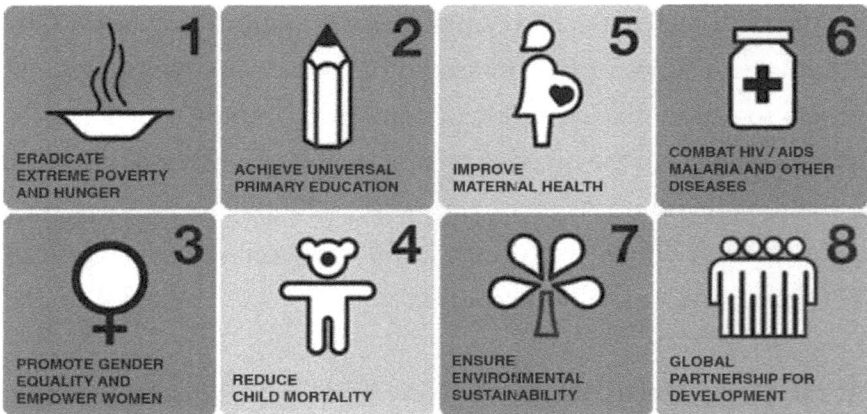

The entire operation has been met with a varied response ranging from those who welcomed a clear statement of intentions and a commitment towards their fulfilment, through those critics who saw them as well-intentioned but irrelevant and finally to those who saw them as a sham designed to deflect attention away from more fundamental critiques of the capitalist system (Hulme, 2009: 4-5). However, there was more detailed criticism. Some pointed to the 'costings' of meeting all these goals, the responsibilities for implementing the policies and the very assumption that success could be 'purchased' by a particular level of financial assistance.

The realisation of many of the aims lay outside the direct remit of the policy-makers, whether it be the underlying level of growth (to provide income and employment) and the underlying international trend in food and energy prices (to cushion the purchasing power of incomes). Equally, many of the social goals relied for their attainment on fundamental changes to family values and attitudes to public health, that are less amenable to short-term change and which made many of the goals simply unattainable (Clemens e.a., 2007). This was considered especially the case for Africa, where the starting position was not as favourable as elsewhere. As a result, it risked being branded a 'failure' despite broad progress on many fronts (Easterly, 2009).

The UN has produced regular reports on the progress towards realising the Millennium Development Goals. Several targets had already been met. Its most recent review claims that the proportion of people living in extreme poverty living on less than $1.25 a day has been halved from 36 per cent in 1990 to 18 per cent in 2010, with most of those who remained poor living in Africa and South Asia. Similarly, the proportion of people living without access to clean drinking water was also halved by 2010. Between 2000 and 2010, global mortality rates from malaria had fallen fell by more than 25 per cent and death rates from tuberculosis at the global level were likely to be halved by 2015. The proportion of undernourished people in developing regions had fallen from 24 per cent in 1990–1992 to 14 per cent in 2011–2013. The UN itself was quick to admit that much of the relief of poverty was due to the accelerated growth in India and China, and some of the improvements in nutrition were already being eroded by higher food prices. Even where improvements were visible, the geographical coverage was patchy (UN, 2014).

The advantage of this 'dashboard' approach over the construction of composite indices is that it offers a way of tracking changes over a range of targets over time. It is true that the UN often has to employ qualitative judgements to compensate for the lack of accurate annual data or of any means for linking expert assessment with those statistical details that it did have (Afful-Dadzie, e.a., 2014). Nevertheless this approach is evidently preferable to reducing complex information of varying quality and covering different dimensions of a problem into a single composite index. Despite the failure of the Millennium Development Goals to meet all its ambitious targets, and the fact that some success derived from factors outside the program itself, there is much to be salvaged from the exercise. Against a backdrop of diminishing enthusiasm for aid-giving, the program has served to keep the concrete issues of poverty in the public eye in both the donor and in the recipient countries. In some areas, it has also led to improved statistical and accounting procedures. If the 'goals' had been expressed as 'benchmarks', and if had they been more nuanced, the prospect of 'failure' would have been less oppressive. For here is surely a lesson – that a programme of definite targets and appropriate means to attain them remains a better policy instrument than all-encompassing composite indices.

## Poverty in the OECD

Thus far our discussion on poverty has centred on 'poor' countries where 'poor people' may be expected to live. However, the concept of poverty contains two dimensions. Most commonly it refers to an inability to access many of the basic requirements of life, such as food, shelter, sanitation, health and education. At a more genteel level, it encompasses being unable to afford goods and services deemed necessary for, and enjoyed by, the majority in a society. To discover just what 'poverty' means in developed countries, we have to turn to the Organisation of Economic Cooperation and Development (OECD) established in 1960 and often known as a 'rich countries' club'.

The OECD defines poverty as a relative phenomenon and just before the recent crisis it published a report entitled *Growing Unequal? Income Distribution and Poverty in OECD Countries* (2008). It suggested a new but simple measure for poverty. The definition it chose was a household income level (after taxes and benefits) equivalent to less than half the median income in that country (the median is the mid-way point in the rank-order, meaning that half the households received more and half less). The sum was then standardised to establish a uniform household size. This was known as the *poverty threshold*. Using that definition, it went on to analyse the incidence of poverty by two measures. The first measure was the so-called poverty rate, the percentage of households living on an income below the poverty threshold. This is shown in the Figure 4.5. The results range from under 6 per cent in Denmark, Sweden and the Czech Republic to over 20 per cent in the Mexico and Israel.

The second measure adopted was the *poverty gap*; the percentage by which the average income of the poor lay under the poverty threshold. The OECD database has chosen a different poverty threshold in compiling these data, namely 60 per cent of the median income rather than the 50 per cent which they use for the data on the poverty gap. This measured the degree of (relative) destitution, and again we have shown the results in the graph below. This data shows the degree to which the average household income of the 'poor' fell below a level of 60 percent of the median income. The results for both of these measures are shown in Figure 4.5.

Figure 4.5: Poverty Rates and the Poverty Gap in OECD countries 2010/11

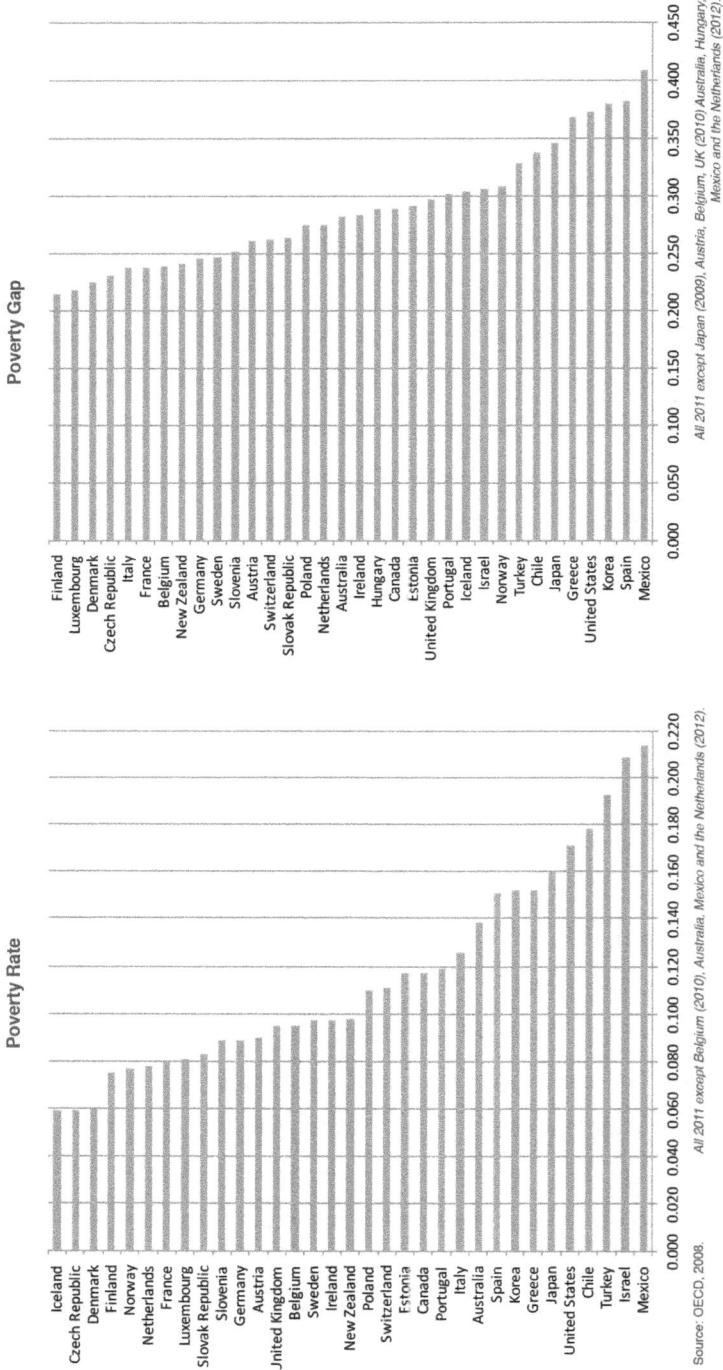

Here there are some interesting shifts in the rank orders. The Scandinavian countries, which performed well in the data for poverty rates, slide down the scale for the poverty gap (Norway to below the OECD average) while the Benelux countries move to occupy three of the four top places. At the bottom, the USA and Mexico remain in the bottom three, now joined by Switzerland. The Swiss households may be (relatively) deprived, but it had fewer 'poor' than the OECD average.

Before we draw the conclusion, for example, that the USA is a terrible place to live (since it has a high percentage of 'poor' and they survive with incomes further below the poverty threshold than do the poor in other countries) it is worth returning to the 'real' world. In 2013 Gallup released the findings of a poll on median household incomes expressed in PPP-dollars (Phelps and Crabtree, 2013). If we take the USA and the country just above it in both the poverty rate and the poverty gap, which happened to be Greece in both cases, we can see why the direct comparison is misleading. To live below the new poverty threshold (taken at 60 per cent median income) would still give an American household almost two and a half times the disposable income of its Greek equivalent. There is no way that the error margins in the PPP-conversion exercise would eliminate a difference of this order of magnitude. Indeed, an American household living at 62 per cent of the poverty threshold would have more disposable income than a poor household in Finland, which ranks at the top of the deprivation index (although this would be partly offset by the free services available to the Finnish population). The US level, however, would be slightly under that enjoyed by the poor in The Netherlands.

It is legitimate in the West to view poverty as a relative concept, but the word itself is politically charged. In the debates on welfare that are raging in many Western countries, the image conjured by the word 'poverty' is often some way divorced from reality. In The Netherlands, the Social Cultural Planning Bureau and the Central Bureau of Statistics jointly produce an annual 'Poverty Survey'. Its most recent report covered the situation in 2013. The survey adopts two definitions of poverty, one linked to the benefit level established in 1979, when the purchasing power was highest, and adjusts it for inflation. The second is a budget calculation for what is needed to have a 'not-much-but-sufficient' level of income. The former gave a higher 'poverty threshold'. In a country of 16.8 million inhabitants as many as 1.4 million people were living in 'poverty' (CBS/SCP 2014, 7). The Report also describes the budget limitations faced by the poor. These were always presented in what the poor could not afford, but it is interesting to turn these around to what they could permit themselves. Over 86 per cent of the poor managed to warm their accommodation properly through the winter and to enjoy a hot meal with either meat or fish or chicken every day. Over seventy-five per cent had family or friends around for dinner at least once a month. 45 per cent could afford to buy new clothes regularly and 40 per cent could afford at least a week away from home on holiday. Over 34 per cent even managed to replace old furniture (CBS/SCP 2014, 44-45). In fact, if we look at poverty in The Netherlands, the only conclusion is that life is not too bad. It is a simple existence that does not allow for much spontaneous luxury, but usually, there is sufficient that, with careful budgeting you can live a satisfactory life. That is not to deny that there are pockets of deprivation, including single mothers and members of large migrant (non-Western) families. However, what is conspicuously absent in the Report is the incidence of alcoholism, drug addiction and mental illness among the poorest segments of society. The fact needs to be faced that at least some of the deprivation revealed by statistics is not the result of inadequate means but of undisciplined expenditure patterns often caused by illness and addiction or by temporary 'life time events'.

Poverty is an emotive concept, wherever it occurs; and it does occur everywhere. In terms of absolute deprivation, the poor in richer Western countries may enjoy a life that would be the envy of someone suffering from hunger and disease in a poorer country. But poverty also acts as an exclusion mechanism, marginalising segments of society and denying them the chances of personal development and improvement. It damages society directly by denying it the human resources necessary for growth and prosperity but it also helps undermine its social cohesion and the levels of trust necessary for it to function. This is a topic we shall return to in the next chapter on Trust.

## Summary

Let us summarise this chapter. It showed that the conversion of per capita GDP data into PPP-adjusted currency was intended to convey the average real purchasing power of the population. This average was adjudged unsatisfactory by the World Bank which, in 1990, defined poverty as those living under a predefined PPP-threshold of one dollar a day. The UNDP in turn considered this monetisation of poverty to be unsatisfactory and constructed its own multi-facetted Human Development Index (HDI), comprising access to health, education and income.

The chapter showed how constructing a composite index requires a standardisation of the data and the selection of weights for the different dimensions. The HDI has been criticised for (still) including a GDP-component, for neglecting quality differences in education and for using life expectancy as a proxy for health. It also employs arbitrary cut-off points to label countries' development as 'very high', 'high', 'medium' and 'low'. The UNDP's attempt to construct a Gender Inequality Index was undermined by choosing a health dimension for women that has no counterpart for men. The chapter also described the UNDP's multidimensional poverty index, before raising the question whether a composite index has any use as a policy instrument. It prefers the approach of the UN's 'Millennium Development Goals', which are each measured separately using a 'scoreboard' or 'dashboard' method.

The chapter subsequently looked at the phenomenon of poverty in richer countries. It showed that poverty was measured relative to prevailing incomes, usually employing the median income and establishing a 'poverty threshold' as a percentage of that income. The 'poverty rate' represents the percentage of the population living below this threshold. The 'poverty gap' represents the extent to which the average income of the poor falls below the threshold.

# Case Study: Human Development in Nepal

Nepal is a mountain state sandwiched between India and China. It has a population of almost 28 million people and a density of 180 per km². It usually escapes any detailed treatment in textbooks with a global or international reach. It owes its position in this volume to the 20th anniversary edition of the UNDP's Human Development Report (2010) that listed it among the 'top movers' (i.e. most improved) states between 1970 and 2010. In April/May 2015 it was hit by a series of earthquakes that killed almost 9,000 inhabitants and injured three times that number. Almost half a million people lost their homes. This disaster almost persuaded me to abandon Nepal as a case study but it would have been a waste of a tale of a well-directed policy with a positive outcome. It shows a determination and resourcefulness upon which the country will have to draw again to overcome its current difficulties.

Before the earthquake, most peoples' knowledge of recent Nepalese history was probably limited to three facts. First, the increased repression by the King of a groundswell protest movement in the 1990's eventually spilling over into a civil war, led by a rebel Maoist army. Second, in 2001 the entire royal family was wiped out by the Crown Pirnce during a family argument, who then shot himself. And finally, in 2006/7 parliament was reinstated, the Maoists entered government and Nepal was declared a republic. It did not seem a promising backdrop for a major improvement in human development levels (Do and Iyer, 2007). But the statistics did not lie. Between 1970 and 2010 Nepal's HDI score rose from 0.22 to 0.50 (on the basis of 2010's calculation system). This represented an improvement of no less than 125 per cent.

If you recall, the HDI is made up of three components, weighted equally – health, education and living standards. So, using the most recent data (and the new calculation method) it was possible to deconstruct Nepal's progress, though only since 1980. The results are illuminating. National income (expressed in PPP dollars, 2005) just about doubles over the period, but this does not appear to boost the HDI. Education increased sharply in the first decade, after which further progress was more muted. Much of this was the result of the introduction of free primary education in 1970. The extension in 2007 of free education to secondary schooling helped raise the expected years at school from four and a half to nine years, but these last measures have yet to impact on actual years of schooling, which has still only reached an average of just over three years. One interesting by-product of the educational effort is a rise in adult literacy rates from 21 to 57 per cent. The driver of the improvement, in the overall index, however, is the increase in life expectancy. Life expectancy at birth stood at 48.2 in 1980 but it has subsequently risen to an impressive 69.1.

In looking through the data for the possible reasons behind this improvement I stumbled across some data that was so unexpected that I originally thought that there had been a misprint. They referred to the maternal mortality rate – the number of women that die during childbirth, expressed as a ratio against 100,000 births. In 2010 this stood at a horrific 830, as opposed to an average of 8 in the OECD countries. In 2013, the corresponding figure had fallen to 170 (with a range 100–250) (UNDP 2013; Sharma e.a., 2014).

One important reason was that women were having fewer children. There were several explanations for this including the fact that female literacy had surged in the last decade from 35 to 57 per cent, which gave women greater empowerment within the family hierarchy. Family planning had also improved and the fact that husbands increasingly found work away from home contributed to the drop in pregnancies. Far more important, however, were a series of targeted public health measures. In 1998, for example, a female health volunteer scheme was launched, which had grown to 58,000 health volunteers. In addition some 4,000 midwives were specifically trained under a scheme initiated in 2006. More recent still, in 2009 subsidies were made available for pregnant mothers to travel to clinics and pre-natal care, more funding was provided for establishing and equipping hospital maternity wards and anti-hemorrhaging drugs were made permanently available at local clinics. The result of these measures was that in the five years 2006-2011 births either at a hospital or with a trained assistant present rose from 32 to 67 per cent. These are indeed impressive achievements, but they also demonstrate the gap between the knowledge imparted by a composite HDI and the detailed data required to target and tackle an individual health-care problem. There was still room for further progress by improving facilities, and attendance at the facilities, in the more mountainous districts but, for the rest, there was a need for better data, including improved 'cause of death' registration. After all, as one commentator implied, we still don't know why these women die (IRIN 2013).

The final observation on this case study, perhaps superfluous, is that the HDI itself would never have identified the problem let alone indicated the way for its solution.

# Chapter Five

# Trust

In the previous chapters, we have analysed the factors explaining population and national income growth. Differences in the rates of growth of both variables have laid the foundations for the geographical distribution of wealth and poverty that configure today's world. We also spent time examining the numbers used to measure these phenomena. We were particularly critical of the official national income data, and the attempts made to eliminate the 'distortions' caused by different price levels. We then spent a whole chapter analysing the phenomenon of poverty and the steps taken to measure it. This concentration of attention at the lower end of the income and wealth spectrum of distribution is because much of the literature explaining income differentials is directed at trying to find answers to the seemingly intractable problem of destitution and misfortune to which a large segment of humanity is condemned.

In the following three chapters, we will examine the concepts of trust, diversity (inequality and fragmentation) and governance, and their interrelationships. We will also investigate how political scientists and economists try to establish a causal link between these variables and questions of relative wealth and relative growth amongst nations. The answers to these questions determine peoples' chances of having been born comfortably off or miserably poor, whether they will live long or die young, whether they will ever see or read a book like this in their entire lives. Central to all of these questions, and all of these issues, is the phenomenon of trust.

## Personal Trust and Generalised Trust

'Trust' is the word we use to define a relationship between individuals and between social groups. It means that in that relationship you can rely on the fact that what you are told is the truth, that you will not be cheated and that the other person has your interests at heart. It is a strange concept, because you do not even need a specific person. Let me explain this with an example. When I drive long distances on a motorway or highway, I usually take a little time to drive 'off-piste' to enjoy the country roads. This is partly to take a break from the monotony of the journey, but mostly to see if I can find some local produce. Usually, this is available from an unmanned small table, just outside a garden gate, laden with pots of home-made jam or bags of home-grown fruit and vegetables, and sometimes even slices of cake. The produce is always labelled with a price, and on the table is a jar in which to leave the money for the purchase, often already containing some cash from earlier visitors. Someone has left their goods and their money outside, unattended and arranged in such a way that any theft of either would be virtually undetectable. It is a naked demonstration of trust in society. Equally, it would never cross my mind to take the food without paying for it, far less to take the money (though I cannot explain to myself why the latter feels more heinous than the former). By reciprocating that initial trust, I am helping to perpetuate the practice and build trust for the future... and doing my bit to ensure that off-piste driving remains adventurous.

What does trust mean? This immediately raises a fundamental point because the (apparently single) concept of trust contains two different dimensions that may or may not be connected: a trust in friends, family and other people individually and a trust in institutions, or informal or formal groups, in society. Many of the problems associated with trust as a concept derive from this ambiguity. As we have already seen, on the level of the individual, trust means that you believe that others will be honest and fair in their relations with you. This is often referred to as 'interpersonal trust'. A quite different kind of trust is the trust one has in institutions and the way that institutions work. This is a more difficult concept. The question is not the same as asking whether one trusts a particular government that happens to be in power at the time, since those who did not vote for the parties in government would probably answer negatively. Instead, what is asked is whether one has trust in the institution that allows a choice in government in the first place For example, most Americans are proud of the US system of government even if the country is torn in two over its party politics. This dimension of trust is referred to in the literature as 'generalised trust'.

The idea of trust has been present in the political science literature since the 1950s, but it did not gain prominence until it became caught up with a new concept called 'social capital'. Growth economists had conceived the idea of 'human capital' in the 1950s as part of an effort to explain productivity. 'Human capital' meant that workers are no longer seen as an amorphous undifferentiated group putting their 'hours' into the production process, but rather that they were endowed with acquired skills that enhanced their contribution to the economy. In measuring this, economists did not get much further than counting years of secondary and post-secondary education, but the concept became an essential part of the 'growth accounting' literature (Becker, 2009).

Social capital is a curious concept. Until the 1990s the it was scarcely used at all but then it literally exploded onto the scene (Woolcock, 2010: 470-471). The concept of social capital embraces many dimensions, such as shared norms and values, but it also operates at an interpersonal level, whereby it embraces the network of relationships, personal and professional. And embedded in all of that is the key concept of trust. The sudden popularity of social capital coincides almost exactly with the end of the Cold War. Having spent nearly four decades looking at the world in terms of superpowers, with the capacity to destroy each other several times over, political scientists suddenly found that their whole analytical framework had become redundant. Into this vacuum came the concept of social capital (Woolcock, 2001). The late 1980s also coincided with some of the more fanciful flowering of the globalisation rhetoric, describing an interdependent world in which market forces and rational 'economic agents' held sway. Many academics, economists included, felt uncomfortable with this reductionist analysis. Markets were not abstract places where economic laws prevailed, but they were social constructs governed by formal and informal rules that depended upon trust in order to function (Williamson, 2000) Thus, at the end of the 1980s, we were at a juncture in history where several old paradigms were becoming seemingly less relevant. Almost immediately, then, social capital became a hot topic, and it was assimilated into the rhetoric of many international organisations, including the World Bank. The World Bank was already looking at concepts of governance, which in turn depended on trust and social capital (Bebbington e.a., 2004).

The leading exponent of the social capital movement became a political scientist called Robert Putnam, who had written a comparative history of North and South Italy. What he described was a divided country, whose roots lay in different cultural backgrounds and the range and effectiveness of civic organisations in each part of the country. Over the centuries, the North had developed a citizenry that bound its identity to a wide range of formal and informal civic institutions, which constituted a horizontal and diverse ordering of social capital. By contrast, the social capital of the South remained constrained by a narrow and closed network based around a strictly hierarchical church and on strong family ties. Putnam attributed the huge divide in levels of development which Italy exhibited by the end of the twentieth century to the persistence of these cultural differences (Putnam e.a., 1994; for criticism see Harris, 2000: 23-28). Now, even in America, Italian history is not material for a bestseller, but Putnam distilled his ideas in an article entitled *Bowling Alone* which he later expanded into a book highlighting the decline in civic engagement in America. He described how, although ten-pin bowling was becoming more and more popular, the number of bowling clubs and associations was on the decline. What he did was to measure the density of civic clubs, associations and networks in a region, and people's identity and involvement with them. By counting membership of church organisations, support groups, sewing clubs and whatever else one could find, it was possible to map civic trust in a society, and then to predict the social consequences. Bowling Alone was a metaphor for the decline of civic engagement in American, which he blamed on the television and the internet. The consequences, he suggested, would not be confined to American governance, but would also impact American growth and ultimately America's entire future (Putnam, 1995, 2000).

Robert Putnam's concept of social capital has been at the receiving end of some trenchant criticism. The concept has been accused of lacking definitional rigour or any grounding in theory. This has served to make it malleable, pliable and therefore unusable. Meanwhile, Putnam has been accused of neglecting almost all the contextual variables that could explain the differences in its developments and the inferences that could be drawn from these. Thus, he tends to neglect the effect of economic power, the existence of conflict, the nature of the state and the role of gender, race, class and ethnicity (Fine, 2010). As for *Bowling Alone*, its claims have been dismissed by some as a product of assertion and exaggeration. The point from which decline was measured represented a high-point in participation, rooted in American post-war history. The existence of these institutions did not create trust, but rather they were reflections of the trust already existing in the society and Putnam was confusing cause and effect. He was also criticised for failing to differentiate among the associations he counted. Not all are the same. One's commitment to a knitting club might be very unlike one's commitment to a church Sunday school; one's commitment to a political party might be quite distinct from one's membership of a book club. In other words, he was failing to distinguish between a dense network (having many civic institutions) and a deep network (civic institutions that really attract the commitment of their members). Finally, he misrepresented and misconstrued the impact of television and the internet on social bonding (Boggs, 2001; Durlauf, 2002).

Let us leave the issue of social capital and return our focus to the central element of trust. The main issue here is the direction of causation. As one author, surveying the literature on the topic, commented, "in dealing with the determinants of generalised trust, one inevitably confronts the task of disentangling several 'bowls of well-tossed spaghetti' since many of the variables claimed to be determinants of generalised trust levels may as well be their effects" (Nannestad, 2008: 422). Putnam's central idea was that participation in civic institutions served as a socialisation mechanism which, through repeated reciprocal actions, would lead to the construction of trust and, from there, the creation of good and effective institutions of government. He recognised that these interactions might lead to introvert behaviour within the group, and so he distinguished between 'bonding social capital' which centred on those similar to oneself and 'bridging social capital' which was outward and beneficial, though he saw a mutually reinforcing link between the two. He was obviously aware of the parallel existence of voluntary organisations and governmental institutions, but he was insistent that the line of causation ran from the first to the second (Putnam, 2000). An alternative approach reverses the causation and argues that it is institutional performance in the form of good governance that engenders feelings of confidence among citizens and creates the trust that underlies participation in civic organisations and the willingness to join voluntary organisations (Dixit, 2004; Newton and Norris, 2000). Finally, social psychologists argue that trust is socialised early in life within the family, and that variations in trust are rooted within long-held cultural traditions that were immune to short-term change. It is trusting people who chose to join voluntary organisations and who comprise their membership (Tabellini, 2008; Uslaner 2008).

## Measuring Trust

Despite the criticism of the role trust plays in the social capital literature, the fact is that it remains a useful concept. Without any trust, society cannot function. The question is how to measure it and, for citizens and policy-makers, how to enhance it.

In 1995, three economists reported the results of an experiment in behavioural economics that they had developed. In the game, the subjects (students from the University of Minnesota) were taken to a room and given an attendance fee of $10. They were then told that they could, if they wished, give-up some of the money, which would then be trebled and given to an unknown subject in another room. This person, in turn, could decide how much to keep and how much, if any, to return to their counterpart. Logically, one should send nothing since it is the same as giving money away to a stranger with no guarantee of return. On the other hand, one might impute a recognition of one's own generosity and the expectation of a reciprocal action that would leave you both better-off than before. In the experiment, with no basis on which to make an assessment, thirty of the thirty-two participants sent money, and an average of $5.16 each, demonstrating that a measurable degree of trust existed in this group. The game was also played in a version that allowed it to be 'repeated' in order to detect the role of 'learning' in influencing behaviour (Berg, Dickhaut and McCabe, 1995). In variation on the original design, the game has also been reported in Harvard in which the pairs were actually introduced to each other before hand, the intention being to examine the impact of the character of the relationship on the game (Glaeser e.a., 2000). Since it was first devised, the 'investment game' has been played in different settings and in different countries, and with different 'social groups'. The results of the proportion of players willing to 'risk' part of their funds' and the share of their 'fee' that they were willing to risk, have been employed as an indicator of trust in a society. A recent survey recorded 162 experiments with 23,000 participants located in 35 countries (Johnson and Meslin, 2011). Another variant of the game incorporated a kind of 'donation' in which part of the 'profit' went into a communal fund to be distributed later among the competitors. What these games discovered was that a willingness to contribute was initially higher than predicted, but that, with repeated rounds, the contributions declined as participants chose to 'free ride" (Chaudhuri, 2011). When the original game was repeated in a different setting, for example, by using non-students, the levels of participation were lower. This implies that the students in the original experiment supposed that their 'unknown' counterparts were fellow students and that this induced implicit assumptions about their behaviour. Similarly, when the potential amounts risked in the game were raised from $10 to $50 or $100, the levels of 'trust' observed also declined (Johnson and Mislin, 2011).

In another often cited experiment, initiated by the Readers' Digest, a wallet containing $50 and the name and address of the owners was dropped in different cities, and the numbers returned were recorded. These results have also been used as a proxy for 'trust' in society (Knack, 2001: 18-19). The most recent experiment was in 2013 when it visited fifteen world cities. Helsinki came out best, with eleven of the twelve wallets returned (Scandinavian cities generally do well). Next was Mumbai with nine, followed by Budapest and New York, with eight each. Amsterdam and Moscow followed, with seven a-piece, though I often wonder how Amsterdam would fare if we used unlocked bicycles instead. Berlin and Ljubljana came in next with six. After that, you have less than a fifty-fifty chance of seeing your wallet again. London and Warsaw, returned five each, Bucharest, Rio and Zurich managed four each, Prague returned three and closing the list, Madrid saw only two. Since 1996, social scientists have been dropping wallets all over the place, which is quite expensive bearing in mind that there is a slightly less than 50:50 chance of seeing them again. Others have circumvented that problem by asking people whether they would expect to have their wallets returned. In any case we should note that the results of the lost wallet test are more of a reflection of trustworthiness rather than of trust, and that there is not necessarily a relation between the two.

Another approach to obtaining evidence of trust in society is simply to ask people. Ever since 1956 when it was conceived by the political scientist Morris Rosenburg (1956), there has been a standard question:

"Generally speaking, would you say that most people can be *trusted* or that you can't be too careful in dealing with them?

- Most people can be trusted.
- You can't be too careful when dealing with others".

The question always has been included in the World Values Survey (WVS) since the project started 1981. The WVS is a cooperative venture by social scientists throughout the world that asks an identical series of questions in opinion surveys. In general, about one thousand adults are surveyed in each country and fifty or so countries are surveyed in each 'wave'. To date, there have been six waves of the survey, the results of the last wave appearing in April 2014. The survey is a veritable treasure trove of what everyone in the world thinks of a whole range of issues, or more accurately, what everyone in the world is asked to think. Based on the results of the surveys, social scientists have built up a huge mountain of literature. In the last wave of WVS, the trust question was question twenty-four.

The archives of the WVS are kept in Madrid, and the answers to the 'trust question' have been compiled into a single index. Using WVS and other local surveys, the database for waves 1-4 integrated details 117 for countries (including 9 small states with less than 1.5 million people). The score is achieved by calculating the percentage that are distrusting, subtracting from this the percentage that are trusting, and adding one hundred to the result. Thus any result over 100 represents a country where more people are trusting than are distrusting. Similarly, a score of less than 100 has a majority of citizens who are distrusting. For the world as a whole, only 26 per cent of respondents replied that they do trust people.

Figure 5.1 integrates the most recent findings from the fifth wave into the database, using the same methodology. The new results raised the total coverage to 122 larger countries. Only eleven had a majority of respondents willing to urge you that you can trust your fellow citizens. These include many of the middle powers with which we are beoming familiar. Norway is the most trusting country, followed by the Netherlands and Denmark. Breaking the pattern, in fourth place, is China but it is then followed by Sweden, Finland, New Zeeland and Switzerland. Saudi Arabia and Vietnam take the next two places in the rankings and the eleventh and last net 'trusting' nation is Australia. Some social scientists using this data have implicitly questioned these results, and several have excluded countries like China from statistical analysis as an 'outlier' (an observation with freak results). One political scientist ascribed China's high score to "social pressures and political control" (Newton, 2001:

208). China, Saudi Arabia and Vietnam are all, effectively, one-party states, with strong continuity in their leadership. They are all relatively homogeneous and they are all societies with firm state control over the media. However, there are other states with these characteristics that do not produce trusting respondents. The other end of the spectrum shows no discernible pattern. The Philippines and Colombia are the least trusting countries followed by Ghana and Turkey. Also in the bottom decile are Romania and Brazil.

## Data Assessment

How much can we trust trust? This is a crucial question. The first problem we have to consider is whether the survey is really random. The answer is that it is not. If one reads through the supporting information, it is clear that the WVS allows for stratified samples. The example they give seems innocent enough – spreading a small number of respondents among three villages where one is much bigger than the other two. Whatever the reason, stratified samples are not random, and if WVS finds it necessary to resolve the issue of a 'fair' spread among villages, one can only speculate what it might do with the 'fair' distribution of far larger blocs among different towns, for example, in a country the size of China.

A far larger concern is at the level of the individual respondent. The trust question might be question twenty-four in the survey, but it is one of over 240 questions and it is conducted on a face-to-face basis. Answering a survey like that is not a ten minute's break on the way to catch a train, but actually takes a couple of hours out of your day. We might have a random sample, but not of the population, but of the one thousand people who like spending two hours answering

Figure 5.1: World Map of Trust, Latest year

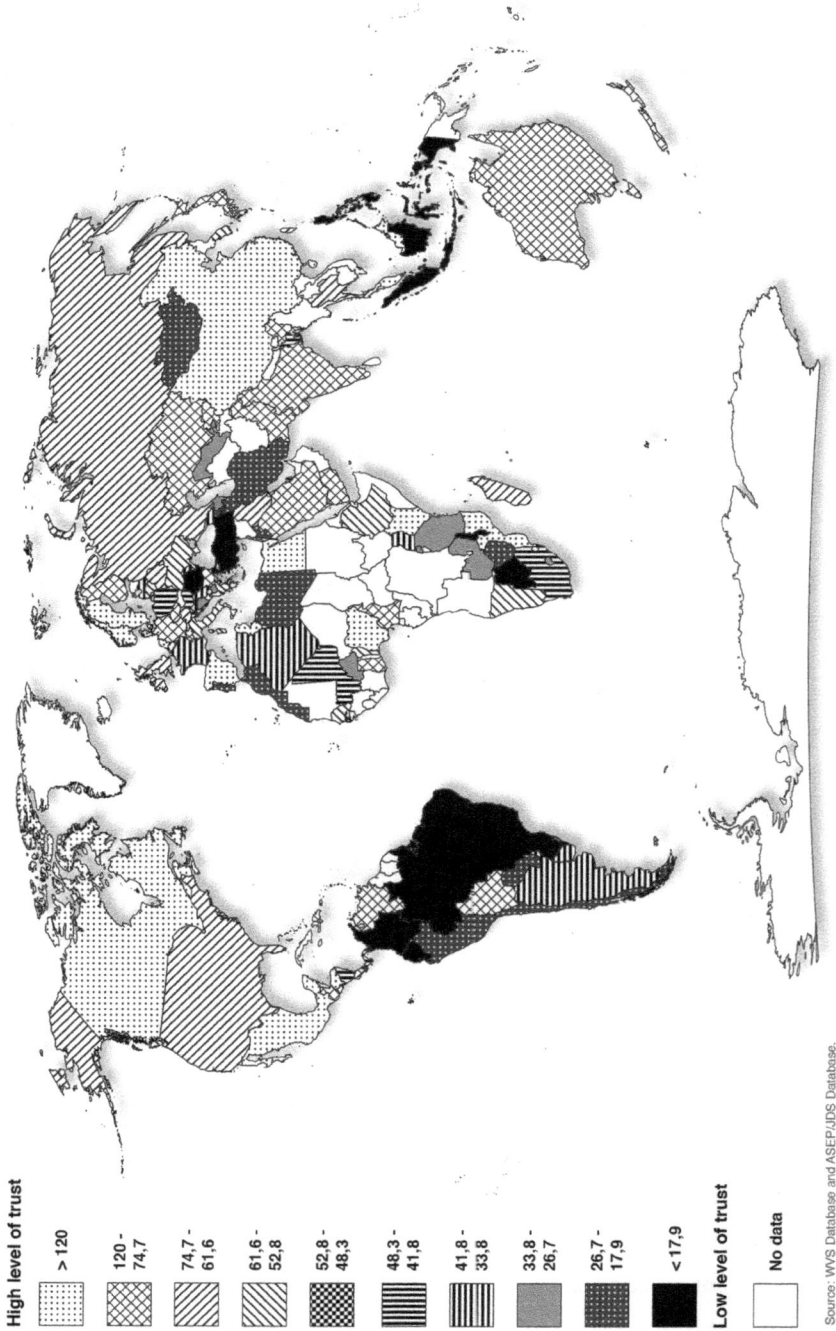

**High level of trust**

- [ ] > 120
- [ ] 120 - 74,7
- [ ] 74,7 - 61,6
- [ ] 61,6 - 52,8
- [ ] 52,8 - 48,3
- [ ] 48,3 - 41,8
- [ ] 41,8 - 33,8
- [ ] 33,8 - 26,7
- [ ] 26,7 - 17,9
- [ ] < 17,9

**Low level of trust**

- [ ] No data

Source: WVS Database and ASEP/JDS Database.

152

240+ inane, unconnected questions. A survey on the effectiveness of postal surveys (not face-to-face) unsurprisingly showed a negative relationship between survey lengths and response rates (Edwards e.a., 2002).

This brings us to the problem whether people answer questions objectively, or whether they actually have any opinion on the issue raised. The fact that the trust question is number twenty-four, means that they have already worked their way through the first twenty-three, including a set of five where the respondent marks on a scale of one-to-ten the five most important features in the raising of children. Here it is:

*Here is a list of qualities that children can be encouraged to learn at home. Which, if any, do you consider to be especially important? Please choose up to five!*

- *Independence*
- *Hard work*
- *Feeling of responsibility*
- *Imagination*
- *Tolerance and respect for other people*
- *Thrift, saving money and things*
- *Determination, perseverance*
- *Religious faith*
- *Unselfishness*
- *Obedience*
- *Self-expression*

After this, there are two hundred more to come. At some point in a survey as large as this, people are likely to switch to automatic pilot. They will either start repeating answers in the pattern already established, in order to stay consistent, or giving the answers they think the interviewer wants to hear.

A far more fundamental problem is to determine exactly what people thought was meant by the trust question in the first place. Literature on trust tends to characterise 'interpersonal trust' as relating either to known friends and acquaintances or as exhibited towards to unknown outsiders. The first is referred to as 'thick' trust and the second as 'thin' trust, and the concept evidently has links to the phenomena of bonding and bridging capital. The latest WVS wave of surveys (for 51 countries) contained not only the general 'trust question' (now question 23) but also a series of questions on trust of different groups, ranging from family and neighbourhood, at one end, to peoples of another religion or nationality, at the other (questions 125-130). The answers to this second batch of questions showed only a weak relationship between the 'radius of trust' (a measure for computing the varying degrees of trust as one slid down the scale) and the original trust question (Delhey e.a., 2011). Although this research attempted to impute what people were thinking of when they answered the trust question, the latest WVS passed up the chance to ask the respondents directly. Thus the possibility remains strong that what we might be measuring is not people's trust, but their interpretation of the question. A couple of years ago, researchers in Southampton University (UK) asked five hundred respondents this supplementary question (as an open-ended question) and obtained results which we might have expected. Among those who trusted others, nearly 40 per cent identified the 'other people' as those they could know personally and slightly less than 20 per cent identified them as 'outside' groups. By contrast only 25 per cent of those urging caution had personal contacts in mind when answering the question and close to 45 per cent associated 'other people' with groups with whom they had no immediate contact (Sturgis and Smith, 2010). I was intrigued by these results and so, when I was teaching at a Summer School at Renmin University 2013, we undertook a pilot study of 144 respondents in Beijing. Since there was no chance of a random survey, we conducted a deliberately stratified survey in several different, carefully selected locations. Although our classification of the answers was less refined than that of the Southampton research, we found exactly the same pattern, namely that those with a trusting attitude to 'others' tended to have 'known others' in mind and the reverse was the case for those tending to urge caution when dealing with 'others'. Incidentally, the pilot confirmed the trustful nature of the Chinese, with 67.4 per cent of respondents stating that they trusted 'other people'. One other dimension we tried to capture in the survey was the percentage of those approached (and actually engaged in conversation with our students) who refused to take the survey. Nearly 40 per cent of those approached declined to take part. This raises the question whether those who chose not to participate did so because they did not trust the exercise. It could be that the random sample is not as random as we try to believe.

Once we get over the problem with 'other people', another question arises over how to interpret the outcomes of the trust question. As it stands, the classic trust question singularly does not address the issue of trust in institutions. It is true that the most recent WVS wave does ask about 'confidence' in the police, the courts and the government but that too carries a problem. For example, do respondents interpret the question on government to mean the parties in government or the system of government. However, there is also a European Value

Survey, which asks a different set of questions and which clusters some of the answers together to represent civic or 'generalised' trust. Their results suggest that in Europe, there is a close link between the two with a very high degree of statistical significance (on which, more below). So, countries where people have a high level of institutional trust, they also tend to have a high level of personal trust and so on down the scale. However, one must bear in mind that the data used only gives a country breakdown. It does it does not allow one to see whether those who distrust other people, whoever they may be, also distrust government, whatever they may understand under the term (Zmerli and Newton, 2008; Boda and Bálint, 2012).

## The Implications of Trust

Trust is the pivot upon which the outcomes of many societal phenomena depend. The questions that need to be answered are: What factors determine trust? and What are the implications of trust for other variables?. Social scientists attempt to answer such questions using correlation and regression analyses, which we examined in Chapter One. Basically, correlation measures how stongly two variables are related to each other, whilst regression calculates the best-fit between the variables, calculates the impact of the one on the other and allows an estimate to be made of the degree of certainty that a researcher can have in the outcome. For example, one variable might be trust and the other might be per capita GDP or an indicatior for corruption. If everything were that easy, we would all be able to read one super-magnum article per subject and settle everything forever. Yet every time one explores a relationship, it seems to give rise to a small library of attacks, disclaimers, revisions and citations,

citations, and citations. Why, when we have all these solid techniques, are there no solid answers?

Statistical techniques only generate mathematical outcomes. They say nothing about the inputs. Most disagreements among economists and social scientists come from one or more of the following sources. First, it is possible that the data is incomplete. Not every country may have the data required and therefore there may be a bias in the data that we have. Second, the data itself is uncertain. Very often variables are entered into a model, ignoring the error margins in the data. Even if the result is statistically significant, it counts for nothing if the original data is suspect. Third, the historical periods chosen for comparison may be different. A more recent article may use more recent data, or researchers may choose different time-spans, and the quality of the data may vary between the intervals chosen. Fourth, the data employed in the analysis might be a proxy for a reality and there may be some disagreement about the whether the evidence covers the issue area as claimed by the researcher. A fifth source of disagreement may be a fundamental dispute over the original hypothesis, making the direction of causality contentious and so invalidating the claimed results. A sixth, and unfortunately common cause of dissent, is that the results are not reported correctly. Many books and articles are happy to present correlations, even weak correlations, as proven outcomes. A simple rule of thumb is to be suspicious of anything without a significance test, and then to see whether the change is of such magnitude as to justify the conclusions drawn. A final source of dispute, which is almost impossible for a lay-man to penetrate, lies in the practice, especially among economists, of constructing 'econometric models' and using them to test new variables. The problem is that these models are built on intrinsic assumptions about interrelationships based on *past performance*. These, of course, may no longer reflect the present reality.

There is a large empirical literature in which trust plays an important role. Let us begin with that strand in the literature that ascribes a positive role to trust. Most of it describes a backward link between trust and the inequality or fragmentation of a society. It suggests that that the more homogeneous a society, the more likely its members are to exhibit a high measure of personal and, by implication, institutional trust. This homogeneity can be exhibited either in the field of income or wealth, or in the area of ethnicity, religion and language.

The link between income inequality and trust runs along two tracks. The first is that wide divisions between income groups translate themselves into closed circles of 'bonding' relationships and provide few opportunities for establishing 'bridging' networks. The second link is that poorer groups simply do not have the resources to participate in the civic institutions that may enhance their 'bridging' networks. A recent cross-country analysis, albeit one confined to Europe, has cautiously suggested that the resource element is the more probable explanatory factor (Lancee and Werfhorst, 2012). Any such caution was thrown to the wind in *The Spirit Level*, by Richard Wilkinson and Kate Pickett, who opted for the first option and argued that income inequality in richer countries violated a sense of fairness. Moreover, income inequality affected not only trust, but a wider range of other economic and social and health phenomena. A more even income distribution would cement a sense of homogeneity that, in its turn, was also strongly reflected in the willingness to entrust greater tasks to governments (and therefore to 'share' what are called 'public goods'), in a greater degree of gender equality and a willingness to contribute to the development assistance to less fortunate countries. Not only did Wilkinson and Pickett argue this, they supported their argument by the positive outcomes of a plethora of correlation and regression analyses (Wilkinson and Pickett, 2010). However, the book has been highly criticised. The literature cited was deliberately distorted to bolster their arguments. The statistical proofs were restricted to a bivariate analysis (inequality was tested one-for-one against variables, and never against several at the same time) and many of the results seem to be over-determined by 'outliers' (or extreme results) and the selection of countries included. For example, if they had omitted the USA (high inequality and high murder rate) and the statistical relationship between inequality and murder rates disappeared. The causation was also often over-simplistic. For example, even if there were a relation between inequality and murder, it may have nothing to do with inequality and everything to do with gun-crime, especially in African-American districts (Saunders, 2010; Snowdon, 2010) None of this seems to matter to those who find their ideas reinforced in the book's text.

The underlying assumption in the literature is that ethnic diversity tends to reinforce 'bonding' activities within ethnic groupsand that this can result in 'crowding-out' bridging networks with other ethnic groups. The result is that participation in civic activities is constrained and that levels of generalised trust diminished. Many of the studies that have been conducted to date have been within individual countries and their questions and methodologies do not easily lend themselves to comparative evaluation. Moreover, the contexts and dynamics of these studies vary greatly. For example, it matters a great deal whether the ethnic groups are firmly established or have been newly created through immigration, and it matters whether there has been a recent past of ethnic discrimination or violence (Nannestad, 2008). The results of cross-country comparisons also point in different directions, with one study of 60 countries engaged in the second and third waves of the WVS suggesting a strong relationship in the Nordic states, but a weaker one elsewhere (Delhey and Newton, 2005). A more recent study, incorporating also the fourth wave of the WVS, found no significant relationship between the two (Bjørnskov, 2007).

Meanwhile, different effects have been found for religiosity. Some argue that religiosity has a negative impact on social (institutional) trust (Berggren and Bjornskov, 2011) whilst a slightly earlier analysis, embracing both individual countries and individual states within the USA, suggests that religiosity has a positive impact on trust in high-income countries, and a negative impact on trust in low-income countries (Bettendorf and Dijkgraaf, 2010). Of course, how one interprets these conclusions depends not only on the model specifications and on the data selection, but also on how and whether these phenomena can be accurately measured. We have already placed a question-mark over the trust data, and in the next chapter we will examine the measures for polarisation or fragmentation in incomes, ethnicity, language and religion.

Having debated the impact on inequality and fragmentation on trust, we now focus on much of the literature that draws a forward link between and trust and effective and efficient institutions of governance and, from there, through to growth and prosperity. People that trust each other, the argument runs, are also more willing to trust non-group members. They are, therefore, more disposed to put their faith in institutions, trusting that outcomes will be untouched by the personal or group interests of those in positions of responsibility. Once that certainty exists, citizns can plan ahead knowing that any changes in circumstances will be evenly applied to all and that all will be judged fairly, and according to open and transparent conditions. This will increase their willingness to undertake business ventures that entail the sacrifice of consumption now in favour of returns in the future. In other words, they will be more willing to invest, confident that they will face fair competition and that the returns will be guaranteed (within the range of anticipated policy shifts, such as changes in taxation and regulation). This extra investment will act as the transmission belt of innovation and productivity gains, and will boost economic growth. This link can run through private commercial operations as well as through governmental organisations. In his monumental book *Trust* Francis Fukuyama (1995) argues that high levels of generalised trust allow the members of society to develop the larger firms that are necessary to exploit the technological frontier. In places where trust is narrowly focused, society will find it difficult to move beyond the family firm and will be forced to rely instead on large, inefficient, subsidised public sector corporations. *Trust* is an interesting work that is stronger on description than analysis and that has an inclination to the selection of stylised facts. In the high trust/large firm category he places Japan, Germany and the USA, and he contrasts their performance with China, Southern Italy and France. It remains to be seen whether history is as unkind to his view of trust as it has been on his prediction of the 'end of history' (Fukuyama, 1992).

Thus far it seems logical that a fragmented society should be marked by an absence of trust, that this should affect the institutions governing society and that this in turn should have an impact on its economic performance. Moreover, there seems to be a wealth of statistical evidence supporting the connection between these variables. However, a statistical connection does not tell the direction of the causation and statistical modelling often embodies assumptions about that direction. Let us start with prosperity. One could easily argue that prosperity enables societies to commit more resources to their institutions of governance, allowing the construction of a better manned, better equipped and better paid institutional infrastructure. Higher levels of education, and an exposure to a wider range of experience and thinking, may also lead to improved levels of trust. Moreover, education is itself a type of socialisation, exposing individuals to a shared sense of common heritage, which is why it was seen as so important in nation-building in the 19th century (Wang and Gordon, 2011). Knowing that these institutions actually work and that there is little incentive for individuals employed to cream-off extras for themselves, would promote trust in them (institutional trust) and diminish the potential for inter-group distributional conflicts (personal trust). However this argument cuts across an almost doctrinal divide in the trust (or social capital) debate that we have already referred to above. On the one hand, there are the 'institutionalists' who believe that the effective defence of individual property rights and good governance can create trust. On the other hand, there are 'culturalists' who believe that trust has deeper historical roots and cannot be created by institutions. Given that the latter will be unconvinced by arguments, to the contrary, we might as well continue with the reverse causation. Once there is good and effective governance, particularly if it is reinforced by a sense of 'ownership' that institutions such as democracy may provide, it can lead to increased trust, and it may help defuse the potential conflicts underlying ethnic fragmentation, especially where there is a dominant group (Collier, 2011).

A review of the trust literature in 2008 had the following to say about the confusing and often contradictory findings on trust. "There are still few stylized facts about generalised trust and its correlates that most or all scholars in the field agree on. In this situation, three possible strategies suggest themselves. One is to acknowledge defeat and withdraw. The second is to keep going, producing ever more empirical findings in the hope that, by a process of scientific Darwinism, knowledge in the end will emerge from continuous variations of existing research programs. But there is a third alternative. Rather than keep adding to the pile of studies already in front of us, the time may have come to start sifting the results to find out which generalise and which do not….. The question of trust is a huge puzzle that is not even near a solution." (Nunnestad, 2008: 431-432). It is still relevant today.

## Summary

In this chapter we learned that 'trust' is used to define both 'personal' trust and 'generalised' trust in institutions, and that the literature assumes there is a link between the two. The concept of trust was subsumed into the concept of 'social capital', which refers to the various formal and informal networks to which individuals belong. The literature distinguishes between 'thick trust' (friends and family) and 'thin trust' (strangers and acquaintances) and it also distinguishes between 'bonding' relationships (among friends and family) and 'bridging' relationships (towards relative strangers). There is a debate on whether trust is culturally determined or a learned experience.

The chapter described some of the experiments used to measure trust before looking at the World Value Survey (WVS) employed a standard 'trust question'. This had been used on the basis for constructing a trust index. However, it questioned the results of the WVS because of the size of the survey, because of the 'radius' of trust and because of uncertainty of the identity of 'other people' who may or may not be trusted.

The chapter explained how the relationship between variables was established by correlation and regression analysis. It suggested that the results of these statistical exercises are often disputed because of differences in the data or the assumptions of causality. Some of the literature explains trust with reference to polarisation of incomes and societal fragmentation while other strands of literature link trust to the performance of institutions.

In the next chapter we will examine the evidence on income inequality and on ethnic, linguistic and religious fragmentation. After that, in chapter seven, we will review the evidence on the nature and effectiveness of governmental institutions. In both cases we will look at the consequences on the levels of trust in society, both as a cause and as an effect.

# Case Study: The Dutch Polder Model

The 'polder model' has become a short-hand way of describing the consensual model of governance adopted in The Netherlands after the Second World War. From the late nineteenth century Dutch politics had become increasingly polarised as society organised itself around vertical 'pillars' defined by political or religious persuasion, under which everything was organised from education, sport, recreation, newspaper, and, of course, church and politics. Members of various Christian denominations, as well as the socialist and liberals, all identified themselves with their particular pillar. The electoral system and the population distribution ensured that the Catholics were always in power and, since (until 1939) they refused to consider any coalition with the socialists, they usually ruled with the liberals and with other Christian parties. After the Second World War that all changed. The Labour Party became a regular coalition partner and a slew of new 'horizontal' institutions was created that brought together labour unions, employers and government officials to prepare economic and social policy. These policy debates were framed by alternative scenarios provided by the economic forecasts of the Central Planning Bureau, headed by Jan Tinbergen. The polder model was born (Van Schendelen, 1984).

Everyone knows that 26 per cent of The Netherlands lies below sea level, and a large proportion more lies below the level of the rivers flowing through the country. The drained land had long ago been reclaimed by the construction of dykes and pumping out water by a system of mills. A polder is the name given to a unit of land linked to the same drainage system. The secret of The Netherlands, which makes it so special, is that you cannot simply drain the land and walk away. Water has a tendency to seek its own level. Left alone, the land would simply become flooded again. So, the water has to be continually pumped out, to the next level (which is someone else's land) until it reaches the sea. Therefore the operation has to be coordinated, regardless of whether you like your neighbours' religious beliefs or life style. The whole operation is even more complex than this. The Netherlands is below sea level, so the water seeping into the coastal polders is salt water which, if left unchecked, will kill off any chance of cultivation. Therefore, in addition to pumping out salt water, regular sluicing is needed to clean the system by pumping in sweet water. Day after day, year after year, this hidden coordinated, cooperative system keeps the country dry.

The polder model for the economy demonstrated its first auspicious 'success' in the 1950s when employers and employees combined to maintain a regime of wage controls that allowed sufficient margins of profits to fund future investment. Wages were initially frozen, and then a carefully calibrated programme of gradual relaxation allowed a trickle down of the benefits of growth. The government eventually abandoned this spell of labour market regulation at the start of the 1960s as labour shortages manifested themselves in demands for wage increases. Although income policies were the most visible part of the model, cooperation also occurred, and persisted for longer, in broader fields of social policy. In the 1970s, however, the model all but collapsed as a high currency, driven upwards by energy revenues, slowed growth, eroded competitiveness and generated unemployment (Fase, 1980; de Haan, 2010).

As the economy seemed about to succumb to 'Dutch disease', it was rescued by a remarkable agreement between employers and employees, known as the Wassenaar Accords. In return for measures to restore employment, the unions agreed to a period of wage moderation that paved the way for recovery. The agreement was lubricated by the government, in its turn, agreeing to tax cuts that would help reflate the economy and cushion the fall in real incomes. The economy did indeed recover and by the 1990s a new period of economic growth was launched. The polder model was back in business (Woldendorp and Keman, 2007; Karsten e.a., 2008).

There are three points to note in this story. The first is that the term 'polder model' was only coined in 1990 and only became popular after 1996, when the Dutch held the chair of the European Union and wished to publicise the success of its particular social model. However, in some form the consensual model of Dutch politics has always been present, but it has varied in its intensity according to the nature of the challenges and the complexion of party politics. The second point is that the so-called 'successes' of the model have often been ascribed to other economic and societal developments that coincided with the policy realisation. For example, the wage restraint of the 1950s has equally been explained by modeling the real-life interaction of macro-economic variables (though, interestingly, the model failed to capture the wage moderation in the more highly productive export sectors). Similarly the progress after the Wassenaar Accords has been ascribed to the coincidence of a more favourable international economic climate. Finally, the 'model' does not rest solely on centuries of learned behavior dating from medieval systems of water management or the parliamentary arithmetic of the electoral system. It is cemented into place by a culture of social responsibility that was once identified with the dominant Protestant culture but which, with the decline in religiosity, now assimilated into popular civic culture. It is further reinforced by a highly developed welfare state to which all layers of society contribute (with high overall rates of taxation) and from which all benefit. Finally, to forego fighting for tangible benefits in the present in return for possible returns in the future requires a certain level of trust.

It is a trust that glues the society together, that helps economic markets function efficiently, and that allows societies to absorb the risks and uncertainties of change. It presence shimmers through the muddy uncertainties of trust statistics but its results are evident in the rankings of many other economic and societal variables. Similar arrangements are found in Scandinavia and the other middle-powers of Europe, each with its own particular national variant and with its own name. In The Netherlands it happens to be called 'the polder model'.

# Chapter Six

# Inequality and Fragmentation

In scientific analysis, researchers often reduce data to averages in order to cope with the complexity of results. In this way they create a 'reality'. However, that 'reality' is a reductionist response to complexity; it is possible to envisage a situation where not one single observation conforms to the 'average'. Since country averages do not necessarily tell the whole story, in this chapter we will look at the range of experience within a society in terms of its coherence or homogeneity, both economic and cultural. On the economic side, we will concentrate on the distribution of income (and less so on wealth, where less data is available). We will examine the debate about the drivers of inequality and discuss the consequences for economic growth. On the cultural side, we will examine the concepts of ethnicity, language and religion. We will not look specifically at the kind of language or the particular religions that characterise a country. Rather we will see whether, and to what extent, the country is marked by diversity. At the same time we will examine the possible causes and consequences of this social and economic fragmentation. What we cannot do is to predict when societal differences will tip a society into discontent and conflict.

# Income and Wealth Inequality

In 2013, a young(ish) French economist called Thomas Piketty published a 685 page volume on income and wealth distribution in the 20th century. When the English translation hit the market in April 2014, it climbed immediately to the top of the USA non-fiction best-seller list. Spanish, German and Chinese editions also appeared and, by January 2015, they had together sold over one and a half-million copies. The central thesis of the book was that as long as capital earned returns in excess of economic growth, the ownership of capital would become increasingly concentrated in the hands of a few and that this will have negative effects on long-run prosperity and social stability (Piketty, 2014).

Let us start with the analysis of income inequality. Much of what is presented for the twentieth century is not new, especially not for the USA. The fact that American income inequality had reached an historic peak on the eve of the Wall Street Crash of 1929 fed into a healthy debate on the causes of the Great Depression. In this debate the skewed distribution of income and wealth was used to support a neo-Marxist 'under-consumption' explanation for the subsequent slump (Temin, 1976). This explanation long outlasted the fact that it had been refuted by an excellent monograph placing the blame firmly on the shoulders of a mistaken monetary policy followed by the Federal Reserve (Friedman and Schwartz, 1965). Equally, it has also been long accepted that income inequality in the USA has tended to be more extreme than that in most developed countries. Finally, it is generally accepted that income differentials have widened since the freeing of capital markets in the 1980's and that they are, once more, approaching levels not seen since the end of the 1920's. This last point might explain the resonance Piketty's work found in the USA – that, and the fact that the American reading population may have recovered sufficiently from the hammering of the most recent financial crash to search for a new scapegoat for its cause. We will focus a great deal on Piketty and the USA in this part of the chapter for two reasons – because the popularity of his book has made it one of the most discussed works on the topic, and because I assume that it was popular because of what it said about America. I doubt whether a book focused on Sweden would have sold so well. Indeed outside the USA, the UK and Canada, using Piketty's definitions and evidence, income inequality in the other countries he has researched actually declined over the twentieth century as a whole.

Figure 6.1: Income Inequality in the United States, 1910-2010

Source: Piketty, Online Techical Appendix, 2014, TS8.2.

One thing that Piketty has done in his best-selling work is to focus his analysis of the top decile and percentile, rather than employ Gini curves[3]. This type of presentation always carries the emotional charge of having a very small 'top' segment of the population consuming a disproportionate share of the cake. Despite his claims to wide historical research, the focus of the comparison is to the USA, the UK and France, with occasional references to Germany and Sweden. For the USA, his findings can be summarised in the Figure 6.1. This shows that indeed the top decile and percentile income shares peaked in 1929 and then fell steeply until after World War Two. The decline continues at a slower pace until the early 1980s, when they both bounce back sharply to reach their previous peaks today. There is very little criticism of this portrayal of developments. We know infinitely more about the distribution of (declared) incomes in developed countries than we do about wealth or capital holdings. Unlike what has been implied by Piketty, the driver behind these higher levels of income inequality since the 1980s has been the returns to income, especially the very top incomes, rather than returns to capital which had been the case in the 1920s (Kopczuk, 2015). Much of the discussion, however, has been on the implications of these changes for the rest of American society.

The data used by Piketty is one of 'primary incomes'. This is data for pre-tax cash market income, including realised capital gains and excluding government transfers (Piketty, 2014: 255). Although Piketty's data shows inequality in primary incomes returning to the previous 'highs' of the 1920s, it ignores the impact of differential taxation of earned incomes which benefited low-income earners, as well as the impact of 'transfer payments' and benefits. In 2008

---

[3] A Gini curve measures the cumulative percentage of total income earned (or wealth held) by the population and the cumulative percentage of people earning that income or holding that wealth and calculates how far that deviates from a perfectly even distribution.

these benefits amounted to 12 per cent of American GDP and they benefited almost entirely the poor. It also ignored the provision of 'free' goods such as primary education and basic healthcare. In other higher-tax, higher-benefit countries as the UK and, more so, the countries of North-West Continental Europe, these countervailing factors are likely to weigh even heavier. In effect, in the USA and other Western countries, Piketty has wiped away the impact of post-war redistributive tax policies and most of the welfare state. Recent research has shown that the top decile or even percentile of income earners is far from the static club that Piketty suggests, but a highly fluid one. Over their working lives, over fifty percent of the American workforce has spent one year in the top decile category, and eleven per cent have reached the top percentile but do not stay there. Less than eight per cent experience ten consecutive years among the top decile, and only 0.6 per cent in the top percentile (Hirschl and Rank, 2015).

Figure 6.2: Wealth Inequality in the United States, 1810-2010

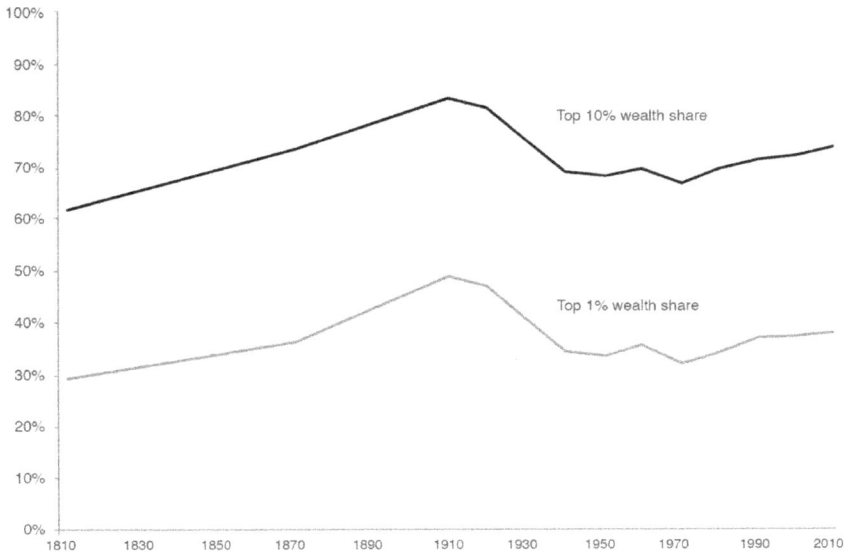

Source: Piketty, Online Techical Appendix, 2014, TS10.1.

The study of wealth inequality in the USA shows a slightly different pattern from incomes. The data is shown in Figure 6.2. The top decile and percentile shares of wealth peaked earlier (in 1910, but possibly earlier still, since there is no real data anchoring 1910 to 1870) before declining until the mid-1950s. From then until the early 1970s, it stabilised, but then it began to climb upwards once more – but not as steeply or a high as had incomes. Throughout the period, inequality of wealth was more pronounced than that of income. Once again, we have to take care with the definition employed. For Piketty, capital is defined as the current market value of personal, exchangeable wealth. There is nothing intrinsically wrong with this definition, but it does carry some important implications. Firstly, wealth is not confined to productive capital. It includes housing and other forms of real estate. On the other hand it excludes wealth that is not personally transferable, such as pension funds. If my savings were in a personal pension fund, they would count towards my wealth, but if they are in a government pension fund, they are not. This would create major distortions in countries like The Netherlands and Switzerland that have generous (non-transferable) pension schemes funded from prior contributions. Fortunately, neither country is included in Piketty's analysis. It also ignores other forms of wealth or capital that are not privately held, such as public parks and museums, publicly-owned utilities and government buildings.

The second problem lies in the fact that reconstructing data to procure chronological series for wealth distribution is infinitely more complicated than building income series. The main series employed by Piketty (on the top percentile only) places the start of the decline later (in 1929), the flattening out earlier (early 1940s) and, at best, it shows only a modest increase from the 1980s onwards. It is only by some undocumented 'augmenting' of the original source (Magness and Murphy 2015) and some ad hoc switching between this and an alternative set of estimates that Piketty obtains his 'rebound' (for the impact of different methods see Kopczuk 2015). Piketty's response to this criticism was to claim that an even newer set of estimates established his 'u-curve' better than he had done. However, the new series employed a different approach. It is based on taxes and is therefore susceptible to changes in the American tax system. The new data shadows existing estimates for much of the century only to diverge in the 1980, when changes in income tax rates may have influenced how people chose to declare their income. Divergent statistical series are not unknown in economic history, but the differences should be confronted, and choices explained, and not concealed altogether (Kopczuk, 2014; Magness and Murphy, 2015). The *Financial Times* made a similar critique of Piketty's construction of the UK's wealth. It accused him of occasional (and surely forgivable in a work of this size) transcription errors, of ad hoc unexplained 'tweaks' to the data, of sliding data along the horizontal axis so that it coincides with decades (but a wealth figure for 1935 is not likely to be the same as one for 1930) and for switching sources when it suits his outcomes. The result is that the upturn of wealth inequality in the 1980s is far less than shown by Piketty's data (Giles, 2014). Incidentally, Swedish commentators have also levelled the same criticis (Sahlén and Furth, 2014).

If we turn now to examine regional differences in inequality, the OECD has recently constructed a series for income inequality for 34 of its own members and for seven emerging economies for the year

2008. These differ from the Piketty's statistics in the construction of data and in the way they are expressed. The OECD statistics refer to disposable income (i.e. after taxes and including transfers) and are adjusted for differences in household size. They still take no account of the provision of 'free' goods and services where these are offered, such as education and primary health care. Moreover, the measure is not the top decile or percentile, but the Gini Index, which measures distribution right across the income spectrum. The Report notes the (obvious) fact that the Gini index for what it calls 'market income' is consistently higher than that for disposable income (including the USA) (OECD, 2011). The results for the 38 economies with populations over 1.5 million are shown in the Figure 6.3. The Index is has a range of one to zero, with the lowest number expressing the greatest degree of homogeneity. The top eighteen countries in terms of income equality are all in Europe – South Korea comes in at 19th and Canada at 21st. The USA is 28th in the list, about the same level as Indonesia. All of the BRICS countries have inequality levels greater than those of the USA and so do Argentina, Chile and Mexico.

Figure 6.3: World Maps of Income Inequality (Gini Indices)

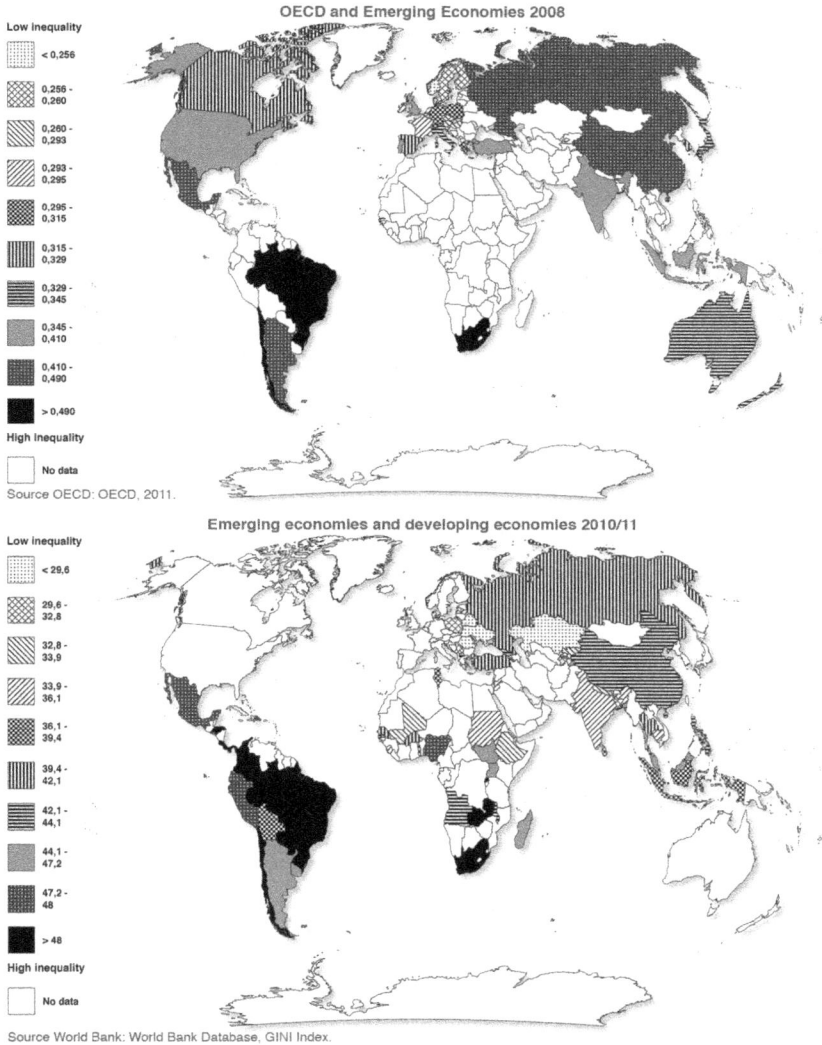

OECD and Emerging Economies 2008

Low inequality

- < 0,256
- 0,256 - 0,260
- 0,260 - 0,293
- 0,293 - 0,295
- 0,295 - 0,315
- 0,315 - 0,329
- 0,329 - 0,345
- 0,345 - 0,410
- 0,410 - 0,490
- > 0,490

High inequality

No data

Source OECD: OECD, 2011.

Emerging economies and developing economies 2010/11

Low inequality

- < 29,6
- 29,6 - 32,8
- 32,8 - 33,9
- 33,9 - 36,1
- 36,1 - 39,4
- 39,4 - 42,1
- 42,1 - 44,1
- 44,1 - 47,2
- 47,2 - 48
- > 48

High inequality

No data

Source World Bank: World Bank Database, GINI Index.

The World Bank has also been responsible for preparing a Gini-index, but this time measured on household expenditure surveys. The results are shown in Figure 6.3. These are not comparable with the data employed in the OECD surveys. The compilers of the index admit that the statistics comprise what is called a 'dirty data-set', but they argue that if they aimed at perfect compatibility, they would have to eliminate too many countries. Moreover, any attempt to 'correct' the data might lead to even more biases than the ones they were trying to eliminate. There are two main issues. First there is no distinction between single earner households and multiple earner households (and the inequality tends to be reduced in multiple earner households). Second, just as with the OECD series, it takes no account of non-income benefits, such as free education or primary health care. The compilers warn "we therefore caution researchers who use these data to interpret the results carefully" (Deliger and Squire, 1996). I have taken data from the years 2010 and 2011, which allows me to cover 60 larger countries. There is some overlap between this series and that provided by the OECD. Indonesia provided a point in the OECD series that came close to that of the USA, and it is 25th in the World Bank series. All the other countries, all of which are far poorer than the USA, are characterised by an even more skewed income distribution. With the noticeable exception of Bolivia, all the Central and Southern American countries and the Caribbean are in the bottom twenty. The list is anchored by South Africa, which is also last in the OECD series.

If we turn first to explaining and remedying income inequality, the OECD suggests that the main cause lies in the changes in the global labour market, where there is far more competition in unskilled jobs than in skilled employment. It acknowledges that some of the consequences could be ameliorated by redistributive government policies. On the other hand, it acknowledges that the mobility of global capital has constrained the scope for a progressive tax policies. This places greater importance on the imbalance in the skill levels within the population, and the OECD sees the main societal challenge in stimulating investment in human capital (OECD, 2011). It is interesting that the OECD makes no mention at all of returns to capital which play such a large role in Thomas Piketty's analysis (Piketty, 2014). It is also interesting that no mention was made of the relative power balance within markets, and the role of labour organisations (trades unions) in helping redress this balance. Trades unions have generally been associated with concentrations of workers in large-scale work places and membership has declines as (decentralised) service industries have replaced manufacturing in many developed Western economies (Hayes and Novitz, 2014). The role of market distortion is dealt with more widely in the context of the American economy, where formal rules and informal association allows the formation of quasi-monopolies within the economy, to the benefit of insiders and the detriment of the rest (Stiglitz, 2012).

As far as the discussion on wealth inequality is concerned, the debate has recently been dominated by Piketty who seems to suggest that the world is returning to a modified version of 19th century rentier capitalism based on lazily harvested returns, and a self-perpetuating elite founded on inherited wealth. Underlying this is the contention that the rates of return to capital will tend to outrun the growth of economies as a whole (Piketty, 2014). There are several problems with this account. The first is that Piketty's concept of wealth/capital includes both productive and residential capital, measured in nominal terms. Much of the increase in wealth inequality in the USA has been accounted for by rises in the price of housing which, in turn, is part of an asset-price bubble fuelled by artificial scarcity resulting from planning processes and monetary policy. Swings in monetary policy and asset prices have little to do with underlying growth rates in the economy (Rognlie, 2014). They can also pave the way for a collapse, as they did in the 1930s, with very visible consequences for Piketty's graph on wealth inequality. A second problem lies in the relationship of (productive) capital to growth. Piketty's choice of capital to output ratio that underpins his thesis on the inexorable rise in the share of capital lies in a choice of a ratio far outside that recorded by most economists (Dubay and Furth, 2014). A final factor to consider is the role of taxation. Living in a high-tax, high-welfare society like The Netherlands, I am always fascinated at how the word 'taxation' can polarise the political debate in the USA. Piketty has been pilloried for suggesting a wealth tax as a means of remedying wealth inequalities (Piketty, 2014) and it seems logical, therefore, to add policies towards inheritance taxes to the list of factors explaining the (in)equalities in wealth.

Before looking at the consequences of income and wealth inequality, we should observe that some inequality is inevitable and even favourable. The important questions are When is enough? and When is too much? Most economists would agree that society needs to offer a return to capital above that earned by labour if it is to provide an incentive to risk one's savings and to reward initiative and enterprise. Inequality also provides a source of funds for investment since low-income households tend to save little and therefore have few investment funds. Finally, the prospect of improvement in incomes often provides an incentive for the schooling and training necessary to upgrade human capital and improve labour productivity. A recent survey of cross-country studies in the relationship between economic growth and levels and trends (since 1980) in income inequality concluded that there was no agreement, either on the direction or on the strength of any relationship. It suggested, however, that the focus on 'top inequality' may be misplaced and that the impact on growth depends more on what is happening with the bottom forty per cent of lower middle class and working-class families. The lowering of incomes in this group (but not the others) has negative implications on educational attainment and employability, and represents a dis-investment in human capital upon which future growth and incomes depend (Cingano, 2014). At the other end of the spectrum, there is a progressive (or leftist) literature that presents a consistently dark picture of the consequences of the widening income and wealth disparities (seemingly regardless of the actual levels). These predictions range from slower and more volatile growth (Piketty 2014), breakdowns in democracy, erosion of the rule of law (Stiglitz, 2012) to the rise in crime and collapse of health (Dorling, 2014; Wilkinson and Pickett, 2010).

Throughout these discussions, the one consoling thought I had was that, although income and wealth distribution within countries may be deteriorating, the growth in emerging economies and the commodity boom that has lifted many families out of poverty, had also resulted in a more even distribution on a global scale (Milanovic, 2012). Imagine, therefore, my disconcertion when, on the eve of the 2015 Davos World Economic Forum, Oxfam published a research report entitled *Wealth: Having it All and Wanting More* (2015) that observed that the wealthiest one per cent of the planet controlled almost half the world's wealth. This was intended to discomfort the champagne-swilling billionaire businessmen and world leaders meeting in the exclusive resort and presumably to awaken the anger of the rest of the population. I too seethed with indignation at this smug self-satisfied one percent, sucking the life-blood of the rest of the world…. until I realised that my mother was one of them. My old, frail widowed mother, living in the modest semi-detached house on the outskirts of London for which she and my father (a woodwork and technical drawing teacher at a local secondary school) had struggled to save a down-payment in the early 1960s, and in which they had raised their four children, was one of the one per cent. The rising incomes and the inflation of the 1960s and early 70s had let them pay off the mortgage. A further forty years more of inflation (especially in London house prices) had helped lift the value of the house until it stood above the 'one percent' threshold of £528,000 (Credeit Suisse, 2014: 11), but it still remains a modest, small family house. My mother, incidentally, stated that she had enough, and did not want more.

The current 'one percent' fad empowers the discourse of envy but although one would expect the poor to harbour some resentment towards the rich, it is rarely enough to translate into conflict. The 'poor' themselves are not a homogeneous group and they usually lack the human and financial resources to channel their resentment into political action. Inequality may certainly erode trust within a society, but a more potent driver is required for it to spill-over into something more decisive. This is often to be found in deeper and longer smouldering resentments (Estaban e.a., 2012).

## Ethnicity

In the 19th century, the concept of ethnicity and eugenics suddenly became very popular. Darwin's theories of evolution, combined with the renewed drive towards imperialism, gave momentum to the idea that there was a definite racial hierarchy in the world and that, at the top were the descendants of the white European 'races'. These ideas held that advanced nations of Western Europe and North

America owed their superiority not simply to their political, military or economic power, but that these were manifestations of their higher position in the Darwinist hierarchy. These convictions led to attempts to deal with the concept of ethnicity in a scientific way employing objective physical criteria. These ideas culminated in the 1920s and 30s in Nazi's ideology that constructed a racial hierarchy dominated by the Aryan race. The Slav races to the East were destined to become the semi-slave 'colony' of the new German Reich or Empire, and below them were the Jews who were initially to be expelled from Europe but who were eventually exterminated. The horrors of Nazi Germany discredited much scientific research into ethnicity and the discourse (and practices) of eugenics. They did not stop race and ethnicity leaving its bloody trail over the map of 19th and 20th-century history.

Ethnicity, then, has acquired a bad name, to put it mildly. It was rather surprising, therefore, when in 1997 two World Bank economists constructed an Ethno-Linguistic Fragmentation (ELF) Index to help explain "Africa's growth tragedy" (Easterly and Levine, 1997). Although most of the material they used had been collected by Soviet ethnographers in the 1960s, the ELF Index was pressed into service by other economists and social scientists in a whole raft of statistical experiments. If critics paused at all to assess the Index, it was usually to observe that the data was old, and that it was unclear upon what basis the variables had been defined. In 2003, therefore, another World Bank team produced an improved ELF Index, based upon an analysis of 650 ethnic groups, 1055 major linguistic groups and about 294 separate religious groups. All that was needed was to see how many of these there were in different countries and to construct an index measuring the degree of fragmentation in each. The measure

Figure 6.4: World Map of Ethnic-Linguistic Fractionalization 2003

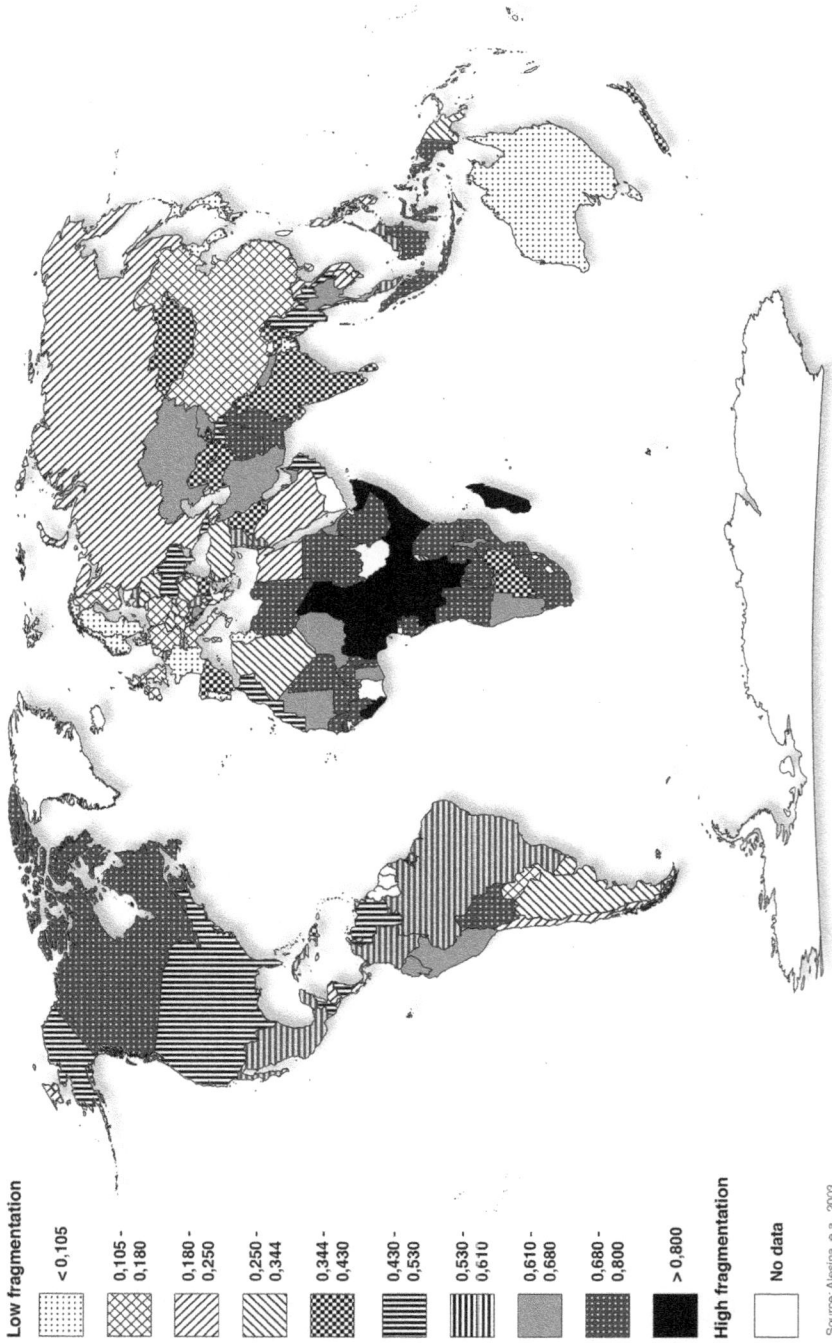

**Low fragmentation**

| | |
|---|---|
| | < 0,105 |
| | 0,105 - 0,180 |
| | 0,180 - 0,250 |
| | 0,250 - 0,344 |
| | 0,344 - 0,430 |
| | 0,430 - 0,530 |
| | 0,530 - 0,610 |
| | 0,610 - 0,680 |
| | 0,680 - 0,800 |
| | > 0,800 |

**High fragmentation**

| | |
|---|---|
| | No data |

Source: Alesina, e.a., 2003.

184

employed is known as the Herfindahl-Hirschman Index (often shortened to the Hirschman Index because it is easier to spell) which is used to calculate both concentration (such as trade concentration) and fragmentation (such a linguistic fragmentation). The new ELF constructed by a team led by Alberto Alesina also separated ethnic, linguistic and religious diversity of the world (Alesina e.a., 2003). Because it is a very authoritative index it is important to examine what lies behind the data and whether it is as solid as is usually claimed. But first, let us examine the results. A word of caution, the way they calculate the Index is such that the higher the number, the more fragmented it is. The outcome is presented in Figure 6.4.

Since both the concept and the definition of ethnicity are highly contested, it is not worth spending too much time on the details of the rankings. Among the fifteen most homogeneous countries are four from East Asia (both North and South Korea, Japan and Hong Kong), seven from Western Europe and the remainder are Bangladesh, Tunisia, Haiti and Australia. At the other end of the spectrum, all of the fifteen are in Sub-Saharan Africa. Alesina and his co-authors admit that ethnicity is a "vague and amorphous concept" but that does not prompt them to abandon their effort to quantify it, nor does it seem to have deterred others from using it. However, as soon as you start prodding the concept, it begins to disintegrate (Lambart, 2010). Most people take race or colour as a starting point, but when you question this assumption, the scope almost immediately spills over into culture. For example, is an African the same as an American-African? Do they have the same ethnicity, or not? Does a black American share the same ethnicity as a white American? They might well share the same cultures, but they do not share the same skin colour, and because of that they may experience the same culture in very different ways. Ethnicity, therefore, is a very difficult concept to operationalise. It certainly involves biological and physiological features, but it is also related to socio-cultural aspirations. A further complication is that ethnicity is both a self-identifier and an external identifier. In other words, ethnicity is a label employed to identify a group and it can shift according to the context and time (Fearon, 2003: 197-200). In Africa, for example, often the only visible sign of your ethnicity is dress or dialect. People can change that quite quickly if necessary or desired. In other words, it is hard to get results, and difficult to interpret them, especially in one is not sure of the context. "Contrary to the assumptions of most scholars who seek to test for the effects of ethnic diversity on growth, there is no single 'correct' accounting for ethnic groups in a country, and thus no single 'correct' fractionalization index value" (Posner, 2004: 850).

Alberto Alesina and his co-authors attempt to deal with these problems by trying to separate ethnicity and language, although the definition of language brings with it a whole new set of questions (which we will examine later in this chapter). At a second level, they do not deal with these problems at all, because they do not do their own research. Instead they build on the work of others. At the time of publication, most of the data was at least a decade old and some stemmed from twenty years earlier. In case of conflicting sources, they opt for the most homogeneous alternative. Their key source is *Encyclopaedia Britannica* which has no uniform system of classification. Much of its data stems from census returns and other counts, which raises two issues – the different circumstances that may influence self-identification and the legal nationality status in different countries.

A second problem lies in the degree of cultural difference, and determining where to split a group. Italy, for example, appears as a relatively ethnically homogenous country, but one could question the closeness in identification between North and South Italians. Similarly, in Africa, many of these so-called ethnicities are fairly close to each other. By contrast, Latin America is ethnically less fragmented but the distance between the dominant ethnicity and the tribal ethnicities is much larger than in Sub-Saharan Africa. Simply counting ethnicities, therefore, tells you little about how they are far apart, culturally or ethnically (Fearon, 2003).

Another criticism of the ideas behind the Index is that it does not matter how many ethnicities there are in a country, what matters is the way they might interact. For example, it is possible to envisage a situation of relative homogeneity but where the minority group is quite distinctly different and has become marginalised in society. In this case, it would be dominance, rather than fragmentation, that would be the operational factor in any further analysis (Collier and Hoeffler, 2004). Another issue is whether groups live separately in a different part of the country, completely isolated from the others or whether they live together in mixed communities. If these groups lived together, their own identity vis-à-vis that of their neighbours would presumably matter less than their definition vis-à-vis outsiders (Posner, 2004; Uslander, 2010). In a second paper, Alesina takes this criticism on board and produces a new series for ninety countries, using data at a sub-national level as a measure for 'segregation'. Unfortunately, although the results are presented in a series of scattergrams, the underlying data was not published, so that it is impossible to control for any individual country (Alesina and Zhuravskaya, 2008).

One final criticism raises the question of 'mobilisation', particularly in the case of Africa. This goes to the heart of the question: why does ethnic fragmentation matter? It matters, of course, because different groups may have different aspirations and because this, in turn, will have an impact on society. However if that is the case, why not go straight to the question of political mobilisation (Chandra and Wilkinson, 2008). For example, Kenya can be divided into nine main ethnicities but most of these distinctions do not matter. The ethnicities cluster around three politicised ethnic groups. Therefore if one is looking at the impact of fragmentation on Kenya, it is these three groups that matter, because that is how people identify themselves for political action (Posner, 2004).

## Language

If ethnicity is a difficult concept to operationalise, it has been suggested that language may hold the answer. Since the core of the problem with fragmentation is communication between groups, then language may offer an alternative way of measurement, literally. Indeed, one author deliberately uses the term "cultural fractionalisation" to refer to linguistic diversity (Fearon, 2003: 211-214). Having seen what a mine-field the measurement of ethnicity is, one could be forgiven for thinking that matters will be more tranquil when we turn to languages. Surely it is only a question of finding out what language people speak. Let's start with the concept of one's mother tongue. Is that the language one speaks at home, or is it the language that is most generally used? They are not necessarily the same, especially in (first- or second- generation) migrant families, but not just there. There are multilingual societies, in which people are genuinely bi-lingual. In Belgium, for example, many citizens could converse in both French and Flemish. The country is becoming politically more polarised but is that related to language or to political issues for which language has become a convenient metaphor (Witte and Van Velthoven, 1999)? Similarly, in many African societies, language groups tend to be fairly close and people often switch between languages (Posner, 2004). Multi-linguality provides situations that cannot be covered by asking which one language is used.

This brings us conveniently to another, more general problem. Where languages are very close, the question arises at what level does one try aggregate languages? When does a language become a dialect, or a dialect become a language? This is a vital issue in constructing an index purporting to be an accurate (and useful) measure of linguistic diversity. Usually, linguists employ a criterion of 'mutual intelligibility', which means that one does not count a speech as a separate language if it can be understood from another language. If we look at the main Scandinavian languages, the Norwegians are the best at understanding both Swedish and Danish, whilst the Danes are the worst (though most can manage), but the levels of comprehension vary by location (neighbouring regions being better able to understand each other) and by age (where mutual-intelligibility among the youth is declining). Most Scandinavians can understand each other, yet they each claim to speak a different language, and the three are still usually listed separately (Gooskens, 2007). The idea of mutual intelligibility is theoretically sound but is difficult to operationalise. Where exactly do you put the line in terms of this intelligibility? Does this understanding have to be two ways, or can it be one-way? Moreover, the 'ability' to understand another language to some extent also depends on the willingness to do so (Posner, 2004). If people do not want to understand a language, they will define it as an ethnically different language and, once this idea had been internalised, it will create a (mental) barrier against understanding.

Clearly the question of language versus dialect is central to any effort, first to count them (and their speakers) and then to measure the degree of fragmentation. And there is a massive difference in data selection. Alesina and his associates plundered *Encyclopaedia Britannica* and the *CIA Factbook* to isolate 1,055 language groups. The rest are merely dialects (Alesina e.a., 2003). On the other hand, since 1951 an international army of linguists, grouped under the Ethnologue project has been engaged in collating the world's living languages and the 2013 edition of their handbook come to a total of no less than 7,105. To be fair, these linguists are enthusiastic collectors of languages and their project is aimed at preserving as many as possible, but the discrepancy is too large to be dismissed as a kind of language fetishism. Of the languages listed, 682 have official recognition, a further 2,502 are described as vigorous (whereby the language is used for face-to-face communication by all generations) and another 1,534 are classified as developing (where the language is in vigorous use, with literature in a standardised form being used by some users, though this is not yet widespread). These 4,718 languages are in use by 98.9 per cent of the world's population. The remainder have small cohorts of users, and as such are unlikely to impact on the calculation of a diversity index (Ethnologue Project Website).

There is clearly a problem in reconciling the 1,055 language groups identified by Alberto Alesina and his group and the 7,105 identified by the Ethnologue project. Somewhere between the two there is a slide from language to dialect, and defining that line is far from easy. At the centre of the definitional problem lies the issue of 'language distance'. Linguists deal with this phenomenon through the use of 'language trees' to cluster 'families' of language together and to measure the distance between them (for example between Italian and French and Italian and Chinese). If we employ language distance to 'weigh' the languages defined in the Ethnologue project, we can resolve the crude over-clustering that is apparent in the Alesina Index. Let us take one example. According to the Ethnologue project Papua New Guinea is the most linguistically fragmented country on Earth. With over 862 languages, Papua New Guinea hosts 13.2 per cent of the world's languages and the Ethnologues calculate a fractionalisation score of 0.990. However, by grouping languages, Alesina calculates Papua New Guinea's fractionalisation score as 0.3526, which would make it linguistically less fragmented than The Netherlands (0.5143). By introducing the notion of distance, Papua New Guinea finally emerges with a score of 0.598 and The Netherlands with a more credible 0.137. Overall the result of the weighted index is to decrease the degree of diversity in Central Africa, which has a large number of languages most of which are rooted in different versions of Bantu. On the other hand, it increases the diversity in Latin America, where most people speak Spanish or Portuguese, but where there is a large distance between those and the many minority languages which share no roots with the European languages, and themselves come from very diverse roots (Desmet e.a., 2009). One final comment on the sources used for the construction of the weighted diversity index is that the Ethnologue database refers only to 'native languages' and therefore offers excludes languages used by the migrant population. The results are shown in Figure 6.5.

Figure 6.5: World Map of Linguistic Fractionalization 2009

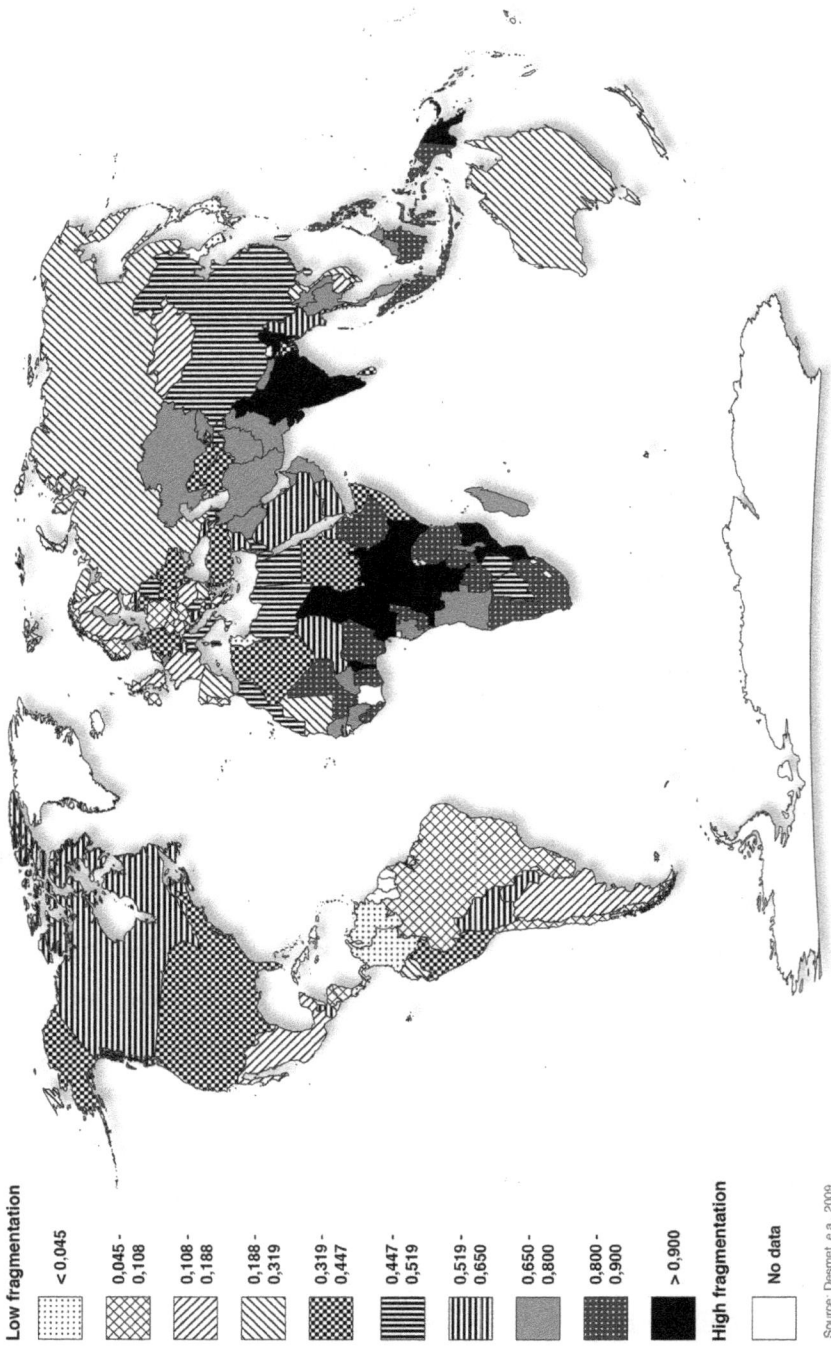

**Low fragmentation**

- < 0,045
- 0,045 - 0,108
- 0,108 - 0,188
- 0,188 - 0,319
- 0,319 - 0,447
- 0,447 - 0,519
- 0,519 - 0,650
- 0,650 - 0,800
- 0,800 - 0,900
- > 0,900

**High fragmentation**

- No data

Source: Desmet, e.a., 2009.

What is interesting here is that most of the diverse countries are near the Equator, and many people have commented on this. To be more precise, the most linguistically diverse areas lie in the forest belts on the Equator, in the jungles in India and in Africa. There are various theories about why these areas should still be highly fragmented. One theory says that because it rains a lot in these areas, they are therefore particularly productive in fruits and other produce. As result, the peoples living there did not face periodic subsistence crises and this, in turn, meant that they could live in relative isolation. Because of this they did not have to trade with other areas in order to sustain their existence and, as a result, they were not exposed to other languages. The other theory is that it is difficult to find other people in a jungle. People living in groups tend to be fragmented around the edge of the jungle. Within the jungle itself they do not meet other people and they do not come into contact with other languages (Nettle, 1998).

Another interesting observation is that rich countries are not particularly diverse in languages. It is true that they are far from the equator, but few ascribe their relative linguistic homogeneity to that. One argument is that these countries are characterised by a high intensity of economic and cultural interaction. For this to occur there has to be a dominant language. Most people learn to accept this need and learn to speak it (possibly along-side a local language). Over the last couple of hundred years, this tendency was accentuated by deliberate strategies of nation-building that stressed the need for a single national language and that constructed universal education systems to cement this (and the other cultural elements attatchd to nationhood) in place (Wright, 2003).

# Religion

Religion can invoke strong emotions. In many ways, it touches the core of a person's existence and self-identification, more so than either ethnicity or language. We can define a religion as containing a shared belief system (in a supernatural being or existence) that is exercised through a set of shared rituals. In this respect, therefore, religion resembles any form of social construction. Note, that what are looking at is societal divisions along religious lines, and not for the impact of specific religions (Iannaconne, 1998; Bednarik and Filipova, 2009).

The problem, then, is how to measure religious diversity. One way is to ask people, but this is often difficult. For some, religion is something to be declared with pride. For others, religion is a deeply personal (and private) relationship which is not readily divulged. For still others, religious identification may be a source of discrimination and persecution, and something to be concealed. A further complication lies in the ambiguity between formal religious identification and religious practice, and the definition of when one ceases to be a 'member' of a religious denomination. This last problem is particularly acute when the religious group itself is the source of the information. Most counts to work on the principle that the only way to leave the religion is to leave this earthly existence at the same time, and they work on the assumption that once one is 'in', it is for life. Alberto Alesina and associates used the *World Christian Encyclopaedia* to compile their index. This probably overstated the representation of Christians but it was meticulous in separating different Christian faiths (Alesina ea 2003. For criticism see Montalvo and Reynal-Querol, 2005a and b).

An alternative way of measuring religion would be to focus on the attendance at the religious rituals and ceremonies. However, in many communities, especially smaller ones, religious ceremonies have a wider social importance. Attendance, therefore, may be more part of a bonding exercise than an outward expression of religious conviction. Non-attendance may lead to social exclusion and discrimination in employment and access to public good (Berggren and Bjørnskov, 2009).

A third alternative is to use self-definition. Questions on religion are rarely contained in census questionnaires (because of the sensitive nature of the religion/state interface). Despite the doubt whether such a question would be answered truthfully anyway, the Pew Research Centre has reconstructed a religious diversity index relying heavily on this census data, adjusted to take account of demographic changes. The methodology relies on the Herfindahl-Hirschman Index but has been standardised to produce a Religious Diversity Index with scores ranging from zero (completely homogeneous) to ten (high fragmentation). The major problem with the compilation is that the data is conflated into eight categories – Christian, Muslim, Hindu, Buddhist, Jewish, Folk Religion, Other religion, and Unaffiliated (Pew 2014). Fortunately it has published separate estimates of the distribution of the Sunnis and Shias (Pew, 2009). I have used these figures (taking the midpoint of the estimates) to recalculate the original data, still leaving the large degree of aggregation still remaining. The results are shown in Figure 6.6.

Figure 6.6: World Map of Religious Fractionalization 2010

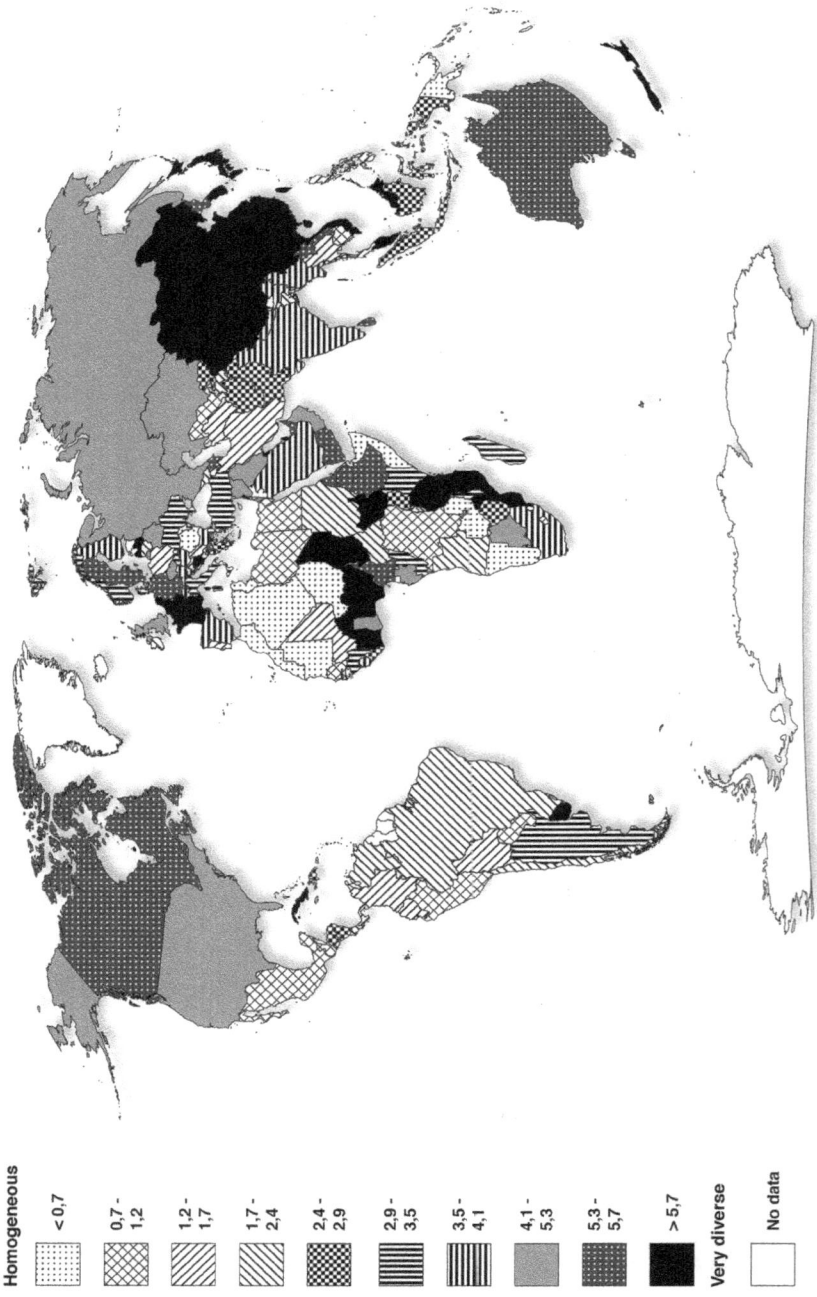

Homogeneous

| | |
|---|---|
| | < 0,7 |
| | 0,7 - 1,2 |
| | 1,2 - 1,7 |
| | 1,7 - 2,4 |
| | 2,4 - 2,9 |
| | 2,9 - 3,5 |
| | 3,5 - 4,1 |
| | 4,1 - 5,3 |
| | 5,3 - 5,7 |
| | > 5,7 |

Very diverse

| | No data |

The results have been modified for Afghanistan, Azerbaijan, India, Iraq, Iran, Kuwait, Lebanon, Nigeria, Oman, Pakistan, Qatar, Saudi Arabia, Syria, Tajikistan, Turkey, UAE and Yemen.

Source: Pew, 2009, 2014.

Since diversity of religion is being investigated not for its own sake, but as a potential input into other social and economic analyses, we have to question the validity of the data and the validity of such an exercise. We have already observed that religion is (also) a social construct and that membership or not of a church, or even the intensity of religious observance, carries with it real benefits and penalties in other areas of daily life. One way to discover the degree of religiosity is to ask a sample of the population about the importance they attach to religion in their daily lives. This is exactly what the Gallup polling organisation did in 2009 for the citizens of 114 countries. The global median was that 84 per cent of adults questioned found that religion was an important part of their daily lives. In the 2010 survey the question asked was "Is religion important in your daily life?" (Crabtree, 2010). The 2012 survey asked, "Irrespective of whether you attend a place of worship or not, would you say you are a religious person, not a religious person or a convinced atheist?" It is interesting that with the new question the global median dropped to 59 per cent. Aside from the change in the question, this fall could be explained by the fact that 3-5 years had passed since the previous surveys and, of course the people surveyed also changed. Moreover, the number of countries sampled was smaller (57 as opposed to 105) and contained 16 new countries (half at the non-religious end of the spectrum). In almost all cases the degree of religiosity fell, most of all in Turkey where 82 per cent had claimed that religion was important in their lives, while only 23 per cent owned up to being a religious person (Gallup, 2012). Generally most of the responses slid downwards but in constructing the map, we chose in favour of the most recent data. The resulting decile changes were rarely more than one position. The 110 countries with populations above 1.5 million are portrayed in the Figure 6.7.

Figure 6.7: World Map of Religiosity

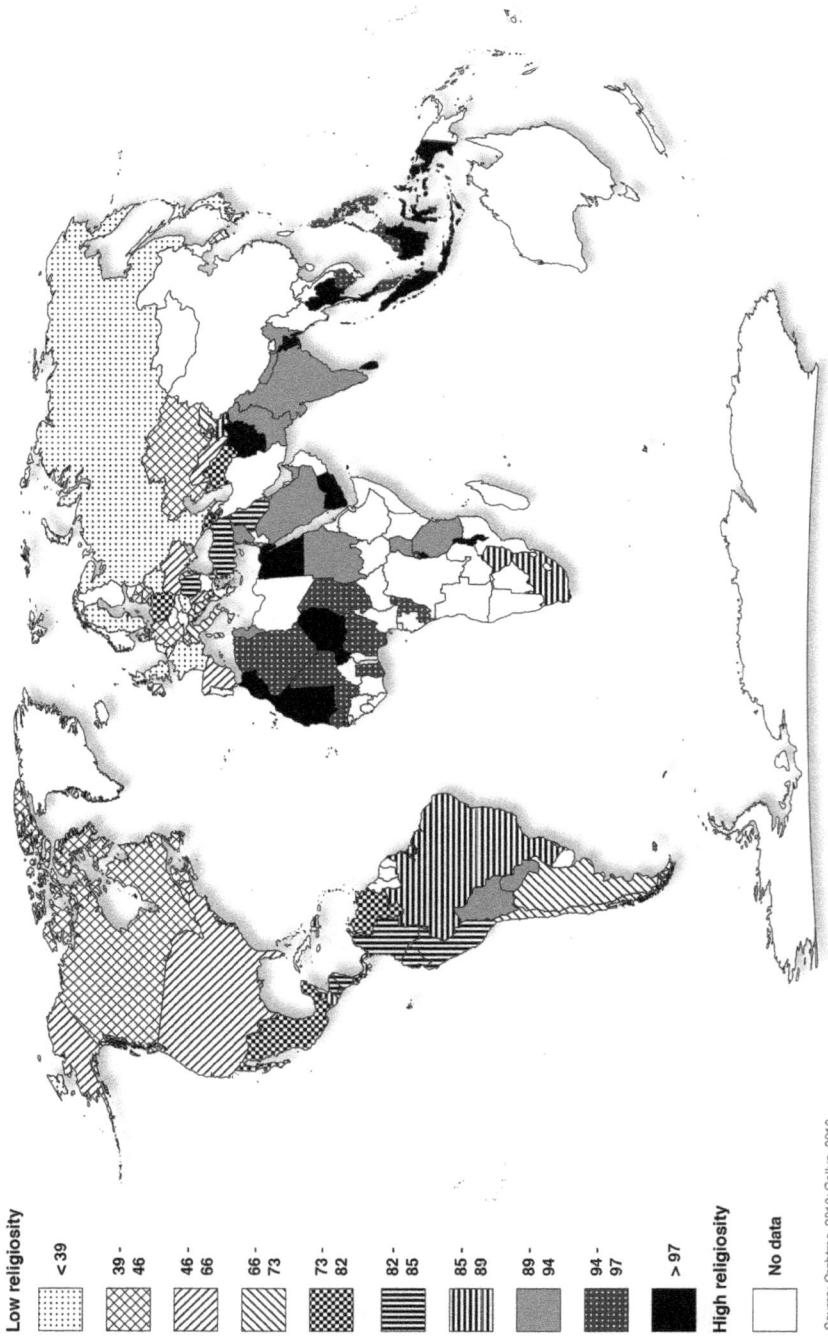

Low religiosity

< 39

39 - 46

46 - 66

66 - 73

73 - 82

82 - 85

85 - 89

89 - 94

94 - 97

> 97

High religiosity

No data

Source: Crabtree, 2010; Gallup, 2012.

Of the 22 countries in which a majority declined to describe themselves as religious, 13 lay in Europe and 3 in East Asia (China, Japan and Hong Kong) and the remainder were Australia, Azerbaijan, Canada, Kazakhstan, Turkey and Vietnam. At the other end of the spectrum of the 29 countries where over 90 per cent contended that religion played an important part in their lives (most of them with data from the earlier surveys) 17 came from Africa and 4 from South-East Asia. But one thing that stands out among the more religious countries is that none of them could be considered rich. One theory suggests that it is the very precariousness of daily existence that reinforces an attachment to the spiritual and supernatural. On the other hand, perhaps it is not religiosity but non-religiosity that needs to be explained. Perhaps, despite the overwhelming arrogance with which many Europeans carry and propagate their non-religious models of society are the current exception.

## Causes and Consequences

It is always easy with back-projection to view a situation of dysfunctional government or economic stagnation and to find some societal disconnect that can be used as an explanation. The object of the exercises in quantification that we have reviewed has been to establish whether gradients in inequality or fragmentation are statistically comparable to gradients in the performance in other variables, such as trust, governance or growth. These measures, it must be remembered, also reflect a choice of mechanism – are we interested in general inequality, or in polarisation at the extremes, or in fragmentation, or marginalisation and dominance, or in segregation? In each case there will be a separate measure available for the calculation. It will be no surprise to learn that surveys of the literature confirm that different fragmentation indices, whether utilising different data sets or different measures, yield different results. However, where the results are positive, there lurks the suspicion that the choice or design of the measure was partly to produce the result wanted. It is very difficult to publish scientific papers that disprove something that no one had thought of in the first place. Thus we will dispense with the statistical models and exercises, and concentrate on the mechanisms by which these phenomena affect levels of trust in society.

Income and wealth inequality may be expected to influence trust levels in several ways. At one level, the 'poor' in society may look towards the 'rich' and feel a degree of powerlessness, not to say resentment, that will prompt them to pull back from civic engagement. Put another way, if society is more equal, its members will look towards each other with a degree of mutual recognition. This will generate an image of a 'shared fate' which in turn will make its members feel more disposed towards common action to solve problems, which will engender trust (Uslaner and Brown, 2005). It has been argued that, once incomes in a country have risen above a certain level, income inequality affects not only the poor, but also the rich. Humans have evolved in small hunter-gatherer communities and have been 'programmed' to function in conditions of social equality. In larger, modern, urbanised, competitive, hierarchical societies, they are exposed to stresses involving self-esteem and self-worth which gnaw at the foundations of trust and well-being (Wilkinson and Pickett, 2010). It should be noted that both the theory and the evidence for this more extreme version of the relationship have been savaged by their critics (Saunders, 2010; Snowden, 2010).

In a fragmented society, different ethnic groups will exhibit different material cultures that may show themselves in different styles of clothing and in tastes and prohibitions of food. This will react directly on trust by reinforcing images of difference. Similarly, differences in languages will inhibit communication, most obviously in direct person-to-person exchange. However, the differences go deeper, since different language groups will access different news media and get exposed to different political messages. This will enhance and perpetuate cultural differences and inhibit the construction of trust. These factors will also affect economic performance not only through the trust mechanism, but also directly by fragmenting markets, raising transaction costs and inhibiting labour productivity (Alesina and La Ferrara, 2004). In a polarised society, the dominant group will tend to use its power to shape policies in its own interests, whether they be defined by class (and income) or ethnicity and culture. If sufficiently powerful, or long-lived, it may even do so at the expense of property rights and civil and human rights, and even democracy itself. Moreover, such dominate groups may promote a 'culture of intolerance' directed against potential dissenters in whatever form and unleash regimes of fear and repression. None of this, of course, is consistent with enhancing trust (La Porta e.a. 1999: 226-234).

Finally, looking at religiosity, the links to trust can run in two directions. On the positive side, many religious teachings emphasise the benefits of generosity and reciprocity towards others. They often also disapprove of anti-social behaviour such as dishonesty and theft, reinforced by the prospect of sanctions in the after-life. These teachings are internalised and passed through generations and they contribute to expectations of similar behaviour in others. Another mechanism lies in the repeated attendance at rituals which help create a shared sense of community and thereby enhance trust.

On the other hand, it is possible to envisage mechanisms that militate against trust creation. The first is that religious teachings and practices prescribe a route to salvation provide a 'sacred umbrella' that is not shared by non-believers and members of other faiths. This will create a clear divide between 'insiders' and 'outsiders', reinforcing 'bonding' trust at the expense of 'bridging' trust. A second link runs through the attitudes of the outsiders themselves towards groups united by exclusive belief system and engaged in their own religious practices. These outsiders may greet such religious observers with suspicion and distrust (Berggren and Bjørnskov, 2009). Finally, we must add Putnam's link to hierarchy in religions (stronger in some than in others) which, through the promotion of vertical bonds of duty and loyalty undermines the incentive to form horizontal bonds (Putnam e.a., 2004).

Before leaving this chapter, there is one issue that we need to address. All the analysis assumes that inequality and diversity are endogenous, that they derive and can be explained entirely from within the explanatory model. However, this is not entirely true. Income inequality may derive purely from the operation of the capitalist market economy in a given resource environment, but it may equally be the outcome of societal preferences deriving from other historical and cultural factors. It may well be these factors that explain not only differences in redistributive policies but also the differences in trust levels which produced them (Katzenstein, 1985). Equally some of the ethnic and linguistic diversity may have stemmed from geographical considerations where, early in history, land endowment and resources determined whether populations settled and acquired layers of cultural attributes, or whether they migrated and formed a more dispersed pattern of ethnic identities (Michalopoulos, 2012).

However, many ethnic differences within countries, especially in Africa, came from the definition of the borders defining the territorial spread of nations. These were drawn by imperialist powers with scant regard for the tribal composition of the areas. Moreover, the very intensity of ethnic divisions may lie not so much in statistical variables as fractionalisation or polarisiation, but in the way in which colonial institutions favoured some tribes above others as part of a deliberate divide-and-rule strategy or the way in which colonial land settlement displaced existing populations (Easterly and Levine, 1997; Leeson, 2005). Moreover, societal cleavages tend to intensify in their effects when they are bound up with distributional conflicts, and this brings the whole discussion back to the nature and degree of inequality (Lichbach, 1989).

## Summary

Let us summarise what we have learned. The chapter started by reviewing the work of Thomas Piketty on income and wealth inequality. It showed that the work concentrates on the top one or ten per cent of the income and wealth holders. Piketty had shown that since the 1980s income inequality in the USA has risen to levels approaching the 1920s, a fact that has been known for some time. His analysis can be criticised for measuring income distribution in terms of primary incomes that excluded taxes and benefits.

The GINI index is preferable as a measure of inequality since this covers the entire spectrum of experience, as opposed to focusing on the top end of the spectrum. The OECD's measure of net disposable income showed the USA as one of the most unequal of the OECD countries but even more unequal were the BRICS. The World Bank's use of household surveys shows that most poorer countries have a worse income distribution than that of the USA. The chapter showed that economists tend to favour some degree of income inequality for economic growth, but they agree that it could be societally dysfunctional.

The chapter introduced the Herfindahl-Hirschmann Index as a useful measure of concentration or dispersion that researchers have applied to analyse societal fragmentation by ethnicity, language and religion. Ethnicity is difficult to define and therefore almost impossible to measure, but that does not stop people trying. The concept of 'language distance' can be used to resolve the problem of distinguishing languages from dialects. It also highlighted the difficulties in recording peoples' religions.

The chapter subsequently examined the imputed links between these societal divisions and trust. It suggested that income inequality can affect trust through diminishing the sense of empowerment and shared fate. Fragmentation generally can lead to lack of understanding between groups and to groups diverting resources in their own favour, which will undermine trust. However, in places where religion is an important element on peoples' lives, it can make differences seem more important than other divides. The chapter also found that the highest levels of religiosity occur among the poorer countries.

In the next Chapter we will consider the extent to which these factors impact on the quality of governance that citizens can expect in society. In particular, we should be alert for the possibility that better governance may diminish the societal impact of these divisions, and whether improved governance can provide the key of unlocking the potential for growth and prosperity.

# Case Study: Race and Trust in the USA

In the Chapter Five we described several problems with the classic 'trust question' and we observed that international comparisons employing the trust question tend to be contradictory and inconclusive. This may be because of the flaws in the trust question itself, or defects in the other fragmentation of growth indices which are usually employed in the analyses. And both of these issues, in their turn, may well stem from the fact that the nation state may not be the best unit of analysis, being simply too large and too insensitive to differences in contexts.

When Robert Putnam's reputation as the oracle of 'social capital' began to take off, he initiated a *US Social Capital Community Benchmark Survey* (SCCBS) based at Harvard University with the idea of harnessing local enthusiasm into conducting parallel social science surveys. The first survey was conducted in the year 2000 and covered 41 locations (towns and districts) and a total of approximately 27,000 respondents in the USA. The survey year coincided with the 2001 US Census, so it became possible to relate the results of the surveys directly with the far wider body of information gathered by the census, including the information of the ethnic diversity of the populations in locations surveyed. All was quiet until Putnam decided to reveal his findings in the *Johan Skytte Prize Lecture* delivered in Uppsala University (Sweden) in 2006. Things did not stay quiet for long.

In October 2006 the *Financial Times* had a headline proclaiming "Study paints bleak picture of ethnic diversity" (8.10.2006). It reported Putnam as stating that the effects of racial diversity were worse than had been expected and suggested that he had delayed publishing the findings, ostensibly until he had been in a position to suggest solutions. Putnam was inundated with emails, not from the politically correct Left but from the xenophobic Right who asserted that he was only saying what they had known that all along. Meanwhile Harvard was embarrassed by the suggestion that a foremost academic was suppressing the publication of results; Putnam claimed that he had been incorrectly quoted. In the event, the national bestselling author of *Bowling Alone* published the results of his path-breaking study on race and social capital in the USA in the journal *Scandinavian Political Studies*. If this had been intended to bury the findings, it was not successful. When I checked in *Google Scholar*, it had been cited over 2,700 times.

Putnam had earlier isolated two types of social capital – 'bonding capital' which involved networking among one's own sort and 'bridging capital' which reached out to 'others'. Previous studies had been based on one of two hypotheses. The contact hypothesis suggested that as one learned to appreciate new groups, there would be an expansion of bridging capital at the expense of bonding capital. The conflict hypothesis, on the other hand suggested that contact with new groups would lead to antagonism or, at best, antipathy, a decline in bridging capital and an increase in bonding capital.

Putnam observed that a zero-sum game was basically assumed in both models and that most of the research had been into 'bridging capital'. Little work had been done on 'bonding capital'. His new results suggested a third alternative, which he labelled a 'constrict theory', namely that racial diversity caused a decline in both bridging and in bonding capital. Respondents withdrew into themselves, rather like a tortoise into its shell, a process he described as 'hunkering down'.

Putnam presented his results at two levels. In the first, in each location, he compared different types of trust (in other races, in one's neighbours and in ones own race) with a fragmentation index of race derived from the census classification (reflecting the distribution of Hispandic, non-Hispandic white, non-Hispandic black and Asian and others). In each case, as levels of racial diversity increased, so the level of trust declined. The outlier at the trusting end of the spectrum is Rural South Dakota where, to paraphrase Putnam, celebrating diversity is like inviting a Norwegian to a Swedish picnic. Anchoring the other end are San Francisco and East Bay, California. Not only do residents in racially fragmented areas trust each other less, they are less likely to register to vote, to expect collective solutions to shared problems, to work on a community project, to give to charity, to have many close friends and confidants and to feel happy.

The second level of Putnam's analysis was to locate each respondents in his/her census track (the +/_ 4000 people living in the same neighbourhood) and to link each person's trust replies individually with all the data on race, income, education, housing etc., in their area using what is called multivariate regression analysis, which allows the importance of all possible variables to be discounted against each other. Now instead of having 41 locations, we had 27,000. The outcome suggested that strongest predictors were at the individual-level variables: age, ethnicity and socioeconomic class. Next in importance, however, were contextual variables: poverty, crime and, once again, ethnic diversity (and in the USA these were interrelated). Putnam confessed to being shocked by his findings but the time he had taken to reflect upon a solution had not yielded much. All he could suggest, to paraphrase him, was not to try to make them like 'us' but to try to create a new sense of 'we'.

Although Putnam never suggested that the findings applied to anywhere other than the USA, the fact that he dared formulate a new theory acted like an open invitation for political scientists to 'test' it elsewhere (Laurence, 2013; Semenas, 2014). Occasionally the same mechanisms were observed, but less strongly. It was suggested that Putnam might be using the wrong variables (attitudes, like 'trust' rather than observed patterns of behaviour) or that he was ignoring variables (underestimating the generational effect) or that the 'hunkering down' may have been a specific response in the American context of (sub-)urban housing. The debate rolls on, but it is ironic that the man who wanted nothing more than getting his fellow Americans to engage in good old-fashioned bowling clubs, should be the one to open the Pandora's box of ethnic diversity.

# Chapter Seven

# Governance

Governance is a concept that describes the processes by which governments, markets or networks decide upon goals and deliver the goods and functions expected of them. It concerns the determination of policies, the exercise of power and the monitoring of results. In this chapter I will limit the concept to governments. Good governance provides the 'public goods' that the society wants and needs, and does so efficiently, fairly and effectively. Bad governance allows itself to be deflected from the demands of its citizens, leaves tasks undone and employs power to favour particular groups. Good governance is predictable, open and fair. It provides a firm foundation for future planning and can be expected to promote a commitment to the future. Bad governance is arbitrary and capricious. It leaves it citizens languishing in uncertainty and encourages short-run maximisation with limited horizons. Good governance is supposed to promoted growth and prosperity, whist bad governance leaves its citizens languishing in stagnation and poverty. Alternatively, rich countries can afford good governance, poor countries cannot. Were life that simple, there would be no need for more nuanced measures. However, governance itself became target for policy, it required an indicator to determine the current situation and to track any improvements.

The quantification and operationalisation of the concept of governance came from the debates on foreign aid, which we will explore in more depth in Chapter Eight. By the 1970s the initial 'technocratic' optimism that had characterised the international aid effort was giving way to a more cautious assessment. The growth in many less-developed countries was failing to match the expectations generated by the resources channelled to that end, and the growth that was taking place was failing to 'trickle down' to the poor. This led to much soul-searching in development circles. Was the direction of aid misplaced? Should we, from the start, have targeted the poor and perhaps directed more resources towards rural areas where most of them lived? Were the projects on too large a scale and too difficult to control? However, a major stream of criticism went in another direction. The fault lay not in what was being done, but how it was done. Was aid too reliant on governments? Governments are not industrialists, and in many developing countries they lacked a sufficiently high level of technological expertise. Was it a problem of 'free goods'? If donors were giving money away, there was little accountability, and few incentives to do things differently. Was there a lack of 'ownership'? Could it be that the recipient countries felt that aid was something that happened to them, dictated by priorities established by the donors, and for which they were not responsible? Was it perhaps not the strategy that was at fault, but the agencies for implementing them?

Out of this thinking came a new approach. One of the debates in these years was on the difference between states and markets. If states were the problem with development aid, markets were the solution. This was an era in which 'globalisation' was being recognised and the phenomenon was being held responsible for the accelerating growth of the world economy. Markets are good, it was argued. They make rational choices and, guided by the price mechanism, they lead to the optimal allocation of resources and the best provision of goods at the prices and quantities demanded. In this view, states simply got in the way – they distorted incentives, manipulated the economy and prevented markets from functioning properly. States, rather than being seen as the intermediary in the aid and development effort, now carried the blame for its failure. If markets were allowed to work, poor countries, with all the natural advantages of the lower wages and strategic resources, would suddenly become attractive to foreign investors as well. In a world awash with capital, there were more investment funds available through foreign capital than the sums donor government were willing to give from their domestic taxpayers. Moreover, foreign investment would encourage market development, responding to and being driven by market signals. FDI would also help close the investment gap and, an additional bonus, it would bring the technology and management expertise required (Arndt and Oman, 2006).

By the mid-1980s, we had entered a new era of thought – one in which aid had a role, but not the primary role in developing economies. It was now argued that if recipient countries could find the right formula, they could achieve the rapid economic growth that would benefit their citizens. All of this hung on the question of governance. It depended on markets being able to function, and states clearing the way to allow that to happen. 'Good governance' became the catch-word of this new way of thinking, often known as the 'Washington Consensus'. This term was coined in 1989 to describe a strategy shared by both the World Bank and the IMF, both of which attached a whole set of structural reforms to the financial aid they gave. At this stage, the idea of good governance was defined as an efficient and effective public sector (World Bank, 1989).

# World Bank Governance Indicators

All that was missing was a set of indicators to measure the governance phenomena, and this was developed in a quite different context. The pioneer was a Harvard-trained economist called Daniel Kaufmann. His early career in the World Bank saw him working in the slums of Cartagena in Colombia, which confronted him with the reality of persistent, abject poverty in the midst of such wealth. The answer that he came to had less to do with economics and more with politics, the politics of patronage and corruption. Missions to Africa confirmed these convictions. When in Tanzania, for example, he saw enterprises securing scarce foreign exchange not based on their economic efficiency but on their proximity to power. However, in an international body like the World Bank, it was almost a taboo to mention that the fault may lie in 'corruption', since that implied that the fault lay in one of the member governments. So he, and others like him, sought empirical ways to describe the phenomena without resorting to politically-charged vocabulary. In this way, they used technocratic language to propose 'technocratic' reforms that indirectly touched politics and the perversion of power. After the collapse of the communist regimes in 1989, and the implosion of the Soviet Union two years later, there was naturally much discussion about what institutional arrangements to put into place, and to measure their performance. Kaufmann was sent to the Ukraine with responsibility for recommending institutional reform, focusing more openly on the rampant corruption in government circles. Measurement techniques, originally conceived in the Ukraine, were further developed in the 1990s in Albania, Georgia, Latvia, Bolivia, Ecuador and Ghana. This 'undercover' approach to politically sensitive issues was successfully extended in the late 1990s and early 2000s to issues such as human

213

rights and democratic accountability (Kaufmann 2008). Kaufmann was by now director of the research arm of the World Bank, the World Bank Institute (WBI), and in 1996, he published the first set of indicators for analyzing 'governance'. The caution was well-placed. In 2007, the World Bank Institute was attacked by nine countries, which questioned whether the Bank should be in the business of 'governance analysis' at all. In particular, Argentina complained about the data showing a decline in governance quality over the previous decade, while China was furious with the low ranking it achieved in 'voice and accountability', questioning the objectivity of the survey information upon which the report was based (Financial Times, 12.7.2007).

In this chapter we will focus on the governance indicators produced by the WBI for three main reasons. First, they come from a recognised international organisation. Second, they are already being used as assessment criteria in the international aid effort, and are employed as a guide to aid allocation, especially the US Millennium Challenge Account (Knoll and Zloczysti, 2012). Thirdly, and finally, they are being increasingly employed as inputs into academic exercises in policy analysis. At the same time, however, as part of our scrutiny of the World Bank's efforts, we will explore some of the alternative measures.

Figure 7.1: World Bank Governance Indicators and the Policy Process

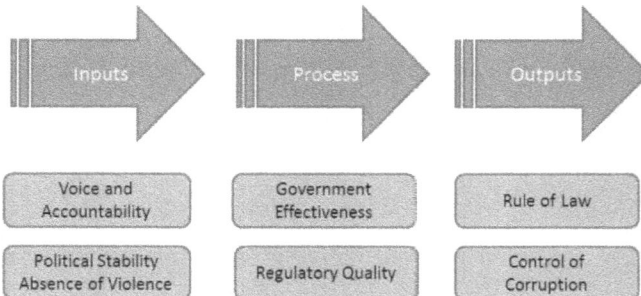

The easiest way to envisage the World Bank indicators is to view governance as a three-step process for each of which the Bank has constructed two separate indicators. These are shown in Figure 7.1. The first step is afforded by inputs into the policy-making process, measured by 'voice and accountability' and by 'political stability and absence of violence'. Thus one can envisage a process starting with elected representatives, chosen in an environment of free information and expression, who are also accountable to the electorate. Moreover, if property rights are to be developed and protected, there is a need for confidence in a fair, open and transparent legal structure that enforces contracts, protects property rights and protects life and property against crime. Systemic change should be possible through constitutional means, without intimidation and violence. The second step can be seen as the process of decision-making, measured by 'government effectiveness' and 'regulatory quality'. In other words, governments should be able to respond to the signals of the electorate without wasteful and cumbersome bureaucracy, and ensure that its decisions are implemented in an efficient manner. Finally, the WBI deals with outputs. These are also defined in political or administrative terms, namely 'rule of law' and 'control of corruption'. These imply that public power is not used for private gain, that corruption is controlled and that property rights and contract are enforceable by an effective and independent judiciary. Thus, we are looking at a very complex set of socio-political processes each of which, the WBI has compressed into one single indicator. This description of the indicators is what one should expect; it is not necessarily what the WBI delivers. Daniel Kaufmann deliberately wanted to de-politicise the indicators in order to allow the Bank to operate in sensitive policy areas. In this respect, the Bank's analysis has slid into the vocabulary of 'new public management' thinking that was emerging in the early 1990s. The basic idea behind this movement was that public management should turn towards markets and that this would provide cost-savings and efficiency benefits (Hood, 1991).

These indicators are cited repeatedly through the literature and through the policy-making process. They have also been employed in various econometric exercises, often very carelessly, but this is something we shall discuss later. To assess the accuracy of the governance indicators, it is necessary to return to the guiding principles behind their construction. The WBI deliberately avoided what it called 'rule-based indicators' – indicators in the form of actual laws and regulations, and the qualitative indicators that often accompanied such analyses. This was because the way in which such factors are recorded does not allow for judging the efficiency in their functioning. Instead, it wanted to assess how governments actually worked, and it chose to do this by looking at the results. 'Outcome-based indicators' seemed to offer the way out. The problem is that these also rely very much on the views and opinions, which invariably carry a measure of subjectivity and which are always difficult to verify (Glaeser, e.a., 2004). On the other hand, the WBI argued that there was much to be said in favour of their use, because they capture the views of stakeholders. The World Bank Governance Indicators (WGI) provides evidence for 214 countries. It then calculates the average of all the observations, to produce a world average, and they award that a value of zero. Individual country results are then awarded a 'plus' if they are above the average and a 'minus' if they are below. The range of possible marks is +2.5 to -2.5. It does give results to two decimal points, so the compression is not as great as it may seem. (Kaufmann, e.a., 2011).

One of the things we criticised when we discussed HDI in Chapter Four was the use of composite indices. These, if you recall, were indices that combine several elements and reduce them to one number. This seems to be exactly what the WBI is doing, so why are the WGI so different? Firstly, instead of combining one or two existing sets of numbers into grand-sounding categories and then turning these into one index number, the World Bank has employed as many as thirty to forty elements into each of its six indicators, and it has resisted the temptation to reduce them all to a single number (and correctly so). Thus, what Bank officials do is to note the kind of information they can extract from a report and to reduce it to a standard set of questions and answers, and allocate a score to each answer. All these answers are then converted onto a standard scale. The Bank would argue that the plurality of different indicators, reflecting different dimensions of complex socio-political phenomena, is preferable to slapping two or three 'proxy' numbers together under a fancy label. They also argue that it has the added advantage of being able to calculate an 'error term' into the estimates (we explained this earlier on pp 21-22). One final thing adjustment is to give different weights to the answers, giving greater weight to answers that are close to each other. However, this contains the danger that if the results are tending to cluster around a central point, this will have the effect of reinforcing the central tendency, and artificially narrowing the room for error. This is worth bearing in mind when looking at the results. The World Bank is very open on its procedures and on the results, but it does not publish the exact questions (though it does indicate the area of inquiry in each source employed) nor does it publish the weights (reinforced or not) employed in the calculations. However, it does publish its error margins. It offers readers a range with a 50 per cent confidence level and an alternative range of 95 per cent certainty, the size of the margin being larger for the latter than for the former. In the gap between those two lies 45 per cent of accuracy (a little better than tossing a coin, but not much). At the bottom decile of the spectrum, over half of the observations (8/15) could be put in any order between these two margins. As Daniel Kaufmann himself warned, "Margins of error are not trivial, and caution in interpreting the results is warranted – one should not precisely rank countries." (Kaufmann, 2005: 41). The worst countries are never going to be at the top of the range, so we can use the data as ballpark figures. Putting them into a demanding statistical exercise is another matter entirely.

In attempting to 'depoliticise' the indicators, Kaufmann initially intended to launch a serious policy debate. However, critics have suggested that the WBI's action has had the opposite effect and has actually narrowed the frame for debate. By objectifying governance, and by doing so in a narrow economistic manner, it has restricted the room for discussion. The focus, it was argued, was no longer on the concept of governance, but on a country's performance in a particular set of definitions. The Bank has responded to this kind of criticism. When some of the indicators were incorporated into the Millennium Development Goals and used for development aid allocation, the Bank stressed more publicly than before the error margins and the dangers of establishing country-rankings too rigorously. In addition, from 2006 onwards, the Bank has begun releasing more of the disaggregated data into the public domain (Erkkilä and Piironen, 2014: 7-9).

The first area of criticism has to do with the global average. For every year and for every indicator, the average for that year is zero. This means that it is impossible to measure change over time, except in relation to the average. In other words, a country can move up or down the rankings, but the goalposts move every year (Arndt and Oman, 2006: 61). The response of the World Bank is to accept the criticism, but to argue that it is still valuable to see countries' performances relative to the average, and relative to each other (Kaufmann, e.a., 2007a: 2-3).

Another criticism is that over time the number of reports employed in the surveys has increased, and so, therefore, has the number of facets that could be incorporated into the calculations. Thus, the argument runs, what one might be seeing over time, relative to other countries, is not the effect of a change in performance, but a change in the types and qualities of the data (Arndt and Oman, 2006; Knack, 2006). The Bank has replied by pointing out (correctly) that if one is employing random pieces of information, then one does not need exactly the same pieces for every exercise. The whole point of using multiple data-points lies in the fact that one is less likely to have any systemic bias in the results and that, anyway, the error margin can easily be adjusted for a smaller number of observations (this used to be done with statistical tables, but everything is now in a computer programme, so that this is not difficult). Although there may be differences between two data sets describing the same phenomenon, it contends that these have not proven to be statistically significant (Kaufmann e.a., 2007a: 5-9).

Having focused on the statistical treatment of the data, it is now time to turn to the nature of the data itself. One area of criticism lies in the nature of the responses used in compiling the indicators. As we have already observed, the World Bank has chosen the side of market capitalism as being the best route for development and has skewed some to the areas of inquiry in this direction. However, in order to answer market-type questions it needs people with market-type knowledge and, as a result, the sources that it employs are produced largely by Western experts. It speaks for itself, therefore, these experts, and the reports they produce, are predisposed towards certain views and are antipathetical towards others. In particular, they will not be favourably inclined towards state-led industrialisation, or state sponsored national champions. Nor, will they be particularly well disposed to the forms of labour market regulation in many welfarist Western economies. So, basically, capitalism is writing its own governance indices (Kutrtz and Schrank, 2007). The World Bank replies to this by insisting that it does not rely exclusively on these commercial reports, but also use sources compiled by governments and NGOs[4]. Moreover, they argue the firms surveyed are not just the multinationals but that "the majority of firms are small- and medium-sized enterprises". They also suggest that if the object is to measure the business climate, the resources employed should reflect that aspect. It is not a bias, they argue, but something inherent in their whole approach (Kaufmann e.a. 2007b: 556-557).

A further criticism of the objectivity of the sources lies in the so-called 'halo effect'. Basically what it suggests is that if a country is performing well, or it is surging up the rankings, experts will tend to judge it favourably. The data, then, would reflect past performance

---

[4] That is true, but an examination of the details extracted from each source does not suggest that the balance is equal.

or reputation, rather than the current picture (Kurtz and Schrank, 2007). The response of the Bank is to run a series of statistical tests and refute the accusation. In effect, their reply is that statistically, for the halo effect to impact on the indicators, it would take an improbably large and immediate shift in opinion (Kaufmann e.a., 2007b, 557-560).

Finally, it has been suggested that the individual indicators are not conceptually distinct, and that there are very clear overlaps in the indicators. If they are not different, it is argued, then the outcomes tend to become mutually reinforcing, and this will affect decisions made on this basis. In fairness, it should be said that this is more the fault of users of the Index than it is of the compilers. However, each component embodies various dimensions, and the selection and allocation of these dimensions among the six components has been accomplished without any formalised theoretical or empirical underpinning (Langbein and Knack, 2010; Thomas 2010). Rather haughtily, the compilers of the indicators "reject this line of criticism entirely as definitional nitpicking" (Kaufmann e.a., 2007a: 24).

There is a whole industry of 'governance' indicators operating at any one point of time as social scientists plunder existing databases or assemble their own in order to develop and test their research hypotheses. Many of these refer only to single years, of specific interests. Of all the indices, the WGIs do have the widest credibility (see Williams and Siddique, 2008 for an overview) but there is one unresolved objection. Occasionally the WGI does take a limited pro-growth and pro-market approach and attach it to a label that is clearly intended to be neutral. In those cases we have tried to find an alternative indicator that seems more consistent with the terminology. Incidentally, in this way we also deal with the 'overlap' criticism that so obviously irritated Kaufmann and his colleagues.

In the next sections we will look at three dimensions of the index that have been most employed in the literature attempting to link governance to questions of prosperity and growth. These are the link between economic performance and the input 'voice and accountability', links with process 'regulatory quality' and the links with the two outputs 'rule of law' and 'control of corruption'. The precondition for growth of 'Political Stability and Absence of Violence' will be dealt with in the next chapter, in the section on state failure (pp 278-282). In each case, we will start with a presentation of the World Bank data, together with any alternatives. After that we will explore the theoretical relationships that tie each indicator with growth and development data, before finally examining the results of empirical studies into the relationship.

## Inputs: Voice and Accountability

The World Bank has defined two inputs as part of the governance indicators – Voice and Accountability and Political Stability and Absence of Violence. We will consider the latter in the next chapter. The World Bank claims that, "Voice and accountability captures perceptions of the extent to which a country's citizens are able to participate in selecting their government, as well as freedom of expression, freedom of association, and a free media". No less than twenty international and regional sources have been used to compile the index, including data on such issues as the freedom of the press, the transparency of information, the honesty in organising elections and the confidence in public institutions. On the other hand, the

Figure 7.2: World Map of Voice and Accountability, 2014

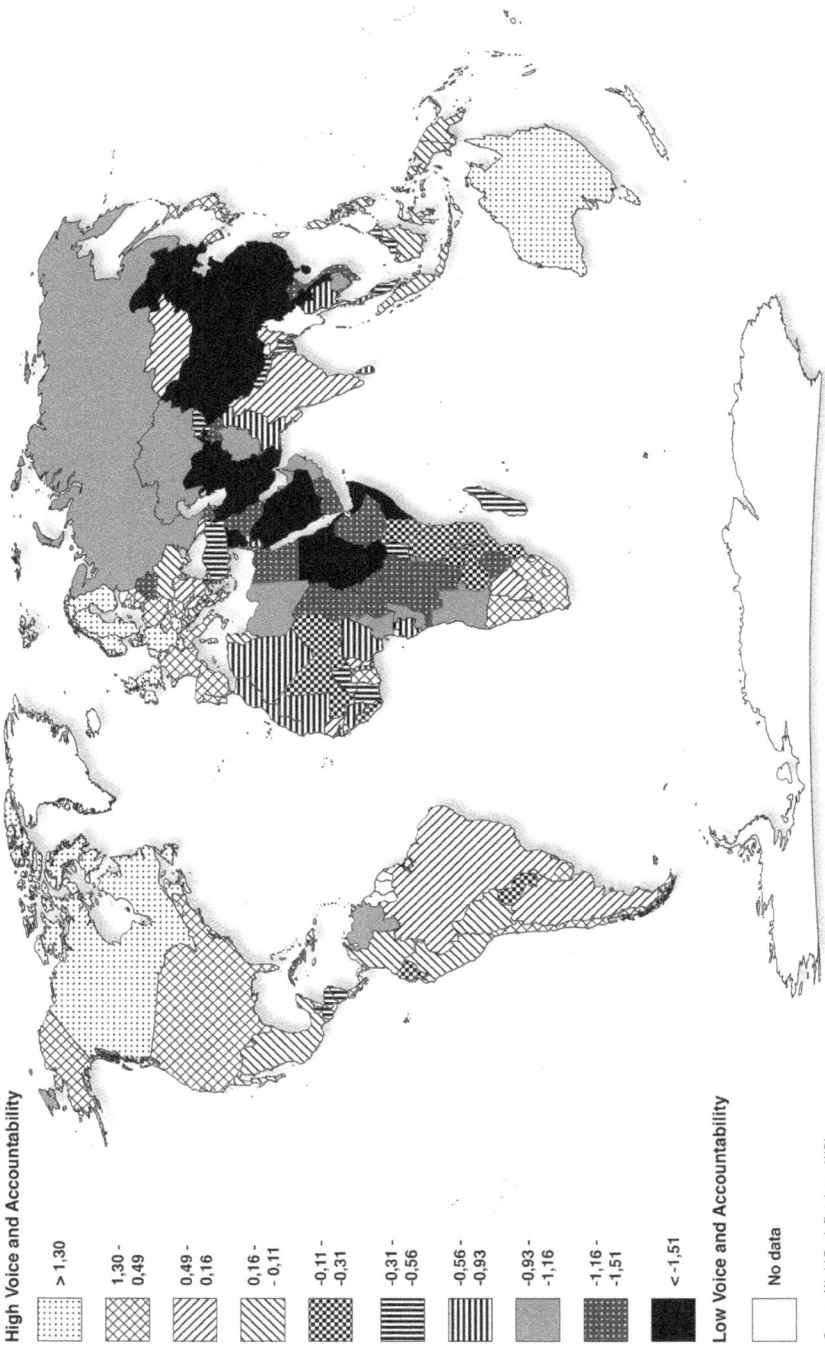

High Voice and Accountability

> 1,30

1,30 -
0,49

0,49 -
0,16

0,16 -
- 0,11

-0,11 -
-0,31

-0,31 -
-0,56

-0,56 -
-0,93

-0,93 -
-1,16

-1,16 -
-1,51

< -1,51

Low Voice and Accountability

No data

Source: World Bank Database WGI

whole edifice is premised on a Western democratic understanding of 'voice and accountability'. In fact, it is difficult to see why economic development should not be compatible with authoritarian state rule, even if, from a Western perspective, the entire process would be morally more satisfying if it were accompanied by increased democratic freedoms. Moreover, from the standpoint of trust, a successful economy and improved perspectives for the future may be as good as a basis for high measures of interpersonal and generalised trust, especially if combined with the semblance of an impartial and efficient bureaucracy. Nevertheless, some form of democratic structure does allow the preferences of citizens to be translated into policies. It also introduces some element of accountability of the elected representatives to the people they are supposed to serve, which should also generate higher levels of trust (always assuming, in both cases, that trust is not purely culturally determined). The indicator, which was completely revised in 2013, covers the years 1996 to 2012.

As we have already stated, in this Chapter we will be examining four of the World Bank Governance Indicators. Of the fifteen countries that represent the top decile, twelve appear in all four lists, though not always in the same order. In alphabetical order they are Australia, Canada, Denmark, Finland, Germany, The Netherlands, New Zeeland, Norway, Sweden, Switzerland and the UK. For Voice and Accountability, they were joined by Austria, Belgium and France. At the other end of the spectrum, only two countries appear in the lowest decile in each of the World Bank Indicators we examine. They are North Korea and Somalia. For Voice and Accountability they are joined by three Sub-Saharan African countries – Eritrea, South Sudan and Sudan. The rest are an interesting collection representing, from worst to least bad, Turkmenistan, Eritrea, Uzbekistan, Syria, Saudi Arabia, Laos, Iran, China, Cuba, Belarus and Tajikistan.

The problem with the Indicator is that in its efforts to absorb as many components as possible, the result has become rather amorphous. It does indeed contain everything that we could understand under the term 'voice and accountability' but rendered in such a way that it is impossible to see which particular dimension might operate in which direction. Moreover, this kind of index offers precious little help if the intention is to go beyond highlighting problems and instead try to actually facilitate improvements in policy. There are plenty of alternatives. There is a virtual industry of 'voice and accountability' indices but approaching the issue from the perspective of democracy.

One of the oldest indices is the *Freedom House Index* which was founded in the USA in 1941 and which has since 1973 published an annual *Freedom in the World Report.* The Index is compiled by a team of experts who answer a total of 25 questions awarding a score 0 to 4 points for each, where a score of 0 represents the smallest degree of freedom. The questions are divided between political rights (10 questions) and civil liberties (15 questions). Based on these scores, countries are rated on a scale of 1-7 each for political rights and for civil liberties, in which the lower number represents the higher degree of freedom (NOTE the switch from the original scores!). The average is then used to classify a country as Free (1.0 to 2.5), Partly Free (3.0 to 5.0), or Not Free (5.5 to 7.0).

There are several problems with the Freedom House Index. The first lies in the experts employed for the entire exercise. Only 32 are listed, so there must be a question-mark, at least, over the range of expertise they represent and their impartiality. This is not to imply that they deliberately collude to influence the outcome, but the methodology does admit that the scores are rarely revised without some objective reason for doing so, which seems to be a way of institutionalising the 'halo-effect'. A second concern lies in the reporting of the results since, having started with a carefully calibrated set of questions (the results of which we do not get to see) any nuances in interpretation are lost by squeezing the results into a narrow range. Commentators felt that the range of 'rights' analysed had been ideologically chosen, and that there was a large measure of subjectivity in determining countries' positions in the rankings. In methodological terms, scholars were especially critical of the fact that Freedom House did not clearly indicate the factors taken into account in drawing up the various scales used and of the fact that the scales were not able to be disaggregated. More specifically, in the 1980s its rankings were subject to harsh criticism because countries generally considered to be broadly comparable emerges with widely divergent rankings. What became obvious was that countries considered friendly to the USA were treated more leniently than the others. Since then the rankings have still been suspected of exercising erratic judgements (Alston, 2005: 76)

The final concern with the Freedom House Index is that democracy is more than the granting of political rights and civil liberties. This need for a wider definition of democracy lies at the heart of the Democracy Index compiled by the *Economist Intelligence Unit* which considered that freedom was an essential but not sufficient ingredient in democracy (EIU, 2013: 43). "Free and fair elections and civil liberties are necessary conditions for democracy, but they are unlikely to be sufficient for a full and consolidated democracy if unaccompanied by transparent and at least minimally efficient government, sufficient political participation and a supportive democratic political culture". (EIU, 2013: 1) It started publishing its own index in 2007 based on five categories and ending with the categorisation of countries in one of four types of regimes: full democracies; flawed democracies; hybrid regimes; and authoritarian regimes.

The Economist Intelligence Unit's Democracy Index is based on the ratings for 60 indicators grouped in five categories: electoral process and pluralism; civil liberties (which are also in the Freedom House Index); the functioning of government; political participation; and political culture. Each category has a rating on a 0 to 10 scale, and the overall index of democracy is the simple average of the five category indexes. It too operates on the basis of a panel of experts and a questionnaire, but instead of allowing a graduated scale of responses, it prefers a simple 1 or 0 (Yes/No) response (though it does allow for half-way opinions), arguing that it leaves less room open for differences in interpretation among the experts. It also includes survey data. The results are mapped in Figure 7.3.

The composition of top decile of this Index is virtually the same as that of the World Bank, with a few changes in the exact rankings. Belgium and France are replaced in the top decile by Uruguay and the USA. There is almost a complete change at the bottom end of the spectrum with only Cuba and Belarus surviving on both lists. The rest, listed from worst to least bad, are Burundi, Angola, Russia, Cameroon, Vietnam, Togo, Ivory Coast, Ethiopia, Nigeria, Gabon, Jordan, Kuwait and Libya.

Figure 7.3: World Map of Democracy, 2014

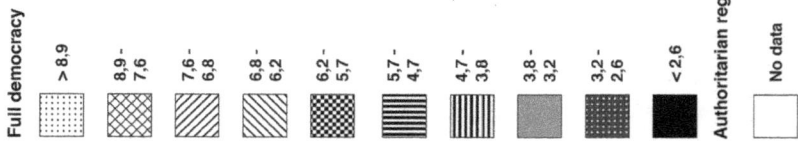

Full democracy

- >8,9
- 8,9 - 7,6
- 7,6 - 6,8
- 6,8 - 6,2
- 6,2 - 5,7
- 5,7 - 4,7
- 4,7 - 3,8
- 3,8 - 3,2
- 3,2 - 2,6
- <2,6

Authoritarian regime

No data

Source: Economist Intelligence Unit, 2015

The link between democracy and growth hinges on the assumption that the granting and reinforcement of individual political rights will lead to the reinforcement of economic rights, in particular what are called 'property rights'. These grant individuals control and decision-making over their own land, labour and capital. If economic rights are guaranteed, individuals and businesses are free to decide for themselves on their levels and distribution of consumption and investment and, collectively, on what they reserve for collective expenditure. Guided by signals from the market, it is presumed that they will make optimal decisions and so achieve the best growth result possible. Moreover, since citizens will control those whom they have chosen to take decisions on their behalves, they will also optimise government expenditure and keep a check on the twin dangers of clientalism and corruption. The one snag in this scenario that is that the power distribution within society may allow some groups of citizens to use the political process to grant themselves 'economic rents' or rewards in excess of what would otherwise be granted under market circumstances. For example, organised groups may allocate themselves subsidies, subventions or other transfer payments from the budget, which lead to a corresponding increase of (other people's) taxes. Equally, labour unions or business associations may lobby successfully for protectionist measures in the forms of regulations that penalise consumers (Barro, 1996; Tavares and Wacziarg, 2001).

However, the whole edifice is premised on a Western democratic understanding of 'voice and accountability'. It has been forcefully argued that early economic development in the West took place against a backdrop of a distinctly undemocratic order, at least in terms of modern conceptions of the term (Kahn, 2012: 51-56). A second question in the causation model is whether democracy is a precondition for the protection of economic rights. The right-wing, conservative, dictatorships, such as the Pinochet regime in Chili and the Fujimora regime in Peru, both successfully supported economic rights and free markets (Barro, 1996). Finally, one could argue that authoritative, non-democratic regimes may promote growth through policies that were not market-enhancing, but which employed state support for 'national champions' to push growth forward. Indeed, in many countries the initial stages of economic growth have been accompanied by active state promotion (Chang 2002). China, of course, is the most recent example of the same phenomenon.

If we turn to examine attempts to establish an empirical link between democracy and growth the evidence is contradictory. Many studies show a strong relationship between levels of GDP and democracy. However, this simply means that richer countries tend to be more democratic but it does not necessarily establish a role for democracy itself. Other studies have suggested a (weak) negative relationship between democracy and growth, only to be outnumbered by those that have established the reverse causation (Butkiewicz and Yanikkaya, 2006: 650). There is little evidence, either, that regime change produces a positive growth effect, and this from studies before the changes brought about by the Arab Spring. One reason for the confusion may be that democracy is too blunt an indicator to cover the complexity of power balances, decision-making structures and institutional forms that exist in the world, and that each has different potential effects (Persson and Tabellini, 2006). The most-recent survey suggests that all studies have different definitions of democracy and different specifications in their models, and all pay too little attention to the range of influences affecting economic growth or the channels through which democracy may affect its dynamics. Its own conclusions are that democratic transitions do have a significant impact on growth through the economic reforms that accompany the transition, the investment in schooling and better health as well as higher levels of investment, better provision of public goods and lower levels of social unrest (Acemoglu e.a., 2014). It is unlikely that this will be the last word on the subject.

## Process: Regulatory Quality

When we turn to consider the World Bank's Regulatory Quality indicator, we face a problem of the use of language. Any neutral interpretation of the term would suggest that what was under consideration was the government's ability to monitor, fairly and transparently, its own policies across a range of policy dimensions, such as health and safety standards, labour legislation, environmental concern, as well as business activities. The World Bank, on the other hand, is primarily concerned with the implementation of policies designed to promote private sector business and to support freer trade. The Bank makes no secret about this, and it is concerned, after all, with the business of developing less developed economies. However, the term, as it is used here, is misleading and it is important to bear this in mind when examining the results. The World Map, shown in Figure 7.4, looks distressingly familiar, with the better performance concentrated among the richer countries and with poor performance concentrated in Africa, parts of Central America and the Middle East. Eleven of the countries in top-15 positions for Regulatory Quality are identical with those appearing in the top of the Voice and Accountability Index (though not in the same order). Topping the regulatory quality list are Singapore and Hong Kong, which are ranked 68th and 39th respectively for Voice and

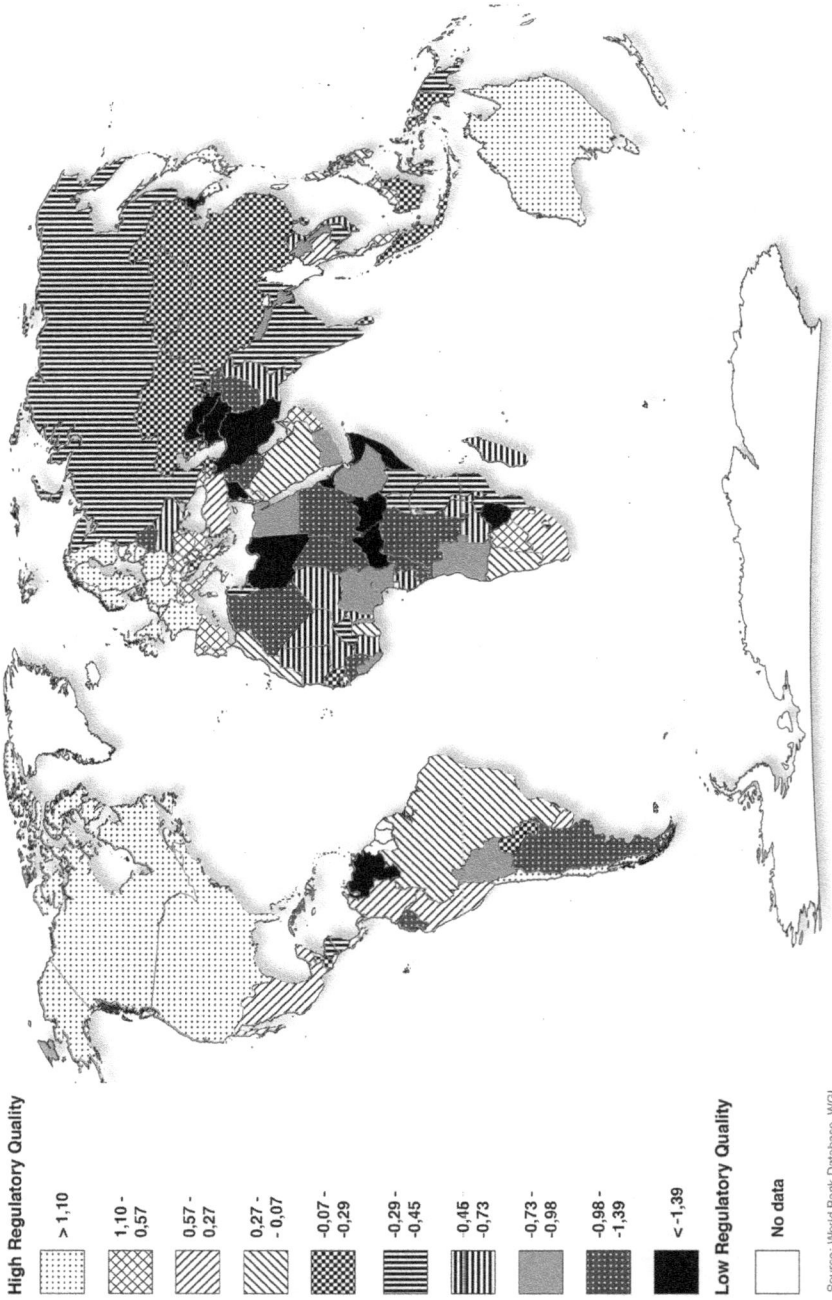

Figure 7.4: World Map of Regulatory Quality, 2014

**High Regulatory Quality**

| | |
|---|---|
| | > 1,10 |
| | 1,10 - 0,57 |
| | 0,57 - 0,27 |
| | 0,27 - -0,07 |
| | -0,07 - -0,29 |
| | -0,29 - -0,45 |
| | -0,46 - -0,73 |
| | -0,73 - -0,98 |
| | -0,98 - -1,39 |
| | < -1,39 |

**Low Regulatory Quality**

| | |
|---|---|
| | No data |

Source: World Bank Database, WGI

Accountability. The other addition to the top decile is Chile, which was 20th in the Voice and Accountability Ranking. Also at the other end of the scale, ten of the bottom-15 countries are also in the same decile for Voice and Accountability. Joining them are the Central African Republic, the Democratic Republic of the Congo, Libya, Venezuela and Zimbabwe.

An attempt to link the WBI governance indicators to growth divided the country sample into 24 'advanced countries' and subdivided 88 developing countries into a group of 53 'diverging countries' and 35 'converging countries' depending on whether they were growing faster or slower than the advanced group in the years 1990-2003. Leave aside, for a moment any doubts about the validity of the growth data. The results discovered no link between the performance of either sub-group and its performance in the regulatory quality index. It did find that the advanced countries had better regulatory quality than the 'diverging' group, but that indicated nothing more than that they could afford it (Khan, 2006).

Although there are studies of regulatory policies on specific issue areas, there is rather less on the expectations from regulation, broadly defined. Among the benefits expected to flow is that, well-designed, regulation can benefit society but that badly defined regulation can have the opposite effect (the too much red-tape syndrome). Insofar as regulation is poorly designed, it can actually reduce growth by inhibiting profitability, investment and entrepreneurship. The costs imposed by regulation can be separated into 'information costs', the costs of obtaining and processing the information necessary to make regulation work, and 'compliance costs', the cost imposed on business in meeting the requirements. Effective legislation should aim at reducing these costs without sacrificing the agreed objective. Many of the statistical tests on the relationship between different (proxy) measures and economic growth do indeed suggest that there is ia link between the 'burden' of regulation and economic growth, but this because many of the proxies have indeed been defined in terms of the measurable or implied 'costs' of regulation. The fact that the regulation itself may be beneficial for the economy, or to society as a whole, is usually ignored (probably because the evidence is too specific). For example, regulation standardising various railway gauges, plug sockets and the like may well yield benefits of economies-of-scale to businesses. Similarly, 'clean-air' legislation may impose costs on business, but reduce the very real social and, often, medical costs. Moreover, even if there is a statistical match, the causality is not necessarily in one direction. For example, it could be that countries with slow growth (for whatever reason) resort to more regulation to attempt to resolve the problem. In addition, it is questionable whether the proxy variables adequately, or consistently, capture the full impact of both administrative and compliance costs. Finally, even when we can establish a relationship, the components have been so aggregated that it is impossible to filter out any sensible policy advice over which part of the policy or regulatory system to alter to have any impact. In fact, most of these elements, that could contribute to 'better regulation' are under-tested or have not been tested at all (Parker and Kirkpatrick, 2012).

## Outputs: Rule of Law

The World Bank's indicator for the Rule of Law suffers the same type of problem, as does its regulatory efficiency indicator, namely it is not about the rule of law as the concept is generally understood by the public. The indicator does not measure human rights, and it does not have a focus on the independence of the judiciary, the principle of equality before the law, the absence of discrimination, and the rights to a fair trial and to appropriate sanctions. Nor does the 'rule of law' mean that all citizens are treated equally, promptly and fairly by the legal system. It also ignores many of the concerns that would be prominent in a list of concerns of the civil rights movements. Instead, the indicator is loaded with an extra dimension in favour of business contract and property and, not surprisingly, the sources employed are biased in that chosen direction (Thomas, 2010). We have to recognise that the World Bank is not an institution for the protection of human rights, and it makes no secret of the direction of its interest in its documentation. The indicator has an economic bias, although it does also concern itself with the incidence of crime, the protection of property, the enforcement of contracts and the confidence in the entire judicial apparatus.

The world map in Figure 7.5 shows the same distribution as all the others – a good performance in the richer states, with most problems concentrated in Africa and South Asia. Among the top-15 fourteen places are shared with the top decile of the Regulatory Quality Index. Chile slips out of the list to be replaced by Austria. The bottom-end of the spectrum only eleven of the countries appear on both lists. New to the poor performers in the Rule of Law list are Afghanistan, Guinea, Iraq, Guinea-Bissau, and Syria. But we have to remember that this index is skewed towards the formulation and implementation of market-friendly economic law. If we want an index for the rule of law, as is generally understood, we have to look elsewhere.

Figure 7.5: World Map of the Rule of Law, 2014

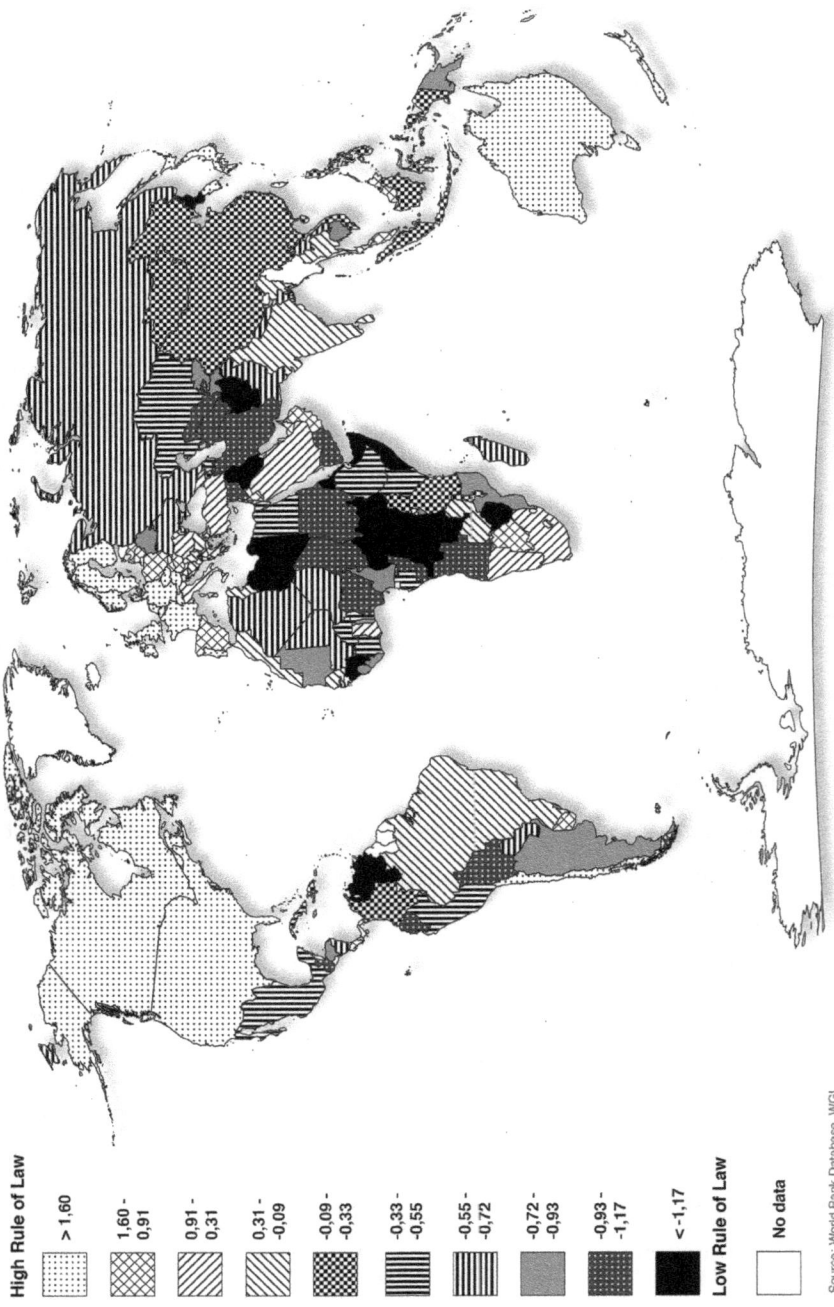

**High Rule of Law**

- > 1,60
- 1,60 - 0,91
- 0,91 - 0,31
- 0,31 - -0,09
- -0,09 - -0,33
- -0,33 - -0,55
- -0,55 - -0,72
- -0,72 - -0,93
- -0,93 - -1,17
- < -1,17

**Low Rule of Law**

No data

Source: World Bank Database, WGI

This gap can be filled by the *World Justice Project*, an independent group of lawyers founded in the USA in 2006 which publishes its own annual 'rule of law' index. Again it is a composite index, based on eight separate elements, weighted equally. Just as the WBI's 'voice and accountability' indicator, it is a little too comprehensive for its own good. Half of it includes what we would happily understand under the 'rule of law' – limitations on government powers, fundamental rights, access to civil justice and effective criminal justice, but the other half lumps together items considered separately by the WGI – order and security, open government, absence of corruption and effective regulation. It mixes results from its own opinion polls with expert polling, both conducted on an impressively large scale, but there are for only 99 countries. Too many countries are missing from Africa and the Middle East to obtain a global picture of performance which is why I have refrained from mapping the results. If its coverage ever improves, it might offer an alternative for the WGI.

So why should the good observation of the rule of law promote economic growth? The logic starts with what is often the most difficult point - an independent judiciary. The appointment of judges should be transparent and not too biased by political preference. If the judiciary is not independent or neutral, the rest quickly becomes a sham. The independent judiciary then ensures that the legal institutions function efficiently and effectively. This also applies to the economic sector, so we should expect all the benefits to flow that arise from the protection of property rights and contracts. Some authors restrict their analysis of the impact of the rule of law to a narrowly economic interpretation that focuses exclusively on property rights and security of contract even if, occasionally, they have a whole book to fill (Dam, 2007). This is also the view implicit in the construction of the WGI on this topic.

Other authors have a wider perspective, arguing that business risk can also be reduced by factors such as helping to provide peace and stability. They even suggest that this wider interpretation may have more explanatory power than the narrow formulation (Barro, 2000: 35-36). This favourable social climate is expected to work particularly in the attraction of FDI. It is interesting that one test found that the narrow definition of the rule of law was significant for developing countries, whilst the wider definition was more important for developed countries. Unfortunately, this study also observed that the results were extremely sensitive to the time periods and the countries chosen (Butkiewicz and Yanikkaya, 2006). It is possible to take the analysis one step further back and observe that a just and effective legal system may help prevent the death and destruction that accompanies state failures and civil wars. This is rarely tested (Haggard e.a., 2007). In addition, the institutions themselves need guarantees that the judiciary is free from political manipulation, but the strength of these may vary according to the issue area involved and the government in power. Again, the support for any link between formal judicial independence and economic growth is weak (Glaeser and Shleifer, 2002) but this may be because studies focus on the higher level courts and not those at a local level.

Finally, there is a feed-back link to levels of trust, especially if you believe that constantly observing the efficient management of judicial affairs socialises people into more trusting modes of thought and behaviour. One difficulty in establishing any relationship between the rule of law and growth is that law is used in different ways, at different levels and with different results, which are difficult to capture with a single measure. On the other hand, pushed to an extreme, a complete absence of the rule of law will almost inevitably end in chaos and possibly economic decline, even if we cannot capture this statistically along the full spectrum of experience.

## Outputs: Control of Corruption

For markets to function effectively, you need to control corruption. This was the first item that pulled the young Daniel Kaufmann into the idea of quantifying governance, and it remains one of the fundamental requirements for the creation of markets. It is always difficult to measure something that borders on the edge of secrecy or even illegality. The number of convictions may reflect the efficiency of the authorities rather than the incidence of corruption itself, while the amounts of money (or favours) involved are guess-work at best. The usual approach to measuring corruption is through business opinion surveys, but since these involve those paying or receiving bribes, there are greater than usual problems of comparability of responses. After all, how much will businesses admit to? Then there is the eternal question of the comparability of the responses across different countries (Galtung, 2006: 101-106). The entire question is also politically highly sensitive. Note that the indicator is called 'control of corruption' and not simply 'corruption'. This name somehow implies that states are at least trying to control corruption. The WBI uses these sources to compile its own indicator. The results are shown in the world map in Figure 7.6.

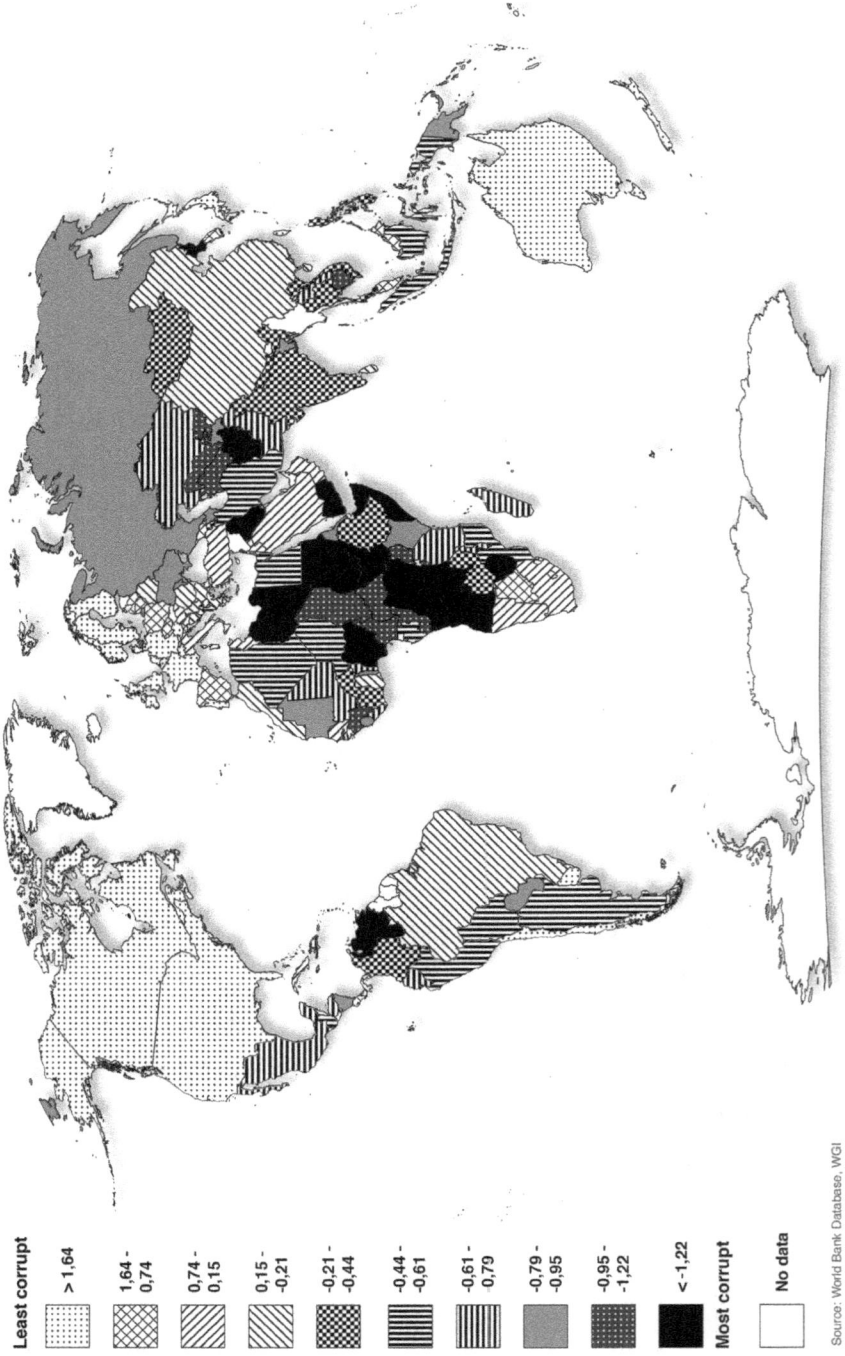

Figure 7.6: World Map of Corruption Control, 2014

Least corrupt
> 1,64

1,64 - 0,74

0,74 - 0,15

0,15 - -0,21

-0,21 - -0,44

-0,44 - -0,61

-0,61 - -0,79

-0,79 - -0,95

-0,95 - -1,22

< -1,22
Most corrupt

No data

Source: World Bank Database, WGI

240

The countries represented at both ends of the spectrum are those with which we have become familiar throughout this Chapter. The top decile comes closest to that found in the Regulatory Quality Index, though with some variation in the exact ranking. The only difference is the replacement of Chile with Japan. There is more change apparent at the lowest decile, where only nine of the countries features in the Regulatory Quality Index also appear in the Corruption Index. The new countries are Yemen, Guinea Bissau, Angola, Iraq, Afghanistan, and Nigeria.

For voice and accountability and the rule of law, we have offered alternative indicators. Here, too, there is one authoritative source, namely Transparency International's 'Corruption Perception Index'. Transparency International was founded in Germany as an independent organisation dedicated to the elimination of corruption, and it started publishing its own index in 1995. It is included among the sources employed by the World Bank, and in this case there is no reason to believe that the results are much different from those we have seen already. One criticism that you could levy at these indices is that they have a narrow definition of corruption. Transparency International was originally established to monitor corruption in business, and like that of the WBI, it too is focused on the business aspects of governance. As a result, these aspects are more likely to pass the review than the equally damaging phenomenon of political corruption. Moreover, in the West we are used to condemning the receipt of cash payments for vague services whereas in the Middle East it is expected to reward politicians for helping set up a deal or transaction. A second criticism is that these indices focus on the bribe takers, and say nothing about the bribe givers (Galtung, 2006: 108-111). In a small and imperfect effort to redress the balance,

Transparency International has also constructed a Bribe Payers Index, which it has published every two years since 1999. For the latest report that covers 2011, it asked over 3,000 senior business executives in 28 countries for their perceptions of the likelihood of companies with which they have dealings, to engage in bribery when doing business in their country. For some reason their survey excluded Denmark, New Zeeland, Finland, Sweden and Norway, which topped the rankings in their own Corruption Perception Index, but all the others in the top decile feature in the top fifteen in the Bribe Payers Index (Transparency International, 2011: 5-7). Bear in mind, too, that it is the banks in many of these countries that open their vaults for the deposit of these illicit gains, and it is in their major cities that those who gathered vast fortunes buy their football clubs or their celebrity mansions.

A recent study opened with the statement "A striking fact about government corruption is that, no matter how you measure it, it is higher in poor countries" (Bai e.a., 2013: 1). The most direct route to measure corruption is directly through its impact on the businesses responsible for generating economic growth. In this respect at one level, corruption is like an invisible tax, a stealth tax. And if it were just that - a cost levied on all business – business would be able to factor it into their cost calculations, although obviously it would diminish profit calculations. A more serious problem with corruption is when it is unpredictable. When you don't know whether a contract may be lost because the backhander you offered was less than that of your competitor, corruption has a more deleterious effect. It is the unpredictability of corruption, as much as its absolute size that destroys the market (Kaufmann and Zoido-Lobaton, 1999)

A causal second route, however, is through the reduction in the volume of public investment and the decline in the quality in the provision of 'public goods' that inevitably follows when significant proportions of taxation are creamed off into private pockets. It reduces the provision of public goods – you get fewer roads, you get unmodernised facilities for your tax money (or for your foreign aid), and this too inhibits growth (Tanzi and Davoodi, 1997). The final route is the feed-back loop into trust. Persistent exposure to the routine of corruption is extremely damaging to the reputation of institutions and must have the effect of undermining levels of generalised trust in societies (Tanzi, 1998).

Among all the governance indicators, corruption is the only one that produces significant results, at least when related to long-run growth. Its impact is particularly strong in low-income countries which, unfortunately, is where corruption is most endemic. A review of 29 studies testing the relationship of corruption to growth, producing a total of no less than 327 results, suggested that there was indeed a weak negative relationship between the two (i.e. that higher estimates of corruption coincided with lower growth). The relationship was stronger if only developing countries were considered, but the number of results (16 of the 327) was small. The review also suggested that the measured effects of corruption were larger when the growth period under review was longer. In all cases, however, the results varied according to the corruption index used. One curious outcome was that journal articles (in contrast to working papers or book chapters) tended to report more negative results which suggests that editors are looking for studies that actually show something (Ugur, 2013).

How can one reduce corruption? The obvious answer is to eliminate its causes. However, sometimes those are deeply embedded in the political (elite) culture of a country. Another answer is to increase the chances of detection and to enforce stricter penalties. This merely transfers the problem to the other dimensions of good governance – efficient institutional controls and open and transparent government systems. A final suggestion is to increase public sector pay, but this is what poorer countries cannot afford to do (Tanzi, 1998).

## Causes and Consequences

So far we have been looking at different aspects of governance as a check-list, one-by-one, and even then we have still not gained any useful policy prescription. It is also worth reflecting that, from our modern perspective, no single country had good governance when it embarked on a prolonged period of economic development and growth but that they were all able to continue growing because they continued to improve their levels of governance. If, therefore, several aspects of the problem were to be approached simultaneously, it might be possible to break out of the 'low development trap'. In other words, efforts to improve democratisation would not only help a real programme for the relief of poverty (which would enhance economic prosperity and which, through a feed-back loop would be expected broaden the democratic base) but it would also mobilise efforts to contain corruption and privilege. This in its turn would strengthen property rights and, if accompanied by the proper reforms, allow governments to adopt both 'growth enhancing' and 'market-promoting' strategies. Markets alone may not be a sufficient condition for growth, but combined with favourable meso- and macro-economic policies, and a commitment to 'improving' governance it might be possible to slowly grow to a more a higher and more sustainable level of development (Kahn, 2012: 51-56).

## Summary

Let us review what we have learned in this chapter. It started by defining governance as the processes by which governments take decisions and their effectiveness in implementing them. In the 1980s the World Bank and the IMF increasingly viewed 'bad governance' as a major hindrance to economic development. This became known as the 'Washington consensus'. To support this analysis, the World Bank constructed six governance indicators; two each for the inputs into and outputs from the policy process and two for the process itself. In general, rich countries dominate the best performing countries while poor countries in Africa and Central Asia tend to occupy the lowest reaches. More specifically, richer, medium-sized countries tend disproportionately to occupy the best performing ranges.

It criticised the world governance indicators (WGI) for misleadingly labelling some of their indicators (rule of law, government effectiveness). It also discussed other criticism and the World Banks's efforts to refute them. It accepted as an advantage that the Bank calculated an error term for all its data and warned about their use in intertemporal comparisons. Finally, it voiced appreciation for the transparent data site, allowing access even at country level to much of the documentation used in the construction of the indicators and allowing results to be presented with different error tolerances. It was not the fault of the Bank that its warnings have been largely ignored.

In the next chapter we will examine how the international community viewed the entire question of international poverty. We will assess their efforts to alleviate world poverty through the employment of development aid, first in conjunction with specific projects, but later with conditions of governance reforms attatched. We will also examine the contention that development efforts failed because aid policy was not directed at poverty relief but at national geo-political goals defined by the climate of the Cold War. We will look at whether efforts to improve governance in developing countries have been successful, and finally, we shall examine what happens when governance and trust both evaporate and states start to fail.

# Case Study: Corruption in Latin America

In October 2015 the Petrobras scandal took the latest of many strange turns. Petrobras is a partly state-owned Brazilian energy company which for many years was seen as a shining example of modern corporate practice. Since March 2014, however, it has been mired in a creeping bribery and corruption scandal. It was then that the police began investigating the finances of Roberto Costa, the head of the refining and supply division, following his aquisition of a new Range Rover from a convicted money changer. In August 2014 he signed a plea-bargaining deal with the police, information in exchange for a lenient sentence. He was the first of many who began to 'sing' and gradually the investigation, and convictions, spread through Petrobras executives, suppliers and contractors, senators and congressmen.

What apparently was happening was this. Petrobras established a list of companies from which it would accept bids for contracts. This is a normal precaution to ensure that the firms have the capacity to deliver and can match the company's technical specifications. What followed was not. The priviledged companies joined together to select who would win the bid, and arranged for, and compensated, the bids of the 'losing' companies. The exhorbitant profit of such arrangements was paid to members of the bidding cartel and to the Petrobras executives who know what was happening (Arruda de Almeida and Zagaris, 2015). The scale of the bribes was revealed when one of the accused offered to repay his share of the gains - $100 million. In an interesting twist, the Petrobras executive added a three percent 'political adjustment levy' onto the final sum which was sluiced into political slushfunds and campaign finances of the ruling political parties. As the scale of corruption became apparent, the Brazilian parliament established its own inquiery and in October 2015 it published its 754 page report. This report exonerated Petrobras from any blame. It, apparently, had been a 'victim' of the cartel. The report also exonerated the current President Dilma Rouseff, and her predecessor, of any knowlegde of the affair. This is surprising since she had been Minister for Energy from 2003-2005 and her own election campaign had been a beneficiary of the slush funds generated by the cartel (*Latin Correspondent*, 27.10.2015). In December 2015 the parliament started impeachment proceedings against the President for illegally using business funding for her political campaigns. Quite clearly the story is not finished yet. Meanwhile the Brazilian consumer has been paying for all of this through the resulting higher energy prices.

Thinking about politics in Latin America and the word 'corruption' almost spontaneously springs to mind, but this is not always and not everywhere the case. The WGI for control of corruption regularly show Chile to have scores rivalling those of the USA and rapidly improving Uruguay not far behind. Of the rest, however, only Costa Rica lies above the world average. Every other country in Central and South America lies below that line. Transparency International's Corruption Perception Index shows exactly the same pattern. In both cases these are perception indices, based on opinions on the problem rather than the experience of the citizens with the problem. In 2014 the *Americas Barometer* probed these twin dimensions of corruption – the day-to-day contact with the payment of bribes and the perception of the bribability of figures in national government (Singer, Carlin, and Love, 2014)

On average 20.5 per cent of respondents to the survey had paid a bribe to a government official in the previous twelve months. The corresponding figure for Europe was only 8 per cent and the only countries reaching the average for the Americas were Bulgaria, Lithuania, Slovakia and Romania (*Eurobarometer* 2012). Now, the exposure to bribe transaction is partially dependent on the probability of contact with a particular situation. For example, only 1.5 per cent of respondents had paid a bribe to the Courts, but few respondents had had recourse to the Courts in the previous year. Fourteen per cent of those who had, had been approached for a bribe, slightly less than the incidence among those who needed dealings with the Municipal Government, which topped the list of situations likely to lead to a bribe transaction. Next in line, ten percent of dealings with school authorities and with the police had also involved the payment of a bribe. The study did not question which party had initiated the bribe transaction - whether the bribe had been solicited or whether it had been offered independently. This was because previous research suggested that respondents were likely to lie if asked this directly. Nonetheless there were interesting variations in exposure to bribery. After discounting for differences in exposure to different situations, men were more likely to report a bribe payment than women. The more wealthy and the more educated were more likely to be involved in bribery but it is unclear whether this is because they were more likely to be specifically targeted or whether it seemed easier for them to bribe their way out of difficulties. Another group disproportionately represented were those on the margins of society who were in receipt of welfare benefits. Less surprisingly, perhaps, there was also a higher rate of bribe victimisation in high-crime areas, presumably in pay-offs to the police, which highlights the downward spiral when standards of local governance deteriorate.

The respondents were then asked whether they had themselves paid a bribe during the previous twelve months, and the results revealed a wide range of victimisation. These are shown in figure 7.7. Topping the list by some considerable margin was Haiti. A staggering 76 per cent of those with dealings with health care had paid a bribe during the previous years and 74 per cent of those with children at school had paid a bribe to the school. If it is any consolation, the police were actually better behaved than the regional average. At the other end of the spectrum, both Chile and Uruguay were relatively bribe-free.

Figure 7.7 Corruption Victimisation in Latin America (per cent)

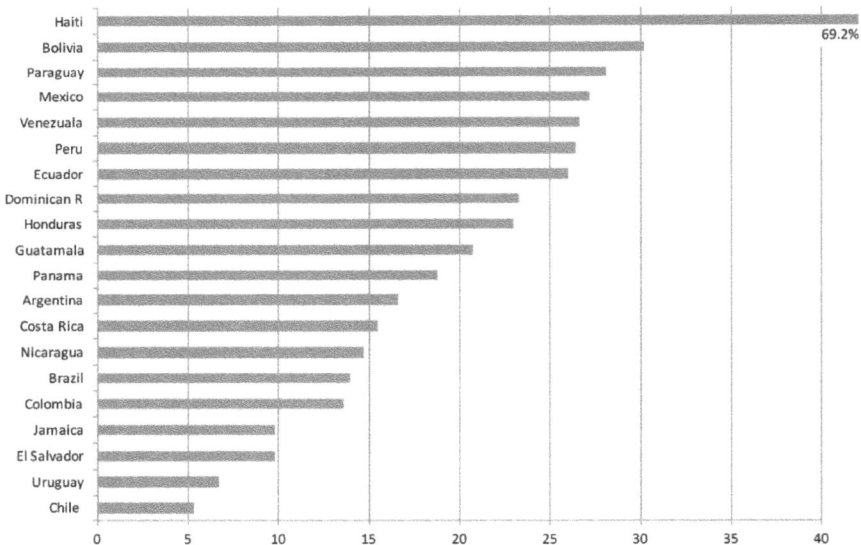

Source: Singer, e.a. 2014, 146.

The range of experience in bribery victimisation was not reflected in the perception of bribery among public officials. Virtually 80 per cent of respondents considered that corruption was either 'very common' or 'common' among public servants, even in countries where bribe payment had been relatively uncommon. Again, Haiti is worth mentioning because despite having the highest incidence of bribery transactions, it had one of the most positive (or least bad) perceptions of officials. It is interesting that, despite their relatively low personal experience with corruption, 75 per cent of European citizens saw corruption as a "major problem" in their country at both local and national level. It is perhaps not surprising to see that the only countries where less than half of respondents considered corruption to be a problem were the high trust countries of Denmark, The Netherlands, Luxembourg, Finland and Sweden (*Eurobarometer* 2011).

At a completely different level, in 2012 Miller & Chevalier and Matteson Ellis Law joined with 12 Latin American law firms in a survey of companies spanning 14 countries in the Americas (including the USA) to gain an understanding of the extent of corruption throughout the region. Their study examined the effects of corruption on companies operating in those countries, perceptions of the effectiveness of regional anti-corruption laws, and the tools that companies are using to address corruption risks (*Latin American Corruption Survey*, 2012). They found that across the region, slightly over 50 per cent of companies considered that they had lost business to competitors who had made illicit payments, though less than 13 per cent had reported their suspicions to the authorities. Of those cases that had been reported to the authorities, only in one third did it lead to an inquiry. It is not surprising to learn that over 70 per cent considered anti-corruption laws to be ineffective in the countries in which they operated. Since these businesses often operate at national levels, it is interesting to see their reflections on the incidence of corruption at different levels of government. Generally, the levels of corruption were judged to be highest in the legislative branch of national government (55 per cent) followed by the judicial and executive branches (47 per cent and 45 per cent respectively). Overall assessments were most favourable for Chile and Uruguay.

There is much more to be teased from surveys such as these. They do not resolve the debate between perception-based versus evidence-based data. Nor do we know who initiates the bribes process. Nevertheless, it is only by penetrating below the level of single all-encompassing composite indices, to the level of who is the victim and who is the bribe-taker that it is possible to begin constructing a strategy for the control of corruption.

# Chapter Eight

# Development Assistance

In the previous chapter, we saw how the World Bank became convinced of the centrality of good governance in the question of economic development in poorer countries. We examined how it defined good governance and how it tried to measure it. We also looked at how social scientists tried to link some of the dimensions of good governance (democracy, the rule of law and the control of corruption) to economic growth. Behind these ideas of governance and growth lies the philosophy and practice of attempting to assist poorer countries to reach higher levels of human development and prosperity, by giving away real resources and cash. In fact, without the 'carrot' of development assistance, it is doubtful whether the concern with governance would have gotten much further than empty rhetoric.

The chapter will begin by looking at the various phases in development aid strategy that preceded the World Bank's focus on good governance. It will then turn its attention to the motivation of aid donors and explore some of the literature examining the question of what determined the volume and direction of aid flows. This kind of analysis tends to follow the big money flows and fails to capture the motivation of aid-donors that are not large in terms of absolute size but which lead the field in terms of their generosity relative to their GNI. This will focus of the four countries that adopted the UN-norm for aid of 0.7 per cent of GNI (Denmark, The Netherlands, Norway, Sweden) in the 1970s and, with small recent lapses, have adhered to it ever since. Included in the contemporary analysis will be the UK, which reached the UN-norm last year.

Having looked at development assistance from the donor perspective, we will turn our attention to the crucial question of aid effectiveness and, in particular, to the question of whether you can promote good governance through the medium of foreign aid. Finally, we will look into the concept of 'state failure'. After all, this is the one real nightmare scenario of a failure to accomplish economic development with adequate levels of good governance.

## History of Development Assistance

There is nothing new under the sun, and the debate on development strategy is no exception. At the one extreme, ideas of development concentrated on industrial progress. This was seen as the locus for productivity advance and the provider of all the accomplishments of modernisation – railways, telegraph, urban lighting, etc. Within this strategy, the function of the state was either to provide a suitable environment for attracting (foreign) capital or for supplying it itself directly. Agriculture was not ignored in this picture, but attention was usually focused on the (large-scale) sector geared for markets that was encouraged to export, to provide a source of foreign exchange. Under Stalin, for example, it was exploited as a source of 'forced saving' directed towards state driven modernisation programmes. The other extreme lay in concentrating on the latent potential of the majority of the population engaged in agriculture. In this scenario, the role of the state is to provide the incentives for land acquisition and consolidation by peasants, and for improved techniques. This has the dual aim of increasing both food marketing and industrial consumption, and of creating a broader political support base for the beleaguered autocratic governments.

Partly under the influence of the success of the Soviet industrialisation campaign of the 1930s in laying the foundation for its success in the Second World War (Coyne and Boettke, 2003), post-war development thinking favoured industrialisation and modernisation. There were, however, two main differences between the Soviet experience and this early thinking. First, the Russian achievements were the result of input-output planning, whereas the first generation of development economists expected them to result naturally from market forces. Second, the 'investment gap' in the Soviet Union was filled by a ruthless exploitation of agriculture, whereas in the West it formed the challenge for rich donor nations. Western models, too, consigned agriculture to a passive role in the industrialisation process, not now as a source of capital but as an unlimited source of cheap industrial labour. Even at the time, there were mainstream development economists who did not share the dominant paradigm. Some pointed to the dangers of dualism and protectionism inherent in unbalanced growth and called for more 'balanced growth' to meet and encourage domestic demand. Others questioned whether the 'trickle-down effect' would really compensate outlying regions for the 'backwash effects' from the favoured core (Maier, 2005).

The post-war origins of development assistance lie in the creation in 1943 of the United Nations Relief and Aid Administration. It came into operation in 1945 with a limited two-years mandate, after which the International Bank for Reconstruction and Development

(IBRD or World Bank) should assume the task of assisting structural development. Before the latter could begin work, Europe was engulfed by a hard-currency crisis that required a separate aid effort on the part of the USA that has gone into history as the Marshall Plan. In 1948, the World Bank made its first loan – to Colombia – but its early development was slow, partly because its loans were only scarcely more attractive than borrowing on the open market (Mason and Asher, 1973; Kapur e.a., 1998). As a result, the USA remained responsible for 66 per cent of aid expenditure in the 1950s, with British and French aid to their (former) colonies accounting for most of the rest (Hjertholm and White, 2000: 10-12).

During the 1950s and early 1960s confidence in the Western development effort was shaken by a series of developments. First, from the mid-1950s, the Soviet Union began a foreign aid offensive in Africa (Lawson, 1988). Second, the peasant revolution in Cuba in 1958 sparked an immediate response in neighbouring Latin America. There the new peasant movements began to receive moral and political support from the local Catholic churches, whilst 'liberation theology' served to link Christian social thought to political empowerment and, ultimately, revolutionary change (Berryman 1987, Smith 1991). Third, a wave of newly-independent countries began to emerge in Africa that provided a fresh constituency for the aid effort. This increased demand for aid coincided with the first balance-of-payments crisis in the USA, and this reinforced American efforts to secure some 'burden sharing' from its Allies (Kaufman, 1982). At the time, the USA was still the source of 40 per cent of total aid expenditures.

The response to these challenges took the form of several declarations and a flurry of institution building. However, behind this outbreak of activity, the aid effort in terms of donor GDP actually fell. Whereas in 1960 the OECD donor countries had contributed 0.51 GNI in 'official development aid', by 1970 this had fallen to 0.34 per cent. Meanwhile a group of developing countries had united to demand a change in the world trading system and to remedy the trend of falling real prices for primary products. In response to this pressure, in 1964 the United Nations Committee for Trade and Development (UNCTAD) was created, but its success, too was limited. Finally in 1970, the UN agreed to a target of 0.7 per cent GNI aid for developed nations. In 1973 Robert McNamara, President of the World Bank called for a reorientation of aid towards the 'Basic Needs' of the poorest 40 per cent of the world's population and a new concentration on agriculture, health and education. Intellectually, a model was developed that completely turned the mainstream orthodoxy on its head. What was required, its exponents argued, was an 'employment-oriented strategy of development' that optimised the benefits of the interdependence between agriculture and industry, starting with labour-intensive sectors of small-scale agriculture and rural industry to meet domestic demand and following a change in trading arrangements, foreign trade (Mellor, 1976). Aside from a small group of countries that achieved and maintained the UN target of 0.7 per cent, these good intentions left little imprint on the overall generosity of the aid effort, though there were shifts in the distribution of aid, most notably towards Sub-Saharan Africa.

Whilst this new aid effort was building momentum, developments in the international economy were about to contribute to a paradigm shift in thinking within the field of development economics. The impact of these changes was to push governments away from large-scale investment policies and (by the start of the 1980s) even from small scale integrated projects. This passed through two overlapping phases – the first was a belief in sound (monetary) policies as a precondition for growth; the second a conviction that good governance (rooted in transparency, democracy and civic society) was the necessary underpinning for well-functioning markets and effective aid.

This shift had several causes. The first was a crisis within development economics itself. During the 1960s, development economists had become increasingly disenchanted by the failure of large-scale government investment to produce the predicted results (Maier, 2000). Whilst development economics was drifting into an intellectual backwater, sociological development theory was being enveloped in a cultural struggle of a different nature. Left-wing critique had always described the West's aid effort as self-serving – whether to procure markets, to meet security goals or simply to perpetuate neo-colonialist pretensions. However, now a wider analysis attributed the failure of development projects to a refusal to recognise historical realities, or even to an attempt deliberately distort them. This soon degenerated into a remorseless post-modernist debate with its emphasis on fragmentation and the endless multiplicity of actor perspectives. The end-result was a failure to produce any fresh, innovatory ideas (Mosse, 2004). Despite the shifts in goals towards human development and despite the new insights into the need to abandon top-down planning, donors persisted with technocratic management techniques, which were becoming increasingly inappropriate (Howes, 1992).

The second factor was the growth of FDI in the global economy. By 1974, the volume of private FDI to Less Developed Countries (LDCs) exceeded official flows of development assistance, and aside from the period 1983-1991 it has remained that way (US Congress, 1997: 19). This coincided with shifts in thinking about the importance of investment in economic growth, which had already started in the late 1950s and had been reinforced by later generations of 'growth accountants'. Embedded technology (i.e. the technology implicit in new investment) and human capital development were increasingly seen as important. FDI, it was argued, not only relieved the public purse from its burden of financing the LDCs, but the market (and market risk) was the best medium for the sectoral allocation of capital. Moreover, investment capital automatically came with the appropriate technology and expertise (Fromhold-Eisebeth, 2002).

Thirdly, the collapse of the Bretton Woods system in 1971-73 and the impact of the first oil-crisis of 1973-4 introduced more volatility into the international system. In particular, the weak states in Latin America had difficulties adjusting to the new world order and now entered a period of typical roller-coaster, high-inflationary growth patterns. The focus of economic analysis, which saw the market response as a normal reaction to the political signals that it had been receiving, now turned to analyse the role of government in distorting those markets. What emerged was the 'Washington consensus' that called for sound fiscal and monetary policies as a precondition for healthy growth and development. As the pattern of debt crises and balance-of-payments problems brought a line of applicants to the IMF and the World Bank for emergency financial assistance, aid for adjustment rather than for development became the operating principle. If necessary, the World Bank and the IMF employed conditionality clauses attached to restructuring and development loans to force governments to sound macro-economic policies (Kapur e.a., 1998). Finally, by the end of the 1980s, the initial enchantment with the monetary reform revolution began to wane. Instead of demanding a retreating government, World Bank thinking now saw the solution in effective government. By reducing uncertainties and transaction costs 'good governance' could enable markets to function efficiently and ensure the effective use of whatever development assistance was available. This lesson was reinforced by the experiences in the transition economies of Eastern Europe as they recovered from the collapse following the end of the Cold War. 'Institutions matter' has become the slogan of the new orthodoxy (Burnside and Dollar, 2000; Collier and Dollar, 2001).

The end of the Cold War also provided the context for a new offensive deliberately directed at human development. In 1990, the first of a rolling series of UN summits was held. In 1990 they addressed issues as education, the least-developed countries and children and poverty which led to the adoption of specific targets on issues such as maternal mortality, primary education and sanitation. As these summits accumulated ever more targets and resolutions, two things were apparent. The conference rhetoric was building up a set of expectations on progress in human development and poverty reduction. At the same time, however, the aid effort, expressed as a percentage of donor GNI, was falling.

The entire process was lacking focus and commitment. Looming ahead was the Millennium. At the start of every decade the UN had made some pious pledge or other to improve the lot of human kind. In the year 2000, something special was required. Sifting through the inheritance of a decade of conferencing, governments began to select their priority issues for inclusion in the final declaration. The results were incorporated in the Millenium Development Goals, which undertook to large reductions in eighteen targets relating to poverty and human development by 2015 (Hulme, 2009). In 2015 these targets were recalibrated, redefined and adopted as seventeen Sustainable Development Goals to be achieved by 2030.

## Explaining Aid Flows

The Figure 8.1 below shows the trends in aid giving by the member states of the OECD both in terms of real dollar expenditure and expressed as a percentage of their combined GNI. In looking at the graph, there are three important things to note. First, it does not represent all development aid transfers, but those that satisfy the OECD qualification, one of which is that each sum must have a grant component of at least 25 per cent. Second, it only includes funds intended for development of the country. It excludes humanitarian aid and military aid, though it does include participation in UN peace-keeping missions, refugee assistance in developing countries and for one year in the donor country (Roodman, 2014). Finally, the aid recorded is not necessarily government-to-government. Government aid to multilateral aid organisations and to domestic NGOs are also included.

Figure 8.1: Total OECD Official Development Aid, 1960-2013

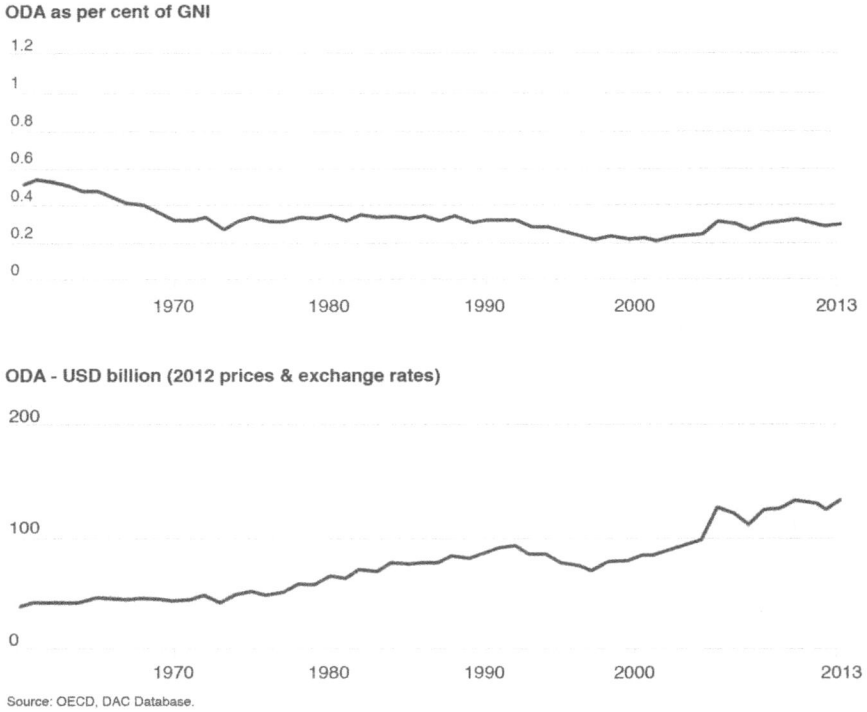

**ODA as per cent of GNI**

**ODA - USD billion (2012 prices & exchange rates)**

Source: OECD, DAC Database.

If we turn to the Figure 8.1, the decline in donor generosity throughout the 1960s is immediately apparent, largely due to the retreat of the USA from its dominant position. Equally striking is the impact of the 1990s 'aid fatigue' on both the real value of development assistance and on the relative generosity of the donor countries. Most of the statistics for the 'Western' aid effort are coordinated by the Development Aid Committee (DAC) of the OECD, and their databases provide a rich resource for the empirical analysis of donor aid behaviour. We will look at the other donors later in this section.

In a pioneering article, Alberto Alesina and David Dollar (2000) took the OECD aid data for the years 1970 to 1995, and they compared the direction of bilateral aid flows with several possible explanatory variables. These included trade openness, democracy, civil liberties, colonial status, FDI, per capita income in 1970, voting patterns in the UN, and the position in the Middle-East (i.e being either Egypt or being Israel). One must bear in mind that in these years, three-quarters of bilateral aid came from five countries – USA, Japan, France, Germany and the UK– and that idiosyncrasies among them can easily skew the results. Nevertheless, the study concluded that there was "considerable evidence that the pattern of aid giving is dictated by political and strategic considerations" (Ibid., 33). On this basis, Alesina and Dollar concluded that one reason why aid did not seem to work was because the aid flows were determined more by political and strategic considerations than by the desire to promote political and economic reforms.

Their analysis was based on a calculation of how far the aid flows diverged from an expected distribution based on recipient income. They suggested that being open and democratic was good. If a country was open, it would result in 20 per cent more aid and that being democratic would increase the aid flow by 39 per cent. More important still was having a long colonial past, which increased the flow of aid by 87 per cent. In fact, being a non-democratic colony allowed a country to receive more aid than a democratic non-colony. The same held true for openness. Countries voting with Japan in the UN received a massive 172 per cent more aid, though interestingly, voting with the USA made no particular difference. This last observation was the result of the fact that the flow of US aid was dominated in these years by its involvement in the Middle East. If you were Egypt, you received a 481 per cent boost in the aid flow, and being Israel was best of all since you received over 400 times the expected aid.

There are two criticisms that can be made of this analysis. The first is that some of the variables employed were suspect or simplistic. For example, Alesina and Dollar used the Freedom House indices for democracy and civil liberties, a crude open/closed dichotomy for gauging trade openness, and their per-capita GDP estimated were based on PPP calculations. Second, their study only establishes a statistical association between variables and, from the results, suggested a causal relationship. What it did not do, however, was demonstrate that such an intention did indeed exist. It is possible, for example, that countries responded to the American call for burden sharing by choosing countries with which they had some cultural experience and affinity (even if in the role of imperial power) and that this coincided with bilateral trade flows, which had been generated by that self-same experience and affinity. Of course, donors supply aid to countries with corrupt, undemocratic governments with bad human rights records because that is where many poor people happen to live. On this last point, there is an interesting possibility that donors prefer to avoid direct contacts with such government and to employ NGOs as the vehicle for development aid (Acht e.a., 2014).

Fifteen years have passed since the Alesina and Dollar article was published – fifteen more years of post-Cold-War experience. So, has the passage of time affected the factors conditioning aid flows? One study using data stretching from 1980 to 2004 and confined to the largest five donors, confirmed the original thesis that donor self-interest continued to play a major role in determining aid flows. The flow of aid tended to follow trade flows and still rewarded the voting pattern in the UN. Countries with better democracy and human rights records were also better rewarded, but not by all donors. The UK and Japan tended to reward democracy, and Germany, France and Japan rewarded human rights. The USA flows seemed indifferent to recipient merit. On the other hand, all donors seemed to allocate more aid to the poorer developing countries (Hoeffler and Outram, 2011).

The problem with the preceding analysis is that the generalisations are determined by the overwhelming weight of five large countries in the total and they say nothing about the determinants of donor generosity. However there exists a separate group of countries that appear more altruistic and more generous than the rest. They emerge quite suddenly, from the mid-1970s and they include Denmark, The Netherlands, Norway and Sweden, all of which reached, and maintained, aid contributions as a percentage of their GNI that exceeded the UN-norm of 0.7 per cent. Moreover, their efforts targeted the poorest nations of the world, and they were extremely early and generous in providing aid in the form of grants rather than loans. Their emergence could be explained by a desire as 'middle powers' to stake out for themselves a credible, independent position in an increasingly polarised world. Another line of explanation is a genuine desire to project their domestic norms and values (characterised by highly-developed welfare social policies) into the international arena. Finally, one should not discount the hope of translating altruistic gestures into commercial opportunities at some stage in the future (Griffiths 2008). What is remarkable, however, is that they maintained this position, with the single exception of the dip in Dutch aid in 2013, right up to the present. 2013 was also the year in which the UK's ODA hit the UN target for the first time.

In March 2015 it took the unusual step of passing parliamentary legislation to ring-fence this commitment into the future.

One aspect that we have not touched upon is the practice of private charitable donations. In the mind of the general public, private charities run on private money, but this is far from the reality. In practice, many governments channel development aid through NGOs because they do not see it as the task of civil servants to promote development in foreign countries, especially when there are voluntary organisations, with more experience, expertise and flexibility willing to do so. Equally, NGOs also seek to attract contributions from the general public. This is partly to legitimise their hand-out from governments, but also as a genuine supplement of their incomes and a reinforcement of their identities since all started as private initiatives. The question remains whether these private funds constitute an important component in the aid effort that has not been captured by the statistical analyses we have been studying. Recently, the Washington based Hudson Institute attempted to quantify global philanthropy for the year 2011. In looking at the results shown in Figure 8.2, it is important to note that the sums also include contributions intended for disaster relief, which is excluded in the ODA statistics. According to their estimates, private philanthropy in 2011 added almost 44 per cent to volume of development aid. Three quarters of this came from the UK, Japan and the USA, where charitable contributions makes a large difference in the share of their GNI devoted to development aid. It also influences the position of several other countries, most noticeably that of Ireland (Hudson Institute, 2013).

Figure 8.2: Net ODA and Private Philanthropy (percentage GNI) 2011

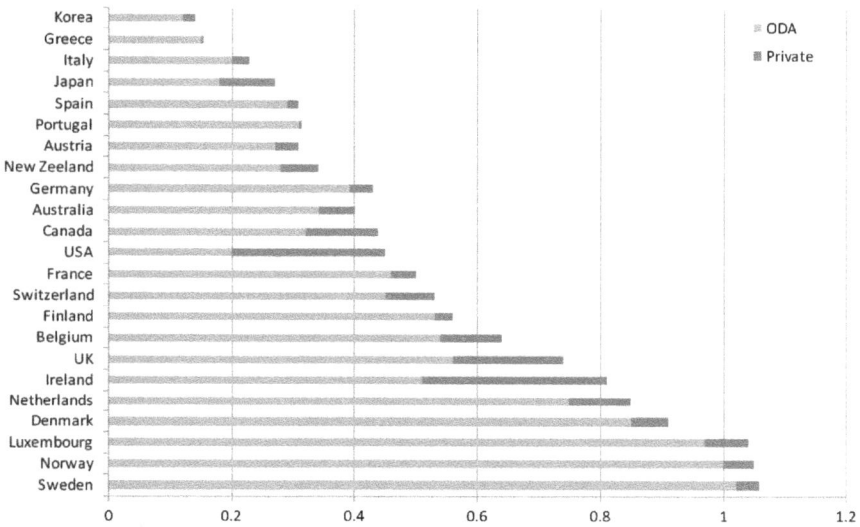

Source: Calculated from Index of Global Philanthropy, 2013, 6, 7, 12.

Although the OECD states, united in the Development Aid Committee, have jointly been the largest aid donors, they have never been the only ones. The first (unwelcome) intrusion into their domination of the aid effort was, as we have noted already, the Soviet Union. In the period 1955 to 1964, the OECD reported Soviet economic aid to non-Communist countries amounted to $2.6 billion, of which only $33 million went to Africa. This was mostly in the form of infrastructural projects. In terms of size it amounted in the beginning to no more than ten percent of the total Western aid effort, but it was targeted at newly independent countries and regimes unsympathetic towards the USA. It was also usually accompanied by military assistance, often in excess of development aid, and which is not included in these totals (Guan-Fu 1983). The Soviet data was always particularly opaque and it was neither collected nor presented in a manner consistent with the DAC definitions. The adjustments rarely favoured Soviet reporting, and sometimes deliberately reduced the force of the aid effort. In 1974, for example, the DAC unilaterally removed price subsidies (for example to Cuba) from the aid classification (Raffer, 1996: 2). The peak of the Soviet aid effort coincided with aftermath of the Yom-Kippur War and the heightened international tension in the Middle East. In the seond half of the 1970s Soviet aid averaged slightly over $1.4 billion a year, equivalent to about 13 per cent of Western aid. By the late 1980s, Soviet aid to non-communist countries had fallen to no more than four per cent of DAC aid. The largest recipients at that point were India and Afghanistan (with 40 per cent and 16.5 per cent respectively) (Graziani and Preeg, 1990: 20).

The second challenge to Western hegemony in the field of development assistance came from the Arab peninsula. In 1973, again against the backdrop of the Yom-Kippur War, the Arab members of OPEC (Organisation of the Petroleum Exporting Countries) decided to test their monopolistic powers by raising prices, restricting production and declaring a boycott of the USA and The Netherlands for their support of Israel. Over the next eighteen months, prices rose dramatically, and they stayed high until after the so-called 'second oil crisis' in 1979. The dramatic shift in the terms of trade brought a flow of oil-revenues into the coffers of the oil producers. They, in their turn, used these revenues to improve their own welfare provision, to increase their foreign investment portfolios, and to stake out an independent position in offering foreign development assistance. From almost nowhere, by 1975 development aid offered by three Arab oil producers alone was equivalent to 40 per cent of that supplied by the OECD countries. Now there may be a degree of underestimation in these figures, but there is also uncertainty about whether amounts qualify as aid under OECD definitions. The Arab aid statistics are more than usually opaque. The conditions of aid are not always specified and some forms of aid remain unreported (such as debt-forgiveness with a political quid-quo-pro, and secret transfers). This is partly the result of the independence of the political elite and a wish to conduct policy away from public scrutiny (Shushan and Marcoux, 2011).

Kuwait, Saudi Arabia and the United Arab Emirates accounted for the bulk of Arab aid throughout the period but the pattern tended to be more volatile than assistance given by the OECD countries, reflecting the strength or weakness of the oil market. From the mid-1980s it falls spectacularly (Neumayer, 2004). In terms of generosity, the three main Arab donors in the first decade after the oil crisis outstripped every aid donor on the planet. In 1975/79 the UAE gave 8 per cent of its GNI in aid, Saudi Arabia 7.6 per cent and Kuwait 5.9 per cent. In the five years that followed five years Saudi Arabia was the most generous donor with a commitment of 4.6 per cent of its GNI, followed by Kuwait with 3.8 and the UAE with 1.9 per cent respectively. Even as the aid effort was evaporating in the second half of the 1980s, the aid of Saudi Arabia and Kuwait still exceeded 1.5 per cent of GNI. Although the volume of aid was high, it tended to be restricted to other Arab countries, mostly focused on front-line states in the conflict with Israel, and countries in Africa and Asia with Islamic populations (Neumayer, 2004). There was also some support for poorer African countries, in the guise of Arab-African solidarity, but it helped if they supported the Arab countries in the UN (Neumayer, 2003). One last observation is that after declining in the 1990s, Arab aid failed to rebound in the commodity boom at the start of the century. There are a couple of plausible explanations for this development. The first is that Western donors have moved into countries, such as Egypt and Jordan that were traditionally the focus of the Arab aid effort. It is equally possible that domestic demands for government funds have become more pressing, particularly in the areas of domestic and military security (Shushan and Marcoux, 2011).

In 2001, the BRIC countries quite literally arrived on the international scene. The acronym for new emerging economies Brazil, Russia, India and China was first coined in 2001 (South Africa was added in 2010). They also started offering development assistance themselves and by 2006 questions were already being raised about the challenge they posed for the existing aid regimes (Goldstein e.a., 2006; Manning, 2006). Soon fears were being raised about 'rogue aid' (Naim, 2007) and questions raised whether a 'silent revolution' might not be afoot (Woods, 2008). Before we examine the nature of the 'problem' it is worth pausing at the data. The last year for which broadly comparable statistics is available is 2012. In that year, the BRICS, together supplied $5billion in development assistance in the form that satisfied the DAC definitions. The sum seems large, but it is only equivalent to four per cent of the aid offered by the OECD DAC donors. China was the largest single donor, but the size of its aid package matched that of Switzerland (OECD, 2014a). The problem is that much of China's assistance is in the form of concessional loans which either fall outside the OECD definition or for which insufficient information is available (this is a problem for the OECD countries as well). Including these would more than double China's aid effort (Development Initiatives, 2013: 226) but that would scarcely be sufficient to destroy the impression that, in terms of size, it is not overwhelmingly large. But it is becoming more distinct and more visible. In 2014 the BRICS agreed to create an *Asia*

*Infrastructure Investment Bank* with an initial capital of $50 billion. By way of contrast, the World Bank has a subscribed capital of $232.8 billion. Although the USA sees the new bank as a direct challenge, several Western OECD donors have agreed to participate.

The rise of the BRICS donors, and certainly their voice, owes much to the disaffection with Western aid donors – the slowness in matching aid promises with resources, the insistence on conditionality and the cumbersome bureaucracy that recipients have to construct to satisfy different conditions and different reporting criteria (Woods, 2008). The new aid sources also reaffirm a hidden preference in developing countries for a government-led growth strategy (Watson e.a., 2013) and an emphasis on obtaining positive results in terms of economic growth. Most South-South assistance is effectively commercial in nature, though often with loans offered on preferential terms. However, the BRICs have constructed a discourse on aid that confers legitimacy on their interventions that Western aid seems to lack. Borrowing much of the rhetoric of the non-aligned movement founded in the early 1960s, and incorporating sanitised versions of the past, the new discourse stresses a common identity based on based on shared colonial/post-colonial exploitation, a shared development status, some geographical communalities, an explicit rejection of hierarchical relationships (and recognition of sovereignty and non-interference) and win-win outcomes. It is this factor, as much as the volume of aid that had shattered the imagined geography of donor-recipient identities held in the West (Mawdsley, 2011).

# Aid Effectiveness

Many studies have tried to measure the effectiveness of aid in terms of whether it contributes to economic growth. However, there are several problems with efforts to establish this statistically. First, if you have been following the chapters and have not just plunged straight into this chapter, you will know that there are many doubts about the current accuracy of GDP data and PPP GDP data, especially for poorer countries. This is likely to be worse, the further back one goes, so that the quality of data for the starting year for the calculation of annual growth is likely to be even poorer. Since the countries being compared in any analysis of aid effectiveness are poorer countries, the growth data is likely to be unreliable. This also applies to the components of GDP such as investment and consumption ratios that are often used to establish the 'production functions' employed in macro-economic analysis. Second, we have seen that although the aid figures are reliable, within the terms of the OECD's DAC, the composition of aid has varied over time. In particular, the share of aid destined for productive investment has declined drastically over the last forty years, a there has also been a fall, albeit less marked, in transport and energy infrastructure. Therefore, 'aid' is not a homogeneous concept and, over time, that component in the aid budget most likely to impact on economic growth has diminished. Similarly, the distribution of aid between categories will also have varied between countries as well as over time. Third, there are many other variables influencing economic growth than the size and distribution of aid so that the influence of any one variable is likely to be relatively small. Some of these variables lie in the area of qualitative research, items that evidently do exist but have no quantifiable definition. In these cases, we invent a category such as 'democracy' or 'good governance, define some proxy variables that capture its essence, start counting something that measures it (constitutional clauses, corruption cases or public opinion) and combine all of this into a number by which countries can be measured and ranked. In the case of the World Bank governance indicators, these all carried margins and warnings not to use them over time. Other indicators do not publish error margins, but that does not mean that they do not exist. But most people measuring aid impacts seem so thankful to have any numbers at all that the data is used regardless. Finally, there is no standard, replicable test of any of the relationships. Different experiments use different survey periods and different countries, employ different definitions of aid, choose different variables and are usually not particularly robust in testing the results (Roodman, 2007).

A survey of 68 of the 100 papers produced on the relationship between aid and growth (chosen for reasons of their comparability) produced between 1970 and 1995 showed that most of the tests showed a small but statistically insignificant positive relationship between aid and growth, but many of the authors were reluctant to draw negative or neutral conclusions from these findings. They suggested that there was a bias in some of the publishing outlets towards articles that concluded in a positive light (Doucouliagos and Paldam, 2008). A similar study by the same authors found a similar situation of the relationship between aid and policy. Good policy influenced growth, but seemed to have little association with the flow of aid (Doucouliagos and Paldam, 2005). By the time they had returned to the question and surveyed an extra decade of publications, they had no cause to shift their positions. There was still a tendency to over-optimistic reporting of marginal results, but no evidence that aid flows were effective in generating economic development (Doucouliagos and Paldam, 2011).

One survey of the aid effectiveness literature suggests that most studies err by comparing aid inputs to short-term, contemporaneous growth and employ too many poor quality variables. By lengthening the survey period and incorporating a time-lag in the effect, and by re-running four influential (but contradictory) studies, it found that inflows of aid were accompanied by modest subsequent growth, but not necessarily that that aid actually caused that growth. This was not surprising because "aid-growth literature does not currently possess a strong and patently valid instrument variable with which to reliably test the hypothesis that aid strictly causes growth" (Clemens e.a., 2011: 613). Their approach was replicated with different methodologies and their findings were confirmed, namely that increases in aid are accompanied by modest economic growth, but without explaining the causal variable (Roodman, 2015).

If there is any agreement in the literature it is that aid is indeed most effective in countries with good governance and strong institutions but that making governance reform a condition for aid does not work. Already in 1998 the World Bank held that aid only had an impact on growth when it was linked to good governance (World Bank, 1998). The research upon which this conclusion was based was widely criticised but the authors, returning to their work several years later and updating the data-base, confirmed their original conclusions. Aid accompanied with poor policies has no effect (or possibly even a negative one) on growth whilst good policies, accompanied by sufficient aid, may have a very positive effect. Whilst most quantitative studies lean towards a negative judgement, most qualitative approaches seem to find more positive results. In other words, while one cannot tie aid to growth, one can demonstrate that efforts to improve health or education do improve health and education. This has been referred to as the "micro-macro paradox" (Mosley, 1987) and it derives from the fact that small improvements are often buried in an unchanging environment or because improvements in social capital (health, hygiene and housing) take time to impact on productivity and growth. Incidentally, attempts to separate productive aid (industry, agriculture, transport and energy) from the rest have floundered on the fact that such evidence is not available for the individual recipient states and that attempts to find proxies have proved disappointing (see Minoiu and Reddy, 2010). A broad survey of sector- and country-specific studies by an IMF 'intergovernmental task force' suggested that where both recipient and donor quality conditions are met, aid does reduce poverty by reducing infant mortality, by increased rural development and by providing wider access to primary education (Cassen e.a., 1986. The second edition (same title) published in 1994 draws the same conclusion, but with more recent examples).

The implication of the finding of most macro-economic aid assessments is that much aid is sub-optimal, and that a reallocation of aid among recipients would improve aid effectiveness. Along these lines, for example, a study for the Dutch foreign ministry suggested that Dutch aid in the 1990s was 10 per cent more efficient in lifting people out of poverty than the average for the ODA, but that it would have been almost 25 per cent more efficient still had it all been concentrated on its 19 focus countries (instead of allocating them only 30 per cent) (Ministerie van Buitenlandse Zaken, 2003). The logical conclusion is that donor aid strategy should concentrate on countries with good governance and strong institutions, but if everyone did this it would mean abandoning the very poorest people, living in weak and corrupt states, the very ones who need help the most.

It does not take much imagination to suggest that, other things being equal, a country with good governance will fare better than a country with bad governance. Add aid to the equation, and the same statement will hold true. The trouble is that 'other things' are never equal and, worse, they are not amenable to measurement either. So, let us leave this range of inquiry and turn to the question of whether aid agencies can create the conditions for good governance. One way in which they have attempted to do this has involved two shifts in aid strategy. The first was the introduction of aid in the form of budget support which, since its introduction in 1987, has grown to over five per cent of the aid given by DAC donors. The second was to introduce ex-post accountability for its use when measured against governance targets. In the years 2000 to 2011, there had been 131 temporary or permanent suspensions in the allocation of budget support, 41 per cent triggered by political events (fraudulent elections, repression of opposition and human rights violations) and a further 31 per cent by evidence of corruption (Molenaers e.a., 2015). The sums, however, tended to remain relatively small and since the other channels of aid remain, offending states could afford to ride out donor disapproval and avoid reform (Hayman, 2011).

A second approach is a bottom–up one whereby donors attempt to promote citizens' 'voice and accountability' in their development projects. This was intended as an instrument to break through the barriers of the democratic deficit and its (assumed) negative impact on aid effectiveness. Instead of looking exclusively at the relationship of host government to its citizens and the host government's bureaucracy with aid agencies and projects, the focus would shift to the relationship between the donor and the consumer of its products (Gaventa and McGee, 2013). In 2007 and 2008 the UK Department for International Development published the results of the efforts of seven donor countries to do exactly this in a total of sixty-seven development projects in which they had participated. The donor countries were in alphabetical order, Belgium, Denmark Germany, Norway, Sweden, Switzerland and the UK. The report concluded that, even at a micro-level, the ability to improve 'voice and accountability' was limited and relatively isolated, and it doubted whether even these local successes could be scaled up. The report also uncovered no evidence that improved voice and accountability made any direct contribution to the alleviation of poverty or to any of the other Millennium Development Goals. Why then did these efforts fail? The report enumerated several problems. First, the donor nations had made a 'misguided assumption' that voice and accountability was even wanted and that more effective institutions would naturally become more accountable. Second, they had proved unable to find a strategy, or even an entry-point, in the complex interaction of power relations and formal and informal institutions. Third, there was a mistaken assumption that there was one unified, but unheard voice of the 'poor' and, that at least among the poor, all voices would be equal. This proved to be far from the case. Finally, they had assumed that there would be time to construct governance frameworks without bringing the timetable for the implementation of projects into difficulties (O'Neil e.a. 2007; Menocal and Sharma, 2008). These are pretty chilling conclusions but they would seem to confirm the observation that "where 'accountability' and 'transparency' are at risk of becoming buzzwords, full of euphemism and normative resonance are all but emptied of their original meaning" (Gaventa and McGee, 2013: 4).

## Failed States

One other change in the discourse on ODA is its increasing militarisation. As UN interventions in conflict areas increases, a growing proportion of development aid goes towards military support. So far the costs of the actual front-line forces are excluded, but the military support operations for the delivery of goods and the provision of services (e.g. building schools, repairing roads etc.) and the training on internal police and security forces all qualify for inclusion as part of ODA (which helps explain the spikes in aid towards Afghanistan and Iraq). There are those who argue that this is a logical extension of the focus on governance and who suggest that there should be more peace-keeping missions, even per-emptive. Civil wars not only destroy lives and capital, but they divert resources from production and provide the context for random, personalised violence. In such circumstances long-term military intervention in post-conflict societies would be justified, even if it involves infringing national sovereignty (Collier, 2007). To conclude this chapter, I want to ask where and when this concern with state failure originated, and to see whether we can actually anticipate when and where states are likely to fail.

The current fixation with state failure coincided with the end of the Cold War, the disintegration of the Soviet Union and the problems at the time in Haiti, Somalia, Sudan, Liberia and Cambodia (Helman and Ratner, 1992). The UN had also failed to prevent the Rwandan genocide or to intervene in the bloody was that accompanied the disintegration of Yugoslavia. To construct a framework for a more pro-active policy a new paradigm was created. A failed state, it was now argued, posed three challenges. It was a challenge for its own citizens by depriving of the public goods they expected. It was a challenge to neighbours, that might be caught by spill-over effects, not least in the form of refugees. It was a challenge to the international community since failed states offered a lawless space where crime and terrorism could flourish. To be fair, in the 1990s terrorism did not loom large on the agenda, but that was to change with the destruction of the World Trade Centre in New York in September 2001. Ignoring the fact that all the bombers were from Saudi Arabia, the US administration focused the blame on Afghanistan, which was seen as a lawless place with an objectionable regime that harboured terrorists. Suddenly, failing states were no longer a burden for their own population and an inconvenience for their neighbours, they were now labelled a 'security threat' and this propelled the failed state concept right up the policy-making agenda. Once the threat had been identified and prioritised, a momentum was building up behind the failed state concept, fuelled by a powerful cocktail of academics and policy-makers, by abstract concepts and bloody realities, by distant sufferings and near-by security threats, and by plenty of research funds. In the midst of this, the World Bank started to get in on the action. If states were at risk of failing, a new direction for funding would be required and new criteria indentified to assess those most at risk. In 2002 it established a special unit 'Low-Income Countries Under Stress' (LICUS) programme to tackle the problem of state failure. This move allowed the Bank to enter the security field, further legitimising its own mandate, while giving an extra (developmental) spin to the concept. It was also in this context that the term 'fragile state' began to come into circulation. (Bueger and Bethke, 2013: 18-19) The term received a further boost in 2005 when the OECD's DAC held two meetings devoted to the idea of fragile states and when it became a topic of a strategy paper for US Aid (Guillaumont and Jeanneney, 2009). Meanwhile, the need was being felt to widen the vocabulary. This was a logical step since, if one was not simply interested in states that had already failed, but in shoring up those that were failing, then presumably one needed to express the degree of failure. A whole plethora of terminology evolved to cover every conceivable variation – anarchic, threatened, failing, weak, captured, fragile and so on. It was just a question of time before someone conceived of an index to quantify it all. In 2006 the *Fund for Peace* published the first composite index (for 2005) and it has been published annually ever since.

The Failed State Index (FSI, renamed Fragile State Index in 2014) is a composite index composed of twelve components (each with an average of fourteen separate elements). Half of these components refer to social and economic indicators and half to political and military indicators. The compilers tell us that it is constructed by data-mining, searching 'millions of documents' and using sophisticated computers to code the results. Now, data-mining is a useful technique involving the searching and analysis of vast quantities of data, often without questions in advance, to throw up unexpected relationships (or hot spots) for further research. However, one could question its use in compiling an index in which everything is reduced to one single number. In the Index itself, each component is given a score out of ten. The scores are added, so that the maximum is 120. The higher the mark, the more fragile is the state. It will be no surprise for you to learn that Finland is the 'least failed' state, in a category all of its own (very sustainable). South Sudan, Somalia, Central African Republic, Democratic Republic of the Congo and Sudan all occupy the bottom category (very high alert).

There are several problems with the index. The first lies in the source of the millions of documents – BBC, CIA, CNN, New York Times and National Public Radio. They are all English-language American or British sources. Analysing millions of documents might remove the danger of systemic bias, but not when the selection itself is biased. Second, there was no attempt to define 'failure'. For example, one of the standard political scientists' definitions of sovereignty is the ability of a state to exercise monopoly control over its own borders and therefore over its own territory. If we were to take this as a standard, it would imply that it harboured no armed terrorists, tolerated no separatists, allowed no rebel movements and experienced no outside intervention in its affairs. However, this kind of judgement would be completely different from one based on how well the state exercises state functions (Malek, 2006; Di John, 2008)

The FSI solves the problem by incorporating all these dimensions. But in doing so it creates another. The index is awfully cluttered. Some elements could be seen as consequences of failure (refugees, outmigration, external intervention and reduced state legitimacy), others provide only a context. At least three and possibly five of the twelve components are derivatives of poverty. But being poor does not automatically lead to state failure. This conflation of context, cause and consequence in the same index limits the ability to predict state failure. But the states ambition of the Index is to do exactly that (it even has a US patent - Patent No; 7092927B2 15.8.2006) and therefore to help prevent failure occurring. The Index is good in seeing extreme failure when the body-bags are piling up but less so at predicting collapse. As little as two years ago, 112 countries were in more danger of failing than Ukraine which has now had the Crimea annexed by Russia and has lost control of swathes of territory to Russian-backed rebels.

The FSI is the best-known of the state-failure indices. It also has the pretension of assisting policy-making[5]. Unfortunately, the entire exercise is flawed. The Index has no theoretical foundation; it confuses cause and effect; it deals largely with non-numerical information sources that are difficult to evaluate; it operates with fuzzy definitions of causal hierarchies and it totally ignores the specific historical contexts (until they come and sting them). Finally, they completely ignore such 'exogenous' factors as great power rivalries and the national interests of their states and the benign or malignant influence of neighbouring states.

States have failed in the past and they will doubtless continue to do so. In almost every case what could not be anticipated in advance can be explained afterwards. Hindsight would be a tremendous gift, but it is not one yet bestowed on mankind. When historians do explain state failures, they usually discover a complex layer of interactions, mostly linked to domestic social, economic and political variables, and often the interplay of external observers (and participants). Even for one state, no historian would attempt to reduce the whole experience into a single all-encompassing number - not even actually knowing the outcome. So why, you should ask, should we expect

---

[5] There are other measures to choose from (Mata and Ziaja, 2009. For an alternative approach see OECD, 2015

more when trying to reduce the experience of *all* states into one index, and without knowing the answer. Fortunately for us, most policy-makers when making decisions rely on far wider input and a far less reductionist perspective than that offered by the FSI.

## Summary

In this chapter we saw that development strategy has swung between promoting industry and stimulating agriculture. Having dominated the provision of aid in the 1950s, the USA called for 'burden sharing' by its Allies in the 1960s. In the 1970s the World Bank called for more focus on the needs of the poor. At the same time attention also began to focus on the need for good governance as a condition for aid effectiveness.

Western donor generosity fell in the 1960s, stabilised until the 1990 and then fell still further. An analysis of the aid flows of the biggest donors suggests that the direction of aid was motivated by donor self-interest. However, an analysis of the four countries that achieved the UN aid-target of 0.7 per cent GNI suggests a different motivation. The domination of aid flows by the OECD countries was interrupted by the Soviet aid offensive from the mid-1950s to the 1980s, the Arab aid push from the mid 1970s to the mid-1980s and the recent emergence of the BRICS. The destination of aid has shifted steadily towards Africa, and its focus has shifted away from economic production and infrastructure to health and social concerns.

The chapter also suggested that, in so far as they are trustworthy, most recent studies made a positive link between aid and growth, especially if it was accompanied by good governance. However, attempts to promote good governance by penalising bad practice or by encouraging citizen participation do not seem to work. The chapter concluded that countries without trust were unlikely to make aid work, and might eventually slip towards state failure. The Failed/ Fragile State Index designed to predict this is deeply flawed, but fortunately most governments relied on a broader range of indicators.

In the next chapter we will examine whether 'very small' states, with populations under 1.5 million, offer specific challenges for economic development. The UN has made small island development states a category deserving special treatment, and there is a significant body of literature that measures state vulnerability and describes their difficulties in economic development.

# Case Study: Microfinance in Bangladesh

In the wake of the famine of 1974, Muhammad Yunus and a class of economics students experimented with a project for a rural credit bank that targeted the poor, for whom access to credit was a dream. Scaling-up the project with help from the local government, in 1976 the Grameen Bank (Bank for the Rural Villages, in Hindi) was born. It was not the only project of its kind initiated at the time. In 1974 the Bangladesh Rural Advancement Committee (BRAC) also began advancing small loans to the poor as part of its rural development work. But the Grameen Bank had several interesting features, including a focus on women, that captured the imagination of the aid-giving community, and it became synonymous with the boom in microfinance (Brau and Woller, 2004). The centre of the microfinance movement remains in Bangladesh, where there are an estimated 30 million members, and the concept has been imitated throughout the world. In 2006 Yunus, and the Grameen Bank, were jointly awarded the Nobel Peace Prize.

The 'headline claim' of the Grameen Bank is that it lifts 5 per cent of its members out of poverty every year. Considering that it has an estimated 9 million members, if true, this is an impressive record of improving peoples' lives. Before examining the claim more closely, let us see first, how the Bank works. The Bank borrows money from other banks, and accepts donations, and uses it to make small loans to very poor villagers who typically have no collateral and, therefore, no access to credit. One definition of its target group is that they own less than half an acre of land. In order to help ensure that the loans are repaid, they are extended mostly to women (who make up 97 per cent of the membership) and who are made collectively responsible in groups of five. The idea is that it is the women who usually control household finances and the 'groups of five' increases social control and help avoid defaults. The credit may be used for consumptive purposes (avoiding the necessity to sell-off assets in times of need) and for promoting small businesses. The loans are usually for six months to a year, and repayments are scheduled weekly. The interest rates are modest and there is a small extra payment (or savings) which builds up a sum the group can use for other objectives. The officials and local representatives also help in other local projects, but that falls outside the main 'micro-finance' focus of its work.

It is easy to see why the Grameen Bank captured the public's attention, at a time when there was increasing disenchantment with large-scale government-funded aid projects. It was an effective and sustainable grass-roots self-help movement, focused directly at the poor, and it also tapped into concern with gender issues becoming popular at the same time. But popularity is not the same as effectiveness. The question remains, does it work?

For the last twenty years a team of economists at the World Bank have been surveying the microcredit scheme in Bangladesh, and in April 2014 they produced their most recent survey. All of them have fulsomely supported the effectiveness of microcredit and have defended their findings against critics. Their study concludes that "A 10% increase in men's borrowing raises household spending by 0.04%....Borrowing by women pushes up household spending by one and a half times as much" (Khandker and Samad 2014, 16). Reading that sentence a second time does not change it impact. It is not really very much. Many of their critics have argues that, at best, the impact of microfinance of the incomes of the poor is marginal

Chowdhury, 2009; Duvendack and Palmer-Jones 2012; Imai and Azam, 2012). Why is this?

One line of argument is that there are effects, but that they may be caused by other factors. Those who take-up loans may already be 'more entrepreneurial' than the average villager and they may already have more capital (the Bank's rules are opaque, but many members have more than the minimum acreage to qualify for loans). The loans do not reach the very poor who, it is argued, tend to be risk-averse and who dislike the collective responsibility of the 'group-of-five'. Moreover, 'success' may well be conditioned by factors other than the loan, such as the proximity to markets or the availability of roads. Another direction of criticism concentrates on the nature of the loans and the uses to which they can be put. It has been suggested that the loans can set in motion chains of debt whereby women, who are unable to pay, borrow from other microfinance lenders, often at higher rates (31 per cent of members have multiple loans). The loans are small, which limits the productive uses to which they can be put, leading to an over-supply of low-productivity enterprises. Moreover, the timescale of the loans and the repayments schedules, that start immediately, militate against the accumulation of capital. The interest rates charged have also been criticised. These average between 10 and 20 per cent, and they are certainly cheaper than borrowing from unregistered banks. A recent study suggests that the rates charged contain premiums of about 3 per cent above the market rate, but argues that this could be justified by the other services offered (reduced transaction costs and help in financial management) (Rosenberg, e.a. 2013). However, there are not many small-scale enterprises that generate returns to afford such interest, as well as the compulsory savings.

It is difficult to resolve the debate here. On both sides, the rhetoric often exceeds the evidence and almost all feasible survey methods have their drawbacks. Most agree that, in a country where there is no welfare state, micro-credit reduces the volatility of consumption and that, for a multitude of reasons, the proportion of poor in Bangladesh is falling. As for the Grameen Bank, in 2011 the government removed Muhammad Yunus from his post as its director and altered its governance structure by reducing the say of representative of the poor on its Board. At the time of writing there was no indication of any change in direction of its operations, but who knows how long that will last. Yunus himself is still touring the world, championing his ideas.

# Chapter Nine

# Small States

Throughout this volume, I have deliberately removed states with populations under 1.5 million from our analysis in order not to disrupt the rankings of the 'larger' states, for which we have almost complete coverage for most indices. The coverage for smaller states is far more random and only a few of them, usually different, would qualify for inclusion in any single index. Moreover, I wanted to avoid the situation where we are comparing larger states, with populations in many millions, with small states, three quarters of which (sixty of the eighty-one) have populations less than 500,000. In fact, of the 81 small states and other territorial entities, only seven have populations in the range of 1-1.5 million and thirty-five of them have populations less than 100,000. Their distribution is shown in Figure 9.1. Most of the small states in the world are found either in the Caribbean or in Melanesia (the scattering of small islands in the Southern Pacific). It would be interesting to see how many of these small states one could name (rather than recognise) without prompting, and, if successful, the majority of states named would probably be close to home. Nevertheless all these small states together provide a home for some 26 million inhabitants. To make life a little easier, the small states are shown above, clustered into the regional groupings defined by the UN.

Figure 9.1: Small States of the World

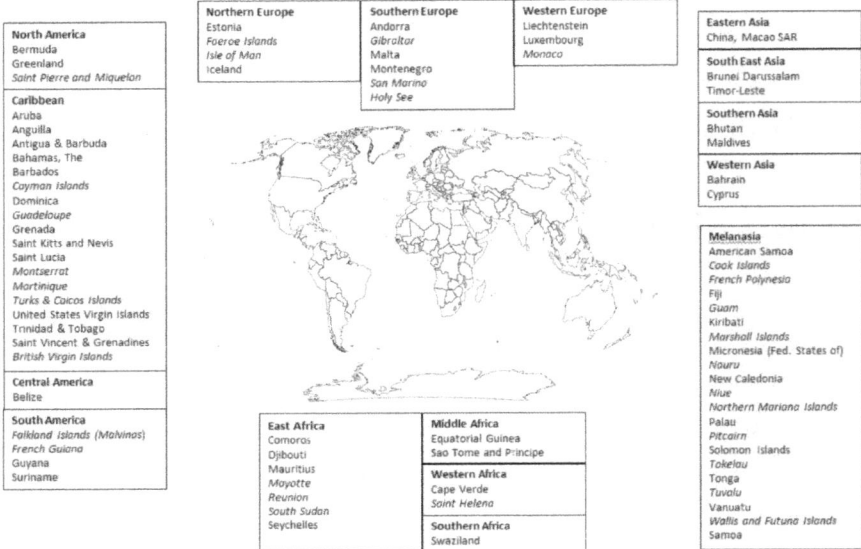

**North America**
Bermuda
Greenland
Saint Pierre and Miquelon

**Caribbean**
Aruba
Anguilla
Antigua & Barbuda
Bahamas, The
Barbados
Cayman Islands
Dominica
Guadeloupe
Grenada
Saint Kitts and Nevis
Saint Lucia
Montserrat
Martinique
Turks & Caicos Islands
United States Virgin Islands
Trinidad & Tobago
Saint Vincent & Grenadines
British Virgin Islands

**Central America**
Belize

**South America**
Falkland Islands (Malvinas)
French Guiana
Guyana
Suriname

**Northern Europe**
Estonia
Faeroe Islands
Isle of Man
Iceland

**Southern Europe**
Andorra
Gibraltar
Malta
Montenegro
San Marino
Holy See

**Western Europe**
Liechtenstein
Luxembourg
Monaco

**Eastern Asia**
China, Macao SAR

**South East Asia**
Brunei Darussalam
Timor-Leste

**Southern Asia**
Bhutan
Maldives

**Western Asia**
Bahrain
Cyprus

**Melanesia**
American Samoa
Cook Islands
French Polynesia
Fiji
Guam
Kiribati
Marshall Islands
Micronesia (Fed. States of)
Nauru
New Caledonia
Niue
Northern Mariana Islands
Palau
Pitcairn
Solomon Islands
Tokelau
Tonga
Tuvalu
Vanuatu
Wallis and Futuna Islands
Samoa

**East Africa**
Comoros
Djibouti
Mauritius
Mayotte
Reunion
South Sudan
Seychelles

**Middle Africa**
Equatorial Guinea
Sao Tome and Principe

**Western Africa**
Cape Verde
Saint Helena

**Southern Africa**
Swaziland

Another reason for treating small states in a separate chapter is that the UN has used the 1.5 million threshold in its definition of 'small island developing states' (SIDS) whose particular problems, it is argues, require special attention (and resources). Whilst the UN approach implies that small states (or small islands) have problems that require special attention, it ignores the possibility that some small states may be very successful and, by excluding them from the analysis, valuable lessons may be missed. But these observations are bringing us too far ahead of ourselves. Before we decide whether size forms an irresolute problem, and whether specific aspects of that problem are emphasised by very small scale, it is worth looking at what, if any, development characteristics are associated with size.

# Small State Characteristics

Small states are obviously different, but the first question we must resolve is *how* they are different. Once this has been established, we can turn to the question whether these differences constitute disadvantages, and whether these disadvantages are insuperable. Many of the differences arising directly from size stem partly from the fact that whereas production is a function of available resources, consumption is a function of income levels (Snorrason, 2012: 47-74). Thus the first hypothesis we can formulate is that the smaller the state, the more limited its range of output is likely to be. This comes from the expectation that small states have supply constraints such as fewer resources (though strictly this is more a function of area and geographical location than of size), less labour, a smaller capital base and fewer entrepreneurs. They are also confronted by demand constraints, the most important of which is a domestic market too small to achieve scale economies, and which makes their production less efficient. But while a small state will not be producing a wide range of products, its consumption patterns will tend to reflect those of other economies with a similar level of income. Thus, the second expectation is that the smaller the size of a state, the larger will be its propensity to import to meet its domestic consumption and investment needs. This high level of import demand will force smaller economies into export markets to earn the foreign exchange necessary to meet the cost of imports, but here again, relative size can be expected to leave its mark on economic structures. Thus, the third expectation is the smaller the state, the more likely that its exports will be concentrated on a narrow range of export products, as the same resource limitations that affected the diversity of output also limit the diversity of exports. Fourth and last, the smaller the state, the more likely that its exports will be concentrated on a smaller group of countries, once again because of restrictions in the amount of human capital available for international marketing (Griffiths, 2014). Despite quibbles over one or two of these expectations most studies conducted at various intervals and with different samples of countries have underlined their basic validity. Thus smaller countries tend to share similar structural patterns deriving from their size and linked directly to their trade dependence. However, these structural patterns do not necessarily translate into factors of vulnerability (Baldacchino and Bertram, 2009: 142). In many cases the factors that turn risk into vulnerability stem from underdevelopment rather than relative size.

## Small State Performance

Before we look at how our select group of small states has performed relative to the rest, we have to make two important reservations. First, poor states tend to have poor numbers. Second, small states tend to have small statistical offices. Combine the two, and we have to face the fact that small, poor states may well have no numbers at all. Of the eighty states in our original selection, thirty had neither GDP data (at least not of a quality recognised by the World Bank) nor HDI data. Most of those states had populations of less than 100,000. Thus, if we try generalising from any subsequent statistical analysis, we have to acknowledge that we are dealing with a 'truncated data-sets' (datasets in which almost all of the observations at one extreme are missing). With that in mind, we can now look at how the remaining small states would have fitted into some of the mapping exercises that we undertook in the previous chapters.

Some time ago, Armstrong and Read (2002) attempted to fill the GDP gaps by employing sources other than the World Bank. In this way they assembled data for sixty of the eighty countries in our small-state list. Not surprisingly, their biggest gap was among states with populations below 50,000 where they managed to collect estimates for only six of the twenty-one states. Given the fragility of some of the estimates, they fitted the data into four broad (World Bank) categories. Their findings dispelled any notion that one may have harboured that small states were uniquely cursed. Indeed, compared with larger states, the small states performed extremely well. Only 10 per cent of the small states sample fell into the lowest category, compared with over 30 per cent of states with populations above three million inhabitants (the cut-off point that Armstrong and Read had adopted for their own analysis). At the other end of the scale, 40 per cent of small states were represented in the top segment, compared with 20 per cent of larger states, again by their definition.

When we employed the most up-to-date data (but with a more limited coverage) of the fourty-one states for which we possess PPP data for per capita GDP, no less than twenty-two (54 per cent) fall within the top 30 per cent of the range and a full twenty-nine (71 per cent) are above the world median GDP. That means, of course, that the remainder fall below the world median, but it is interesting that only two small states (5 per cent) are represented in the bottom two deciles. On balance, therefore, small states, measured by GDP, seem to do relatively well.

Figure 9.2: GDP per capita of Small States (ppp dollars) 2011

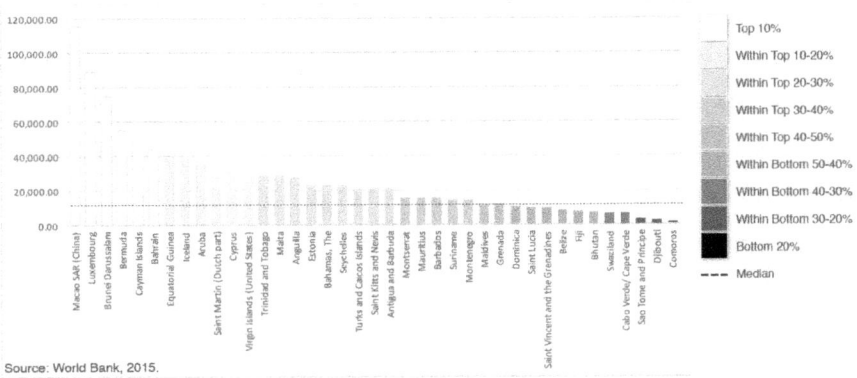

Source: World Bank, 2015.

In Figure 9.2, the small states are categorised as if they occupied the same decile range occupied by the larger states when they were analysed in their various chapters.

If we turn to the Human Development Index, which you will recall combines GDP with equal measures of longevity and access to education, we have a slightly larger data-base (41 instead of 38) but with a slightly different composition. In the analysis of HDI, the distinction between small states and larger states is less marked, but such difference that exists works in favour of the small states. In Figure 9.3 we can see that, interestingly, again no small states are to be found in the very bottom decile and only two (Djibouti and Comoros) in the one above it.

Figure 9.3: HDI of Small States 2014

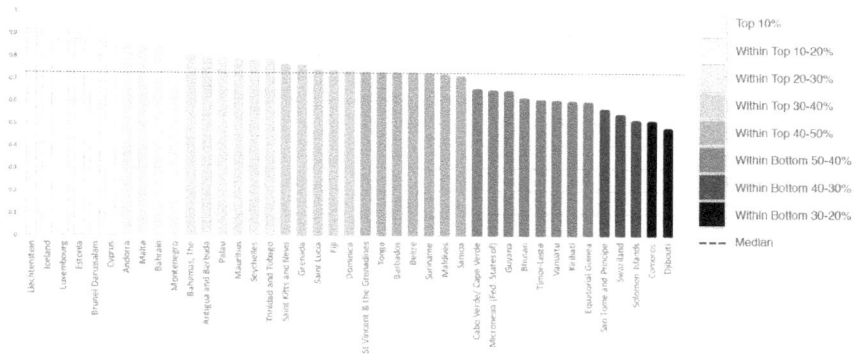

Source: UNDP, Human Development Report, Database.

When we examined the World Bank governance indices, we noted in the chapter that very small states were overwhelmingly represented in the very top echelon of the Political Stability and Absence of Violence indicator. In Figure 9.4 we have shown the small states performance in three other indices. The Voice and Accountability indicator may be viewed as a short-hand indicator for democracy, and the evidence gathered by the World Bank covers almost 60 per cent of small states that we have identified. In the bar-diagram below, the zero line marks the world average experience and the vast majority of the small states in the sample find themselves above that line. Indeed, just over half have scores equivalent to those registered by the top two deciles of the larger states.

# Figure 9.4: Small States and Governance

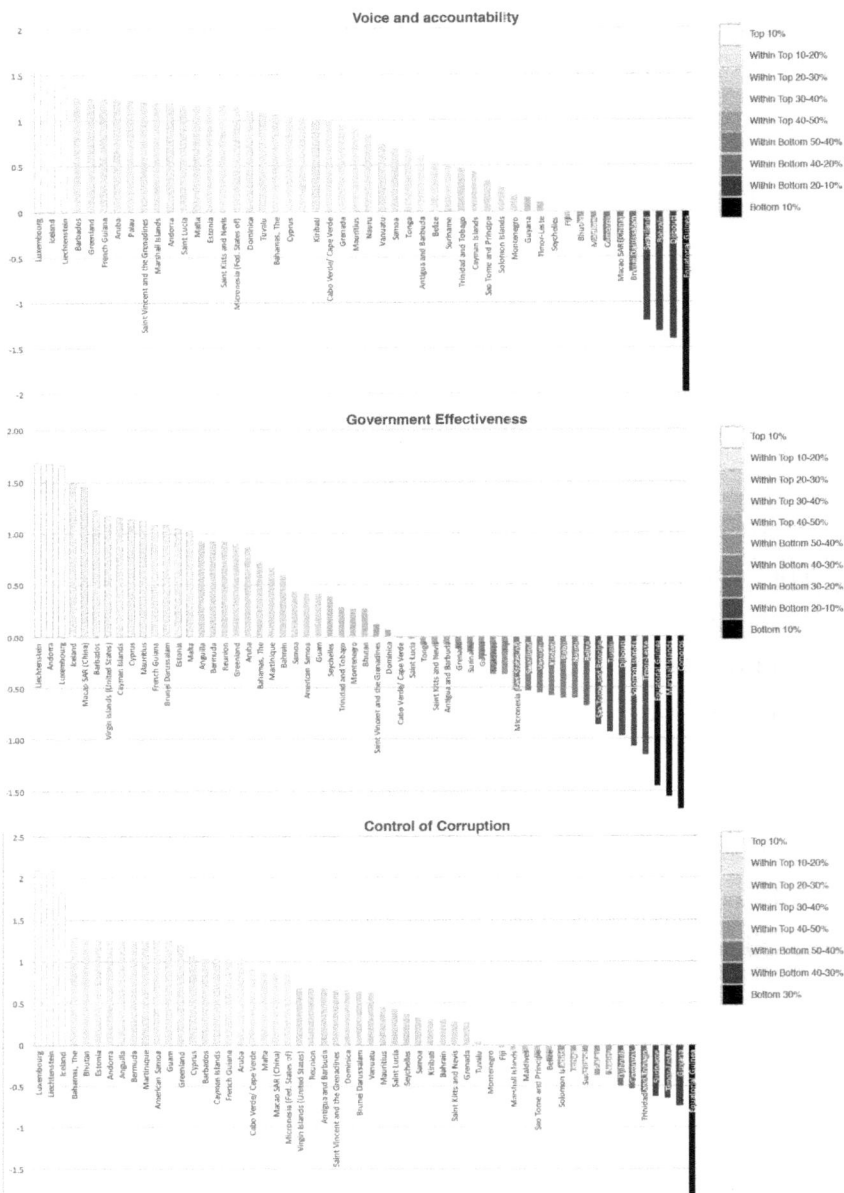

Voice and accountability

Government Effectiveness

Control of Corruption

Source: Source: World Bank Database, WGI

This image of predominantly peaceable, open democratic states, extends to other areas of governance, but to a lesser extent. For Government Effectiveness, almost half of the smaller states (46 per cent) recorded scores that would have placed them among the top 30 per cent of the larger states although 44 per cent register a performance below the world average. Looking at the indicator for Control of Corruption, exactly two thirds of small states achieved scores that would have placed them among the top thirty per cent of larger states. In total 32 per cent fell below the world average and but only one state (Equatorial Guinea) would have been among the bottom two deciles of the scores achieved by the larger states.

## Small States and Vulnerability

Since small states seem to perform economically no worse than their larger counterparts, and to be no worse managed, one could be forgiven for asking why they should merit special consideration. The answer is that their lobby within the British Commonwealth (whose membership included many Caribbean and Pacific island states) published a seminal text way back in 1985, pointing to their unique development challenges. The small states concerned then began to organise themselves itself under the auspices of the UNCTAD and at the *UN Conference on Environment and Development* held in Rio de Janeiro in 1982 they succeeded in obtaining recognition for the special problems confronted by small island developing states (SIDS). Two years later the first *Global Conference on the Sustainable Development of Small Island States* was held in Barbados which also created a permanent framework for research and cooperation among the SIDS. It also established criteria for membership. It recommended a maximum size for inclusion in the group of 1.5 million, and linked this to a maximum threshold of per capita income (Commonwealth Advisory Group, 1997). The UN currently classifies 52 countries and territories under this heading. At the same time, within the World Trade Organisation, a group of small countries pressed for special recognition and for new trade rule to accommodate their problems. Their claim was recognised in 2001 at the Doha Ministerial meeting. This opened the way for them to obtain special treatment but difficulty in agreeing either to the exact criteria needed to qualify for special treatment or to the nature of the concessions that would be granted, kept the issue off the agenda for the next decade. It also helped keep the research agenda alive ever since (Corrales-Leal e.a., 2007; Sutton, 2011: 146-150).

The central problem faced by small states was conceived as lying in their insecurity. It is a truism to suggest that every development that is not completely predictable is, by definition, risky, but a risk can always have two outcomes – both positive and negative. Insecurity implies that there is a greater than average chance that, in a given situation, the outcomes will be negative, and that it will be more than usually difficult to absorb the effects of those outcomes. Insecurity, therefore, implies a greater than otherwise risk of negative impact of exogenous developments and a lack of mechanisms for coping with these external shocks. Most authors opt for the term 'vulnerability' to capture this mixture of elements (Combes and Guillaumont, 2002; Seth and Ragab, 2012).

Once the concept had been formulated, groups of social scientists tried to specify the elements that should fall under the definition and (no surprises here) how to measure it, preferably within a single index. The first steps towards the construction of an Economic Vulnerability Index (EVI) were taken at a Small Island Developing States (SIDS) meeting held in 1990 under the auspices of UNCTAD. This marked the beginning of serious efforts towards developing an index. The work was undertaken under the auspices of the British Commonwealth. A final study tested 30 variables against the performance of 111 developing countries, including 34 small states, but narrowed the relevant variables down to three – export dependence, lack of diversification and a proneness to natural disasters. Of the thirty most vulnerable countries, by this measure, all but two were small states (Atkins e.a., 2001). Working in parallel to these initiatives, a team at the *Island and Small States Institute* at the University of Malta was preparing its own index. It comprised four indicators (weighted equally) including two for openness and diversification, which it shared with the Commonwealth Index, but with proxies added to represent peripherality and strategic import (i.e. energy) dependence. At the same time, it omitted the disaster component. The Malta team included eighteen developed states in its analysis, alongside 99 developing states. However, only eighteen of the 34 SIDS captured by the Commonwealth appeared in its analysis. Once again, small states anchored the range of the most vulnerable in the series.

In 1998, the UNDP began work on its own index. Its EVI has been continuously refined and in its 2011 incarnation, it represents the most comprehensive and up-to-date index available. For this reason, we will pause and examine it in more detail (Cariolle and Goujon, 2013). First of all, we must acknowledge that it is a composite index, with all the drawbacks that we have grown to associate with this genre. On the other hand, it uses exclusively quantifiable indicators, and it embraces most of the elements included in earlier indices. The EVI is made up of two main sub-indices, weighted equally – exposure and shock. The exposure sub-index concentrates on static, structural factors that might influence vulnerability. These include population size, remoteness, economic structure (share of GDP in primary production and the concentration of exports) and the percentage of the population living in coastal areas. The shock sub-index includes external exogenous factors that might destabilise an economy. These include the volatility of agricultural production, the victims of natural disasters and the instability of exports. In all cases, the variables were standardised into a given range. It is worth stressing, at this point, that unlike the previous indices, the UNDP was not exclusively or even primarily concerned with small states. But, equally, it was not interested in states, big or small, that had escaped the development trap.

If we look at the exposure sub-index, which is made up of four elements, you will notice at once that the first element is population size. Most of the previous efforts focusing on the problem of size had excluded it from an index because it was inconsistent to include as a variable when it was also supposed to be the object of the empirical testing (some indices did use GDP size as an indicator of resilience, which seems a little inconsistent – but let's let that pass). Since the UNDP had no such intention, it can hardly be faulted for its inclusion, but anyway it only forms of one eight elements in the total index. For remoteness, the authors have used the average physical distance to markets representing fifty per cent of their exports (with a slight correction to take into account whether the countries were land-locked, and therefore without access to a national harbour). The degree of export concentration was obtained directly from UNCTAD, which calculates a Herfindhal-Hirschman index for the commodity concentration of trade. This, as we have seen, is one of the classic expectations deriving from 'small state' theories. A second part of the economic structure element is the share of agriculture, forestry and fisheries in GDP, with information drawn from UN statistics. This has been included since the share of agriculture is usually (negatively) associated with the level of economic development and since it will also be echoed in the shock index. A final element, which has also been suggested in earlier efforts, is the proportion of the population living in 'low elevation coastal zones', reflecting the potential damage caused by cyclones, earthquakes and hurricanes and, particularly, affect small island states in the tropics, and along the world's earthquake zones. Because a higher proportion of the small state's population are likely to be affected, its capacity to fund recovery and reconstruction efforts and so to 'bounce back' from a disaster, are also limited.

The shock sub-index had three elements, of which calculates the volatility of export earnings[6]. It is a well known fact that the prices for 'primary products' fluctuate far more wildly than do those for manufactured goods and within the category of 'primary products' there are also large differences. The remaining two

---

[6] It takes the quarterly changes in export earnings and then deflates them by an IMF Index for the average unit price for imports from 'developing and emerging countries'. In this way, the indicator comes close to representing what economists call 'the barter terms of trade' which measures the change in the average unit value of exports against the change in the average unit value of imports. In this way, for example, it measures how much maize, rice, copper or oil one has to export to but a specific quantity of imported consumer goods or machinery.

indicators, which together account for a quarter of the total are self-explanatory. The instability of agricultural production, at the mercy of vaguaries in weather and harvest, has historically proved more extreme than changes in manufacturing, and this element mirrors the share of agriculture indicator in the exposure index. Similarly, the victims of natural disasters indicator reflects its equivalent in the exposure index.

All the components of the index are built from quantified data adjusted with tried and tested stamndardisation procedures. All are relevant to the question of vulnerability. The only criticisms could lie in the balance of the components; whether the proneness to natural disasters or the weight of agriculture (in their various guises) should each be one quarter of the total, whether population size should be only one eighth, or whether it should be included at all. However, on balance, it seems a solid approach to the problem. In examining the results, on the basis of data supplied by the authors, we have split the analysis into two stages – first those states with populations above 1.5 million and second, immediately afterwards, those smaller states with populations below 1.5 million.

Figure 9.5a: Map of Economic Vulnerability of Developing countries 2011

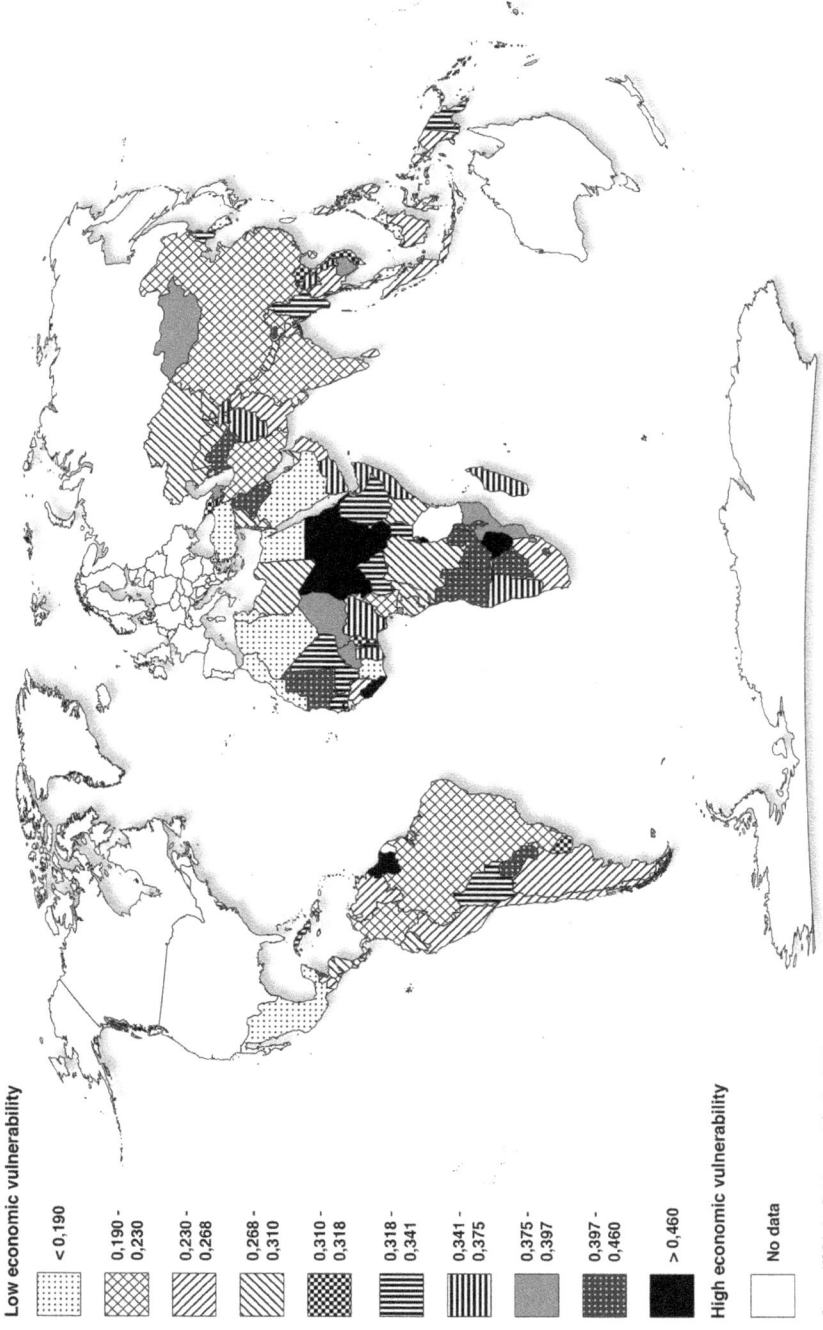

**Low economic vulnerability**

< 0,190

0,190 - 0,230

0,230 - 0,268

0,268 - 0,310

0,310 - 0,318

0,318 - 0,341

0,341 - 0,375

0,375 - 0,397

0,397 - 0,460

> 0,460

**High economic vulnerability**

No data

Source: KOF Index Database and Goujon, 2013.

The results for the larger states are shown in Figure 9.5a. First we should note that the developed world has (almost) totally been removed from the sample of countries analysed, which is consistent with the UNDP mandate. Even so, the inclusion of South Korea and Saudi Arabia, both of which appear among the least vulnerable, is curious since neither could be considered a developing country. Generally, larger and (comparatively) richer states seem to cluster among the least vulnerable and the rural poor occupy the lowest regions. It is when we look at the 32 small states for which data was available the results, which are shown in Figure 9.5b, are striking. Only four small states (12.5 per cent) are located among the top half of the less vulnerable, and twelve (33 per cent) are anchored among the bottom two deciles of economically vulnerable. Among the poorest developing states, acute small size seems to offer an extra development challenge.

Figure 9.5b: Small States and Economic Vulnerability 2011

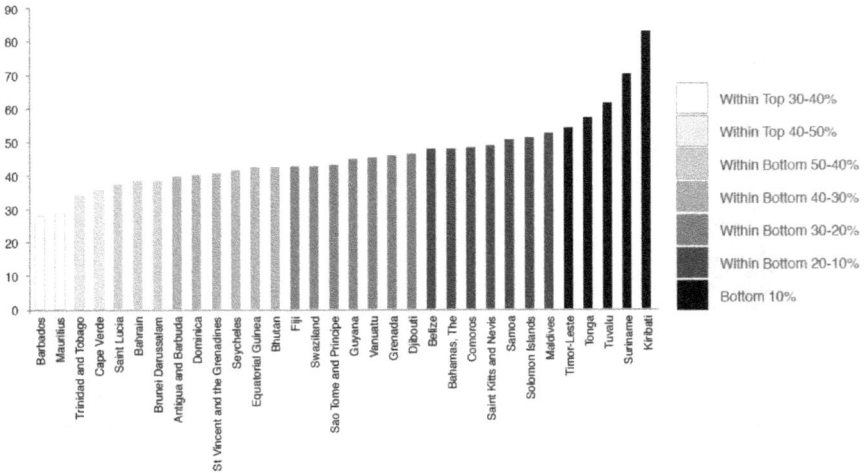

Source: Cariolle and Goujon, 2013.

One of the problems of all the EVI indices is that they may be useful for analysing past crises but that they fail to anticipate future ones. One noteable omission is the absence of financial variables in any of the analyses. As a result, they fail utterly to capture the kind of financial meltdown that almost destroyed Iceland's economy in 2008 following the collapse of its three largest banks (Griffiths, 2014). At the time the IMF was preparing its own index, but had published no detailed country data. Their 'Overall Vulnerability Index' is built-up of three components of which the largest (55 per cent) is the recent economic growth record of the country, combined with the IMF's own internal institutional assessment. The performance of public sector finances including the weight of sovereign debt, the fiscal balance and the size of the public sector comes next. Finally 25 per cent of the Index is made up of the external sector, represented by the size of currency reserves and the dependence of exports (Dabla-Norris and Gündüz, 2012).

Two things are particularly interesting in the Index. The first is the importance attached to economic growth, which accounts for over one third of the whole index. For an organisation that, in the past, has been associated with austerity programmes piled on already ailing economies, this is at first sight surprising. On the other hand, it does reflect its recent stances in the Euro-crisis and its implicit criticism on the European Central Bank and the European Commission for piling austerity on the Greek economy and for doing little to reflate 'surplus economies' like Germany. The second surprise is that the Index takes no account of the private financial sector, where most of the recent crises have originated. In Ireland's case, for example, the public sector data was resoundingly positive until the state, acting as lender of last resort, effectively nationalised the country's bad debts.

By this stage, the crisis had become irreversible. I suspect that the omission can be explained by data availability. If the IMF could not compile an index for developing countries, using easily available public sector data, the task would have been even more difficult if it added private financial data to the whole.

The IMF has released their data to me for the purposes of this publication. Its intention was to compile long-run statistics from 1990 to the present (to 2011, actually) for seventy less-developed countries, including fourteen that could be classified as small countries (i.e. less than 1.5 million inhabitants). However, for the year 2011 it had only managed to complete the Index for twenty-seven states and adding those countries with complete data for 2010 extended the range to thirty-eight, of which nine are small states. These results are too fragmentary to draw any meaningful conclusions. The nine small countries are scattered throughout the sample. In due course, and extended to cover developed economies as well, the new Index could be a welcome tool for small state analysis. Unfortunately, that moment has not yet come.

## Vulnerability and Security Strategies

Small states have been portrayed as being uniquely vulnerable, largely because of the size and their openness. Indices have been compiled to define and quantify the 'problem' and, basically, have shown this to be true. The latest EVI compiled by the UNDP and discussed in this chapter, produces the same results as earlier less sophisticated indices. These results have been used as an instrument to lobby on their behalf for special consideration in questions of trade liberalisation and trade obligations. Free(er) trade and globalisation are portrayed almost as threats to their survival rather than as routes towards greater wealth and prosperity. By conveniently creating a category of small developing states (island states or otherwise), they have effectively expunged small developed states from the analysis. As we saw at the start of this chapter, not all states are condemned to live in the shadow of poverty, or a fear of a return to poverty. Many have broken out of their dependence on agriculture and a reliance on cash crops whose output is hostage to the caprices of the weather and whose prices are regularly destabilised by world market forces beyond farmers' control. Moreover, their access to world markets and their freedom from the constraints of a small domestic demand base have often provided the foundations for success. Openness and foreign dependence may make states more vulnerable (even more so if they are at a stage of their development which accentuates a reliance on primary products) but there are offsetting strategies that have allowed them to prosper. And, even if Iceland has lost ten per cent of its GDP in the recent crisis, it still enjoys levels of income and lifestyles that would be the envy of most of the world's population in far larger states. Despite their inherent vulnerability, small states still tend to perform relatively well. Armstrong and Read (2003) have demonstrated that small states in Western Europe outperform their neighbouring regions in larger states. Baldacchino and Bertram (2009, 147-150) raid the library of available statistical indicators to demonstrate the robustness of small state performance. Reviewing the recent of the literature, Bishop (2012: 949) summarised the state of play by declaring that "almost all small states are doing 'better' developmentally than the least-developed countries in the world, some spectacularly so". By isolating small (island) developing states from the wider body of comparable entities, social scientists and policy-makers risk losing the chance of any policy-learning from their experiences.

The small state literature also suggests that (richer) smaller states have developed successful security strategies that may not shield them from powerful economic forces emanating from abroad, but which allows them successfully to adapt. In his classic study of small European economies (all much larger than the ones we are considering in this chapter) Peter Katzenstein (1985) argued that the paramount need for small countries to remain competitive contributed directly to their development of high welfare expenditure and neo-corporatist governance structures. Potentially damaging private wage demands were bought-off with public goods, including a voice in policy-making, and welfare payments eased the risk to citizens in making structural adjustments to the economy. Consensus was more easily achieved around sound policy measures and inefficient, rent-seeking sectors were more readily sacrificed as industrial policy targeted potential growth areas (See also Midttun e.a., 2006). Criticised by those who interpreted this as prescriptive rather than descriptive, Katzenstein later modified this position to stress that the main advantage available to small states lay in their ability to adapt quickly to changing circumstances, which was itself a reflection of the social cohesion that they had been able to engineer (Katzenstein, 2003). Another insight was afforded by comparing (European) small countries or entities (mostly with populations under 1.5 million) with neighbouring regions of larger countries. This was made possible by the regional accounting procedures adopted by the European Union. In almost every case and in almost every measure of performance, the small states did better than their neighbouring region, although it had all the apparent disadvantages of market size and none of the fall-back options of transfer payments and support from central government. The compensatory advantage, it was suggested, was to be found in their independence in defining their own sectoral and other meso-economic policies (Armstrong and Read 2003).

Thus smaller richer states have the advantages of possessing economic resources to sustain good governance structures and to support strong social cohesion around policies of adjustment and adaptation. Their position is a far cry from the picture of the small island developing states in the Pacific and the Caribbean that is painted by the Commonwealth, World Bank and UNDP. And yet, there is no barrier to these small developing states adopting the same governance practices and encouraging the same strategic adaptability as demonstrated by the success stories in Western Europe and elsewhere. In a challenge to the institutional pessimism of the vulnerability school, Baldaccino and Bertram (2009) suggest that this is exactly what many of them are already doing. They are not entirely without security strategies and, without being exhaustive, in the rest of this chapter, we will attempt to cover some of these, starting with vulnerabilities stemming from the classical 'small state' literature.

Most literature stresses that foreign trade dependence is more of an advantage than a structural disadvantage but, by itself, it is unpredictable, and it leaves countries especially vulnerable to policy changes by major trading partners. One solution is to tie oneself as closely as possible to important trading partners through a customs union or else through another form of preferential trading arrangement (Mansfield and Reinhardt, 2008). This was a prime motivation of the Benelux countries in the early stages of European integration, and same logic prevails. Whatever loss they incurred in trade policy independence is outweighed by the guarantees against the independent policies of their larger partner states. Small states love international agreements, the more complex and more binding the better.

This then brings the discussion to the volatility in export earnings caused by an extreme reliance to particular primary products. This has been referred to in the literature as a 'resource curse' but recent research on the period since 1970 (when the price trend was upwards) has suggested that the long-term effects of abundant resources on growth has been positive. It is the short-term instability that creates the problem (Cavalcanti e.a., 2012). One answer would be to combine with similar producers and form an international commodity agreement cartel, but past experience suggests that this is rarely a permanent solution. In some cases, prices are stabilised at too high a level, and this attracts outside competitors, as has been the case with OPEC. In others, the high prices stimulated overproduction and the agreement collapsed because it could not bear the costs of maintain ever-growing stockpiles – coffee and tin are good examples. Another danger is that individual members start 'cheating' by increasing their own output to take full benefit of high prices maintained by everyone else restricting theirs, as proved the case in the international steel cartel between the wars.

If an international solution does not serve the problem of price volatility, then a stabilisation fund may well so. In this case, one puts (part of) the government's income in good years into a savings account upon which it can draw when prices are low. It does mean, however, that those resources cannot be used for investment (UN, 2008: 45-48). Moreover, while the idea is simple, the implementation is fraught with difficulties. Politicians will inevitably be tempted to use the account to reward party allies and to buy votes in the build-up to elections. And dictators will always be tempted to add a wing to a palace, to buy yet another pair of shoes of to add a few more noughts to a Swiss bank account. However, a still greater temptation is to assume that an upward trend is permanent, and to abandon the programme prematurely.

The above solutions proscribed for the volatility issue are really 'coping' mechanisms. The way to obtain greater security in the longer term is to diversify output and sources of export earnings. A recent review explained that "for most developing countries, economic insecurity is first and foremost a development challenge (that) calls for economic diversification and policies that foster productive investment" (UN, 2008: 7). This does not necessarily mean developing a whole new range of commodity exports or even commercialising some colourful local custom to attract the odd cruise ship for a stop-over. One way is to allow labour to find more productive and better paid work abroad and to send money back home. For many small islands, such as Tonga and Samoa, remittances are equivalent to over thirty per cent of GDP and they serve not only to boost family consumption but also to allow families to invest in small businesses and to diversify their own sources of income (Connell, 2011: 4-6). The risk, of course, is to undermine the population base, possibly almost to extinction. Alternatively, attracting some FDI that will allow the development of some link or component in an international supply chain may be sufficient to stimulate the economy and establish the beginnings of a niche sector. For that to happen, the investment climate must be favourable. That means that it must be stable, transparent, well-regulated and predictable. And this is often where the problems really start.

## Government Capacities

There is a large body of literature associating good governance with growth and democracy. However, before we consider this literature in the context of the small states under discussion in this chapter, we will examine two further challenges posed by the scale of operations. These are education and health care. In both cases, the difficulties of size are compounded by distance.

The problem with education is the challenge in offering an appropriate range of courses for at the levels required. There are various specialist skills needed for the provision of basic services and administration. Moreover local labour markets require skills attuned to local conditions and contexts and this needs locally relevant tertiary education. Small states generally have made rapid progress in the universal provision of primary education and information technology has eased contacts with other centres of education and to reduce their isolation. New syllabi have been designed that are sensitive to local needs and challenges. And regional universities exist along side many forms of localised institutions of tertiary education, one serving the Caribbean and the other in the South Pacific (Brock and Crossley, 2013). One side-effect of the relative success of small states in raising education standards is the high propensity of trained people to emigrate. Smallness has an impact on emigration because opportunities for advancement and because the social and cultural milieu is less glamorous that that offered in urban environments in larger countries. It is particularly harmful if it involves strategic occupations, such as teachers and doctors. One study suggests that between 1990 and 2000 on average 50 per cent of the high-skilled labour force in the SIDS have emigrated. In some countries rates exceeded 70 per cent. By contrast, the emigration rate of graduates in larger developing states was about 15 per cent[7]. The close family ties in small communities have helped cement a new 'status-quo' of (partial) reliance on remittance incomes and the migrant may himself or herself often become part of a pattern of 'chain migration'. It is a sad fact that without migration many SIDS would have skill ratios comparable to those of developed economies (de la Croix, e.a., 2014).

Migration is almost embedded in the culture of many small societies, and it would be unrealistic to think that healthcare could escape. This is even more the case when the training occurs abroad, when the dividing-line between home and abroad has already become blurred. Moreover in the health sector migration is seen as modernising and status-enhancing. Traditionally, nursing was seen as a lower-class activity, but being a nurse abroad is seen as modern – clean uniforms, new buildings, and advanced machinery. At no time has there been any substantial return migration, and when it does occur, it is usually not to practice one's profession, but to open a local business with the repatriated savings (Connell, 2014).

A major problem with healthcare is that providing even a basic package of care is already expensive for a small country, with a comparatively small tax base. A minimum system requires the training and retention of a range of health-care professionals as well as an infrastructure of hospitals, research facilities and pharmaceutical services. Many of these facilities would be cheaper if they were connected through a central medical school, but few small countries

[7] In alphabetical order these are Grenada, Guyana, Haiti, Jamaica, Saint Lucia, St Vincent and Grenadines, Samoa and Tonga

have the capacities to fund and staff such a facility (Tremblay, 2012). The lack of specialist knowledge can be partly compensated by embracing in telemedicine – the provision of diagnosis and advice over the internet. In 1990 the first ever program started in the Pacific islands, linking several islands to the American army facilities in Hawaii. However, the contribution that telemedicine can make to small states is limited. Many forms of invasive surgery or implants are ruled out because of the impossibility of guaranteeing follow-up care. Lack of access to advanced imaging technologies and well-equipped laboratories often handicaps good diagnoses. Finally, shortages of basic drugs and medicines undermine effective treatment (Person, 2014).

Securing adequate supplies of drugs at a reasonable price is another problem confronting small states. Pooling resources offers a way out but in remote island environments remoteness from each other as well as the distance to suppliers serves to negate much of the potential savings. However this was not the only problem. Partners had difficulties in agreeing on the overhead costs of any arrangement or on sharing the benefits. This helped undermine governments' commitment to regional solutions and this reluctance was reinforced by the lack of political spin-off accruing to the politicians responsible. Much of the credit for any perceived success went to the regional organisation rather than to the governments. This problem was exacerbated by the tendency of the regional organisation to push its own agenda. The fact that many regional experiments were funded by foreign donors, increased this tendency since management tried to please the paymasters rather than the governments it was supposed to serve (Dornan and Newton Cain, 2013).

It is interesting that it was the politics of regional cooperation rather than the economics that have been held responsible for such problems.

It has long been held that because of their relative homogeneity, small states are and more likely to be governed democratically and consensually (Dahl and Tufte, 1973). A recent article offers five reasons why this should be so. Small states are more likely to be democratic because they allow for a more direct participation of large sections of the citizenry in the political process. Moreover, they tend to be more responsive to needs of citizens because the bureaucratic distance is less. Furthermore, in larger states, the business of politics has become increasingly professionalised and its practitioners have become insulated from their electorates by party bureaucracies, which pay more attention to the moneyed interests, who fund their campaigns than to citizen needs. Politicians in small states have been spared these temptations. In addition, the small size of the state is supposed to provide a structural bulwark against authoritarian rule. Finally, in small states the losers at an election are more willing to accept the results of the popular ballot because, it is argued, they disperse power more evenly through different levels of the government (Diamond and Tsalik, 1999). Personally I feel that there is a great deal of wish fulfilment in this reasoning, but it has received some empirical support. Using the Freedom House Index for democracy, with its crude three-step categorisation, it has been suggested that since the 1970s there has been a rise in democratisation among states with among states with a population below 1 million inhabitants. Moreover they have continually performed better in the 'free and 'partly free' categories than larger states. Much of this performance, however, was concentrated in states below 500,000, seemingly reinforcing the "small is beautiful" perspective on the world (Anckar, 2010).

This paints a rather too rosy picture. The label of democracy hides many practices that are distinctly 'less democratic', and small states are prone to most of them. Far from encouraging a kind of grass-roots democratic representation, politics in many small states is either dominated by elites or riven by deeply fractionalised groups. In such circumstances the route to power is through patronage and vote buying, and a powerful culture of compliance often serves to marginalise the voice and interests of minorities. Bureaucratic distance might indeed be less, but that can also mean that the bureaucracy and legislature are both under resourced. Moreover, because many in power fulfil multiple roles, the lines of accountability become blurred, giving rise to deep-rooted practices of nepotism and corruption. Politics and administration in some of the 'amateur' quality that it has long been lost in other parts of the world but that does not mean their politicians are necessarily closer to the people. Politicians in small states still tend to belong to the elites, and the 'amateur' nature of politics may contribute to their isolation from their constituents. Given this situation, it is difficult to imagine why they should be immune from authoritarian tendencies. Several small states, including Fiji, Grenada, Seychelles, and Suriname have reverted to authoritarian rule. Others have kept a facade of democracy while affording little scope to dissident voices (Veenendaal and Corbett, 2015).

Meanwhile endemic corruption, capricious decision-making, cronyism and nepotism are blights over almost all developing economies, large or small. In small states the weakness of enforcement mechanisms and the personalisation of politics exacerbate the problem. As long as that state of affairs is allowed to prevail, an honest, responsive democracy and a higher degree of economic security will both remain distant dreams for many small developing states.

# Summary

This chapter focused on the 81 small states and territories with populations under 1.5 million, thirty of which had populations less than 100,000. It identified four 'classic' hypotheses associated with size, related to small states' economic openness, their narrow range of output and their relatively concentrated direction of trade and product composition of exports. Despite the pessimistic tone of much of the literature, small states seem to perform relatively well.

It described how the concept of small island developing state (SIDS) was formulated in the late 1980s to extract concessions in multilateral trade negotiations. The Economic Vulnerability Index (EVI) shows small developing states relatively more vulnerable than larger developing states. However, the experience of richer small states suggests that the availability of larger foreign markets provides a foundation for their success.

The experience of 'medium-sized' countries suggests strategies for dealing with vulnerability. These include adaptability, sharing the risks of structural adjustment and policies aimed at sectoral adaptation. Further policy options for small developing states include trade alliances, producer agreements, stabilisation funds, encouraging remittances, attracting FDI and improving governance.

The chapter acknowledged the difficulties that SIDs confront in offering a full range of health care and education. They also face problems from the emigration of higher educated workers. Despite claims of success in securing democracy, many SIDSs remain susceptible to clientalism, nepotism and corruption.

For small states openness is both an opportunity and a source. In the next chapter we will review the increased openness of the world economy that had become known as 'globalisation'. We shall look at the debate on whether we are entering a new phase of historical development, and whether this is good or bad, permanent or reversible. We will attempt to configure the world in terms of trade investment and financial services to see which aspects of globalisation have developed the furthest, and touch on the risks for all that this might entail.

# Case Study: Heirs of the Bounty Mutineers

In 1789 in the still sultry seas of the Southern Pacific, the crew of HMS Bounty, led by the ship's master Fletcher Christian mutinied and cast the Captain, William Bligh and eighteen of his crew adrift in the open ocean. By an amazing feat of seamanship, Bligh navigated the boat over 6000 kms to safety. The mutineers, meanwhile, returned to Tahiti for women and food, and a bit of the 'good life', but the fear of being caught was always present. Fletcher Christian with eight crew, six Tahitian males and eighteen women, returned to the Bounty and sailed in search of a remote island where they could settle. In January 1790 they landed on the largest of the Pitcairn Islands, an island of barely 5 square kilometers. Drunken squabbles among the crew spilled over into open warfare and by 1793 five of the crew and all of the Tahitian men were dead. The survivors struggled to rebuild a community. Their descendants are still there today (Alexander, 2003). But not all of them.

By the 1850s Pitcairn's population had swollen to nearly 200. The agricultural resources were being stretched to the limit and a recent mud-slide had driven away the fish stock upon which they relied to supplement their diet. The islanders appealed to the British government for assistance and in 1856 the whole population of 194 was relocated to nearby Norfolk Island, six thousand kilometers away. Norfolk Island had been abandoned as a penal colony the previous year, and its buildings were still intact. After recovering, two groups of islanders returned to Pitcairn; the remainder continued to live on Norfolk Island.

Pitcairn Island (now a British overseas territory) is the smallest national jurisdiction in the world. It is also in danger, literally, of dying out. It has only 49 permanent residents and seven non-residents (government representative, teacher, doctor, police officer, family and community advisor and their partners). There are only eight children and it is expected that once they go to New Zeeland to complete their secondary education, they are unlikely to return. There are only seven persons aged between 18 and 40, and no new births are expected from them. The current labour force numbers 31 (all of whom work in part-time government functions), and eighteen of those are already over 50 years old. The island desperately needs new blood. Two things stand in the way.

The first problem is the island's unsavory reputation (Marks, 2009). With the island run by a small clique and without a police presence (or even a law book) it had become the custom for the ruling males to take and rape the young girls. This fact had only come to light when in 1997 the UK government sent a police woman to the island. Eventually, six islanders found guilty on 55 charges and six former inhabitants guilty on 41 charges. This explains the presence of a police officer and a family and community advisor among the non-resident staff, and also why no children are allowed to visit the island alone. This is hardly an advertisement for young couples settle there, but the history of child-abuse and rape has cast a long shadow over the diaspora. Not one single person has elected to return to his or her former home. A wider campaign to attract immigrants produced over 550 enquiries, but so far without a single result.

The second question is one of economics (Solomon and Burnett, 2014). The islanders live a simple day-to-day life on local food. Taxes take the form of free labour service to repair roads etc. Residents have a small cash income from tourism and souvenirs sales. Both of these are limited since the island is off the main cruise routes and because it is utterly impossible to land anything on the island other than in the islands traditional long-boats. The main cash income is from the sales of stamps and coins and this is earmarked for covering government expenses. By the early 1990s, the income had been sufficient to channel the surplus into an investment fund which had reached $3.4 million and had generated a healthy flow of interest payments. But over the next decade, the fall in interest rates, the stagnation in stamp sales and withdrawals of capital to fund a couple of bad fiscal years had combined to wipe out the fund entirely. By 2004, nothing was left. When, in that same year the government decided that the stamp operation should be funded from its own revenues, the 'profitability' collapsed. Basically, Pitcairn survives on UK government subsidies, the occasional EU grant and donor aid.

Matters are a little better on Norfolk Island. Half of its 1600 residents descend from the families of the mutineers and half are from the Australian mainland. Recently, it has seen the settlement of richer migrants attracted by the life-style and cheap tax regime. The island is a self-governing territory, not of the UK but of Australia. It too is in dire financial trouble, prompted largely by a decline in tourism following the financial crash of 2008. But it is not without hope. In 2010 its convict buildings were listed with others in Australia as a World Heritage Site. Proposals are in place to improve the piers and harbour facilities, to reform air services and to improve the road and telecommunication infrastructure. There is also a realisation by the Australian authorities that, just as with other small, isolated communities there will always be a need for budget subsidies. The breaking point for Norfolk Island is its governance.

Concealed behind an appeal to a 'Norfolk way' or a 'Pitcairn way', in 2003, an Australian Committee of Inquiry found evidence of state capture exploiting a weak governance system (JCS, 2003). It found systematic use of intimidation against critics and the use of political patronage to place incompetents in positions of authority. It argued that the principles of good governance were neither understood nor accepted, and that the problems had been remained neglected for the previous fifteen years. A decade later, with progress stalled on the front of economic reforms, Canberra's patience is finally exhausted and the government proposed bringing Norfolk Island firmly and formally under national control (Parliament of the Commonwealth of Australia, 2014). The Islanders are mounting a protest campaign but with the local economy shrinking and Treasury empty, there are few options left. In October 2014, at the opening of the Royal Agricultural and Horticultural Show they protested by singing the Pitcairn anthem and 'God Save the Queen' rather than the Australian anthem (*Daily Telegraph*, 16.10.2014). It did not work. In May 2015 the Australian Parliament finally revoked Norfolk Island's autonomous status (*The Guardian*, 21.5.2015).

# Chapter Ten

# Globalisation

It is almost impossible to read anything touching on economics today without stumbling on some reference to its global nature and either the challenges that it brings or the opportunities that it affords. A search Google Scholar for the year 2015 (only) for books and articles with 'globalisation' in the title (spelt both with an 's' and a 'z') will reveal 3,070 hits; Chinese will offer an additional 1,150 options. It is interesting to reflect that Google is scarcely more than ten years old. Before then scholars had to search through databases in print. My favourite used to be the Journal of Economic Literature (JEL) which every quarter published lists of articles published in economic journals, all classified into separate categories according to the topic covered. It still took ages to compile a bibliography. Nowadays, even these databases are available electronically. A search of the JEL database today would reveal that not one single article with the word 'globalisation' in the title had been published before 1984.

Globalisation is the kind of term that everyone claims to understand but where no two strangers will agree on a definition. Is it a question of more international contacts or connections, or does it imply a greater dependence or interdependence on those contacts? What are the drivers of the process – the inexorable push of markets, the transforming power of technology or the mobilisers of capital? Is the word 'international' sufficient or should we separate the local or regional from the more truly global? Should we distinguish among different dimensions of globalisation – the economic dimension, the cultural sphere and areas of governance? If it is economic, to what should we attach more importance – to trade, to business, to labour or to communications? If it is governance, where should we concentrate – cooperation among governments, the role of international bodies or the influence of civic society and NGO's? Finally, within all of this, what role do we leave for the national state (the unit upon which we lavished so much attention in this book).

In 1999 a team led by David Held, of the Open University, published a book entitled *Global Transformations*, which described the parameters of the discussion and which still, largely, holds true for today. They divided the different authors into three camps – Hyperglobalists, Sceptics and Transformationalists. The Hyperglobalists see the present globalisation as something new and unique. They argue that market forces have undermined state control over national economies, and are weakening the authority of states (examples of key publications are Albrow, 1996; Friedman, 2005; Ohmae, 1990, 1994; Micklethwait and Woodridge 2000; Reich, 1992). Some Sceptics argue that current globalisation resemble developments in an earlier period, 1870-1913, which in some respects went further and were more truly global (Hirst and Thompson, 1996). Others argue that there are limits to its so-called benefits, and that it can only work when the benefits are fairly distributed and are seen to be so. Ironically the most open countries are those with the biggest governments, the most extensive and effective regulation, and the widest social safety nets. Until market forces are brought under some control, further market liberalisation will be counter-productive (Rodrik, 2011). The Transformationalists argue that globalisation is more complex than mere economics or the freeing of markets (involving also sociological, political and cultural factors), and they refuse to commit themselves on where it is heading or whether the process is reversible (examples of key publications are Castells, 1996; Ghemawat, 2011; Hay and Marsh, 2000; Held, 1999). Not only do authors disagree on the nature of the process; they also argue whether it is beneficial or not. At one extreme, the Hyperglobalists assert that markets decide the optimal use of the world's resources and that globalisation is bringing the world's citizens a wider range of products at lower costs. Poverty exists because governments persist in maintaining protection, and depriving their citizens from benefitting fully from these developments. And with the 'market' come other benefits of western civilisation, such as democracy and human rights. The Sceptics, on the other hand, argue that the process has gone too far; that it is driving down employment and wages in developed economies and penalising the vulnerable in developing countries. Far from enriching countries, the penetration of western culture is homogenising local cultures and aggravating the conditions for cultural conflict.

Another source of disagreement is on the ability (or even the desirability) of states to do anything to change the course of globalisation. Calls by Sceptics for states to protect the vulnerable have to confront a reality that protective legislation or higher welfare expenditure will lead to capital relocating to states with lower standards and lower taxation, taking even more jobs and incomes with them. Hyperglobalists, and others, argue that the state is already being bypassed. The world economy is coalescing around production and service 'hubs' or agglomerations which function independently from the states nominally controlling them. Transformationalists, and some Sceptics, would respond that globalisation is not making the state irrelevant, but that it is placing a premium on the quality of what the state supplies, a premium on good governance. They also argue that international institutions occupy a supra-territorial space and are therefore already in a position to manage the changes that globalisation is generating (Held, 1999) and that many medium 'welfarist' states have been proactive in successfully adjusting their social security systems to accommodate the changes imposed by the international environment (van Hemerijk, 2013).

Others commentators have described the debate in terms of successive 'waves'. In this line of analysis the first wave started by making exaggerated claims for the demise of the state and the inevitability of a global economy, but it later altered this position to leave a role for the state, albeit in a modified and reduced form. The second wave offers a more nuanced view of the extent of recent change, and it allows the state more room for a response, and therefore, a more variegated impact on different national economies. In this way changes in the world economy have helped create different varieties of capitalism (Hall and Soskice, 2001). It accepts that change is inevitable, but is not deterministic about its direction. Thus far the wave analysis subsumes elements of all three of the camps identified in *Global Transformations*. The third wave accepts the descriptions of change offered by the first two waves, but is more interested in the processes that lie behind it. In doing so, it certainly disengages from the view of the inevitable victory of markets and democracy that offered both an explanation and a justification for first-wave theorists. However, this has also reopened the question of what needs to be included in the definition of globalisation. Moreover, in rejecting the implicit dichotomy between global and national, the third-wave has reintroduced not only different spatial dimensions such as cities and regions, but also the dimension of class. This has opened a discourse of whether the whole concept of globalisation, should not itself be investigated – why has it clustered this particular set of ideas around itself, and who stands to benefit from framing the discourse in this particular way (Bruff, 2005; Berry, 2008; Keller, 2014)?

In many ways this attempt to organise the debate on globalisation is itself simplistic and positions often overlap. For example, both neo-liberals and neo-Marxists can share a Hyperglobalist standpoint on the inexorable and irreversible nature of globalisation whilst disagreeing profoundly on the nature of the engine of change. However, if we take the three waves as reflections of the (overlapping) chronology of the debate, then it is striking that the 2008/9 financial crisis has done little to deflect any of the waves from their pre-determined course. The debate seems cemented in a structuralist (even transformationalist) framework and almost immune from any (re-)incorporation of cyclical analysis. The idea that there might be a 'trade cycle' (waves of intensification and slackening in rates of growth every 7-9 years, or every 50 years, depending on the focus of analysis), let alone any whiff of the danger of systemic collapse, failed to penetrate the core of the globalisation discourse (See Reinhart and Rogoff, 2009) until the financial meltdown of 2008 (Heemerijk, Knapen and van Doorn, 2009; Wolf, 2014). The intellectual electricity that crackled over the initial discussion has died as political scientists, sociologists and IPE specialists have entered the semantic playpen of defining, dissecting and idealising the concepts while retreating from the material shifts that promoted the original discussion.

## Globalisation Index

If globalisation can evoke different responses from national governments, this may either stem from the degree to which the national economy is part of the globalised economy or equally, the policy responses adopted may determine the degree of its exposure. In other words, the degree to which a country could be considered 'globalised' may be either a cause or an effect of the policy options available or exercised. For this reason, it is important to assess the extent to which countries are globalised. It will be no surprise that there is not one, but several, indices available for the purpose. All of these contain components that might have been better kept separate. All contain an economic and a political component, but there is some variation in the nature and number of the rest (Caselli, 2012; Martens e.a., 2014).

Since our primary concern is with the economic component, and since the indicators available for political globalisation are a pretty poor proxy for what could be understood by the concept, the only question that remains is which index to choose. All the economic components include data for trade and investment flows; some include portfolio transactions as well. However, one index stands out by including not only cross-border transactions, but also by incorporating measures that have the effect, if not the intention, of restricting those flows (Apostoaie, 2011). The KOF Index was first constructed in 2002 by the *Konjunkturforschungsstelle* of the *Eidgenössische Technische Hochschule* in Zürich and it covers the period from 1970. The most recent year covered is 2012. Even so, it is not perfect. The index is evenly split between 'actual flows'and 'restrictions'. Each has four elements. However, three of the elements in the flows category refer to financial flows and only one to trade flows whereas the balance of the elements considered under 'restrictions' is the reverse. Most of the individual elements in the KOF index are quantitative measures that have been derived from international reports. There is one proxy index, namely payments made to foreign nationals (persons and companies), which has been included to reflect foreign involvement in the production process. There is also one slightly dubious measure. The element 'restrictions on capital account' does not estimate the impact at all. Instead it takes the thirteen types of restrictions identified by the IMF and counts the number in force in every country, regardless of whether they have a token impact or amount to a total prohibition. Finally, before we turn to the results themselves, there is one last criticism that we should make. In the presentation of the results, kindly made available in an online database, countries are included in the final index even when data for fully one half of the index is missing[8]. One observation we could make is that smaller countries tend to be overrepresented in the more globalised end of the spectrum. This impression would have been strengthened had we included the small states with populations under 1.5 million in the analysis (Dreher, 2006; KOF Website). One experiment in constructing a globalisation index attempted to correct for size. The author found that although larger countries improved their scores, smaller states still tended to dominate the list because they really were more globalised (Vujakovic, 2010). The most recent results are shown in Figure 10.1.

---

[8] Of the larger countries, the Democratic Republic of the Congo, Myanmar, Qatar and the United Arab Emirates appear in the overall list even though they have no data indicated in the 'actual flows' component and Belarus and Swaziland appear even though they are absent from the 'restrictions'.

Figure 10.1: World Map of Economic Globalisation (Index) 2012

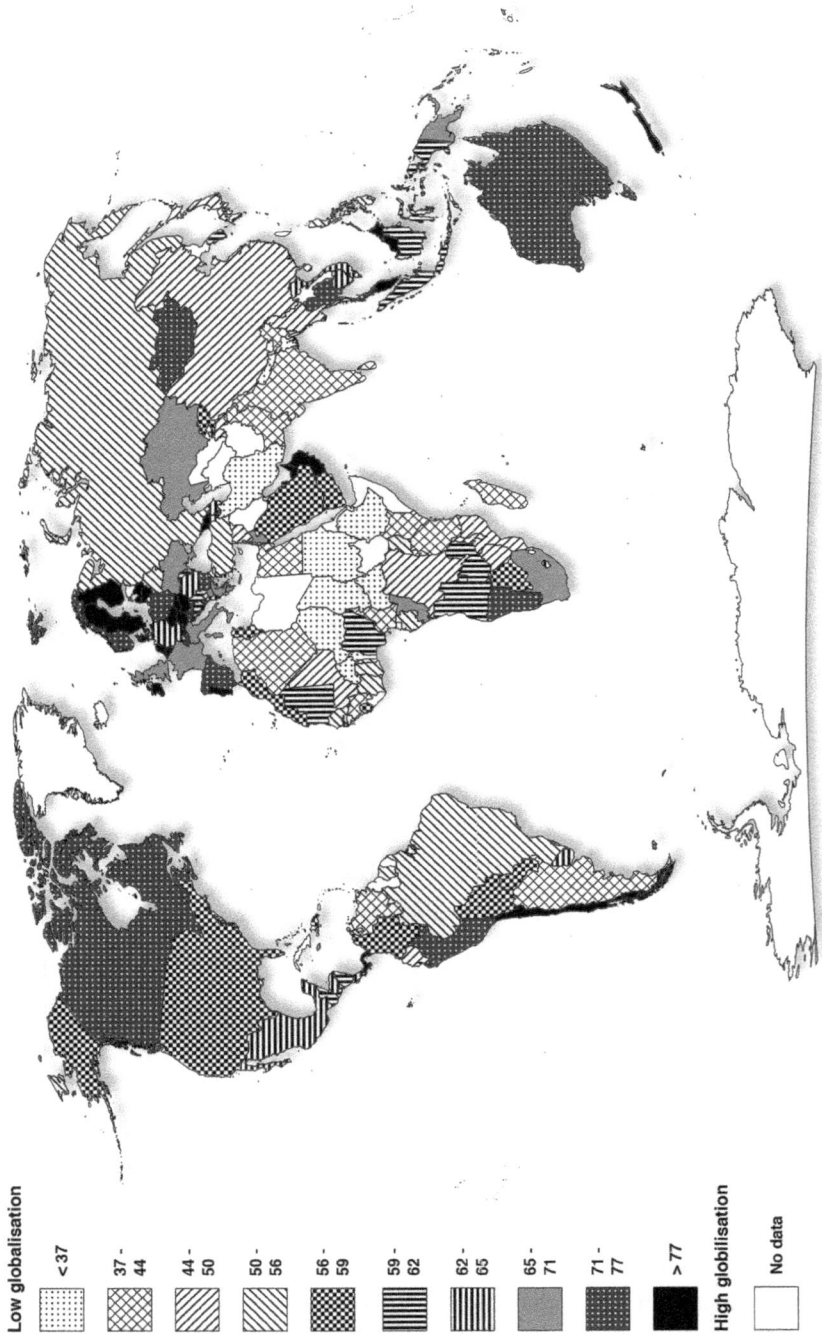

Low globalisation

<37

37 - 44

44 - 50

50 - 56

56 - 59

59 - 62

62 - 65

65 - 71

71 - 77

>77

High globilisation

No data

Source: KOF Index Database and Goujon, 2013.

The most globalised economies are dominated by the smaller, more developed economies. The other end of the spectrum is anchored by Uzbekistan and Turkmenistan, Laos and Iraq. The KOF Index also publishes regional aggregate data stretching back to 1970. In terms of actual flows (which, it must be remembered, are dominated by investment and financial flows), Europe is the most globalised region by some considerable margin, with the start of the surge in its performance coinciding with the opening-up of the former planned economies of the East-bloc. Until that surge twenty years ago, South America was ahead of Europe and it still outperforms the other world regions. If we turn globalisation in terms of restrictions (notably trade restrictions), the KOF index shows Europe as clearly the most liberalised area in the world, though drifting backwards since 2004 (well before the recent financial crisis). Asia emerges as the second most open area, and remains so throughout the entire period. One phenomenon all share in recent years, in the aftermath of the financial crisis of 2008-9, is the reversal in progress in removing restrictions (KOF Website).

In the following sections we shall examine in more detail the main types of international transactions – trade in goods and services, FDI and finally, other financial transactions.

## International trade

Although international trade covers trade in both goods and services, for reasons of space, and a paucity of literature, I will concentrate here entirely on trade in goods (but see Borchert e.a., 2014). One of the oldest sets of statistics available to historians, other than those relating to population, are those covering foreign trade. This is probably because taxes were collected on trade (because of the relative ease of collection and their effect of protecting domestic production). In fact, the trade data often provided the first step in the reconstruction of output indices, and ultimately national income indices, for earlier periods. The trade data does have gaps in the coverage (non-dutiable items, transit trade, non-registration, and smuggling, converting volume to value) and matters are not helped when it is juxtaposed against less than exact GDP data, but the picture fits well with other indicators (shipping and rail freight) to give a general picture of long term developments.

Trade openness increases from the mid-1840s, coinciding with the UK's 'free trade' acts, which contained reciprocity clauses that encouraged trade liberalisation in other countries. It was also facilitated by the spread of railways, and to a lesser extent of steam shipping. The peak in the early 1870s coincided with a dramatic fall in agricultural prices, with the opening up of the plains and prairies of North and South America and the fall in ocean shipping rates, which precipitated a surge in agricultural protectionism. Prices revived in the early 1890s and the 'second industrial revolution' kicked-in, giving birth to a whole range of new business opportunities, but this episode was ended by the outbreak of the First World War (Chase-Dunn e.a., 2000). International trade never fully recovered in the inter-war years. The Russian Revolution, the effect of the disruption of European borders, the economic problems of the Weimar Republic, the overvaluation of sterling and the overhangs of productive capacity from the War years all helped to limit trade growth. The onset of the Great Depression in 1929, and the rising tide of protectionism that accompanied it choked off openings for international trade (Kindleberger, 1973). It was not until the end of the 1950s that the world finally unravelled the network of protection in which it had become entangled, but from then onwards trade growth continued to outstrip gains in GDP. This was accompanied by some interesting shifts in its composition. From about the 1870s to the end of the 1930s, the pattern of world trade could be typified as an exchange between a core of industrial countries and a global periphery, in which manufactured goods were traded for food and raw materials. Indeed, so entrenched was this idea that an influential study published immediately after World War II urged the revival of this trade pattern as the motor for the growth of the world economy (Maizels, 1945). Instead, something completely different happened. The fastest growing sector of world trade became the exchange of increasingly sophisticated industrial products between rich industrial nations, and to a large extent, within the context of multinational companies situated in different countries (Grubel and Lloyd, 1971). In 1990, the share of what we can call North–North trade reached 56 per cent of total world trade. After that, the pattern has begun to reverse as consumption in large underdeveloped economies began to grow, and as their exports began to increase their market share in the imports of richer nations. By 2011, the share of world trade conducted between industrial countries had declined to 36 per cent. The share of manufactured goods in world trade continued to increase until 2000, when it reached 75 per cent. Since then it has fallen to 65 per cent, with most of the difference being made up by a surge in demand for fuel and raw materials (WTO, 2013). Once we have eliminated flows within regions, the pattern of world trade today is dominated (in order of size) by the flows between Europe and Asia, Asia and North America, and North America and Europe. These, and the other flows, are shown in Figure 10.2.

Figure 10.2: Network of World Trade 2011(measured by exports fob, $ billion)

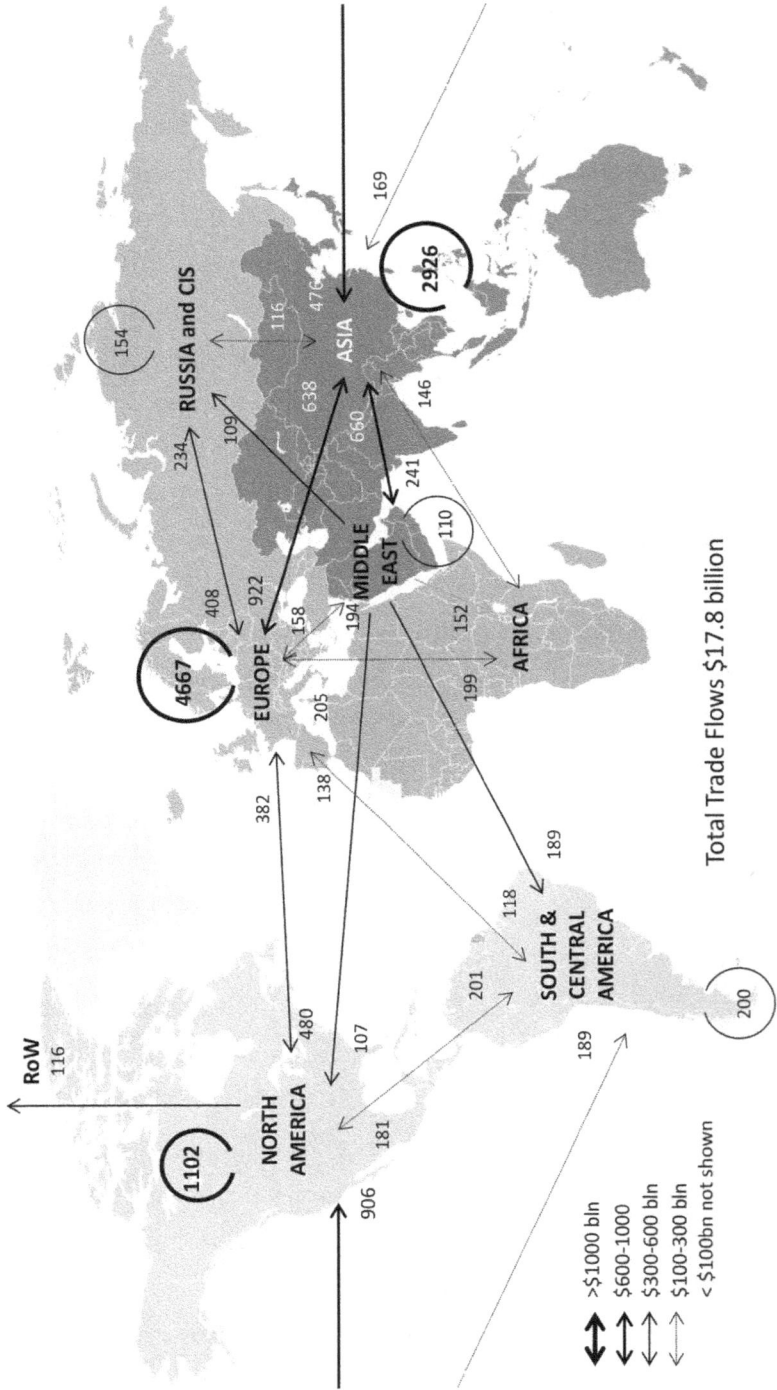

Total Trade Flows $17.8 billion

RoW
116

RUSSIA and CIS
154
116
476
169
2926
ASIA
638
660
146
234
109
241
MIDDLE EAST
110
408
922
158
194
205
AFRICA
152
199
382
138
EUROPE
4667
189
118
SOUTH & CENTRAL AMERICA
201
NORTH AMERICA
1102
480
107
181
906
189
200

>$1000 bln
$600-1000
$300-600 bln
$100-300 bln
< $100bn not shown

Source: WTO, 2014. Table A2.

There are a couple of problems with international trade statistics. Firstly, national income is a sum of 'values added' whereas international trade measures the total value of a product is counted every time it crosses a border. This is not as complicated as it sounds. The diagram in Figure 10.3 attempts to show the difference. Imagine a raw material, for example, cotton, going through several production processes before reaching its destination. Each process is in a different country. The top row shows the value-added (shaded) that would enter the GDP calculations of the countries either for the additional process itself or for the transport, insurance and freight services between countries. The lower row shows the total values (shaded) that would enter the trade statistics. So, when people talk about the importance of trade as a percentage of GDP, we are not comparing like with like.

A second problem is that when a country exports a finished product to another country, a proportion of its value may well have originated as imports further back along what is often called a 'value chain'. Let me give one true example. Let us suppose China exports an iPod to the USA for $150. That figure appears in China's export statistics and in its balance of payments data, but only $4 of the value is added in China. The R&D and design values originate in the USA and the parts in the USA and Japan. Similarly, less than $10 of the value of an iPod selling for $290 is accounted for by labour costs paid in China (Linden e.a., 2009, Kraemer e.a., 2011).

Figure 10.3: Differences between GDP and Trade Statistics

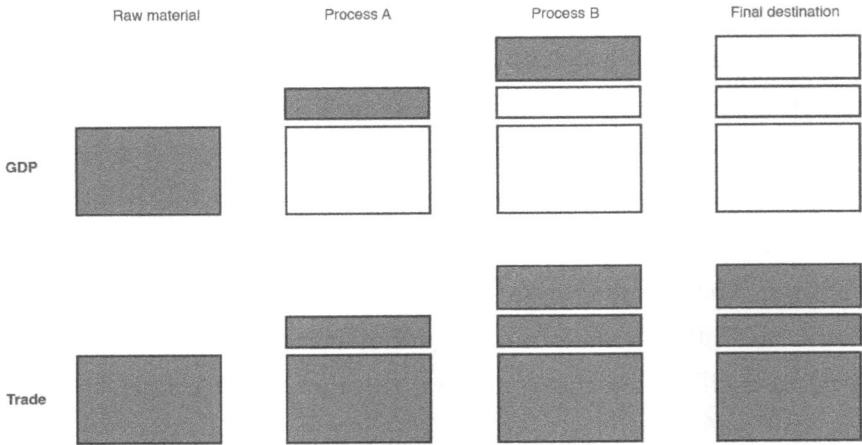

This phenomenon has several implications for policy-makers. For example, trade negotiations are still conducted by national representatives (or by those of regional customs unions like the European Union) but nowadays neither imports nor exports constitute purely national interests. Equally, the calculation of the beneficial effects of international trade, traditionally employing national trade data needs to be recast along a different paradigm. It also complicates the already difficult task of designing purely national polices to deal with crises like the 2008 financial crisis (Jara and Escaith, 2012). The OECD, in partnership with the WTO has attempted to calculate the proportion of foreign content in the exports of 61 countries. The results are eye-opening. Almost one-third of the value China's recorded exports is accounted for by foreign content. In Ireland, Taiwan and Korea the share tops 40 per cent. The overall pattern reveals high foreign contents in trade dependent countries. Countries reliant on primary product exports (minerals or agriculture) perform relatively better in this respect (OECD-WTO database). It has been estimated that 22 per cent of the total value of world exports originated outside the 'exporting' country (Koopman e.a., 2011).

A third problem is that trade is counted only when trade flows are recorded. If Dutch truck crosses the border between The Netherlands and Germany and fills its tank with German petrol, the transaction does not appear as trade. If, on the other hand, German petrol is delivered to a Dutch petrol station, it will be counted as foreign trade. In Africa, where much cross-border trade is unrecorded, this can lead to major distortions. Finally, there are bigger problems in Africa. Official national trade statistics have frequent gaps. Only six African countries have complete series of annual statistics from 2000 to the present. Many statistics do not conform to international definitions or standards. In such cases the gaps have to be filled from the statistics of their trading partners, which is far from being a satisfactory solution (WTO, 2013: 4–5).

Of course, world trade cannot grow if it is discouraged and disadvantaged by high-cost penalties that operate to discriminate against foreign goods. This is not to say that the growth of trade is primarily driven by such barriers, but the fact remains that if trade barriers are prohibitive, goods will not move across international borders. In the past, much work and emphasis was placed on the removal of barriers to trade that had been erected by governments (Love and Lattimore, 2009). The first barrier to trade that we will consider is tariffs. These are taxes levied on imports either as a fixed charge or as a percentage on a sliding scale. Since the 1960s, tariff rates have been progressively reduced. In 2008, the OECD countries charged an average tariff of only 2.8 per cent on industrial goods, but 10.8 on agricultural products. The rates in developing countries were significantly higher

(13.9 per cent) for industrial goods but slightly lower (9.5 per cent) for agricultural products (World Bank Database, Data on Trade and Import Barriers, Dec. 2011) Another restriction is quotas, which place a fixed limit on imports, regardless of the level of prices or demand. In Western Europe, most of these were phased out in the 1950s but their use has continued elsewhere, mostly in agriculture. In 1999, for example, Uruguay Round replaced over 1300 existing outright bans or quantitative restrictions in agriculture alone with slightly less restrictive 'tariff-rate quotas' (Skully, 2001) At least lists of quotas are usually published, but this is not the case for exchange controls. These became common in the 1930s, originally to control speculative movements of currency, but they quickly became powerful weapons in trade manipulation. If an importer could not obtain foreign currency to pay for the goods, the transaction very often could not take place. In most Western countries, these controls had also been phased out by the end of the 1950s, although in the 1970s quotas on textile were reintroduced (Love and Lattimore, 2009: 56-58).

The last category of official controls is the so-called non-tariff barriers, usually in the form of regulations. Technical barriers, such as minimum safety standards, or hygiene regulations against imports of (possibly) infected food products, may just have a legitimate function, but they do have a negative impact on imports - often deliberately so. In many cases in developing countries, these have become more important than tariffs in regulating trade. For example, in Latin America, the applied tariff on agricultural goods is 6.6 per cent, whereas the tariff-equivalent effect of non-tariff barriers is an estimated 21.5 per cent (Hoekman and Nicita, 2011: 2071). Another category is regulations over what are called 'government procurements' or purchases made by governments. These can amount to between 15 and 20 per cent of GDP, and the allocation of contracts was often biased to favour of domestic suppliers – at the expense of imports. Since 1996, this practice has been gradually dismantled (Cole and Davies, 2014). A final barrier to imports is what I refer to as 'private protection' in the form of cartels. These are voluntary agreements by business to restrict market access in order to force up prices and extract 'monopoly profits'. In many countries such agreements are outlawed, but they are difficult to police and the penalties are often insufficient to act as deterrents (Levenstine and Suslow, 2012).

It is not only government action that restricts trade, there are other cost penalties, known as 'transaction costs'. All import statistics are expressed as including cost, insurance and freight (cif) whereas they are recorded at point of origin as free-on-board (fob). One study, by collating both sets of data, suggests that in 1990 the difference between the two represented 28 per cent of the import price. The survey's coverage was large, but not perfectly representative, so this should be taken as no more than a ball-park figure with massive variations between individual cases (Limão and Venables, 2001). The first costs of these involve the transport of goods from one country to another, which obviously differs according to the nature of the product, the distance travelled and the means of transport. Matters do not end, however, when goods arrive at a port. They have to be unloaded, recorded, and released for further transhipment to their final destination. One well-known study estimated that, for developed countries, total border costs were twice as high as international transport costs and that only a small part of that (less than a fifth) was due to traditional measures such as tariffs (Anderson and van Wincoop, 2004). The World Bank has calculated the administrative costs (documents, admin fees, handing charges and inland transport) of exporting or importing a 20-foot container to or from a ship in 2013. The delay in the port of a container of imports averaged ten days in high-income OECD countries, they reached 38 days in Sub-Saharan Africa (and over three months in Uzbekistan, Chad and South Sudan). In high-income OECD countries the whole exercise costs about $1000, but it cost more than double that amount in Eastern Europe and Central Asia and in Sub-Saharan Africa. The sad thing is that these did not just hamper imports, thereby affording some measure of protection to domestic producers, but that the same type of red-tape and high costs strangled their own exporters as they try to break into world markets (WB 'Trading Across Borders' database). At Bali in December 2013, the WTO reached an agreement on measures which, if fully implemented, would reduce these administrative costs by between 13 and 15 per cent (OECD, 2014 b).

Although much attention in the literature concentrates on the removal of trade barriers, once they are reduced, the real motors of trade growth lie elsewhere. One way in which trade grows, is to have fast economic growth in one's traditional trading partners, especially if this translated into import demand. Since much trade is 'neighbourhood' trade, this dynamic has been translated into 'gravity models' of trade which add distance, connectivity and cultural similarity to the explanation (Teh and Piermartini 2005). Another way to perform comparatively well in international trade is to have a domestic production structure that is concentrated on goods for which world demand is growing faster. Then, even if one just keeps a 'constant market share', a country with a specialisation in a fast growing sector will experience a higher growth of trade (Feng e.a., 2014). And a final way to experience relatively fast growth is to increase one's competitiveness. The only sustainable way to do this is to produce more goods for the same amount of inputs and this requires access to more capital and better technology. And one short-cut way to get that is through FDI, which we will look at next.

## Foreign Direct Investment

FDI involves the purchase (or expansion) of (the whole or part) of a business in one country by an individual or business in another. It can take one of four forms – the purchase of shares in a foreign company, a merger with, or acquisition of, a foreign company, the establishment of new business facilities in a foreign country and, finally, the enlargement of existing foreign business in a foreign country. The definition of FDI does not, however, include the purchase of local or national government bonds.

Unlike international trade statistics which require documentation covering all consignments of good crossing international borders, there is no such attempt at the systematic collection of information on FDI. The data is usually solicited from individual companies, and that is where the problems start. Let us look, for example, at the USA which is the largest owner of FDI assets in the world. It owns 22 per cent of the world's total FDI (UNCTAD statistical database). The authorities collect annual data from what is supposed to be a representative sample of larger firms, with the argument that they account for most of it. Every five years, they hold a 'benchmark' survey, covering a far wider range of business. However, even with the benchmark survey not all firms are equally interrogated. Less information is collected on the foreign-owned firms in the USA (reflected in the inward flows/ stocks) than for American firms (reflected in the outwards flows/

stocks). In addition, the authorities also have three different forms, varying in the refinement of the information solicited, and the most detailed information is only required from firms with a turnover of more than $150 million (Feenstra e.a., 2010). I did some work on the American statistics some years back, looking at a brief period in the 1970s when The Netherlands were the largest foreign direct investor in the USA, and I found significant difference between benchmark and the annual surveys with both the volume and destinations of American FDI. I assume that the situation has improved since then (the benchmark surveys I used were some of the first ever produced), but if this is the situation in the USA, one can imagine what happens as we slide down the scale towards less rich states and less efficient administrations.

Immediately after the Second World War, there was only one source of foreign capital and that was the USA. It was only after Europe had replenished its depleted reserves of foreign exchange, at the end of the 1950s, it began to re-enter the FDI market. From that moment onwards the volume of annual FDI flows has grown apace, from $13 billion in 1970 to $1.3 trillion in 2012 (UNCTAD statistical database). This is a one-thousand-fold increase, while American price levels had increased by a factor of six. Behind this explosive growth of FDI there has been an interesting shift in its destination. Initially, three quarters of all FDI went to other developed economies. Even as late as 1990, the share of FDI going to developing economies was still less than 20 per cent. Since then, however it has grown steadily and, by 2012, it has reached over 50 per cent (UNCTAD statistical database). This has still to impact fully on the pattern of FDI stocks, which records the investment holding accumulated over six decades or more.

Figure 10.4: World Top-10 Countries FDI Stocks, 2014

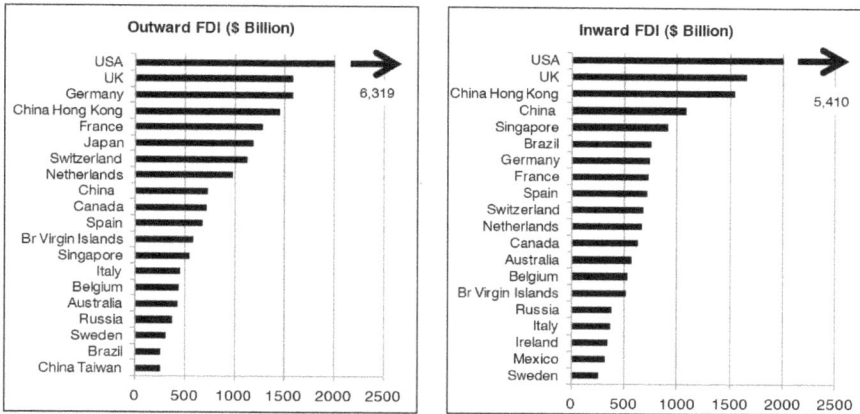

If we look at the diagram for the stock of outward investment in Figure 10.4, we can see that the USA still holds an impressive 22 per cent of the world's FDI assets, but this has fallen from a peak of 45 per cent in 1986. Even so, it remains far ahead of the next ranked economies – the UK and Germany. The appearance of Hong Kong, in fourth place is rather interesting. It functions as a gate-away to China, and as late as 1989 it held only 0.5 per cent of world FDI. The British Virgin Islands, a little tax paradise in twelvth place, was too small even to register on the statistics before 1988. Turning to the data on inward stocks, the USA is also the world's largest destination for FDI (though it still has a substantial outward balance) followed by the UK. Hong Kong is in third place but its position as a conduit for funds towards China has substantially diminished since the 1980s, and China is emerging as a major foreign investor in its own right, in fourth place.

What determines FDI? Before answering that, it is useful to distinguish three different forms. The first involves investment into broadly similar activities as those of the investing company.

One example is automobile company investment in assembly and production facilities abroad. We can call this 'horizontal' investment. The second is towards activities higher or lower in the production chain. For example, an oil drilling firm may branch into shipping, refining and retail outlets. We can call this 'vertical' investment. Finally, we have examples of firms that shift FDI, and even their head-quarters, to profit from differences in regulatory regimes and tax levels. I suppose we can call this 'tactical' investment (Grubert, 2003). For example, for tax reasons the iconic Swedish furniture giant, IKEA (with 349 stores in 43 countries and earnings of four billion dollars) is not based in Sweden but in the university town of Leiden, in The Netherlands, about ten-minute cycle ride from my home. For each of these forms there are different determinants.

One factor uniting all forms of FDI, is the regulatory framework in the home country. Although the international financial system established after the war witnessed the freeing of commercial transactions (i.e. payments for trade and associated services) many countries maintained controls over capital flows until deep into the 1980s. One exception was the USA. The UK also freed FDI, but only in countries trading in sterling (which meant, basically, its colonies and some of the Commonwealth) (Schenk, 1994). Since the 1990s, until the recent financial crisis, there has been an acceleration in the number of countries, and the number of measures, aimed at liberalising FDI (Contessi and Weinberger, 2009).

A second factor, common in horizontal FDI, was determined by the desire to leap-frog international trade barriers and get access to markets on the same basis as domestic producers. However, as the impact of trade barriers diminished, so too did the power of this explanation (Dunning, 1998; Vernon, 1974). This brings us to a third factor. In situations where trade barriers do not play such a major role, the same kinds of gravity models employed for international trade are popular. Such explanations are based on the specific size of markets for the products concerned and the geographical (and cultural) distance. Add to this some economic specifications for cost differentials, and much of the horizontal (North-North) FDI flow could be explained (Blonigen and Piger, 2011). If we look at horizontal FDI towards less developed countries, then the balance of explanation would need to shift away from an accent on markets and towards an emphasis on the type of enterprise (labour intensive) and the factor advantage (low labour costs). Here one would need to know why there is a preference for 'ownership' rather than 'outsourcing'. One important factor influencing the choice is the 'knowledge intensity' of the product. If you own the business, you can control access to technology and preserve conditions of monopoly, whereas if you outsource the product, you lose control over these competitive advantages. On the other hand, these factors are unlikely to operate in the same way for vertical investment, especially now that FDI of this kind in developing countries has increased so markedly in recent years. In this case the explanation would lie in gaining access to raw material supplies and securing that access by investing along the 'supply chain'. As for the final category of 'tactical' investment, there is not much evidence that such considerations play an important role in the overall pattern of FDI location (Blonigen, 2005). IKEA is the exception rather than the rule.

## Financial Markets

So far, in this chapter we have looked at transactions in goods (and services) and by implication, the cash that changed hands to effect the change in ownership. We have also looked at transactions to acquire increased business assets abroad, and again, by implication, the cash that has changed hands. Financial markets cover the cash transactions for what is left. But what is left? There are four main categories namely bonds, equities, derivatives and foreign exchange transactions.

Bonds are fixed income, fixed-term loans, usually issued by governments (both national and local) but occasionally also by businesses. A typical bond would be a five or ten-year loan for a fixed amount carrying a fixed rate of interest (e.g. a ten year $1,000 bond at a rate of interest 3.5 per cent to the Greek government). During the period of the bond, the government would pay an annual interest ($35) and at the end of the period, it would redeem the bond for $1,000. If at any time investors doubted the ability of the government to meet its obligations, he or she might try to sell the bond, even at a loss. For example, he might sell the bond for $500. The government would still be paying an annual $35, so that the effective rate of interest would now be 7 per cent. This is what is called the 'yield'. Governments regularly roll-over their outstanding bonds, re-borrowing the money that they pay out. However, any new bonds issues by the government would have to match the yield of existing bonds and this is how 'government debt crises' develop.

Equities refer to ownership of assets (including company stocks and shares). Here a firm or corporation sells off a share of the ownership in return for a share in the profits. The return is not stipulated in advance, but it is fixed in relation to the 'share'. If a firm is in difficulties, share-holders may sell, even at a loss, but the new owner will still get whatever percentage of the profits represented by the nominal value of the share. If the firm then issues more shares, each owner of an existing share will get proportionally less of the total paid-out profits. This may reduce the attraction of holding those shares, and the owner might sell at a loss. On the other hand, if he expects profits to rise as a result of the new investment, then the whole scenario needs reassessment.

Derivatives are financial contracts that derive (note the word) their value from the performance of another asset. Stripped down to the basics, an investor would agree to buy an asset (grain, currency, stock and shares... it makes no difference) at a fixed price at some stipulated time in the future. This contract is secured by the payment of part of the value of the goods (as a deposit). This allows the buyer of 'insure' themselves against unfavourable price movements in the future. The owner of the asset in question is guaranteed that price, but might have to forego the opportunity to sell at an even higher price. At this level, derivatives are not difficult to understand, but it does not explain why they are so popular. The secret lies in the deposit. For a relatively small part of the final price (for example, one twentieth), the investor can secure 'ownership' of an asset. So if he were to commit the entire 'final' price at the beginning, he can secure twenty times the final volume of the asset, and if the asset has meanwhile risen in price, he gets twenty times the difference. This is called leverage, and it is a very clever concept. Of course, if the final price has fallen, the whole mechanism operates in reverse.

Foreign exchange transactions involve the buying and selling of currencies. One can imagine that many of the financial transactions that have been mentioned in this section, as well as the transactions in the purchase of foreign goods and services (and FDI) involve buyers and sellers located in different countries. Of course, they might be willing to accept payment in a currency not their own (most international enterprises hold some balances in 'international' currencies as dollars or euros) but most will ultimately want payment in their own currency (or the currency of the country in which the asset is purchased). So far, this is not difficult to understand. Of course, usually the currency does not move at all. Most of the transactions involve altering balances held in different columns of accounts. However, there is usually a small difference between the buying and selling price of a currency and by tracking these differences, and electronically transferring currencies to take advantage of the differences, large-volume transactions at even small differences can yield considerable profits. There is one last element to consider, and that is what is known as 'swaps' of currencies between central banks. These are usually conducted in secret, and the aim is to help national banks manage the supply and demand for their currencies, to stabilise their exchange rates.

It is generally agreed that financial markets have expanded rapidly, especially since the 1970s, but there is little consistent data to measure this exactly. Moreover, there is also general agreement that they have grown faster than world GDP, faster than world trade and faster even than world FDI. In my opinion, if there is a radical departure from the previous period of globalisation in 1870-1913, it lies precisely in the growth of the international financial markets. Persistent sceptics of globalisation could respond to this in two ways – that most bonds and equities are still traded nationally and that much international financial trading is still largely regional, or at most, shared among the richer nations in the world economy. However, they, too, would still agree that it has grown.

There are many factors that help explain this growth, but we will generalise about them in four categories, namely: the available currency, government policy, technology and innovation.

Traditionally, in the past, most foreign exchange was held by national banks, although some international companies might hold some as trading reserves. After the Second World War, dollars were scarce, and any surplus dollars earned from the USA were used to replenish domestic foreign-exchange reserves. By the end of the 1950s, most West European national banks, had sufficient dollars, but the US balance-of-payments deficit continued to pump money into the world economy (Schenk, 1998). Right up to today, the US is still running a deficit. These reserves, then, were accumulated in private banks and other financial institutions, where they were used for international transactions. Second, increasingly from the 1980s, restrictions on financial transactions were gradually relaxed. Western governments began to remove controls over financial markets, allowing foreign banks and other financial institutions to establish branches in, and to trade in each other's markets. The IMF also used its leverage in bailing countries out of financial crises to insist on deregulation in this area as well, spreading the area of liberalisation through Latin America, Asia and Africa (Stiglitz, 2000). Third, this was the era of increased speeds in international communications. If there is one sector of the economy that has been utterly transformed by increase in computer speeds and the transmission times through the internet, it is the financial markets. Computers are now programmed to track price movements and instructed to react instantaneously to price fluctuations with buying and selling orders. Indeed, so far has this developed, that major financial companies have powerful servers in close proximity to their offices to reduce speeds even further (and so steal an advantage over their competitors) (Sharma e.a., 2014). Finally, with all this cash available, with lax regulation (and even laxer supervision and virtually no enforcement) and with the means of almost instantaneous communication throughout the world, financial institutions devised new products to sell. And nowhere was this more apparent than in the market for derivatives (Caprio, 2013). The next question is to estimate the size of the international financial sector. Basically, we are dealing with very large numbers. These run into trillions - one thousand billion - and a billion is one thousand million. A trillion dollars looks like this: $1,000,000,000,000.

Bonds are fixed interest, fixed-term loans. The size of the international bond market (in other words, the total accumulated value of all bonds) at the end of 2013 stood at $22.8 trillion. Net issues (new issues minus matured and retired bonds) in 2013 were $0.5 trillion (BIS Statistical database 11A international debt securities – all issuers). At the end of 2013, the global value of equities on the main world stock markets stood at $64.2 trillion with a turnover within the year of $55 trillion (WFE 2014a). At the end of 2013 the total amount outstanding of (OTC over-the-counter) derivatives was $710.6 trillion. The market value of trades in one month (December) alone was $18.8 trillion, but the credit exposure was only $3 trillion (BIS Statistical database 19 Amount of OTC derivatives). The total annual turnover of nominal value of derivatives on official exchanges in 2013 was $2020.3 trillion (WFE/IOMA 2014) The problem here lies in the fact that what you pay for a derivative is only a small percentage of its (probable) future value. As a result, the actual money changing hands is much less than this. If we take the credit exposure and trade figures from December 2013, we get a deposit figure of 15 per cent (BIS 2013a, 10). One must remember that there are also unofficial transactions that escape the records. In 2012 the *Economist* reported their size as adding about 12 per cent to the total nominal value (Economist, 7.4.2012).

Data for foreign exchange transactions is available from the Bank of International Settlements, stretching back to 1989. In April 2013, the daily value of currency transactions stood at $5.3 trillion of which $2.2 trillion took the form of foreign exchange swaps, most of it for less than a week (BIS 2013b). If we multiply the figure by a conservative 350 (we can allow traders a few holidays) we obtain an annual value of transactions of $1855 trillion. Again, it could be argued that this is not really a true value of the transactions, since a large part of this activity is simply a swap, a like-for-like exchange. Nevertheless a dollar is not a euro, so the transaction does involve a transfer of ownership of a real asset.

## A Globalised World Economy

In trying to piece together the world economy, we face one big problem. All the components have been calculated in different ways and for different purposes and it is impossible to put them all together with any degree of accuracy. However, to say that we cannot say anything accurately does not mean that we cannot say anything at all.

Let us start with a base-line number. GDP, for all its shortcomings, is still the best measure we have for the output of goods and services in a society. Many economists express many other variables in terms of the relation to their size to a GDP data. In 2012, the world's GDP in current dollars was estimated as $72.2 trillion (World Bank database). As we have seen, the value of world trade in that year was $18.2 trillion, which would make its value equivalent to about 25 per cent of GDP. It is here, however, that we confront our first problem. When calculating GDP, the only part of a transaction that was counted was the value-added whereas in foreign trade statistics, the whole value is added every time. So, this is there is some degree of double-counting. If we adjust for that by reducing the trade figure by a fifth (see p 337) we arrive at an estimate closer to 20 per cent, but we must remember that none of the historical data available for comparison will have made a similar adjustment. Next, we can turn to FDI. Here there are probably all kinds of uncertainties, and my own guess is that the official data might tend to underestimate the reality. The reported statistics give a value of FDI in 2012 of $1.45 trillion, which would be equivalent to 2 per cent of GDP. Increasing the FDI estimate by 15-20 per cent would not change the fact that it seems relatively small.

Now we turn our attention away from the 'real economy' to the financial sector, starting with equities, stocks and shares. We have a total value $64.2 trillion and a trading volume of $55 trillion. However, foreign ownership is not likely to be large. If we assume that it is 10 per cent, it would give us an international trading figure of $5.5 trillion, equivalent to 7.6 per cent of GDP. Turning to bonds, we have a figure for the end year value of assets of internationally held bonds, which was $22.8 trillion. If we assume that the trading behaviour mirrors that of equities, then we could assume a trading volume of $19.5 trillion, or 27 per cent of GDP. For derivatives, we had a total turnover of the nominal value in 2013 of $2020.3 trillion. However, we noted that only the small down payment changed hands. How small is small? The official reports suggest that it is 15 per cent. If we use this as a base we arrive at a value of $300 trillion, which we should raise by 12 per cent to capture the unofficial trading (assuming the same pattern as that captured in 2012), giving a figure of $340 trillion. This is equivalent to 470 per cent of GDP. However, note that if anything does go wrong, then the investor can get stung for the whole sum. Finally, we arrive at foreign exchange transactions where we put a value of $1855 trillion which are equivalent to 25-times the value of GDP.

These numbers are mind–boggling, so let us try to put it in another context. Imagine that our GDP is a globe - that it is the planet Earth - and on top of that we start layering our globalisation components in the form of one hundred dollar bills, each 0.0124cms thick.[9] Let us run through our numbers again. FDI would reach 1,485 kms into space. This would be at the upper end of low Earth orbit, and already way beyond the International Space Station. Once we add foreign trade, the pile reaches 20,122 kms, which would put us at a level where most GPS satellites are parked. Then we have the financial sector. If we add to this the equities and the bonds, which buy ownership of assets or debts, we reach 45,722 kms into space.

---

[9] I have tried to re-locate where I first found this analogy but got no further than this statement, referring to 1998, "The daily trading on foreign exchange markets alone is US$ 2.0 trillion per day. Those numbers are almost beyond comprehension. A million one hundred dollar bills stacked one on top of the other would stand two metres tall. Two trillion one hundred dollar bills stacked one on top of the other would be forty times the height of Mount Everest" (Round, 2001).

Matters begin to get really interesting when we add an estimate for the payment (not the value) of contracts for derivatives and we reach almost 400,000 kilometres into space, passing the moon on our way. Then we add the follow exchange transactions, and we reach almost 2.3 million kilometres into space. We could easily get to the moon and back twice over and still have a small fortune left. If we had simply carried on, we would have left the moon far behind us and be on our way to Mars. Had we done this exercise in one dollar bills, we would have been there and back already.

What this exercise shows is that around the core of a globalised real world – buying and selling real goods and services and investing in real business – we have a much larger world of financial markets involving infinitely larger volumes of transactions. But where do we find these numbers in the GDP statistics? Remember that the calculations of GDP deal only with the 'value-added' to the stock of wealth generated by the economy. So, all these financial transactions appear in various national accounts as the labour costs and the profits generated by the financial services sector. In developed economies with large financial service sectors, like the Netherlands and the UK, this can account for up to 10 per cent of GDP. In the USA, the figure is a more modest 7 per cent. However, these figures also include the value-added by all the insurance, mortgage and banking services that we consume domestically.

To conclude, therefore, we are faced with a situation where transactions, exceeding in multiples what we deal with in the real world, that make only a modest contribution to a relatively small sector in relatively rich countries. We are dealing with massive volumes, for small margins, but entailing huge financial risks that affect the prosperity of us all.

## Summary

In this chapter we saw that the term 'globalisation' only entered academic discourse in 1984. The debate on the topic was polarised between the Hyperglobalists for whom it represented a real break with the past and posed a real challenge to the state, and the Sceptics and Transformationalists who argue that there was no trend-break and that states can still retain control. The chapter introduced and criticised the Globalisation Index that measures the openness of economies in trade and finance. The Index shows that in terms of both trade and FDI flows and restrictions, Europe led the rest of the world. It suggests that the world's openness to trade peaked in the 1870s and returned to (and surpassed) that level in the 1980s. The share of North-North trade in the world peaked in 1990.

Industrial tariffs of OECD countries averaged 2.8 per cent as opposed to 13.9 per cent in developing countries. The corresponding figures for agricultural were 13.9 and 9.5 per cent respectively. The greatest barriers to trade today are non-tariff barriers and transaction costs. The USA holds the largest stock of FDI in the world, but it is also the largest borrower.

The chapter showed that the volume of financial transactions eclipsed the size of international transaction in goods and services and FDI flows. Financial markets represented trade in bonds, equities, derivatives and foreign exchange transactions. Their growth had been fuelled by available foreign exchange, deregulation, improvements in electronic communications and innovations in banking practice. The value-added of financial markets reaches no more than ten per cent of the GNI of those advanced states (as the UK) specialising in this sector. The chapter warns that the weight of foot-loose capital and the risks that it poses for the whole world economy do weigh up against the benefits it is supposed to bring.

Where does control over the world economy lie? In the next chapter we examine this question by examining the role of international organisations in the field of regulating trade and finance, the role of cities, international business and transnational advocacy groups

# Case Study: Nick Leeson and the Barings Bank

The Barings Bank was established in London in 1762 by John and Francis Baring, second generation German immigrants whose family had earned their wealth in the wool trade. By the 1995 it had acquired a reputation for being a solid, safe, conservative bank. It had become England's oldest merchant bank, and it was the personal bank of Queen Elizabeth II. In that year, however, it went spectacularly bankrupt.

Being solid and a little dull meant that the Bank was missing out on the large profits made by other financial institutions during the postwar boom, and the increasing deregulation and globalisation of financial markets. In the 1980s, therefore, it created within the Bank a new organisation called *Barings Securities*. It started operations by investing in Japanese financial assets, linked to the value of the Japanese stock exchange. It was a high-volume, low margin business, but Barings Securities appeared to have secured for itself a nice-earning niche market. The operation soon garnered large profits, both from transactions and from the appreciation of the Yen, and afforded nice bonuses for the Bank's directors. When the success of the operations momentarily stalled, they simply replaced the head of the division and waited for the profits and bonuses to return (Greener, 2006).

In 1989 a young man, with only high school education and with only four years' experience as a clerk with banks, began working for Barings in London and quickly learned the business. His name was Nick Leeson and in 1992 he was sent to manage the new Singapore Office. Soon after his arrival, he obtained a trader's license and started trading on the Singapore Exchange. He was now managing the back-office (his original appointment) while also engaged in the front-office activities, making him is own controller. When larger-than-expected profits began to appear to the books, London was pleasantly surprised, and disinclined to probe deeper into their source. In 1995 Leeson's trading was responsible for 10 per cent of the bank's profits. He was twenty-five years old.

With profits and bonuses rising, both the directors and their 'star' trader became locked into keeping things that way. And a glitch in the computer package also helped to conceal what was going on in Singapore. The package proved incapable to handling the complex accounts and an 'error' account was created to park the leads and lags in the accounts. It was a technical solution and, over time, it was all supposed to balance, so London declared that it was not interested in seeing the 'balance of error' accounts (account number 99905). Leeson amended his package to create a parallel account which he called 88888 (eight being a lucky number in Singapore).

Nick Leeson traded in derivatives. He operated in futures, which involves trying to predict the value of shares at a date in the future. He could 'go long' whereby he would take an option to buy, and take delivery of shares at a fixed price at a date in the future. For the contract, he paid the equivalent of a small percentage of the price of the share. If, by the due date, the price of the share was higher than the contract, he collected the difference. Let us take an example. The shares in Firm-X were trading at $95 each and Leeson expected the price to rise. He took out a contract for $1,000 to buy 5,000 shares in one week's time. On the due date, the price had risen to $96.50

so he sold the contract and made a profit of $1.50 on each share – totaling $7,500 on an outlay of $1,000 (which is 650 per cent). If the price had failed to rise, he would not exercise the option and would forfeit the contract price. He could also have 'gone short' and gambled on a fall in prices, in which case he would sell shares now and enter a contract to repurchase them at lower price in the future. In this case, however, should the price fall even lower, the owner of the contract would exercise the option to sell at the price, even if the asset had become worthless. In this extreme example, the loss would be $95,000 (though Leeson would probably have taken measures to stem the losses before reaching that point). Because only relatively small deposits are involved, small changes in share prices can generate large percentage profits and losses. While these transactions were gestating, Leeson would park the asset in account 88888. It was also where he could hide any losses.

Leeson's trading strategy took this practice one step further. It is called a 'short straddle' and it involves betting on price changes in both directions for the same asset and at the same time. Let us return to the example. The shares are trading at $95 so he sells an option to sell 10,000 shares at $95 and sells a second option to buy 10,000 at $95, each costing $1,000. If the price stays at $95, neither the buying nor the seller will exercise the option and he will keep the $2,000. If, on the other hand, the price rises to $95.10 his customer will use the buy option to buy at $95 and he will have to secure the shares at $95.10 and so make a loss of $,10 on each share, totaling $1,000. He will however be able to keep the $1,000 from the buying, since the customer will be selling his own shares at the higher price. As long as the price fluctuations remain small, there seems to be little risk, but in order to make much money, you need large volumes. The problems start when price fluctuations are greater. Let us suppose that the price rises to $96.50. Nobody is going to sell to him for $95, so the price for that option contract remains as 'profit'. He is committed to selling shares at $95, which he has to buy at $96.50, losing him $15,000 (Stonham, 1996).

Whatever good fortune had smiled on his initial ventures seemed already to have deserted him. An external audit had discovered a gap of £50 million, but the Barings Board was disinclined to examine his flimsy excuses too closely and Leeson was allowed to continue trading. By now, he was trading in Japanese shares, using the short straddle strategy (or a variant called a 'short spread' which anticipated, and sought to profit from an upward or downward drift). Basically Leeson was betting that the Japanese exchange would show little volatility while continuing a modest recovery, and he was taking out very large contracts. Without anyone knowing, Leeson's accumulated losses had already climbed to just under $300 million. On January 17th, the city of Kobe (30kms from Osaka) was struck by the largest earthquake experienced in Japan since 1923. The stock market responded by beginning to fall, and it continued to fall, with scarcely a pause, for the next six months (not just because of the earthquake, but also fears of the effect of a rising Yen on Japanese exports). As Japanese share prices fell, so did the potential losses on Leeson's option positions. Instead of reining back the losses, Leeson did the reverse. He started 'doubling'. He had done it before 'with success' in 1993 and he was to do it again. Like a roulette player that has lost his stake on red, he doubles the stake next time, in the hope of recouping the losses (Brown and Steenbeek, 2001). By the end of January the losses approached $350 million. Fellow traders began to wonder how long this could continue. Bankers who had lent funds started to get nervous. The Board in London started to worry. And still, Leeson continued trading.

On February 23rd 1995 Leeson did not arrive for work. He left behind a note saying "I'm sorry". By the time auditors had unraveled the mess he had left behind, the losses had mounted to $1.4 billion. Barings Bank was bankrupt. It was later taken over by the Dutch bank ING for a symbolic amount of £1. Leeson was arrested and sentenced to six-and-a-half years imprisonment for fraud. He now lives in Ireland, and earns his income in the after-dinner speech circuit lecturing to bankers on complacency and the need for proper surveillance. He was both the symbol and the victim the 'casino capitalism' that accompanied the deregulation of financial markets in the 1980s.

# Chapter Eleven

# The Locus of Control

In the previous chapter, we examined the increasing internationalisation of the world economy. We suggested that while international trade and investment might have reached fresh heights relative to the scale of global output, the really significant change was in the area of financial services. These had boomed on the back of improved technologies of communication and the development of new instruments of credit and insurance. Hyperglobalist rhetoric suggests that national states are losing the ability to shape events against the remorseless pull exerted by the forces of globalisation. Without necessarily conceding this standpoint, this chapter will examine alternative sources of potential power capable of exercising some control over the international economy.

We will begin by looking at the principal institutions of global economic governance that were established in the shadow of the Second World War. Notwithstanding some considerable doubts at the time of their creation, these institutions had not only survived but have recorded some very real results, but in limited fields. The international trade system has reduced levels of world protection, but it still seems to satisfy neither rich nor poor. The international financial system has adapted to the business of crisis management, but has yet to prove itself effective as an agent of crisis avoidance. It is possible that institutions designed initially to pull states out of cycles of autarchy and protectionism might yet prove incapable of controlling the global forces responsible for (and yet threatening of) their security and prosperity. For if hyperglobalist rhetoric is to be believed, states are ready to be swept aside by remorseless march of globalisation.

If we look to the future for the locus of control, there are several possibilities. The first that we will examine are cities. Despite the popularity of the idea that global forces are somehow transient of national borders and national controls, every single business has some physical location down on Earth, and for many of those businesses that place is in a city. So we will be asking if cities, rather than states, should be the focus of attention in the future and even whether their bosses, rather than national governments, should be left in command of managing the world. After that, we will direct our attention at the role of business, acting individually or in consort, in formulating government policy, and see whether the spectre of a world managed and manipulated by big business is close to reality or a fear of delusional anti-global protestors. Finally, we will turn our attention to the "white knights", the NGOs and lobby groups that hold the world's conscience in their hands and who campaign remorselessly for the 'good causes' that we all espouse; all too often without success.

## International Organisations

The first truly international organisation was the International Telegraph Union, established in 1865 to establish common standards for international telegraph communications. Close on its heels came the General Postal Union created in 1874 to establish common rates for international postage, to ensure that post in one country would be delivered in another and to establish the precedent that the country in which the mail was posted would keep all the revenues. Both of these still exist today, under the umbrella of the UN. However, the roots of the current international order lie in the failure of international organisations in the inter-war years. After the end of the First World War the victorious allies had, in 1920, created the League of Nations. This was an international body designed primarily to guarantee peace and security by resolving international disputes by negotiation and arbitration. By the time the world collapsed into a Second World War, it was evident that the League had catastrophically failed to fulfil this aim. There were several reasons offered for its failure. First, the fact that the USA failed to join the organisation robbed it of some of its legitimacy and clout. On the other hand, given the fact that US policy was becoming increasingly isolationist anyway, it is difficult to say what difference its membership would have made to the course of events. Second, when countries considered that their (expansionist) national ambitions were threatened, they simply left the organisation. Germany did this in 1933, when the Nazi's came to power, Japan walked out the same year after the condemnation of its invasion of Manchuria and Italy abandoned the organisation in 1937 following its invasion of Abyssinia (Northedge, 1986).

Equally important but less well-known are the activities of the League of Nations in the field of economics. After the dismemberment of the Austro-Hungarian Empire after the First World War, the successor states adopted aggressive, protectionist trade policies to help recreate viable national economies. The League held a succession of conferences to bring down levels of import tariffs, all without success. After the Great Depression began to take hold, the League tried, again in vain, to halt the upward drift of restrictive trade measures, such as tariffs and quotas, as countries tried to isolate their national economies from the downwards global spiral. Following the devaluation of sterling, in 1931, it again tried (and failed) to discourage the manipulation of exchange-rates to secure national trade advantages. Finally, when a large international conference, designed to link all these issues, convened in London in 1933, collapsed without any result the League of Nations finally abandoned its ambitions in this direction. There were several reasons for this failure. First, there always seemed to be a problem about agreeing strategy towards tackling issues. At a slightly deeper level was the fact that the groundwork for discussions was never adequately prepared in advance. The League never had sufficient staff and, more important still, no one saw a need for more. League officials never saw it as their task to prepare detailed recommendations, partly because the League was reluctant to interfere with domestic policy matters. This reluctance to overstep some invisible line between commercial policies on the one hand and general economic policy on the other also contributed to an artificial compartmentalisation of problems; commercial policy was an integral part of economic policy as a whole, or was at least rapidly becoming so (League of Nations, 1942; Eichengreen and Uzan, 1990).

Among American policy-makers, surveying the collapse of collective security and the disintegration of the world economy, there was a general mind-set that linked the War directly to the Depression. The Depression had contributed to a rise of protectionism and behind these protectionist barriers, dictatorships had been able to emerge and this, in turn, had led to war. Post-war policy should be directed at avoiding any reoccurrence. One must also remember that the ruling Democrats, led by President Roosevelt, had already promoted wide-spread government intervention in the national economy, in the form of the New Deal, and were ready to employ the same approach to international problems. During the various meetings among the Allies held in the closing years of the War. President Roosevelt gave a high priority to the creation of a new world order – one to which the USA would be committed and one which would also include the Soviet Union (Ikenberry, 1992). The work was continued after his death. Anchoring the entire structure would be the United Nations. Its highest body would be the Security Council which would be primarily responsible to maintaining world peace. This is one aspect we will not be discussing in this lecture. Trade and employment issues would be entrusted to an International Trade Organisation (ITO). Monetary questions would fall under the remit of an International Monetary Fund. Problems of post-war reconstruction would be tackled by for two years by a UN Relief and Aid Administration, and when its mandate had lapsed, responsibility for promoting economic development would fall to an International Bank for Reconstruction and Development, commonly known as the World Bank (Schlesinger, 2009).

## Trade

If we turn first to the field of trade, it is important to realise that the initial American ambitions were far more ambitious than the eventual outcome. In 1947 the Economic and Social Committee of the UN convened an international conference on Trade and Employment in Havana. It is interesting to note that international trade was deliberately linked to the maintenance of domestic full-employment and the promotion of industrial development among poorer nations. The conference indeed reached an agreement on an ambitious programme for comprehensive rules governing tariffs, quotas, subsidies, state trading, cartels and international commodity agreements. Governing the whole structure was to be the ITO, with its own investigative arm and with policy decisions taken by majority voting. Fifty-three countries signed the agreement in March 1948. It was then that things started to go wrong. Although, for the Americans, the agreement had been negotiated by a Democrat Administration, Congress was under the control of the Republicans and was resentful about sacrificing such sweeping powers (especially its own powers) to an international organisation. As a result, the Administration held off from presenting the agreement for ratification, and as long as the USA was unwilling to ratify its own creation, everyone else waited, and waited. When the Republican President Eisenhower was elected, the plans for ratification were quietly forgotten (Diebold, 1952; Toye, 2003).

The ITO was never formed. Instead the world had to wait until 1995 for a permanent organisation to 'govern' world trade. Meanwhile, early in 1947 a provisional framework for agreeing tariffs had been negotiated and in January 1948 it came into effect for the twenty-three founding countries (Zeiler, 1999; McKenzie, 2008). The General Agreement on Tariffs and Trade (GATT) provided for non-discrimination among members and created procedures for negotiating tariff reductions and rules for the creation of free trade areas and customs unions. The tariff reductions are usually conducted in 'rounds' under what is called the 'principal supplier' rule. Basically what it involves is that the largest suppliers of goods will approach representatives of their main markets and ask for improved access in the form of lower tariffs, and they will make concessions in return. In this way a network of provisional bilateral agreements will be concluded among the major trading partners, and when these are folded into each other, their benefits will extend to all member states (regardless of their participation) under the non-discrimination principle (Hoda, 2001).

By the early 1960s the argument began to gain ground that developments in the 'terms of trade' (in other words, the failure of commodity prices to keep up with those in manufactured goods) meant that the less developed countries were losing out from the growth of international trade. The initial ITO had a mandate to tackle such problems, but the GATT did not. The underdeveloped countries responded by pressuring the UN to call a special conference on trade and development (UNCTAD) to discuss the problem. This met in Geneva in 1964. Aside from granting GATT members the opportunity to offer trade preferences to poorer countries and obtaining extra borrowing facilities from the IMF, the meeting agreed to establish UNCTAD as a standing conference, meeting every four years. After an early success in the creation of non-reciprocal preference arrangements for the poorest countries, UNCTAD conferences soon degenerated into confrontations between mutually antagonistic clubs of rich and poor, or North and South (Cox, 1979; Dell, 1984). Meanwhile, it was not as though GATT had failed. On the contrary, especially since the 1960s, it had contributed to a significant reduction in industrial tariffs, especially in the developed industrial countries of the world, and it has prevented any recourse to protectionism in times of crisis (Baccini and Kim, 2012). However, many problems persisted. Agricultural protection remained pervasive and import restrictions often remained in the sectors of textiles and electronics. Non-tariff barriers became more importance in trade policy. Trade preferences extended to poorer countries removed pressure on them to reduce tariffs. In addition, huge swathes of the economy, including purchases by governments and the whole service sector seemed to escape the pressure to become more open. Finally, trade disputes, especially between the USA and Europe and between the USA and Japan, were allowed to fester without resolve (Irwin, 1995).

It was partly because of these difficulties that the GATT was replaced by the World Trade Organisation (WTO) in 1995. One important change was to establish the WTO as a permanent organisation, with a permanent structure and a supervisory function. It also established a dispute-settlement mechanism with the possibility of imposing sanctions and penalties. It has been relatively underused, and the debate is still on-going whether simply having it as a threat might have made a difference. Finally the WTO's remit was extended to cover trade in services and trade-related implications of intellectual property rights (van Grasstek, 2013). Even so, the new organisation had problems, not least of which was the Doha Round of trade talks that started in 2001. The only result to have emerged was an agreement reached in Bali in December 2013 for a reduction in bureaucratic barriers to trade (Bellman, 2014). The Doha Round itself was finally concluded, without result, in December 2015. All the other questions bedevilling the GATT seem to have carried over into the WTO. Trade, and trade policy, still tends to be seen as separate from other concerns as employment, development and the environment.

Richard T. Griffiths

## Finance

Let us now turn to the institutions governing the international financial system. The basis was created in July 1944, when representatives from forty-four countries met at a resort hotel in New Hampshire called 'Bretton Woods'. The 'system' they created still bears the hotel's name. It was designed to prevent a recurrence of the problems that had bedevilled the 1930s. After the financial crisis of 1931, many countries had controlled access to foreign currency and this had allowed them to manipulate trade for political purposes (i.e. war). So, the first principle was the free convertibility of all currencies with each other. At the same time, the dollar was made convertible to gold at an exchange rate of $32 an ounce. In this way, all currencies were also linked to gold. The USA delegation was also obsessed by the phenomenon of 'competitive devaluations'. When the dollar devalued in 1933, sterling (which had earlier devalued in 1931) drifted downwards as well, so maintaining its competitive advantage. To avoid a repetition of this, the new system was to be based on fixed exchange rates. Parities were to be maintained within very small, and strictly defined, limits. Any deviation from them would only be allowed in exceptional circumstances. Finally, to prevent countries being forced to devalue because of speculation against their currencies, a fund – the IMF was established from which they could borrow. The Fund was financed by contributions from the member states (Boughton, 2002; Giovannini, 1993).

This was the system that managed the world economy until the early 1970s. And, in terms of managing exchange rates it seemed pretty successful, at least between the main trading currencies (the dollar, sterling and the main European currencies). After a large-scale realignment of exchange-rates in 1949, exchange rates remained remarkably stable.[10] However, the rules had never been fully implemented. First, all European countries had maintained currency controls, even on commercial transactions, until 1959 (Kaplan and Schleiminger, 1989) and controls over capital movements persisted until the 1980s. Second, from the early 1960s dollars began entering the system at a rate faster than central banks were willing to accumulate them. The cause of the dollar deficits were several (US inflation was higher than its competitors, the government was spending more than it raised in taxes, US firms were investing abroad etc.) but the effect was to allow to build-up of stateless capital in the hands of financial institutions (Bordo, 1993).

There is a concept in institutional economics called 'credible commitment' which means that markets will believe in a country's policies only when backed by measures which are consistent with them (North, 1993). Since American policies were not consistent with those necessary to maintain the exchange rate, speculation built up against the dollar. In 1971, the American government suspended convertibility and, a few months later, devalued the currency as part of a currency realignment similar to that of 1949. For a while, it looked as though the system might just hold together, but by 1973 most countries had let their currencies float against each other, and the regime of fixed exchange-rates came to an end. The only part of the system that remained was the IMF itself, intervening to help countries with foreign payments problems and supporting them to

---

[10] However, there were French devaluations in 1957 and 1958, a small German revaluation in 1961, sterling devaluation in 1967, a French devaluation and a German revaluation in 1969.

get back on their feet to a sustainable future (Garber, 1993). At least that is the 'official' version.

Critics of the Fund accuse it of protecting the interests of international finance (bankers and speculators) and of pushing the burden of readjustment onto the shoulders of those least able to bear it. What the IMF does when it offers financial assistance is to negotiate a deal with the creditors, insist that debtors stabilise their fiscal and monetary policy and it often also uses the opportunity to impose structural reforms. All of this involves some (temporary) surrender of sovereignty and that is generally resented, certainly when the conditions attached to the aid packages are painful. The IMF is seen as undemocratic and bullying, and seems itself to be unaccountable (Klein 2007). On the other hand, time is not usually a luxury in crisis situations, and financial crises are no exception. The criticism is sharper when it extends to the measures imposed. In almost every crisis, government expenditure is too high, and so too is the level of inflation. The correction, however, is painful. The criticism is often that the IMF's measures are too fast and too severe and that the downward pressure placed on the real economy actually impairs recovery; a criticism, for example, that is levelled at the measures imposed on Greece. A further criticism is that some of the measures imposed go further than those necessary to restore equilibrium, but impinge on a country's freedom to choose its own development strategies. The Fund's pro-market policies often demand the sale of public assets and reforms in tax and subsidy structures (Featherstone, 2014).

# Evaluation

In Chapters Five, Six and Seven of this book we focused on the triangle: fragmentation, governance and trust. It is worth pausing to reflect that the international community is more fragmented than any national society could be. Its membership differs vastly in economic size, in population size and military might. Its communication is conducted in a myriad of tongues. Its cultures have been shaped by thousands of years of history (often a shared history, but not always on the same side). Its citizens pray to different gods, and their days-to-day existence ranges from obscene luxury to dire, abject poverty. So what, we should ask, is the role of international governance? Why do international organisations survive at all? Can they make a difference and, if so, for whom?

Standing in the aftermath of the death and destruction of the Second World War, it was difficult to be optimistic on the future of the myriad of organisations created under the umbrella of the UN. The dominant paradigm of political scientists at the time was a belief termed 'realism'. This argued that the world was in a state of almost permanent anarchy and the only guiding principle for states must be the promotion of their own national interest. International organisations would exist only for as long as they did not interfere with the pursuit of national interest and as long as they provided some service towards that goal. The expectation was that that would not be for long. Yet, they still survive today (Cozette, 2008; Williams, 2004). At this stage, the 'realists' modified their position and became 'neo-'(or 'new') realists. They now argued that international organisations had survived because they did convey real benefits. One tangible benefit was information. At a minimum they provided a regular check on what other parties were thinking, or saying. A second benefit was that they provided a regular forum for interaction. Organisations existed, with rules, procedures, agendas and meeting places, and all of this was much easier than having to start afresh every time (Schweller and Priess, 1997). A third benefit worth mentioning is that international organisations often provided a system for monitoring whether agreements were kept. If one party in an agreement reneges on its obligations, then it often undermines the commitment of others, and this monitoring is best done by a 'neutral' third party than by the parties involved (Jervis, 1999). A final benefit was that international organisations were predictable and, for the larger parties, controllable (Schweller and Priess, 1997).

This control of UN bodies was exercised through the privileged position secured for themselves by the richer Western nations. In the Security Council of the UN, the larger powers made sure that they were permanently represented and that they had a veto. The USA and Europe happily controlled the top positions in the World Bank and the IMF. Moroever, if that were not enough, the voting rules were fixed to ensure that they would always have a sympathetic majority. In the IMF, for example, the USA controls 16.75 per cent of the votes, the EU collectively represents another 29.69 per cent. Other friendly powers controlled a further 11.75 per cent. The chances of being outvoted were remote. The BRICS, for example, collectively control 11.03 per cent (IMF Site). In the World Bank, the BRICS control 13.17 per cent of the votes (WTO Site) and it would take a large upscaling of their contributions to make any impact on its policies (Lane and Maeland, 2011). This fact alone might help explain why in 2014 they created their own development bank (Lam, 2014).

This pretty minimalist view of international organisations was challenged from several angles. There were those who argued that collaborative behaviour could actual operate for the benefit of all, creating win-win situations. Benefits did not have to be obtained at each step in a series of one-off games. Depending on the range of issues, it was possible to benefit from 'diffuse reciprocity' (gains and benefits further down the line) and this, in turn, would help to create compliant behaviour (Grieco, 1988). Another argument was that statesmen have actually grown to like international organisations. At a basic level, it allows them to strut on the World stage, and raise their profile against domestic contenders for power. They also provide the possibility for 'agenda-setting' allowing policy-makers to raise the stakes in an essentially domestic matter, that might otherwise face difficulties in passing through domestic legislatures, by making it part of a larger, international set of decisions (Gourevitch, 1978; Putnam, 1988). A good example of this was Marshall Aid, which was transformed from an expensive way of getting rid of American stockpiles of food and raw materials into an aid programme to help establish a free world and protect it from the encroachments of Communism. Others argued that continuous participation in organisations could socialise its members. The benefits of this process ran in two directions. Some emphasised how officials working together to solve problems, would extend that experience to other problems they faced, and advocate similar solutions, a line of thinking known as 'neo-functionalism' (Schmitter, 2004). On the other hand, working together also facilitated the production of a coherent, shared framework of discourse and observed behaviour. This could even help contribute towards policy change within an organisation, independent of the direction of the participating countries (Wendt, 1992; Chwieroth, 2014), although member states could always block this at a later stage.

This picture of shared rituals, experience and discourse is one we recognised when we were looking at issues of trust and governance on a national scale, and it is an attractive one. It suggests a community of high-minded diplomats working together to solve common problems. But are they? Or is this a veneer over a system whose dynamics lie elsewhere? Is the system in the process of becoming atomised and returning to a situation of 'anarchy', but at a level below the state? Alternatively, is the system empowered by movements of money, and controlled by those who hold access to most of it? Or is it not controlled by anyone at all?

## Metropoles and Cities

Cities have a good record in economic history. They have proved to be centres of learning and innovation where different streams of science and logic meet and merge, and where the dead-hand of social control is at its lightest. Merchant cities were particularly valued in this respect (on pre-industrial city networks see Taylor, 2012). The decision by China, for example, to close its cities off from foreign trade and foreign contacts in 15th century has been seen by some historians as a major factor in the origins of the 'great divergence' between China and the West (for a review of the debate see Broadberry, 2013). The city states of Renaissance Italy, the merchant towns of the Low Countries, and the industrial cities of the UK, Europe and the USA drove forward the innovations that made today's world. But not all cities have been successful in the past. The ruins of the great ancient city Kingdoms of the Middle East and of Asia bear testimony to flowering of art and culture, but all were bled dry as the institutions of the ruling elite sucked in the available capital and resources for purposes of luxury and adornment.

Today, half the world's population live in towns and cities and together they produce over 80 per cent of the world's GDP. However, this power is concentrated in the bigger cities. The top 600 cities in the world account for 22 per cent of the world's population, but are responsible for 60 per cent of the world's GDP. At the moment, the most productive of these are in the 'developed world' and its 380 city regions located there contributed 50 per cent to world GDP. The relative size of the world's largest cities in terms of GDP is shown in the Figure 11.1a below. Tokyo, in Japan, is by far the largest metropolitan urban area in the world. With a total income of over $1500 billion, its economy rivals that of the whole of Australia. Asia occupies eight places in the top twenty and this is but the tip of a development that is being characterised by the emergece of large urban conurbations in China, India and Latin America. The twenty-three megacities (with populations of more than 10 million) are together responsible for 14 per cent of the world's GDP. Of these, sixteen are located in the developing world. However, it is also interesting that it is not the mega-cities that contribute most to world growth in recent years, but the group below immediately them (Dobbs e.a., 2011). A somewhat different picture emerges if we look not at the total size but at the relative prosperity of these cities. These are also shown in Figure 11.1a with a list led by Zurich where every man, woman and child generates an average income of over $82,000 a year.

Figure 11.1a: World Top-20 cities by GDP

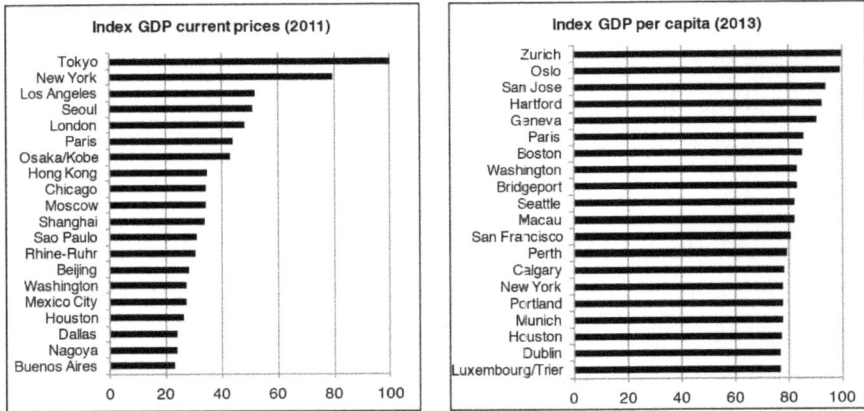

Cities are big, but that does not explain the dynamic of what makes them important. In his classic book, *The Competitive Advantage of Nations* (1990) Michael Porter emphasised the importance of agglomerations or clusters of skills and activities in providing firms with 'externalities' (such as shared pools of skilled labour) and reduced 'transaction costs' (the costs of obtaining information and concluding transactions). Cities, especially big cities, are the real spaces where all the transactions in this whirling globalised, internationalised world eventually come to rest. And these transactions extend into the social and cultural spheres. Cities are where things happen. There are over 150 surveys in the world that attempt to identify the dynamics of cities. Only a few attempt to capture a city in its totality[11] and it will be no surprise to discover that they disagree in what to measure in its rankings and the weight given to different factors (Moonen and Clark, 2013).

---

[11] Some try just to capture certain facets of urban development. The most common are the quality of life (29), business environment (25), infrastructure and real estate (19).

The idea of the creative soup that makes up major cities is best captured by the Global Cities Index which analyses 84 of the world cities. It is a composite index that allocates 30 per cent of the weighting each to 'business activity'and 'human capital', 15 per cent each to 'information exchange' and 'cultural experience' and the remaining 10 per cent to 'political engagement'. At first sight the overall composition may seem reasonable, but the individual components could be questioned. For example, there is no effort to incorporate city GDP into the business activity component or R&D expenditure into human capital. In fact the entire data collection assembled to measure 'human capital' seems pretty tangential to the concept. Moreover, there is no mention of internet access or transport links under information exchange. Finally, one could question the weightings. Given what is included under 'information exchange' is it not perhaps overweighted in comparison with 'political engagement', and does the cultural experience really justify its 15 per cent contribution to the whole? (ATKearney, 2015) Despite its shortcomings, the Global Cities Index[12], is the best available. The results for the top-30 are shown in the Figure 11.1b. It is interesting that slightly under two-thirds overlaps with the global cities defined by GDP. One should also note that below the very top, the rankings are very sensitive to changes in the weights of the individual components.

---

[12] There is one other up–and–coming index that is being used by social scientists and that is the Global Power City Index created by the Mori Memorial Foundation Institute in Japan. It has six components – economy, R&D, cultural interaction, liveability, ecology and environment and accessibility – but it fails to stipulate publically their relative weightings. Moreover its analysis rests on a pre-selection of 40 cities, chosen to represent all regions, and this is a fatal disadvantage in any truly comparative analysis (MMF, 2014).

Figure 11.1b: World Top-20 cities. Composite Indices

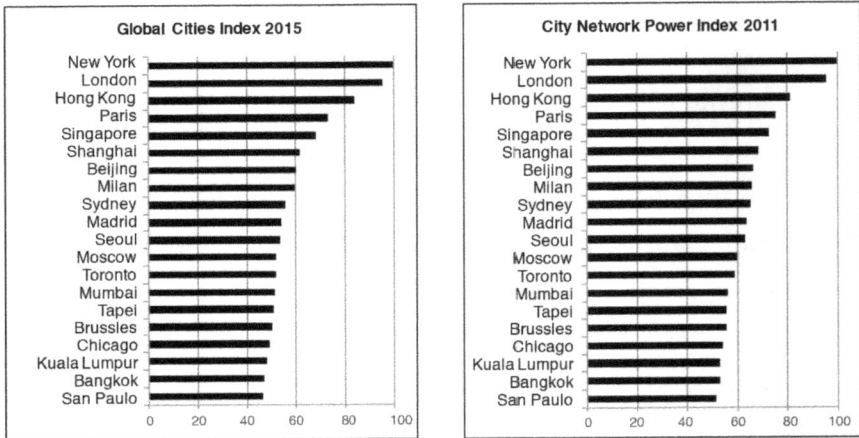

The fact that cities have the potential to be, or to become, global cities says nothing about their place in a growing and shifting world economy. For years Peter Taylor has been a pioneer in documenting and quantifying the interconnectivity of cities. He and his associates see the world economy as one composed of three interlocking networks – the international flows of goods and services (that we have analysed in Chapter Ten), the interconnection of cities in which the production of goods and services are located and the 'service' firms that provide the conduits through which the cities are interconnected. These 'advanced service providers' are the agents for interconnectivity, and have also become the object of the Taylor's analysis. What his team have done is to identify the offices and affiliates of global service firms and to record their size and location. They took the 75 financial service sector firms (banking, finance and insurance) and the top 25 firms in each of five service sectors – accountancy, advertising, law and management consultancy and media. Each office is with a score for its importance (head-office down to a minor local office) and for the relative size of the firm. On this basis they calculated a city network power, which measures not only the size of the firms but also their global reach. The calculations are made for fifty cities, but only the top-30 of which are also shown in the Figure 11.1b. Because of the importance attached to spatial dimensions of the index, the poorer countries are better represented than if the analysis had remained purely focused on size (Taylor e.a., 2011). The network is illustrated in Figure 11.2 below in which the circle size corresponds to the number of firms located in individual cities and the width and shade of the lines correspond to the proportional strength of economic contacts. The dominance of the NewYork–London nexus comes across clearly (Liu e.a., 2014).

Figure 11.2: The Inter-city Corporate Network 2010

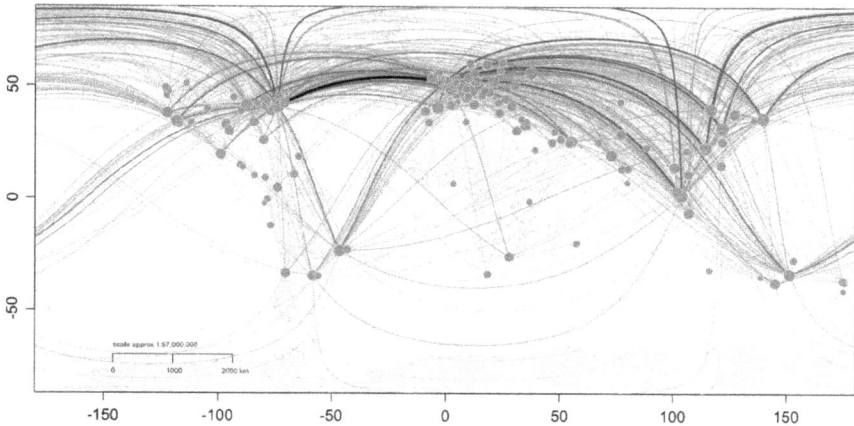

Source: Liu, e.a., 2014.

Not only are cities becoming more interdependent, they are also becoming more democratic, with local elections, local councils and local mayors. And unlike the sleepy small-town image of local government (I speak from a UK viewpoint here) cities authorities have to act, if only to prevent the entire conurbation from seizing-up. The leaders of big-cities are beginning to become well-known and popular, attracting public support and legitimacy. In *The Size of Nations*, Alesina and Spolaore (2003) describe a tension between the scale of governance and its legitimacy. Big nations can do more things more efficiently, goes the logic, but local entities identify less with it. National citizenship is remote and abstract compared with the concerns with day-to-day existence in our neighbourhoods and workplaces. Are cities, then, the optimal size of states in a globalised world?

In his new book *If Mayors ruled the World* (2013) Benjamin Barber argues that cities are the motors for change, that they are closer than national governments to their citizens, that they do not have hang-ups about borders and sovereignty and that, therefore, the world would be better-off it were ruled by mayors. It would allow citizens to participate locally and cooperate globally, and to replace the defunct top-down system presided over by states. Cities are already starting to establish the beginnings of a foreign policy whereby they collaborate and compete with each other. A good example of collaboration is the C40 City Initiative for climate change (started with 40 cities but with a current membership of 63) whose aim is to share experiences in lowering greenhouse gas emissions. And Barber lists over thirty other trans-border collaborative networks, all with permanent secretariats and head-quarters. Such collaborative action, he claims, is already starting to accomplish that which states, in their international negotiating frameworks, are failing to achieve (Barber 2013). But - there is always a 'but' - many of the city examples he cites, such as Delhi and Rio de Janiero, are not really such as to make citizens rub their eyes with wonder, and some of the mayors that he adulates are not particularly noted for their concerns with citizens' rights and welfare. Other questions also arise. Are cities any more capable of controlling world events than states? Do they, any more than the governments they are supposed to supersede, have the financial resources to withstand waves of speculation from edgy financial markets? Do they have the capacities to control international movements of illegal goods and criminal activities? Are they any more immune from corruption and cronyism than the states where they are presently located? And is a world of city-states today any less predisposed towards protectionist tendencies and petty quarrels than were their counterpart in the fifteenth and sixteenth centuries?

## Big Business

Economic activities may take place in cities and connect through networks of facilitators, but a business still remains a business, each with its own structure and its own interests. International business, however, in the form of multinational corporations (MNCs) are in a class of their own. These can be defined as enterprises with assets (presumably productive assets) in more than one country. This means that within one single business structure or organisation they have to coordinate their activities in more than one country. In this book, we have already met them briefly when talking about poverty in Chapter Four. There we saw how their proponents argued that they brought scarce capital into a country and that with that capital came technology, employment and income. We even saw their proponents argue that they could help foster good and responsible governance. So how have they obtained such a fearsome reputation in some left-wing circles?

We can start to answer the question by returning to the definition – MNCs coordinate activities in different countries within a single business structure. This means that their business strategy is determined centrally, at headquarters, regardless of the needs of individual countries or the consequences of their decisions for those countries. Whilst the opening of a new branch is usually welcomed by a country, its closure within the context of a 'global reorganisation' is usually seen as callous and capricious. MNCs also determine their own prices, including the prices MNCs charge themselves for goods and services transferred within the organisation. This allows them to manipulate the countries in which profits appear and, therefore, where they pay their taxes (Sikka and Willmott, 2010; Davies e.a., 2014). The fact that firms are doing nothing illegal, but are using the opportunities offered by same differences tax regimes that make 'tax havens' possible does little to assuage public concern. In 2012, for example, it appeared that Starbucks had recorded sales of over £3billion in the UK since 1998, and had paid only £8.3 million UK taxes. This had not only annoyed the UK tax authorities, but had caught the attention of the European Commission (Guardian, 11.6.2014). But possibly the biggest problem is simply that multinationals are also big; very big. You may have read, for example, that Walmart (the largest multinational when measured in terms of turnover) is as big as Belgium. This is not strictly true since it is spurious to compare the total revenues of Walmart with the value-added within Belgium, but it conveys the idea. In fact, when examined in some years ago, in terms of value added Walmart was about as big as Pakistan, but smaller than 43 countries ranked higher (De Grauwe and Camerman, 2002). In the year 2000 the total revenues of the Top-200 approached the equivalent of 27.5 per cent of world GDP (Anderson and Cavanagh, 2000) and all the evidence suggests that their share has since grown even higher. Multinational companies also control a sizeable part of the international economy. According to the UNCTAD database, in 2010 there were over 103,000 multinationals in the world, 70 per cent based in one of the richer economies. Together they controlled 892,000 foreign affiliates, 58 per cent of them located in less developed countries. In 2013 they controlled 80 per cent of global value chain (i.e. world trade after elimination of double-counting), about half of that representing trade within multinationals themselves (which shows the capacity they have for manipulating transfer pricing) (UNCTAD, 2013).

The fact that MNCs command considerable resources, and that they have a range of plausible alternative locations, helps place them in a strong position when dealing with national governments. It is true that the bargaining strength of MNCs varies according to the nature of the firms (high-tech or resource based) and the nature of the host country (developed or less developed) and even the government to government bargaining that might have preceded any agreement (Bakir 2015). Nonetheless, their size and flexibility often enables MNCs to extract a range of concessions (often kept secret) from governments in the form of tax exemptions and waivers of legal requirements. In addition, MNCs regularly use their funds and expertise to influence government legislation and regulation through lobbying. This is effective because they can marshal resources beyond the capacities of national and local groups. They also use campaign financing to assist the election of favourable governments. Moreover, if officials and elites are corrupt, guess who it is who is paying the bribes. Finally, MNCs also have an unhappy history of assisting in the overthrow of governments they do not like. A survey of over 100 years of American foreign policy showed that the USA had organised the overthrow of foreign governments no less than 14 times, often at the instigation of MNCs or in defence of their interests (Kinzer, 2006). Meanwhile, the British governments attempts since the 1920s to reshape the Middle East to best reflect UK oil interests is unravelling, for all to see.

To see how large corporations try to influence governments, let us turn first to the USA which is the home of more MNCs than any other country in the world. One way in which firms can try to determine outcomes is to influence the complexion of the legislature by trying to get candidates who are sympathetic to their cause elected to influential posts, or trying to get candidates elected who are sufficiently compliant to repay the favour by viewing their cause sympathetically. In both cases campaign funding serves as an entry point for future lobbying activity with the favoured candidate. In the American electoral campaign contributions are restricted to $5,000 a candidate but that does not prevent firms from creating, and supporting Political Action Committees (PACs). This all assumes that firms, and even directors within firms, are in agreement over the political colour of the candidates they support. An analysis of the individual behaviour of corporate executives and board members of the top *Fortune-500* companies shows that during the 2012 campaign no less than 83 per cent of their number made political contributions and they tended to lean towards the Republicans (like most American middle-ages white males). They rarely switched sides, and would be more likely to reflect their coolness towards 'their' presidential candidate by withholding funds (Bonica, 2013)

A survey of firms' PAC and lobbying behaviour in the USA suggests that larger firms spend more on lobbying than smaller firms (no surprises there!) but also that firms that do get involved in election campaigns are also more likely to engage in lobbying activity and to spend more on lobbying than those that did not get involved in the first place (Hill e.a., 2013). However, in the USA campaign funding is not the main path to influence, at least when measured in terms of expenditure. Over the 2011/2012 election cycle PACs and other organisations spent an average of $750 million a year. By contrast expenditure on lobbying at the federal level alone was $3.5 billion annually (De Figueiredo and Richter, 2013).

The *Centre for Responsible Politics* has collated all the materials submitted to the Senate Office of Public Records to obtain a picture of corporate lobbying in the USA. The amounts spent annually have risen from $1.45 billion in 1998 to $3.24 billion in 2013. The data is broken into 120 industries, but the twenty most active in 2013 together accounted for 63.5 per cent of total expenditure on lobbying in the entire country. Given the polarised political situation surrounding health-care it is not surprising to find five of the sectors involved in this big–spenders list. With an expenditure of $630 million, they accounted for one fifth of the total expenditure.

One important question is whether all this expenditure actually produces results. This, of course depends on the object of the exercise and on the external institutional constraints that exist. Looking at lobbyists' intentions one could assume that it is important whether they are trying to achieve a one-off concession within an existing legislative framework (a clause in a trade agreement, a piece of tax legislation or work and safety legislation) or whether they are trying to shape the legislative environment itself. In the first case there is an immediate and identifiable pay-off in what is really a series of repeated 'games' within a familiar context. By contrast the second case offers the chance to shape the 'rules-of-the-game'. This may help explain why various branches directly involved in US healthcare have been so active of late. Firms may also lobby (competitively) if the government is also the customer for its products, which is clearly the case of the defence industry but also the firms providing medical equipment and prescription medicines. Getting empirical results on the impact of lobbying is beset by difficulties – how to isolate the lobbyists' goals, how to define 'success', how to isolate the lobbying effort from other possible causal variables and, finally, how to obtain the necessary data (De Figueiredo and Richter, 2013).

We can view another angle on how MNCs exercise influence by turning our attention to the EU. The EU may only spend one per cent of their members' GDP, but it is widely described as being responsible for 90 per cent of the legislation. However, policy is not made exclusively in Brussels. It is made by the national governments and the European Parliament, agreeing together, and the European Commission, which prepares and presents the legislation. So, if a firm wants to influence policy it should approach all three institutions, preferably simultaneously. At first sight the easiest to influence is the national government – through the national press, through the political parties and through the members of national parliaments. But, by itself, this route is the least likely to bring rewards since there are still twenty-seven other states to get on-side. A better way is for the firm to approach the officials in the European Commission and get the bits that it wants (the levels of chemicals permitted, the banned substances, the safety stipulations, the exact concessions in a trade deal) all slotted into the proposal before it is even published. At the same time, it could tackle the European Parliaments specialist committees, established to examine fields of legislation. The Parliament tends to vote in 'party blocs', so win one or two of those over and the legislation is home and dry (Beyers and Kerremans, 2012; Dür and Mateo, 2012; Greenwood, 2013, 23-52).

There are 30,000 lobbyists active in Brussels (Guardian 8.5.2014). A body called *Corporate Europe Observatory* tries to keep an eye on their activities. And the European Commission, responsible for the formulation of legislative proposals, works particularly closely with the business lobby. The Directorate in charge of trade negotiations (active right now, for example, in negotiating trade deals with India and the USA) works especially closely with big business. This obviously offers advantages to business. For example, it is no coincidence that the EU's proposals of legislative cooperation in the Trade and Investment agreement with the USA (giving industry wide powers to establish rules in finance, food labelling and environmental standards) mirrors the plans articulated by *BusinessEurope* and the US Chamber of Commerce. Again, on the question of improving 'competitiveness' (which involves reducing labour protection) the Commission has held joint consultations with the European Round Table of Industrialists, resulting in the creation of a Franco-German working group chaired by two of its members (Corporate Europe Observatory, 2014). A more direct way to influence EU policy is to obtain representation on one or more of the 778 'Commission expert groups'. At first sight, these seem to be under the grip of national governments, whose representatives occupy 61 per cent of the total number of seats available. The distribution of the remainder shows little evidence of a pro-business bias. Not surprisingly, interest groups with larger financial resources and more staff do seem to obtain representation in more expert groups (but it is difficult to say in which direction the causation runs) and it is difficult to say how this spread of influence could be translated into depth (Chalmers, 2014).

The picture changes when we stop looking at how broadly a sector is represented or at how many seats an organisation manages to 'capture', and look instead at the composition of the expert-groups themselves, especially at some of the more important ones. For example, in the Directorate for Tax and Customs, responsible for customs duties and direct and indirect taxation, no less than 79 per cent of the seats in expert groups are occupied by corporate interests compared with three per cent for 'small and medium enterprises' (SME). A similar picture emerges in the Directorate for DG Enterprise and Industry that operates the internal market, sets environmental and emissions standards and is responsible for space and satellite activities. There 62 per cent of the experts are from corporate interests, compared with three per cent from SMEs. Finally the Secretariat-General looks at debt redemption, business regulation and deregulation and also sets the agenda for the Commission's work draws 64 per cent of its experts from corporate interests as opposed to eight per cent from SMEs. Even this picture is misleading since many supposedly 'independent' academics are tied in some way to corporate interests. Moreover, in all these areas trade unions and civic advocacy groups are seriously under-represented (ALTER-EU, 2013). To this mixture we can add well-paid firms of lobbyists offering 'briefing papers' to members of the European Parliament, and trying to maintain links with those involved in scrutinising different types of legislation. And if we then top this with the fact that monetary policy, settled by the European Central Bank in Frankfurt, is also under the sway and influence of financial interests, we can see that we have a serious problem of 'institutional capture' at the centre of EU decision-making.

One question we still have to resolve is the extent to which, if any, these firms operate together. We already know that many of them are combined in trade associations that campaign and lobby jointly at all levels of decision-making. Recent research, however, has allowed us to dig deeper. One line of research has been into the interconnectivity of memberships of the Executive Boards of corporate enterprises, in other words the extent to which top business executives are represented on each other's Board of Directors. It has recently been demonstrated that the phenomenon of interlocking board memberships has been expanding in Europe, to the extent that it has begun eclipsing in importance the more traditional trans-Atlantic connections. Within this group, international financial corporations were over-represented, acting as the glue that binds the network together. The core of the network could be best described as one of industrialists with financial connections (Carroll e.a., 2010). A more recent study based on Europe's top 300 firms (by share value) has shown that even in the five years between 2005 and 2010, despite the impact of the financial crisis, the network has increased in size and cohesion. By 2010, slightly over 90 per cent of these firms were connected with each other. Slightly under 40 per cent of the firms were connected in this way to others of the group located outside their own borders. The core of this network spans the industrial heartland of Continental Europe, with France the most dominant country. Germany was only modestly engaged in cross border connectivity which is surprising given the size of its economy and the importance of its manufacturing sector (Heemskerk, 2013).

It is not known how far this Board overlap represents the creation of a pan-European (capitalist) class, far less whether it contributes to the exercise of more powerful, concerted pressure on governments. It is, however, surely disingenuous to suggest that this is unlikely simply because an analysis of (recorded) cartels reveals 'very few' cases where the colluding companies had previously been connected through interlocking directorates (Buch-Hansen, and Levallois, 2015). On the other hand, not only did major European firms engage in executive interlocks, they were also represented in a club called the *European Round Table* (ERT) Of the fifty or so members, no less than 37 would have met each other in one or more of the Boards of the largest European firms. The ERT is a network created by European industrialists and its membership is still dominated by industry and services, rather than finance. According to its own website (2014) brings together some fifty executives from European multinationals, with a combined turnover of over € 1,300 billion, and employing 6.8 million people in Europe alone (Farnsworth, 2005). It is doubtful that they they meet each other to compare golf handicaps over a cup of tea. Meanwhile, the bankers and financiers are having fun elsewhere.

If European firms create formal and informal means of cooperation and influence, the next logical question is whether large and powerful multinational corporations are doing something similar on a global scale. These factors have to be considered when looking at the balance of power in any dealings with governments, international organisations or NGOs. But are we justified in seeing them as a common force, beyond, of course, the Marxist categorisation of them all as 'capitalists' or is this just the fantasy of conspiracy theorists? Part of the answer to this conundrum is offered by an interesting piece of research conducted by the Swiss Federal Institute of Technology, not a body normally associated with this kind of research. The researchers are 'complex-system theorists' who use advanced mathematics to model natural phenomena. Their results have been endorsed by the influential *'New Scientist'* (Coghlan and MacKenzie, 2011). What the Zurich scientists did was to plunder a database of 37 million worldwide companies and investors called the *Orbis* database and extract from it the details of 43,000 multinational corporations. They then looked for patterns of ownership among them, and uncovered over one million 'ownership ties'. These they then linked to their size (expressed in terms of operating revenue) and calculated a 'network of control' (in terms of share ownership) over the network as a whole. As we saw above, the network of multinational corporations make up a sizeable chunk of world trade and production.

Their analysis managed to isolate a group of 737 companies that controlled 80 per cent of the revenues of network. Within that group they located a 'core' of 147 'super-entities' that controlled almost 40 per cent of the network, and which was virtually exclusively controlled or owned, within itself[13]. In this elite core, 79 per cent of corporations were active in the financial sector and they were responsible for 93 per cent of the revenues of the core group. American and British-based firms together accounted for over half of the revenues of these core corporations. The wider group of 737 companies, controlling 80 per cent of the network was more diverse. Financial corporations represented 35 per cent of the group's total,

---

[13] Note that this core is identified by its interdependence and impenetrability and not by their relative or absolute size. In fact the largest 94 enterprises already 'controlled' half the network.

but they were responsible for slightly over 66 per cent of its revenues (Vitali e.a., 2011 supplemented by details supplied by the authors).

Given the explosive nature of these revelations, it is surprising that they have not been more widely debated in academic and policy circles. The world is characterised by an enormous concentration of control over its wealth and activities in the hands of a super-elite of institutions, but the 'control' is one of ownership. The crucial question is how far and how often it is used. Ownership of shares conveys voting rights, but financial institutions do not usually attempt to influence the strategic direction of companies in which they have invested. There is no evidence that they do operate in concert, but the domination of financial institutions among them may lead to a preponderance of 'share-holder value' rather than long-term viability in their thinking and dealings, and a certain uniformity of their message in dealings with governments. Whereas they may compete against each other in the market-place, they will surely combine in their own defence against any systemic attack on their position. And, finally, we have already seen the nature of connectivity the financial meltdown of 2008/9. Here it is, laid out before us. If things go wrong again at the core, the impact will indeed be truly global.

## Transnational Advocacy Groups

Juxtaposed against this corporate world we have civic society, organised at various levels – local, national and international. Some of these provide goods and services to the communities they serve, others act as spokespersons for specific interest and some do both. Many are also organised at all three levels, with their peak organization operating at the regional or international level. In total there are about 25,000 international non-governmental organisations in the world, and in this section we will concentrate on those espousing a specific cause or interest. In the literature they have become known as 'transnational advocacy groups'. Some are professional groups (teachers, lawyers, accountants etc.) but many represent major societal interests. Several of these are extremely well-known. For example Human Rights Watch and Amnesty International are active in the human rights field; Oxfam and Save-the-Children deal with humanitarian issues, Green Peace and Friends of the Earth represent environmental concerns. Acting at an international level, they are able to bring larger resources than could be mobilised domestically to the aid of citizens in national states (for example in the fields of environment and human rights) and in this way, just as international business has been doing, they too are blurring the frontiers of national sovereignty (Keck and Sikkink, 1998, 1999). They are a long way, however, from forming a cohesive network – a global form of civic society similar in nature, if not (yet) in power, to the corporate networks. Leaving aside the difficulties in establishing cross-issue alliances, there are often considerable asymmetries in resources within international networks, for example between North and South. Moreover they often differ in their priorities. Northern environmental groups often have ideological or political goals that are not shared by developing nations, and poorer countries have different priorities, such as a greater concern for basic environmental protection of air and water quality than with carbon emissions. In addition, many groups in developing countries are wary of becoming dependent clients of their richer partners and even the scent that they are becoming so may actually undermine their effectiveness in advocacy of local causes (Rohrschneider and Dalton, 2002). Rather than being a reflection of the health of international civic society, the proliferation of transnational advocacy groups on a particular issue may serve to increase competition, uncertainty and insecurity for all (Cooley and Ron, 2002). Faced with a relative paucity of material resources, advocacy groups often try to alter the framework within which an issue is being discussed. These 'framing' tactics include disseminating information, engaging in symbolic actions, mobilising more powerful actors and calling businesses and governments to account on the basis of vague policies and principles they have previously endorsed. In this way they try to construct a coherent internal story which will help shift the political frame of the debate. The intention is to transform an appeal from the margins into a central part of the political culture (Keck and Sikkink, 1998, 1999).

The power of the peoples' voice against organised big-business is a popular image. But what factors determine the success of advocacy groups? Obviously, this depends not only on their own organisational ability and strategy, but also on the permeability of the body they are trying to influence and the organisation, strength and tenacity of the influence groups ranked against them. In the case where they are pitched against corporate interests, transnational advocacy groups face a double imbalance. There is often an imbalance in the resources (in terms of funding, access and expertise) that can be mobilised by an advocacy group compared with those mobilised by organised big-business. For example, a study on the USA published about a decade ago revealed that, at a federal level, corporations and trade associations represented 84 per cent of total lobbing expenditure while 'ideology membership groups' represented only two per cent. At the state level the situation was scarcely any better. Expenditure at corporations and trade associations there represented 86 per cent of payment for lobbyists while ideology membership groups accounted for seven per cent (De Figueiredo and Kim, 2004). But there is a second imbalance, and that is the importance of the issue for the two parties. Here we do not mean the advocacy group itself (the issue is always very important to them) but the citizens' interest that they claim to represent.

Let me take a simple example. Several years ago I worked on the question why, when almost all economists condemned the common agricultural policy of the EU as illogical, inefficient and counterproductive, the policy seemed so resistant to change. One thing to emerge was that the farmers' lobby was extremely well-organised at both the national level (where many had been active since the agricultural crisis of the 1880s) and at the international level. Of all the interest groups, they were the most active, bombarding governments and parliaments with policy advice at both national and European levels. They were far more active (and probably far better resourced) than the consumer groups lobbying against them. But why was this so? This led me to look a little further. The GATT had calculated that in the 1970s and 80s over half of farmers' incomes were derived from 'producer subsidy equivalents' (but note that the impact of American and Japanese support measures were also high). No wonder they were so active. On the other hand the extra burden imposed by these measures on consumers, as a percentage of their expenditures was far, far smaller. Not only had the proportion of 'food' in consumers budgets been falling for the past thirty years, but the proposition of farm–gate prices (what the farmer received) in the final market price (when the product had been transported, processed, packages and arranged neatly in a convenient shop) was also relatively small (Griffiths, 2002).

The sad fact is that, for all the justification for the cause adopted by an advocacy group, it does not usually impact immediately on the life of a citizen. This is the same whether it is the price of butter, the tortured cries of a prisoner in a god-forsaken gaol, the starving child at the other end of a television documentary or that little bit of extra carbon footprint that the car journey to the shops involved. So much less, therefore, is the public concerned by the additives in foods, the exact safety standard or the legal responsibility of banks. For corporate interests, on the other hand, these questions do matter. They matter a lot. They immediately show up on balance sheets, on profit and loss accounts and on share-holder value. And they will use all channels – the regular contacts with national officials as well as special pleadings with relevant ministers and decision-makers – to be heard. Corporate interest groups have deep reserves of patience and deep pockets of cash.

The other fact is that the status quo usually wins. This is because change almost always has budgetary implications and this involves reallocations of material resources. Whatever the initial argument, the decision will often turn on the question of real costs against potential risks. Moreover, the existing policy is likely to reflect the power balance that brought it about in the first place, and this is unlikely to have changed significantly. Much professional lobbying activity therefore is directed at obtaining marginal adjustment to existing policy. On the other hand, this does not mean that policy change is at best incremental. Often, when there is change, it can be dramatic. This suggests that sometimes a 'frictional' or 'crisis' model of change might be more appropriate, rather like tectonic plates absorbing pressures until a quake becomes inevitable, at least with hind-sight. This prospect of large opportunities holds the focus of transnational advocacy groups, even if the probability of change occurring is low (Baumgartner e.a., 2009).

On the other hand, transnational groups have difficulties in maintaining focus. Many advocacy groups have overlapping, and competing ambitions. Not for nothing did I give two examples for each of the three fields we mentioned. However, the fragmentation goes far deeper. In as far as these advocacy groups rely upon citizens' support; this is more easily obtained if the issue has some popular resonance and if it is addressed in a proper cultural context. The result is the emergence of what have been called 'maps of grievance' where different groups identify with different causes, or different slivers of causes. Local (and regional) advocacy groups, therefore, tend to compete with existing transnational groups, squeezing resources and blurring focus (Schwenger e.a., 2013). The challenge of advocacy groups is agenda-setting. They need to raise the level of consciousness on an issue so as to galvanise a larger constituency and, more difficult still, they need to keep it there. One of the problems, apart from capturing citizens' attention in the first place, is the so-called free rider problem. It is difficult to sustain interest when any positive achievements are shared by society whether citizens have even thought about an issue, let alone joined or helped fund any such group. Equally, advocacy groups are also immobilised by those who simply do not care. Although this group may be invisible, they usually form an important component of the electorate and weigh heavily on the perception of elected officials (Baumgartner e.a., 2009: 74-77).

# Summary

This chapter began by examining why international organisations, led by the League of Nations, proved unable to check nationalist tendencies between the wars. It saw how after the Second World War the USA led the movement to recreate a global order based upon the UN and its affiliates. After the failure of the ITO, the management of trade fell under the remit of the GATT, which was the agent for large reductions of tariffs. The international monetary system, based on the IMF, maintained a regime of fixed-exchange rates until the 1970s. Since then it has acted as a lender of last resort. Despite original scepticism, international organisations have survived because they offer states advantages in their dealings with each other.

The chapter then looked at other possible agents of control. It observed that cities are becoming the locus of world production because they reap the benefits of agglomeration and encourage creativity. However, cities are unlikely to replace states as agents for international cooperation.

International business is another possible agent of control. MNCs have great flexibility in their choice to locate in different countries. They also spent a great deal of effort and money to increase their span of influence. US firms spend huge sums on sponsoring and lobbying. Evidence from the EU shows how firms trying to influence legislation target the European Commission, which does little to prevent them from dominating key expert groups. EU evidence also shows a high degree of board-room interlocks, which could be (but need not be) the base of concerted action.

Finally, research from investigators in Zurich shows a high degree of mutual share ownership among MNCs, whereby the assets of 80 per cent of the largest multinationals are 'controlled' by 737 companies, with only 147 'controlling' 40 per cent. However, the chapter questioned the degree to which these activities actually constitute control.

Finally, the chapter reviewed the position of transnational advocacy groups. They face a double imbalance: a relative paucity of resources and a relative low issue salience. They also confront decision-makers predisposed to maintaining the status quo. Research suggests that when changes do occur, these can sometimes be very significant, resembling tectonic plate shifts rather than incremental changes.

# Case Study: Goldman Sachs and the Fed

Goldman Sachs is the third largest investment bank in the world and sits among the top-20 of the 147 'super entities' that we have already discussed. As an investment bank, it advises clients, including corporations and governments on their financial transactions, and it engages in buying and selling of financial instruments on its own account. Left alone, there is no telling what it could do from this powerful and privileged position. For example, it could sell-off dubious credit instruments before the public caught wind and lost confidence. It could help national governments conceal their true level of indebtedness from international regulators. It could collude with other banks in manipulating exchange rates or lend a helping hand to raise the price of aluminium in glutted world markets. It is a good job, therefore, that a regulatory agency exists in the form of the 'Fed' – in this case the Federal Reserve Bank of New York (FRBNY) – which is charged with the task of supervising the banks in the state of New York, including the large 'Wall Street' banks like Goldman Sachs. It regularly checks the operations of the banks under its remit, to control their soundness and, therefore, the soundness of the banking system as a whole. Occasionally, something goes a little wrong.

In September 2008 Lehmann Brothers filed for bankruptcy. At the time, it was the fourth largest investment bank in the USA, and its collapse triggered a credit constriction that plunged the world economy into its worst crisis since the Wall Street crash of 1929. Several years earlier Lehmann had acquired five mortgage companies and, with house prices booming, it looked a good investment. However, in 2007 the property boom seemed over, and the number of mortgage defaults began to rise. Lehmann attempted to correct for its over-exposure, but too little and too late. By September investor confidence had evaporated and with Lehmann hemorrhaging money faster than it could raise more on credit markets, bankruptcy was inevitable. The bank had been overstretched and overexposed. But this was exactly what the supervisory function of the Fed had been intended to prevent.

The FRBNY was conscious of its failings in the Lehmann case, and it was also aware that its supervisory reach would have to extend beyond single institutions and into the entire interlocking system of financial institutions, if it were to prevent a similar crash in the future. To help reform its management procedures, it commissioned a confidential report led by David Beim of Colombia Business School. The Report was leaked (FRBNY, 2009). Its findings were damning. Although the Fed had observed potential problems before the crash, it had not acted upon them. This was partly because the upper echelons of the management had held too simple a faith in the self-correcting power of markets and had been insufficiently alert to the interconnectivity of the system. However, in addition, the management culture within the Fed had been too deferential to the hierarchy in its own structure and too chummy with the institutions it had been supposed to be supervising. There had been a fear of confrontation, a culture of consensus and a distinct lack of initiative and responsibility within the organisation. The report transformed all these findings into recommendations and urged the Fed to use these new insights to guide it in the hiring of staff. "Much has been done well during the crisis and much has been learned" the Report concluded, "The good parts are those where cooperation and frank debate have occurred, where people have taken the risk of speaking out and taking responsibility. The bad parts are those where information hoarding, excessive deference and risk aversion have prevailed."

How had the Fed adapted to the new regime? In October 2011 the Fed hired an experienced lawyer, well-acquainted with big banks and the financial sector, called Carmen Segarra and added her to the team supervising the activities of Goldman Sachs. The Fed team actually operates from a set of offices in the Goldman Sachs Building itself, so that maintaining distance and independence is even more essential. Segarra became so alarmed at what was happening that she started secretly recording meetings and conversations with which she was involved. Seven months later she was sacked. So now, in addition to a report we were not supposed to read, we have tapes of meetings we were not supposed to hear. What had triggered Segerra's concern in the first place was when a Goldman staff member suggested that, above a certain size, clients (presumably like itself) deserved special treatment. Instead of vigorously rebutting the suggestion, embarrassed Fed officials tried to pretend that it had not been meant. Later, her immediate supervisor pressured her to soften the tone of her minutes of meetings she had attended. In January, under the cover of a national holiday in Spain, she observed Goldman undertaking a deal on behalf of the Spanish Banco Santander that allowed it to manipulate its reported exposure (indebtedness) for the EU bank regulators. Although Goldman had agreed to obtain the Fed's approval before undertaking any such deal, they had failed to do so. Yet, instead of pursuing the matter, the Fed officials confined themselves to a solitary comment, not even a reprimand. The motivation, apparently, was 'not to discourage' Goldman from disclosing information in the future. This supine attitude towards the banks had been one of issues highlighted in Professor Beim's report. Another issue was a disagreement with Segarra's boss over whether to state in some minutes that Goldman had no 'conflict of interest policy', as Segarra insisted, or whether to muffle the observation under some more ambiguous form of words. Although Segarra eventually gave way on the point, the Fed summarily dismissed her for insubordination.

Throughout the World, government institutions like the FRBNY are supposed to be protecting us from a systemic bank collapse in the future. Yet they seem incapable of doing the job effectively. All the possible things mentioned in the first paragraph that a bank could do were it not properly supervised are, in fact, charges that have been levied at Goldman Sachs since 2008.

# Final Reflections

This has been a complex book, touching on a wide range of issues. However there are some underlying themes that go beyond the materials I have been able to deal with in the chapters and case studies. In these final pages I want to discuss some of the wider implications of the book.

We live in a society that uses numbers for the simple reason that they express more gradations between variables than is possible using words. For example, simply by using simple percentage differences between the best performer and the rest allows one hundred positions; putting one number after the point extends the range to a thousand. We cannot uninvent numbers, but we can try to understand them, and what lies behind their construction. In fact, we should do so. Matters as happiness and misery, faith or agnosticism cannot be captured in simple numbers, and neither can trust, governance or democracy. All composite numbers contain implicit value-judgements by those who invent them, and selection criteria and data manipulation by those who compile them. Thus the first lesson of the book is to exercise a healthy degree of scepticism when presented with such data, and if you intend to use it, to find out what exactly it involves. Indeed, unwrapping numbers into their component parts often reveals insights that become lost when they have been compressed to express the single number to enter into some statistical analysis.

The fact that numbers are not perfect does not mean that they are not useful. They contain different margins of error but they often still provide 'ball park' figures of the reality they claim to represent. However statistics are not homogeneous and not all data series have the same quality throughout. Generally, you can assume that the poorer the country, the fewer resources it can devote to data collection and the less reliable will be the outcome. Equally, the further back in time the source of the statistic is, the less trustworthy it will be. This means, for example, that any analysis of income differentials involving poorer countries must necessarily be suspect, and any analysis of poorer countries involving economic growth, which by definition must employ earlier statistics, are more suspect still. Unfortunately, this is where so much important work needs to be done. Thus the second lesson of the book is to exercise a degree of caution when statistics are used to explain differences between developing countries. The book has also given several examples to dent one's faith in statistics of more developed countries as well.

Even if we conclude that we cannot prove that a causal relationship exists between two or more variables, this does not mean that it is not there. Much of the literature employing more advanced statistical methods tends to be impenetrable for ordinary readers, and this tends to impart an aura of 'scientific accuracy' to their conclusions. The third lesson of the book, therefore, is a simple one. You should never suspend your own judgement when confronting demonstrations of statistical relationships. Leaving aside the quality of the data, not all explanatory variables lend themselves easily to quantification and few models succeed in capturing the complexity of the interrelation between economic, political and societal variables.

The fourth lesson of the book might be a little unexpected. The book has been fairly critical of the 'trust' literature. However, it still carries the message that trust is central to the functioning of society and the economy upon which it depends. Moreover, trust and good governance are inextricably intertwined and together they can render differences in ethnicity, language or religion irrelevant for the development of a country as a whole.

The fifth lesson is that government, even big government is not bad. Markets do not float to Earth from thin air; they require good and effective governance to function. It is surely no coincidence that the world maps in the book (and the evidence in the databases) show clusters of medium sized countries with welfarist policies and relatively big budgets near the head of almost every international ranking, including those based on the suspect trust data. They are rich, peaceful, happy, healthy, well-educated, efficient and competitive. Hyperglobalist rhetoric would have them as the losers from globalisation.

The sixth lesson that we can draw as the book moves towards its close is that within the global economic system there are potentially dangerous and destabilising concentrations of economic and political power. At present there are few countervailing forces to constrain their action. The answer does not lie in a retreat into cynicism. Good governance depends on political processes and the active involvement of citizens. It also requires trust, which in turn depends on the active engagement of citizens in the daily concerns and activities of those around them.

Finally, good governance requires an informed and critical citizenry, immune from the blandishments of popularist politicians and the pseudo-science that backs many of their claims. If this book helps contribute to that end, it will have served its purpose.

# Bibliography

Acht, M., Omar Mahmoud, T. and Thiele, R. (2014) *Corrupt Governments Receive Less Bilateral Aid: Governance and the Delivery of Foreign Aid Through Non-Government Actors* (No. 1901). Kiel Institute for the World Economy, Working Paper, 1901, Kiel.

Afful-Dadzie, E., Afful-Dadzie, A. and Oplatková, Z.K. (2014) "Measuring progress of the millennium development goals: A fuzzy comprehensive evaluation approach", *Applied Artificial Intelligence*, *28, 1,* 1-15.

Al-Momani, M. (2011) "The Arab 'Youth Quake': Implications on Democratization and Stability", *Middle East Law and Governance*, 3, 1-2, 159 -170.

Albrow, M. (1996). *Global Age, State and Society beyond Modernity*, Cambridge, Ma.

Alesina, A. and Dollar, D. (2000) "Who Gives Foreign Aid toWhom and Why?", *Journal of Economic Growth*, 5, 1, 33-63.

Alesina, A., Devleeschauwer, A., Easterly, W., Kurlat, S. and Wacziarg, R. (2003) "Fractionalization", *Journal of Economic Growth*, 8, 2, 155-194.

Alesina, A. and La Ferrara, E. (2004). *Ethnic Diversity and Economic Performance.* National Bureau of Economic Research Working Paper 10313, Cambridge, Ma.

Alesina, A. and Spolaore, E. (2003) *The Size of Nations*, Cambridge, Ma.

Alesina, A. and Zhuravskaya, E. (2008) *Segregation and the quality of government in a cross-section of countries*, National Bureau of Economic Research Working Paper No14316., Cambridge, Ma.

A later expanded but unpublished version is on the Harvard University website http://scholar.harvard.edu/alesina/files/segregationandthequalityofgovern mentinacross-sectionofcountries.pdf

Alexander, C. (2003) *The Bounty: The true story of the mutiny on the Bounty*, New York.

Alkire, S. and Santos, M.E (2010) *Acute Multidimensional Poverty: A New Index for Developing Countries*, Oxford Poverty and Human Development Initiative Working Paper 38, Oxford.

Allum, N., Patulny, R., Read, S., & Sturgis, P. (2010) "Re-Evaluating the Links between Social Trust, Institutional Trust and Civic Association" In

J. Stillwell, P. Norman, C. Thomas and P. Surridge (eds.) *Spatial and Social Disparities*, Dordrecht, 199-215.

Alston, P. (2005) "Richard Lillich memorial lecture: promoting the accountability of members of the new UN Human Rights Council", *Journal of Transnational Law and* Policy, 15, 49-96.

Alter-EU (2013) *A Year of Broken Promises. Big business still put in charge of EU Expert Groups, despite commitment to reform*, Brussels.

Anckar, D (2010) "Small is Democratic: But who is small?", *Arts and Social Science Journal*, 2, 1-10.

Anderson, B.A. (2002) "Russia faces depopulation? Dynamics of population decline", *Population and Environment*, 23, 5, 437-464.

Anderson, J.E. and van Wincoop, E. (2004) "Trade Costs", *Journal of Economic Literature*, 42, 3, 691-751.

Anderson, L. (2011) "Demystifying the Arab Spring: parsing the differences between Tunisia, Egypt, and Libya", *Foreign Affairs*, 90, 2, 2-7.

Anderson, S. and Cavanagh, J. (2010) *Top 200: The Rise of Corporate Global Power*, Institute of Policy Studies, Washington, DC.

Apostoaie, M.C. (2011) "Measuring Economic Globalization – Facts and Figures", *The Annals of The "Ştefan cel Mare" University of Suceava*, 11, 2(14), 99-109.

Armstrong, H.W. and Read, R. (2002) "The phantom of liberty?: economic growth and the vulnerability of small states", *Journal of International Development*, 14, 4, 435-458.

Armstrong, H.W. and Read, R. (2003) "Microstates and subnational regions: Mutual industrial policy lessons", *International Regional Science Review*, 26, 1, 117-141.

Arndt, C. and Oman, C. (2006) *Uses and Abuses of Governance Indicators*, Paris.

Arnold, F., Kishor, S. and Roy, T.K. (2002) "Sex-Selective Abortions in India", *Population and Development Review*, 28, 4, 759-785.

Arruda de Almeida, M. and Zagaris, B. (2015) "Political Capture in the Petrobus Corruption Scandal: The Sad Tale of an Oil Giant" *Fletcher Forum for World Affairs*, 39, 1, 87-99.

AT Kearney (2015) *Global Cities 2015: The Race Accelerates*, Amsterdam.

Atkins, J.P., Mazzi, S.A. and Easter C.D. (2000). *Commonwealth Vulnerability Index for Developing Countries*. Commonwealth Secretariat Economic Paper, 40, London

Australian Bureau of Statistics (2012) *2940.0 - Census of Population and Housing - Details of Undercount, 2011.* Canberra.

Axford, B. (2007). "In at the death? Reflections on Justin Rosenberg's 'Post-mortem'on globalization", *Globalizations*, 4, 2, 171-191.

Baccini, L. and Kim, S.Y. (2012) "Preventing protectionism: International institutions and trade policy", *The Review of International Organizations*, 7, 4, 369-398.

Bakir, C. (2015) "Bargaining with Multinationals: Why State Capacity Matters", *New Political Economy*, 20, 1, 63-84.

Bakker, G.P den (1992) *Origin and Development of the Dutch National Accounts*, Paper presented at 22[th] General Conference of the International Association for Research in Income and Wealth, Flims, Switzerland, August 30 - September 5, 1992.

Balaam D.N. and Veseth, M (1996) *Introduction to International Political Economy*, New Jersey.

Baldacchino, G. and Bertram, G (2009). "The Beak of the Finch: Insights into the Economic Development of Small Economies", *The Round Table: Commonwealth Journal of International Affairs*, 98, 401, 141-160.

Barber, B (2013), *If Mayors Ruled the World: Dysfunctional Nations, Rising Cities*, New Haven, CT.

Barro, R. J. and McCleary, R. (2003) "Religion and Economic Growth across countries", *American Sociological Review*, 68, 5, 760-781.

Barron, A. (2011) "Exploring national culture's consequences on international business lobbying", *Journal of World Business*, 46, 3, 320-327.

Baumgartner, F.R., Berry, J.M., Hojnacki, M., Kimball, D.C. and Leech, B.L. (2009) *Lobbying and Policy Change: Who Wins, Who Loses, and Why*. Chicago, Ill.

Becker, A.C. (1994) "Intelligence fiasco or reasoned accounting? CIA estimates of Soviet GNP", *Post-Soviet Affairs*, 10, 4, 291-329.

Bebbington, A., Guggenheim, S., Olson, E., and Woolcock, M. (2004) "Exploring Social Capital Debates at the World Bank", *Journal of Development Studies*, 40, 5, 33-64.

Becker, G. S. (2009) *Human Capital: A Theoretical and Empirical Analysis, with Special Reference To Education*, Chicago Ill.

Bednarik, R. and Filipova, L. (2009) *The Role of Religion and Political Regime for Human Capital and Economic Development*. MPRA Paper 14556, Munich.

Bellmann, C. (2014) "The Bali Agreement: Implications for Development and the WTO", *International Development Policy| Revue internationale de politique de développement*, 5, 2.

Berg, J., Dickhaut, J. and McCabe, K. (1995) "Trust, Reciprocity, and Social History", *Games and Economic Behavior*, 10, 1, 122-142.

Berggren, N. and Bjørnskov, C. (2009*). Does Religiosity Promote or Discourage Social Trust? Evidence from Cross-Country and Cross-State Comparisons*. Paper presented at the social dimensions of religion in civil society at Ersta Sköndal University College in Stockholm, October.

413

Berggren, N. and Bjørnskov, C. (2011) "Is the Importance of Religion in Daily Life Related to Social Trust? Cross–Country and Cross-State Comparisons", *Journal of Economic Behavior and Organization*, 80, 3, 459-480.

Berry, C. (2008) *International political economy, the globalisation debate and the analysis of globalisation discourse.* University of Warwick CSGR Working Paper 247/08, Coventry.

Berryman, P. (1987), *Liberation Theology*, New York.

Bettendorf, L. and Dijkgraaf, E. (2010) "Religion and Income: Heterogeneity between Countries", *Journal of Economic Behavior and Organization*, 74, 1, 12-29.

Beyers, J. and Kerremans, B. (2012). Domestic embeddedness and the dynamics of multilevel venue shopping in four EU member states. *Governance*, 25, 2, 263-290

BIS (2013a) *Macroeconomic impact assessment of OTC derivatives regulatory reforms*, Basel.

BIS (2013b) *Triennial Central Bank Survey Foreign Exchange turnover in 2013*, Basel.

Bishop, M.L. (2012). "The political economy of small states: Enduring vulnerability", *Review of International Political Economy*, 19, 5, 942-960.

Bjørnskov, C. (2007) "Determinants of Generalized Trust: A Cross-country Comparison", *Public Choice*, 130, 1-2, 1-21.

Blonigen, B.A. (2005) "A Review of the Empirical Literature on FDI Determinants", *Atlantic Economic Journal*, 33, 4, 383–40.

Blonigen, B.A. and Piger, J. (2011) *Determinants of Foreign Direct Investment*, National Bureau of Economic Research Working paper, 16704, Cambridge, Ma.

Blundell, R., Dearden, L., Meghir, C. and Sianesi, B. (1999) "Human Capital Investment: The Returns from Education and Training to the Individual, the Firm and the Economy", *Fiscal Studies*, 20, 1, 1-23.

Boda, Z., & Medve Bálint, G. (2012) "Intézményi bizalom Európa régi és új demokráciáiban" *Politikatudományi Szemle*, 2, 27-51. (English language summary here http://bit.ly/OV8PrG.)

Boehmke, F.J., Gailmard, S. and Patty, J.W. (2013) "Business as usual: interest group access and representation across policy-making venues", *Journal of Public Policy*, 33, 1, 3-33.

Boggs, C. (2001) "Social Capital and Political Fantasy: Robert Putnam's Bowling Alone", *Theory and Society*, 30, 2, 281-297.

Bolt, J. and Zanden, J.L. van (2013) *The First Update of the Maddison Project; Re-Estimating Growth Before 1820*. Maddison-Project Working Paper WP-4, Groningen.

Bolt, J. and J. L. van Zanden (2014). "The Maddison Project: collaborative research on historical national accounts", *The Economic History Review*, 67 (3): 627–651.

Bonica, A. (2013). *Avenues of Influence: On the Political Expenditures of Corporations and Their Directors and Executives.* Available at Social Science Research Network 2313232.

Booysen, F. (2002) "An Overview and Evaluation of Composite Indices of Development", *Social Indicators Research*, 59, 2, 115-151.

Borchert, I., Gootiiz, B. and Mattoo, A. (2014) "Policy barriers to international trade in services: evidence from a new database", *The World Bank Economic Review*, 28, 1, 162-188.

Bordo, M. D. "The Bretton Woods International Monetary System: A Historical Overview", in M.D. Bordo and B. Eichengreen (eds) *A Retrospective on the Bretton Woods System, Lessons for International Monetary Reform*, Chicago Ill.

Bos, F. (2008) *Uses of National Accounts; History, International Standardization and Applications in the Netherlands*, MPRA Paper No. 9387, Munich.

Botero, J.C. and Ponce, A. (2010) *Measuring the Rule of Law*, World Justice Project Working Paper 1, Washington DC.

Boughton, J.M. (2002) "Why White, Not Keynes? Inventing the Post-War International Monetary System" in A. Arie and W. Young (eds.) *The Open Economy Macromodel: Past, Present and Future*, Boston, Mass., 73-102.

Brau, J.C. and Woller, G. M. (2004) "Microfinance: A comprehensive review of the existing literature", *Journal of Entrepreneurial Finance*, 9, 1, 1-27.

Breeding, M. (2012) "India-Gulf Migration: Corruption and Capacity in Regulating Recruitment Agencies" in M. Kamrava and Z. Babar (eds.), *Migrant Labor in the Persian Gulf*, London, 137-156.

Bresson F and Duclod, J-Y (2014) *More on multidimensional, intertemporal and chronic poverty orderings*

Brewster, K L. and Rindfuss, R.R. (2000) "Fertility and Women's Employment in Industrialized Nations", *Annual Review of Sociology*, 26, 271-296.

Broadberry, S. (2013) *Accounting for the Great Divergence*, Economic History Working Papers, 184/2013, London School of Economics and Political Science, London.

Brock, C. and Crossley, M. (2013) "Revisiting scale, comparative research and education in small states", *Comparative Education*, 49, 3, 388-403.

Brookings Institute (2014) *Global MetroMonitor An Uncertain Recovery* 20/14,Washington, DC.

Brown, S.J. and Steenbeek, O.E. (2001) "Doubling: Nick Leeson's trading strategy" *Pacific Basin Finance Journal*, 9, 2, 83-99.

Bruff, I. (2005) "Making Sense of The Globalisation Debate when Engaging in Political Economy Analysis", *The British Journal of Politics & International Relations*, 7, 2, 261-280.

Buch-Hansen, H.L. and Levallois, C. (2015) "The Scale and Geography of Collusion in the European Market: A Longitudinal View", *Journal of Common Market Studies*, 53, 4, 737-752.

Bueger, C. and Bethke, F. (2014) "Actor-networking the 'failed state'- an enquiry into the life of concepts", *Journal of International Relations and Development*, 17, 1, 30-60.

Burnside, C. and Dollar, D. (2000) "Aid, policies, and growth", *American Economic Review*, 90, 4, 847–68.

Burnside, C. and Dollar, D. (2004) *Aid, Policies, and Growth: Revisiting the Evidence*, World Bank, Policy Research Paper O-2834, Washington, DC.


Caldwell, J.C. (2006) *Demographic transition theory*. London.

Caldwell, J.C. and Schindlmayr, T. (2003) "Explanations of the fertility crisis in modern societies: A search for commonalities", *Population Studies*, 57, 3, 241-263.

Campante, F.R. and Char, D. (2012) "Why was the Arab World Poised for Revolution? Schooling, Economic Opportunities, and the Arab Spring", *Journal of Economic Perspectives*, 26, 2, 167-187.

Carroll, W.K., Fennema, M. and Heemskerx, E.M. (2010) "Constituting Corporate Europe: A Study of Elite Social Organization", *Antipode*, 42, 4, 811-843.

Caprio, G. (2013) *Financial Regulation After the Crisis: How Did We Get Here, and How Do We Get Out?* LSE Financial Markets Group Special Paper Series, Special Paper 226, London.

Cariolle, J. and Goujon, M. (2013) *A Retrospective Economic Vulnerability Index, 1990-2011using the 2012 UN-CDP definitions*, FERDi Working Paper, 17, Clermont-Ferrand.

Caselli, M. (2012) *Trying to Measure Globalization: Experiences, critical issues and perspectives*, Dordrecht.

Cassen R., e.a. (1986, 1995) *Does Aid Work? Report to an Intergovernmental Task Force,* Oxford.

Castells, M. (1996) *The Network Society*. London.

Cavalcanti, T.V., Mohaddes, K and Raissi, M. (2012). *Commodity Price Volatility and the Sources of Growth*, IMF Working Paper WP/12/12, New York.

Centraal Bureau voor de Statistiek and Sociaal en Cultureel Planbureau (2013), *Armoedesignalement 2013*, The Hague

Chalmers, A. W. (2014) "Getting a Seat at the Table: Capital, Capture and Expert Groups in the European Union" *West European Politics*, 37(5), 976-992.

Chandra, K. and Wilkinson, S. (2008) "Measuring the Effect of 'Ethnicity'", *Comparative Political Studies*, 41, 4/5, 151-563.

Chase-Dunn, C., Kawano, Y. and Brewer, B.D. (2000) "Trade globalization since 1795: Waves of integration in the world-system", *American Sociological Review*, 65, 1, 77-95.

Chaudhuri, A. (2011) "Sustaining Cooperation in Laboratory Public Goods Experiments: A Selective Survey of the Literature", *Experimental Economics*, 14, 1, 47-83.

Cingano, F. (2014) *Trends in Income Inequality and its Impact on Economic Growth*, OECD Social, Employment and Migration Working Papers, 163, Paris.

Chowdhury, A. (2009) *Microfinance as a poverty reduction tool—A critical assessment.* United Nations: Department of Economic and Social Affairs (DESA) Working Paper, 89, New York.

Chwieroth, J.M. (2014) "Controlling Capital: The International Monetary Fund and Transformative Incremental Change from Within International Organisations", *New Political Economy*, 19, 3, 445-469.

Clemens, M.A., Kenny, C.J., & Moss, T.J. (2007) "The Trouble with the MDGs: Confronting Expectations of Aid and Development success", *World Development*, 35, 5, 735-751.

Clemens, M. A., Radelet, S., Bhavnani, R. R. and Bazzi, S. (2012) "Counting Chickens when They Hatch: Timing and The Effects of Aid on Growth", *The Economic Journal*, 122, 561, 590-617.

Coase, R.H. (1937) "The Nature of the Firm", *Economica*, 16, 4, 386-405.

Cocuzza, M. and Esteves S.C (2014) "Shedding light on the controversy surrounding the temporal decline in human sperm counts: A systematic review", *The Scientific World Journal*, Article ID 365691.

Coghlan, A., and MacKenzie, D. (2011) "Revealed–the capitalist network that runs the world", *New Scientist*, 24.

Cohen, B.J. (2007) "The transatlantic divide: Why are American and British IPE so different?", *Review of International Political Economy*, 14, 2, 197-219.

Cole, M.T. and Davies, R.B. (2014) *Foreign Bidders Going Once, Going Twice... Protection in Government Procurement Auctions* UDC Centre for Economic Research Working Paper, 14/01, Dublin.

Colletta, N. J. and Cullen, M. L. (2000) *Violent Conflict and the Transformation of Social Capital: Lessons from Cambodia, Rwanda, Guatemala, and Somalia*, Washington, DC.

Collier, P. (2007) *The Bottom Billion: Why the Poorest Countries Are Failing and What Can Be Done About it*, Oxford.

Collier, P. and Dollar, D. (2001) "Can the world cut poverty in half? How policy reform and effective aid can meet the international development goals", *World Development*, 29, 11, 1787–1802.

Collier, P. and Hoeffler, A. (2004) "Greed and Grievance in Civil War", *Oxford Economic Papers*, 56, 4, 563-595.

Combes J-L. and Guillaumont (2002) "Commodity Price Volatility, Vulnerability and Development", *Development Policy Review*, 20, 1, 25-39.

Commonwealth Advisory Group (1997) *A Future for Small States: Overcoming vulnerability*, London

Commonwealth Secretariat/World Bank Joint Task Force on Small States (2000). *Small States: Meeting Challenges in the Global Economy*, Washington, DC.

Congressional Budget Office, US Congress (1997) *The Role of Foreign Aid in Development*, Washington DC.

Connell, J. (2014) "The two cultures of health worker migration: A Pacific perspective", *Social Science and Medicine*, 116, 73-81.

Contessi, S. and Weinberger, A. (2009) "Foreign Direct investment, Productivity and Country Growth: An Overview", *Federal Reserve Bank of St. Louis Review*, 91, 2, 61-78.

Cooley, A. and Ron, J. (2002) "The NGO Scramble: Organizational Insecurity and the Political Economy of Transnational Action", *International Security*, 27, 1, 5-39.

Corporate Europe Observatory (2014) *The Record of a Captive Commission. The 'black book' on the corporate agenda of the Barroso Commission*, Brussels.

Corrales-Leal, W., Baritto, F. and Mohan, S.A. (2007) *Special and Differential Treatment for Small and Vulnerable Countries based on the Situational Approach*, ICTSD Issue paper 2, Geneva.

Coyne, C.J. and Boettke, P.J. (2003) *The Role of the Economist in Economic Development*, Global Prosperity Initiative, Working Paper 32, Mercatus Center, George Mason University, Fairfax, VA.

Cox, R.W. (1979) "Ideologies and the New International Economic Order: Reflections on some recent literature", *International Organization*, 33, 2, 257-302.

Cox, R.W. (1981) "Social forces, states and world orders: beyond international relations theory", *Millennium: Journal of International Studies*, 10, 2, 126-155.

Cozette, M. (2008) "What lies ahead: Classical realism on the future of international relations", *International Studies Review*, 10, 4, 667-679.

Crabtree, S. (2010) "Religiosity Highest in World's Poorest Nations", Gallup Polling Report, Washington, DC

Crafts, N. F. R and Harley, C.K. (1992) "Output Growth and the British Industrial Revolution: A Restatement of the Crafts-Harley View", *The Economic History Review* , 45, 4 (1992) 703-730.

Crediet Suisse (2014), *Global Wealth Report*, Zurich.


Dabla-Norris, E. and Gündüz, Y.B (2012) *Exogenous Shocks and Growth Crises in Low-Income Countries: A Vulnerability Index*, IMF Working Paper 12/264, New York.

418

Dahl, R.A. and Tufte, E.R. (1973) *Size and Democracy*, Stanford, Ca.

Davies, R.B., Martin, J., Parenti, M., and Toubal, F. (2014) *Knocking on Tax Heaven's Door: Multinational Firms and Transfer Pricing*, CESifo Working Paper 5132, Munich.

de la Croix, D., Docquier, F. and Schiff, M. (2014) "Brain Drain and Economic Performance in Small Island Developing States" in A. Artal-Tur, G. Peri and F. Rilenqua-Silvente (eds) *The Socio-Economic Impact of Migration Flows*, Heidelberg, New York, Dordrecht, London, 123-144.

De Figueiredo, J. M. and Kim, J. J. (2004) " When do firms hire lobbyists? The organization of lobbying at the Federal Communications Commission", *Industrial and Corporate Change*, 13, 6, 883-900.

De Figueiredo, J.M. and Richter, B.K. (2013) *Advancing the Empirical Research on Lobbying*, National Bureau of Economic Research. Working Paper 19698, Cambridge, Ma.

De Grauwe, P. and Camerman, F. (2002) "How Big are the Big Multinational Companies?", *Tijdschrift voor economie en management*, 47, 3, 311-326.

Deaton, A. and Aten, B. (2014) *Trying to Understand the PPPs in ICP2011: Why are the Results so Different?* National Bureau of Economic Research Working Paper 20244, Cambridge Ma.

Deaton, A. and Heston, A. (2008) *Understanding PPPs and PPP-based National Accounts,* National Bureau of Economic Research Working Paper 14499, Cambridge Ma.

Delhey, J. and Newton, K. (2005) "Predicting Cross-National Levels of Social Trust: Global Pattern or Nordic Exceptionalism?" *European Sociological Review*, 21, 4, 311-327.

Delhey, J., Newton, K. and Welzel, C. (2011). "How general is trust in "most people"? Solving the radius of trust problem", *American Sociological Review*, 76, 5, 786-807.

Deliger, K. and Squire, L. (1996) "A New Data Set Measuring Income Inequality", *World Bank Economic Review*, 10, 3, 565-591.

Dell, E. (1984) "The origins of UNCTAD" in M.Z. Cutajar (ed.) *UNCTAD and the South-North Dialogue: The First Twenty Years : Essays in Honour of W.R. Malinowski*, Oxford, 10-32.

Deutsch, J. and Silber, J. (2005) "Measuring Multidimensional Poverty: An empirical comparison of various approaches", *Review of Income and Wealth*, 51, 1, 145-174.

Desmet, K., Weber, S. and Ortuño-Ortín, I. (2009) "Linguistic Diversity and Redistribution", *Journal of the European Economic Association*, 7, 6, 1291-1318.

Di John, J. (2008) *Conceptualising the Causes and Consequences of Failed States: A Critical Review of the Literature*, LSE, Crisis States Research Centre Working paper No 25, London.

Diamond, L.J. and Tsalik, S. (1999) "Size and democracy: The case for decentralization" in L. J. Diamond (Ed.), *Developing democracy: Towards consolidation*, Baltimore, MD, 117-160.

Dixit, A. (2004) *Lawlessness and Economics*, Princeton NJ.

Do, Q.T. and Iyer, L. (2007) *Poverty, Social Divisions, and Conflict in Nepal*. World Bank Policy Research Working Paper, WPS4228, Washington.

Dorling, D. (2014) *Inequality and the 1%*, London, New York

Dornan, M. and Newton Cain, T. (2013) *Regional Service Delivery Among Small Island Developing States of the Pacific: An Assessment*, Asia and pacific Policy Studies Working Paper 04/2013, Canberra.

Doucouliagos, H. and Paldam, M. (2005) Conditional aid effectiveness. *Aarhus University Economics Paper*, No 14, Aarhus.

Doucouliagos, H. and Paldam, M. (2008) "Aid effectiveness on growth: A meta study", *European Journal of Political Economy*, 24, 1, 1-24.

Doucouliagos, H. and Paldam, M. (2011) "The ineffectiveness of development aid on growth: An update", *European Journal of Political Economy*, 27, 2, 399-404.

Diebold, W. (1952). *The End of the ITO*, Princeton NJ.

Dobbs, R., Smit, S., Remes, J., Manyika, J., Roxburgh, C. and Restrepo, A. (2011) *Urban world: Mapping the economic power of cities*, Washington DC

Dreher, A. (2006) "Does globalization affect growth? Evidence from a new index of globalization" *Applied Economics*, 38, 10, 1091-1110.

Dreher, A., Nunnenkamp, P. and Thiele, R. (2011) "Are 'new'donors different? Comparing the allocation of bilateral aid between nonDAC and DAC donor countries", *World Development*, 39, 11, 1950-1968.

Dubay, C.S. and Furth, S. (2014) "Understanding Thomas Piketty and his Critics" *Heritage Foundation*, 12.9.2014, Washington DC.

Dunning, J. H. (1998) " Location and the Multinational Enterprise: A Neglected Factor?", *Journal of International Business Studies*, 29, 1, 45-66.

Dür, A., and Mateo, G. (2012) "Who Lobbies the European Union? National Interest Groups In a Multilevel Polity", *Journal of European Public Policy*, 19, 7, 969-987.

Durlauf, S. N. (2002) "Bowling Alone: a review essay", *Journal of Economic Behavior and Organization*, 47, 3, 259-273.

Duvendack, M. and Palmer-Jones, R. (2012) "High noon for microfinance impact evaluations: re-investigating the evidence from Bangladesh", *The Journal of Development Studies*, 48, 12, 1864-1880.


Easterly, W. (2009) "How the Millennium Development Goals are unfair to Africa", *World Development*, 37, 1, 26-35.

Easterly, W. and Levine, R. (1997) "Africa's growth tragedy: policies and ethnic divisions", *The Quarterly Journal of Economics*, 112, 4, 1203-1250.

Economist (2011) "The Shoe-Thrower's index", *The Economist*, 9.2.2011.

Economist Intelligence Unit (2015) *Democracy Index 2014. Democracy and its Discontents*, London

Edwards, P., Roberts, I., Clarke, M., DiGuiseppi, C., Pratap, S., Wentz, R., and Kwan, I. (2002) "Increasing Response Rates To Postal Questionnaires: Systematic Review", British Medical Journal, 324, 7347, 1183.

Eichengreen, B and Uzan, M. (1990). *The 1933 World Economic Conference as an Instance of Failed International Cooperation.* Department of Economics, UCB, Working Paper 90-149, Berkeley, Ca.

Engman, A. (2013) "Is there life after P< 0.05? Statistical significance and quantitative sociology", *Quality and Quantity*, 47, 1, 257-270.

Engsted, T. (2009) "Statistical vs. economic significance in economics and econometrics: further comments on McCloskey and Ziliak", *Journal of Economic Methodology*, 16, 4, 393-408.

Erkkilä, T. and Piironen, O. (2014) "(De) politicizing good governance: the World Bank Institute, the OECD and the politics of governance indicators", *Innovation: The European Journal of Social Science Research*, 27,4, 344-360.

Esteban, J., Mayoral, L. and Ray, D. (2012) "Ethnicity and conflict: An empirical study" *The American Economic Review*, 102, 4, 1310-1342.

Eurostat (2015) *Asylum quarterly report. First time asylum applicants and first instance decisions on asylum applications: second quarter 2015*, Brussels.


Faist, T. (2012) "Migration" , *The Wiley-Blackwell Encyclopedia of Globalization*, Chichester.

Farnsworth, K. (2005) "Promoting Business-Centred Welfare: International and European Business Perspectives on Social Policy", *Journal of European Social Policy*, 15(1), 65-80.

Fase, W.J.P.M (1980) *Vijfendertig jaar loonbeleid in Nederland: terugblik en perspectief.* PhD thesis, KUB, Tilburg.

Fearon, J.D. (2003) "Ethnic and Cultural Diversity by Country", *Journal of Economic Growth*, 8, 2, 195-222.

Featherstone, K. (2015) "External conditionality and the debt crisis: the 'Troika'and public administration reform in Greece", *Journal of European Public Policy*, 22, 3, 295-314.

Feenstra, R.C., Lipsey, R.E., Branstetter, L.G., Fritz Foley, Harrigan, J., Bradford Jensen, J., Kletzer, L., Mann, C. Schott, P.K. and Greg C. Wright, G.C. (2010) *Report on the State of Available Data for the Study of International Trade and Foreign Direct Investment*, National Bureau of Economic Research Working Paper, 16254, Cambridge, Ma.

Feld, L.P. and Schneider, F. (2010) "Survey on The Shadow Economy and Undeclared Earnings in OECD Countries", *German Economic Review*, 11, 2, 109-149.

Feng, W., Cai, Y. and Gu, B. (2012) "Population, Policy, and Politics: How Will History Judge China's One-Child Policy?", *Population and Development Review*, 38 (Supplement): 115–129.

Feng, Y. Guo, Z. and Peitz, C. (2014) "A Tree-Form Constant Market Share Model For Growth Causes in International Trade based on Multi-Level Classification", *Journal of Industry, Competition and Trade*, 14, 2, 207-228.

Ferreira, F. H. and Lugo, M. A. (2013) "Multidimensional Poverty Analysis: Looking for a middle ground", *The World Bank Research Observer*, 28, 2, 220-235.

Fine, B. (2010) *Theories of Social Capital. Researchers Behaving Badly*, London/New York.

Fioramonti, L. (2013) *Gross Domestic Problem. The Politics behind the World's most Powerful Number*, London, New York.

Firth, N.E. and Noren, J.H. (1998) *Soviet Defense Spending: A History of CIA Estimates, 1950-1990*, College Station, Tx.

Fogel, R.W. (1964) *Railroads and American Economic Growth: Essays in Economic History*, Baltimore, Ma.

Fogel R.W. and Engerman, S.L. (1974) *Time on the Cross: The Economics of American Negro Slavery*, Boston, Ma.

Folbre, N. (2006) "Measuring care: Gender, empowerment, and the care economy", *Journal of Human Development*, 7, 2, 183-199.

Forstenlechner, I. and Rutledge, E.J. (2011) "The GCC's 'Demographic Imbalance': Perceptions, Realities and Policy Options", *Middle East Policy*, 18, 4, 25-43.

FRBNY, Federal Reserve Bank of New York (2009) *Report on Systemic Risk and Bank Supervision Draft*, 18.8.2009, New York.

Friedman, M. and Schwartz, A.J. (1965) *The Great Contraction 1929-1933*, Princeton NJ.

Friedman, T. (2005) *The World is Flat: A Brief History Of The Globalized World in the 21st Century*. London

Fromhold-Eisebith M. (2002) "Regional cycles of learning: foreign multinationals as agents of technological upgrading in less developed countries", *Environment and Planning* 34, 12, 2155–2173.

Fukuyama, F. (1995) *Trust. The Social Virtues and the Creation of Prosperity*, London/New York

Fukuyama, F. (1992) *The End of History and The Last Man*, New York.

Fund for Peace (2012) *Failed State Index 2012*, Washington, DC.

Fund for Peace (2014) *Fragile State Index 2014*, Washington, DC.

Gallup (2012) *Global Index of Religiosity and Atheism, 2012*, Washington, DC.

Galtung, F. (2006) "Measuring the Immeasurable. Boundaries and Functions of (Macro) Corruption Indices" in C.J. Sampford, A. Shacklock and C. Connors (eds.) *Measuring corruption*, Farnham.

Garber, P.M. (1993) "The collapse of the Bretton Woods fixed exchange rate system" in M.D. Bordo and B. Eichengreen (eds.) *A Retrospective on the Bretton Woods System: Lessons for International Monetary Reform*, Chicago, 461-494.

Gardner, A. (2012) "Why Do They Keep Coming? Labor Migrants in the Gulf States" in M. Kamrava and Z. Babar (eds.), *Migrant Labor in the Persian Gulf*, London, 41-58.

Gaventa, J. and McGee, R. (2013) "The Impact of Transparency and Accountability Initiatives", *Development Policy Review*, 31, s1, 3-28.

Georgiadis G., Pineda, J. and Rodriguez, F. (2010) *Has the Preston Curve Broken Down?* Human Development Research Paper 2010/32, New York.

Ghemawat, P (2011) *World 3.0. Global Prosperity and How to Achieve it*, Canbridge, Ma.

Gilbar G.G. (1997) *Population Dilemmas in the Middle East: Essays in Political Demography and Economy*, Abingdon/ New York.

Giles, C. (2014) "Data problems with Capital in the 21$^{st}$ Century", *Financial Times*, 23.5.2014

Gill, J. (1999) "The Insignificance of Null Hypothesis Significance Testing", *Political Research Quarterly*, 52, 3, 647-674.

Ginneken, J.K.van (1974) "Prolonged breastfeeding as a birth spacing method", *Studies in Family Planning*, 5, 6, 201-206.

Giovannini, A (1993) "Bretton Woods and Its Precursors: Rules versus Discretion in the History of International Monetary Regimes" in M.D. Bordo and B. Eichengreen (eds.) *A Retrospective on the Bretton Woods System: Lessons for International Monetary Reform*, Chicago

Glaeser, E.L., Laibson, D.I., Scheinkman, J.A. and Soutter, C.L. (2000) "Measuring Trust", *The Quarterly Journal of Economics*, 115, 3, 811-846.

Glaeser, E.L., La Porta, R., Lopez-de-Silanes, F. and Shleifer, A. (2004). "Do institutions cause growth?", *Journal of Economic Growth*, 9, 3, 271-303.

Goldfinch, S., DeRouen Jr., K., Biglaiser, G. and Staats, J. (2012) *What makes a state stable and peaceful? Good governance, legitimacy and legal-rationality matter even more for low income countries*, Paper delivery at the 2012 Annual Meeting of the American Political Science Association, August 30-September 2, 2012

Goldstein, A., Pinaud, N., Reisen, H. and Chen, X (2006) *China and India: What's in it for Africa?* Paris.

Gooskens, C. (2007) "The Contribution of Linguistic Factors to the Intelligibility of Closely Related Languages", *Journal of Multilingual and Multicultural Development*, 28, 6, 445-467.

Gourevitch, P. (1978) "The Second Image Reversed: The International Sources of Domestic Politics", *International Organization*, 32, 4, 881-912.

Grasstek C. van (2013) *The History and Future of the World Trade Organization*, Geneva.

Graziani, G. and Preeg, H. (1990). *Gorbachev's Economic Strategy in the Third World*, New York.

Greener, I (2006) "Nick Leeson and the Collapse of Barings bank: Socio-Technical Networks and the 'Rogue Trader'", *Organization*, 13, 3, 421-441

Greenwood, J. (2013) *Interest Representation in the European Union* (3rd ed) Houndsville.

Grieco, J.M. (1988) "Anarchy and the Limits of Cooperation: A Realist Critique of the Newest Liberal Institutionalism", *International Organization*, 42, 3, 485-507.

Griffiths, R.T. (2002) "Waarom kunnen wij het GLB niet hervormen?" in W. Asbeek Brusse, J Bouma and R.T. Griffiths (eds.) *De toekomst van het Europees Gemeenschappelijk Landbouwbeleid.Actusle vraagstukken end perspectieven voor Nederland*, Utrecht, 2002, 49-62.

Griffiths, R.T. (2008) "Development Aid: Some Reference Points for Historical Research" in H. Pharo and M. Pohle (eds.), *The Aid Rush: Aid Regimes in Northern Europe during the Cold War*, Volume One, Olso, 17-40.

Griffiths, R.T. (2014) "Economic Security and Size" in C. Archer, A.J.K Bailes and A. Wivel (eds) *Small States and International Security. Europe and Beyond*, Abingdon, New York, 46-65.

Grigoriadis, I. N. (2009) "Islam and Democratization in Turkey: Secularism and Trust in a Divided Society", *Democratization*, 16, 6, 1194-1213.

Griliches, Z. (1995). *The Discovery of the Residual: an historical note*, National Bureau of Economic Research Working Paper 5348, Cambridge, Ma..

Grubel, H.G. and Lloyd, P.J. (1971) "The Empirical Measurement of Intra-Industry Trade",*Economic Record*, 47, 4, 494-517.

Grubert, H. (2003) "Intangible Income, Intercompany Transactions, Income Shifting, and the Choice of Location", *National Tax Journal*, 56, 2, 221-242.

Gu, B (n.d.) *Demographic Transition in China* (s.l)

Guan-Fu, G. (1983) "Soviet Aid to the Third World: an Analysis of its Strategy", *Soviet Studies*, 35, 1, 71-89.

Guengant, J.P. (2002) "The proximate determinants during the fertility transition" *Population Bulletin of the UN* Special Issues 48/49 (*Completing the Fertility Transition*), New York, 308-329.

Guillaumont, P. and Jeanneney, S. G. (2009). *State fragility and economic vulnerability: what is measured and why?* European Report on Development, Ferdi Working paper, 07, Clermont-Ferrand.

Haan, I. de (2010) "Parlementaire democratie en maatschappelijke organisatie: de politieke context van de Sociaal_Economische Raad" in T. Jaspers, B van Bavel and J. Peet (eds.) *SER, 1950-2010. Zestig jaar denkwerk voor draagvlak advies voor economie en samenleving*, Amsterdam.

Haas, E.B. (1958) *The Uniting of Europe*. Stanford, Ca.

Haggard, S. and Tiede, L. (2011) "The Rule of Law and Economic Growth: Where are We?", *World Development*, 39, 5, 673-685.

Hall P.A. (ed.) (1989) *The Political Power of Economic Ideas: Keynesianism across Nations*, Princeton, NJ.

Hall, P.A. and Soskice, D (eds.) (2001) *Varieties of Capitalism. The Institutional Foundations of Comparative Advantage*, Oxford .

ul Haq, M (1976) *The Poverty Curtain. Choices for the Third World*, New York.

Harrigan, J. (2011) *Did Food Prices Plant the Seeds of the Arab Spring?* SOAS Inaugural Lecture series, London.

Harris, J. (2002) *Depoliticizing Development: The World Bank and Social Capital*, London

Harttgen, K. and Klasen, S. (2012) "A Household-Based Human Development Index", *World Development*, 40, 5, 878-899.

Haub, C. (2002) "How many People have ever lived on Earth?", *World*, 6, 23, 983-987.

Hay, C. and Marsh, D. (eds.). (2000) *Demystifying Globalization. Globalization and Governance*, Basingstoke.

Hayes, L. and Novitz, T. (2014) *Trade Unions and Economic Inequality*, Liverpool..

Hayman, R. "Budget support and Conditionality: a twist in the conditionality tail", *Third World Quarterly*, 32, 4, 673-688.

Hear, N. van, Bakewell, O. and Long, K (2012) *Drivers Of Migration* Migrating out of Poverty Research Programme Consortium, Working Paper 1, London.

Heemskerk, E.M. (2013) "The Rise of the European Corporate Elite: Evidence from the Network of Interlocking Directorates in 2005 and 2010", *Economy and Society*, 42, 1, 74-101.

Held, D. (1999) *Global transformations: Politics, economics and culture*. Stanford, Ca.

Helman, G.B and Ratner, S.R. (1992) "Saving Failed States", *Foreign Policy* 89 (Winter, 1992-1993), 3-20.

Hemerijck, A. (2013) *Changing Welfare States*, Oxford.

Hemerijck, A., Knapen B. and van Doorne, E. (2009) *Aftershocks, Economic Crisis and Institutional Choice*, Amsterdam.

Hill, M.D., Kelly, G.W., Lockhart, G.B., and Ness, R.A. (2013) "Determinants and Effects of Corporate Lobbying", *Financial Management*, 42, 4, 931-957.

Hill, R.J. and Syed, I. (2011). *Improving International Comparisons of Real Income. The ICP 2005 Benchmark and Its Implications for the Gap between the West and*

*China*, ICP 5th Technical Advisory Group Meeting, Washington, 18-19 April 2011.

Hirschl T.A. and Rank M.R. (2015) "The Life Course Dynamics of Affluence", *PLoS ONE* 10, 1: e0116370. doi:10.1371/journal.pone.0116370

Hirst, P., & Thompson, G. (1996) *Globalization in question: the internatioonal economy and the possibilities of governance*, Cambridge, Ma.

Hjertholm, P. and White, H. (2000) *Survey of Foreign Aid: History, Trends and Allocation*. Institute of Economics Discussion Paper 00-04, Copenhagen.

Hoda, A (2001) *Tariff Negotiations and Renegotiations under the GATT and the WTO: Procedures and Practices*, Cambridge.

Hoekman, B. and Nicita, A. (2011) "Trade Policy, Trade Costs, and Developing Country Trade", *World Development*, 39, 12, 2069-2079.

Hoeffler, A. and Outram, V. (2011) "Need, Merit, or Self-Interest—What Determines the Allocation of Aid?", *Review of Development Economics*, 15, 2, 237-250.

Hoffmann, M. and Jamal, A. (2012) "The Youth and the Arab Spring: Cohort Differences and Similarities" ,*Middle East Law and Governance*, 4, 1, 168-188.

Hood, C. (1991) "A Public Management for All Seasons", *Public Administration*, 69, 1, 3-19.

Hoover, K.D. and Siegler, M.V. (2008) "Sound and fury: McCloskey and significance testing in economics", *Journal of Economic Methodology*, 15, 1, 1-37.

Hou, J., Walsh, P.P. and Zhang, J. (2015) "The dynamics of Human Development Index", *The Social Science Journal*, 52, 331-347.

Howes, M. (1992) "Linking Paradigms and Practice: Key Issues in the Appraisal, Monitoring and Evaluation of British NGO Projects", *Journal of International Development*, 4, 4, 375-396.

Høyland, B., Moene, K. and Willumsen, F. (2012) "The tyranny of international index rankings", *Journal of Development Economics*, 97, 1, 1-14.

Hudson Institute (2013) *The Index of Global Philanthropy and Remittances 2013*, Washington, DC.

Hulme, D. (2009). *The Millennium Development Goals (MDGs): a short history of the world's biggest promise*, BWPI Working Paper 100, Manchester

Hurley, K. (2013) *An Inspection of the London Borough of Newham Law Enforcement Division*, Office of the Police and Crime Commissioner for Surry, s.l.

Iannaccone, L.R. (1998) "Introduction to the Economics of Religion", *Journal of Economic Literature*, 36, 3, 1465-1496.

Ikenberry, G.J. (1992) "A world economy restored: expert consensus and the Anglo-American postwar settlement", *International Organization*, 46, 1, 289-321.

Imai, K.S. and Azam, M.S. (2012) "Does microfinance reduce poverty in Bangladesh? New evidence from household panel data", *Journal of Development Studies*, 48, 5, 633-653.

Imam, P (2013) 'Demographic shift and the Financial Sector Stability: the case of Japan" , *Population Ageing*, 6, 269-303.

Inglehart, R. (1997) *Modernization and Postmodernization: Cultural, Economic, and Political Change in 43 Societies*, Princeton, NJ.

Inglehart, R., Moaddel, M. and Tessler, M. (2006). "Xenophobia and In-Group Solidarity an Iraq: A Natural Experiment on the Impact of Insecurity", *Perspectives on Politics*, 4, 3, 495-505.

Inklaar, R. and Prasada Rao D.S. (2014) *Cross-country income levels over time: did the developing world suddenly become much richer?* Groningen Growth and Development Centre Working Paper 151, Groningen.

IRIN (2013) *Nepal's Maternal Mortality Decline Paradox* , Integrated Regional Information Networks Analysis, Nairobi, 18.3.2013

Irwin, D.A. (1995) "The GATT in Historical Perspective", *The American Economic Review* 85, 2, 323-328.


Jansen, M. (2004) *Income Volatility in small and developing economies: export concentration matters*, WTO Discussion Paper No 3, Geneva.

Jara, A. and Escaith, H. (2012) "Global Value Chains, International Trade Statistics and Policymaking in a Flattening World", *World Economics*, 13, 4, 5-18.

JCS (2003) *Quis custodiet ipsos custodes? Inquiry into Governance on Norfolk Island Joint Standing Committee on the National Capital and External Territories*, Canberra.

Jerven, M. (2012) "An unlevel playing field: national income estimates and reciprocal comparison in global economic history" *Journal of Global History*, 7, 107–12

Jerven, M. (2013) *Poor Numbers. How we are misled by African Development Statistics and what to do about it*, Ithica, London.

Jervis, R. (1999) "Realism, Neoliberalism, and Cooperation: Understanding the Debate", *International Security*, 24, 1, 42-63.

Johnson, N.D. and Mislin, A. A. (2011). "Trust games: A meta-analysis", *Journal of Economic Psychology*, 32, 5, 865-889.

Johnson, S., Larson, W., Papageorgiou, C. and Subramanian, A. (2009) *Is Newer Better? Penn World Table Revisions and their Impact on Growth Estimates*, National Bureau of Economic Research Working Paper, 15455, Cambridge Ma.

Johnstone, S. and Mazo, J. (2011) "Global warming and the Arab Spring", *Survival*, 53, 2, 11-17.


Kahn, M.H. (2012 ) "Governance and Growth: History, Ideology and Methods of Proof" in A. Noman, K. Botchwey, H. Stein and J.E. Stiglitz (eds.) *Good*

*Growth and Governance in Africa: Rethinking Development Strategies*, Oxford, 51-79.

Kale, Y (2014) *Measuring better. Preliminary Results of the Rebased Nominal Gross Domestic Product (GDP) Estimate for Nigeria 2010 to 2013.* Speech by Statitician General, 6.4.2014

Kaplan, J.J. and Schleiminger.G. (1989) *European Payments Union: Financial Diplomacy in the 1950s.* Oxford.

Kapur, D., Lewis, J.P. and Webb, R. (1998) *The World Bank. Its First Half Century. Volume One: History*, Washington DC.

Karsten, L., Veen, K. van, Wulfften Palthe, A. van (2008) "What happened to the popularity of the Polder Model? Emergence and Disappearance of a Political Fashion". *International Sociology*, 23, 1, 35-65.

Kasahara, S. (2004) *The Flying Geese Paradigm: a critical Study of its Application to East Asian regional development*, UNCTAD Discussion Paper, Geneva, 169.

Katzenstein, P.J. (1985) *Small States in World Markets: Industrial Policy in Europe*, Ithica, NY.

Katzenstein, P.J. (2003)m"'Small states' and small states revisited", *New Political Economy*, 8, 1, 9-30.

Kaufman, B.L. (1982) *Trade not Aid: Eisenhower's Foreign Economic Policy, 1953-1961*, Baltimore, Ma.

Kaufmann, D (2008) *Governance, Crisis, and the Longer View: Unorthodox Reflections on the New Reality Reflections on a Journey, Doubts at the crossroads*, Farewell presentation at the World Bank, Washington, D.C. 9.12.2008.

Kaufmann, D., Kraay, A. and Mastruzzi, M. (2007a) *The Worldwide Governance Indicators Project: Answering the Critics*, World Bank Policy Research Working Paper 4149, Washington, DC.

Kaufmann, D., Kraay, A. and Mastruzzi, M. (2007b) "Growth and Governance: A Reply", *Journal of Politics*, 69, 2, 555-562.

Kaufmann, D., Kraay, A. and Mastruzzi, M. (2011) "The Worldwide Governance Indicators: Methodology and Analytical Issues", *Hague Journal on the Rule of Law*, 3, 2, 220-246.

Kaufmann, D., & Zoido-Lobaton, P. (1999). *Corruption, Unpredictability and Performance.* World Bank: Washington DC.

Keck, M.E and Sikkink, K. (1998) *Activists Beyond Borders: Advocacy Networks in International Politics*, Ithaca, NY.

Keck, M.E. and Sikkink, K. (1999) "Transnational advocacy networks in international and regional politics" *International Social Science Journal*, 51, 159, 89-101.

Kekic, Laza (2007). The Economist Intelligence Unit's Index of Democracy. The World in 2007. London: *The Economist*. [http://www.economist.com/media/pdf/DEMOCRACY_INDEX_2007_v3.pdf]

Kendrick, J.W. (1970) "The Historical Development of National-Income Accounts", *History of Political Economy*, 2, 2, 284-315.

Keynes, J.M. (1936/2013) *The General Theory of Employment, Interest and Money*, (available in Kindle)

Khan, M. (2006) *Governance, Economic Growth and Development since the 1960s: Background Paper for the World Economic and Social Survey 2006.* New York.

Khan, M.H. (2012 ) "Governance and Growth: History, Ideology and Methods of Proof" in A. Noman, K. Botchwey, H. Stein and J.E. Stiglitz (eds.) *Good Growth and Governance in Africa: Rethinking Development Strategies*, Oxford, 51-79.

Khandker, S.R. and Samad, H.A. (2014) *Dynamic Effects of Microcredit in Bangladesh*, World Bank Policy Research Paper WPS 6821, Washington D.C.

Kindleberger, C.P. (1973) *The World in Depression, 1929-1939*, Berkeley Ca.

Kinzer, S (2006) *Overthrow: America's Century of Regime Change from Hawaii to Iraq*, New York.

Kirk, D. (1996) "Demographic Transition Theory", *Population Studies*, 50, 3, 361-387.

Klein, N. (2007) *The Shock Doctrine, The Rise of Disaster Capitalism*, London.

Klugman, J., Rodríguez, F., & Choi, H. J. (2011). "The HDI 2010: new controversies, old critiques", *The Journal of Economic Inequality*, 9, 2, 249-288.

Knack, S. (2002) *Governance and growth: measurement and evidence*, Iris Paper 02/05, Adelphi, Ma.

Knack, S.F. (2006) *Measuring corruption in Eastern Europe and Central Asia: a critique of the cross-country indicators.* World Bank Policy Research Working Paper Vol. 3968, Washington D.C.

Knack, S. (2010) *Trust, Associational Life, and Economic Performance*, MPRA Working Paper No. 27247, Munich

Knack, S. and Keefer, P. (1997) "Does Social Capital have an Economic Payoff? A Cross-Country Investigation", *The Quarterly Journal of Economics*, 112, 4, 1251-1288.

Knoll, M. and Zloczysti, P. (2012) "The Good Governance Indicators of the Millennium Challenge Account: How Many Dimensions are Really Being Measured?", *World Development*, 40, 5, 900-915.

Koopman, R., Powers, W., Wang, Z. and Wei, S.J. (2010) *Give credit where credit is due: Tracing value added in global production chains* (No. w16426). National Bureau of Economic Research, Working Paper 16426, Cambridge, Ma.

Kopczuk, W. (2015) "What do we know about the Evolution of Top Wealth Shares in the United States", *Journal of Economic Perspectives*, 29, 1, 47-66.

Kreager, P. (2014) "On the History of Malthusian Thought: A Review Essay", *Population and Development Review*, 40, 4, 731–742.

Kraemer, K., Linden, G., & Dedrick, J. (2011). *Capturing value in Global Networks: Apple's iPad and iPhone*, PCIC Working Paper, Irving, Ca.

Kneller, D. (2014) "Dialectics of Globalization. From theory to practice" in S. Dasgupta and P. Kivisto (eds) *Postmodernism in a Global Perspective*, New York, 4-29.

Kulu, H. (2013) "Why do fertility levels vary between urban and rural areas?", *Regional Studies*, 47, 6, 895-912.

Kurtz, M. and Shrank, A. (2006) "Growth and Governance: Models, Measures, and Mechanisms", *Journal of Politics*, 69, 2, 538-554.


La Porta, R., Lopez-de-Silanes, F., Shleifer, A. and Vishny, R. (1999) "The Quality of Government", *Journal of Law, Economics, and Organization*, 15, 1, 222-279.

Labart, K. (2010) *What is hidden behind the indicators of ethno-linguistic fragmentation?* Fondation pour les Etudes et Recherches sur le Developpement International, Working paper Idi10, Clermont-Ferrand.

Lam, P.E. (2014). "China's Asian Infrastructure Investment Bank: East Asian Responses", *East Asian Policy*, 6, 4, 127-135.

Lambart, K. (2010) *What is hidden behind the indicators of ethno-linguistic fragmentation?* Fondation pour les Etudes et Recherches sur le Developpement International Working Paper 7, Clermont-Ferrand.

Lancee, B., and Werfhorst, H. G. van de (2012) "Income Inequality and Participation: A comparison of 24 European countries", *Social science research*, 41, 5, 1166-1178.

Lane, J.E. and Maeland, R. (2011) "Global Financial Crisis and International Institutions: Challenges, Opportunities and Change", *Public Organization Review*, 11, 1, 29-43.

Langbein, L. and Knack, S. (2010) "The Worldwide Governance Indicators: Six, One, or None?", *The Journal of Development Studies*, 46, 2, 350-370.

*Latin America Corruption Survey* June 2012

Laurence, J. (2013). "'Hunkering Down or Hunkering Away?' The Effect of Community Ethnic Diversity on Residents' Social Networks", *Journal of Elections, Public Opinion and Parties*, 23, 3, 255-278.

Lawson, C.W. (1988) "Soviet Economic Aid to Africa", *African Affairs*, 87, 349, 501-518.

League of Nations (1942), *Commercial Policy in the Inter-war Period. International Proposals and National Policies*, Geneva.

Leeson, P.T. (2005) "Endogenizing Fractionalization", *Journal of Institutional Economics*, 1, 1, 75-98.

Levenstein, M. and Suslow, V. (2012) *Cartels and Collusion - Empirical Evidence*, Ross School of Business Working Paper 1182, Ann Arbor, Mi.

Lichbach, M.I. (1989) "An Evaluation of 'does economic inequality breed political conflict?' Studies", *World Politics*, 41, 4, 431-470.

Limão, N. and Venables, A. (2001), "Infrastructure, Geographical Disadvantage, Transport Costs and Trade", *World Bank Economic Review*, 15 (3), 451-479.

Lindberg, L (1963) *The Political Dynamics of European Economic Integration*. Stanford, Ca.

Linden, G., Kraemer, K.L. and Dedrick, J. (2009) "Who captures value in a global innovation network?: the case of Apple's iPod", *Communications of the ACM*, 52, 3, 140-144.

Linn, J.F. (2004) *Economic (Dis)Integration Matters: The Soviet Collapse Revisited*, Paper prepared for a conference on "Transition in the CIS: Achievements and Challenges" at the Academy for National Economy, Moscow, September 13-14, 2004.

Liu, X., Derudder, B., & Taylor, P. (2014). "Mapping the evolution of hierarchical and regional tendencies in the world city network, 2000–2010", *Computers, Environment and Urban Systems,* 43, 51-66.

Lockwood, B. and Redoano, M. (2005) *The CSGR Globalisation Index: An introductory guide.* Centre for the Study of Globalisation and Regionalisation Working Paper, 155(04), Coventry.

Louçã, F. (2007) *The Years of High Econometrics: A Short History of the Generation that Reinvented Economics*, London/New York.

Love, P. and Lattimore, R. (2009) "Protectionism? Tariffs and Other Barriers to Trade"in P. Love and R. Lattimore, *International trade. Free, Fair and Open?*, OECD Publishing, Paris

Lozano, R. e.a. (2013) "Global and regional mortality from 235 causes of death for 20 age groups in 1990 and 2010: a systematic analysis for the Global Burden of Disease Study 2010" , *The Lancet*, 380, 9859, 2095-2128.

Lynch, M., Freelon, D. and Aday, S. (2014) "Syria in the Arab Spring: The integration of Syria's conflict with the Arab uprisings, 2011–201", *Research and Politics*, 1, 3, 1-7.


Maddison, A. (1998) "Measuring the Performance of a Communist Command Economy: an Assessment of the CIA Estimates for the USSR", *Review of Income and Wealth*, 44, 3, 307-323.

Maddison, A. (1995) *Monitoring the World Economy, 1820-1992*, OECD, Paris

Maddison, A. (2001) *The World Economy. A millennial Perspective*, OECD, Paris.

Magness, P.W. and Murphy, R P. (2015) "Challenging the Empirical Contribution of Thomas Piketty's Capital in the 21st Century" *Journal of Private Enterprise*, 30, 1, 1-34.

Maizels, A. (1945) *Industrialization and Foreign Trade*, Geneva.

Malek, M. (2006) "State failure in the South Caucasus: proposals for an analytical framework", *Transition Studies Review*, 13, 2, 441-460.

Maliniak, D. and Tierney, M.J. (2009) "The American school of IPE", *Review of International Political Economy*, 16, 1, 6-33.

Malmberg, B. (2008) *Demography and the development potential of Sub-Saharan Africa*, Stockholm.

Malthus, T. (1798/2015) *An Essay on the Principle of Population'*, London.

Manning, R. (2006) "Will 'Emerging Donors' Change the Face of International Co-operation?", *Development Policy Review*, 24, 4, 371-385.

Mansfield, E.D. and Reinhardt, E. (2008). "International Institutions and the Volatility of International Trade" , *International Organization*, 46, 4, 621-652.

Marks, K. (2009) *Lost paradise: From Mutiny on the Bounty to a modern-day legacy of sexual mayhem, the dark secrets of Pitcairn Island revealed*, New York, 2009.

Marshall, A. (1890/2013) *The Principles of Economics*, London.

Martell, L. (2007) "The third wave in globalization theory", *International Studies Review*, 9, 2, 173-196.

Martens, P., Caselli, M., De Lombaerde, P., Figge, L. and Scholte, J.A. (2014) "New Directions in Globalization Indices", *Globalizations*, 14, 1-12.

Marx, K. (1867/2014) *Das Kapital* (Reprint of 1883 English language edition, London)

Mason, M.S. and Asher, R.E. (1973) *The World Bank since Bretton Woods*, Washington DC.

Mata, J.F. and Ziaja, S. (2009) *Users' Guide on Measuring Fragility*, DIE/UNDP, Bonn/Oslo

Mawdsley, E. (2012) "The changing geographies of foreign aid and development cooperation: contributions from gift theory", *Transactions of the Institute of British Geographers*, 37, 2, 256-272.

Mayer, T. (2006)"The empirical significance of econometric models", in M. Boumans, *Measurement in Economics*. Amsterdam. 321-340.

Mayer, T. (2012) "Ziliak and McCloskey's Criticism of Significance Tests: An Assessment", *Economic Journal Watch*, 9, 3, 256-297.

MMF, Institute for Unban Strategies (2014) *Global Power City Index 2014*, Tokyo.

McKenzie, F. (2008) "GATT and the Cold War: Accession debates, institutional development, and the western alliance, 1947–1959", *Journal of Cold War Studies*, 10, 3, 78-109.

McNamara, K.R. (2009) "Of intellectual monocultures and the study of IPE", *Review of International Political Economy*, 16, 1, 72-84.

Meadows, D.H (1972) *The Limits to Growth*, Washington, DC.

Meier, G.M. "The Old Generation of Development Economics and the New" in G.M. Meier and J.E. Stiglitz (eds.) *Frontiers of Development Economics. The Future in Perspective*, Oxford.

Meier, G.M. (2005), *Biography of a Subject. An Evolution of Development Economics,* Oxford.

Mellor, J.W. (1976) *The New Economics of Growth: A Strategy for India and the Developing World.* Ithaca, NY.

Menocal, A.R. and Sharma, B (2008) *Joint Evaluation of Citizens' Voice and Accountability. Synthesis Report,* London

Michalopoulos, S. (2012) "The Origins of Ethnolinguistic Diversity", *The American Economic Review,* 102, 4, 1508-1539.

Midttun, A., Gautesen, K. and Gjolberg, M. (2006) "The political economy of corporate social responsibility in Western Europe", *Corporate Governance,* 6, 4, 369-385

Milanovic, B (2012) *Global Income Inequality by the Numbers: in History and Now. An Overview,* World Bank Policy Research Working Paper 6259, Washington, DC.

Milner, H.V. (1998) "Rationalizing Politics: The Emerging Synthesis of International, American, and Comparative Politics", *International Organization,* 52, 4, 759-786.

Ministerie van Buitenlandse Zaken (2003) *Effectiviteit en coherentie van ontwikkelings-samenwerking. Eindrapport van de werkgroep Effectiviteit en coherentie van ontwikkelings-samenwerking,* Interdepartementaal Beleidsonderzoek, 2002-2003, nr. 1, The Hague.

Minoiu, C. and Reddy, S.G. (2010) "Development aid and economic growth: A positive long-run relation", *The Quarterly Review of Economics and Finance,* 50, 1, 27-39.

Mokyr, J. (1998) "The Second Industrial Revolution, 1870-1914", *Storia dell'economia Mondiale,* Bari, 219-45.

Molenaers, N., Gagiano, A., Smets, L. and Dellepiane, S. (2015) "What Determines the Suspension of Budget Support?", *World Development,* 15, c, 62-73.

Montalvo, J.G. and Reynal-Querol, M. (2005a) "Ethnic Polarization, Potential Conflict, and Civil Wars" *American Economic Review,* 95, 3, 796-816.

Montalvo, J.G. and Reynal-Querol, M. (2005b) "Ethnic Diversity and Economic Development", *Journal of Development Economics,* 76, 293-323.

Moonen T. and Clark, G. (2013) *The Business of Cities 2013. What do 150 city indices and benchmarking studies tell us about the urban world in 2013,* No location

Morehouse, C. and Blomfield, M. (2011) *Migration in Europe – Doubts about the Effectiveness of Control Strategies,* Migration Policy Institute, Washington DC.

Morse, S. (2014) "Stirring the pot. Influence of changes in methodology of the Human Development Index on reporting by the press", *Ecological Indicators,* 45, 245-254.

Mosley, P. (1987) *Overseas Aid: Its Defence and Reform,* Brighton.

Mosse, D. (2005) *Cultivating Development: An Ethnography of Aid Policy and Practice (Anthropology, Culture and Society Series)*. London.

Mosse, D. (2004) "Is Good Policy Unimplementable? Reflections on the Ethnography of Aid Policy and Practice", *Development and Change*, 35, 4, 639-671.

Mudasiru, S., & Adabonyon, O. (2001) "The Nigerian Economy under Obasanjo", *Development Policy Management Network Bulletin*, 8, 3, 10-13.

Mueller, S.D. (2011) "Dying to win: Elections, political violence, and institutional decay in Kenya" *Journal of Contemporary African Studies*, 29, 1, 99-117.

Murphy, C.N. and Nelson, D.R. (2001). "International political economy: a tale of two heterodoxies", *The British Journal of Politics and International Relations*, 3, 3, 393-412.

Muramatsu, N. and Akiyama, H. (2011) "Japan: Super-Aging Society Preparing for the Future", *The Gerontologist,* 51, 4, 425-432.

Myrskylä, M., Goldstein, J.R. and Cheng, Y.H.A. (2013) "New cohort fertility forecasts for the developed world: rises, falls, and reversals", *Population and Development Review*, 39, 1, 31-56.

Naim, M. (2007) "Rogue Aid" , *Foreign Policy,* 159, 95-96.

Nannestad, P. (2008) "What Have We Learned About Generalized Trust, If Anything?", *Annual Review of Political Science*, 11, 413-436.

Nettle, D. (1998) "Explaining Global Patterns of Language Diversity" *Journal of Anthropological Archaeology*, 17, 354-374.

Newham Council (2010) *Childcare Sufficiency Assessment Annual Update March 2010*

Newton, K. (2001) "Trust, Social Capital, Civil Society, and Democracy", *International Political Science Review*, 22, 2, 201-214.

Newton, K. and Norris, P. (2000) "Confidence in Public Institutions: Faith, Culture or Performance" in S.J. Parr and R.D. Putnam (eds) *Disaffected Democracies: What's troubling the Trilateral countries*, Princeton NJ, 52-73.

Neumayer, E. (2003) "What factors determine the allocation of aid by Arab countries and multilateral agencies?", *Journal of Development Studies*, 39, 4, 134-147.

Neumayer, E. (2004) "Arab-related Bilateral and Multilateral Sources of Development Finance: Issues, Trends, and the Way Forward", *The World Economy*, 27, 2, 281-300.

North, D.C. (1989) *Institutions and economic growth: An historical introduction*, Leiden.

North, D.C. (1990) *Institutions, Institutional Change and Economic Performance*, Cambridge.

North, D.C. (1991) "Institutions", *The Journal of Economic Perspectives*, 5, 1, 97–112,

North, D.C. and Weingast, B.R. (1989). "Constitutions and commitment: the evolution of institutions governing public choice in seventeenth-century England", *The Journal of Economic History*, 49, 4, 803-832.

Northedge, F.S. (1986) *The League of Nations: its life and times, 1920-1946*, Leicester.

O'Brien, P. and Kayder, C. (1978) *Economic Growth in Britain and France 1780-1914: Two Paths to the Twentieth Century*, London.

OECD (2011) *Divided We Stand: Why Inequality Keeps Rising*, Paris.

OECD (2014a) *Development Cooperation Report*, Paris.

OECD (2014b) *The WTO Trade Facilitation Agreement – Potential Impact on Trade Costs*, Paris.

OECD (2015) *State of Fragility. Meeting post-2015 ambitions*, Paris.

Ohmae, K (1995) *The End of the Nation State, The rise of Regional Economies*, New York.

Ohmae, K. (1994). *The Borderless World: Power and Strategy in the Global Marketplace*, New York.

Ogawa, N and Matsukura, R. (2007) "Ageing in Japan: The Health and Wealth of Older Persons", *United Nations Expert Group Meeting on Social and Economic Implications of Changing Population Age Structures. 31 August– 2 September, 2005, Mexico City*. New York, 199– 220.

O'Neil, T., Foresti, M. and Hudson, A. (2007) *Evaluation of Citizens' Voice and Accountability: review of the Literature and Donor Approaches*, London.

Parker, D. and Kirkpatrick, C. (2012). *Measuring Regulatory Performance. The Economic Impact of Regulatory Policy: A Literature Review of Quantitative Evidence*, Paris.

Parliament of the Commonwealth of Australia (2014) *Same Country: different worlds. The future of Norfolk Island*, Canberra.

Pathak, K.B., Feeney, G. and Luther, N.Y. (1998) *Alternative Contraceptive Methods and Fertility Decline in India*, National Family Health Survey Subject Reports, 7, Mumbai.

Permanyer, I. (2013) "A critical assessment of the UNDP's Gender Inequality Index", *Feminist Economics*, 19, 2, 1-32.

Pettman, R. (1996) *Understanding International Political Economy, with readings for the fatigued*, Boulder Co.

Person, D.A. (2014) "The Pacific Island Health Care Project" *Frontiers in Public Health*, 2, Article 175, 1-5.

Pew Research Center (2009) *Mapping the Global Muslim Population*, Washington DC.

Pew Research Center (2014) *Global Religious Diversity*, Washington DC.

Phelps, G. and Crabtree, S. (2013) *Worldwide, Median Household Income About $10,000*, Gallup News Release, 16.12.2013

Piketty, T. (2014) *Capital in the Twenty-First Century*, Cambridge Ma., London.

Pockney, B.D. (1991) *Soviet Statistics since 1950*, London.

Porter, M. (1990) *The Competitive Advantage of Nations*, New York.

Posner, D.N. (2004) "Measuring Ethnic Fractionalization in Africa", *American Journal of Political Science*, 48, 4, 849-863.

Prebisch, R. (1950) *The Economic Development of Latin America and its Principal Problems*, New York.

Prebisch, R. (1959) "Commercial Policy in the Underdeveloped Countries", *American Economic Review*, 49 2, 251-273

Preston, S.H. (1975) "The Changing Relation between Mortality and Level of Economic Development" . *Population Studies*, 29, 2,. 231-248.

Preston, S.H. (1986) "Changing Values and Falling Birth Rates" *Population and Development Review*, 12, Supplement, 176-195.

Putnam, R.D. (1988) "Diplomacy and Domestic Politics: The Logic of Two-Level Games", *International Organization*, 42, 3, 427-460.

Putnam, R. D. (1995) "Bowling alone: America's declining social capital", *Journal of Democracy*, 6, 1, 65-78.

Putnam, R. D. (2000) *Bowling Alone: The Collapse and Revival of American Community*, New York.

Putnam, R.D. (2007) "E pluribus unum: Diversity and community in the twenty-first century the 2006 Johan Skytte Prize Lecture", *Scandinavian Political Studies*, 30, 2, 137-174.

Putnam, R., Leonardi, R. and Nanetti, R.Y. (1994) *Making Democracy Work: Civic Traditions in Modern Italy*, Princeton NJ.


Quirk, J. and Vigneswaran, D. (2005) "The construction of an edifice: the story of a First Great Debate", *Review of International Studies*, 31, 01, 89-107.


Raffer, K. (1996) *Looking a Gift Horse in the Mouth: Analysing Donors' Aid Statistics*. Paper presented at Annual Conference of the Development Studies Association at Reading (UK), 18 - 20 September 1996

Raftery, A. E., Alkema, L., & Gerland, P. (2013) "Bayesian population projections for the United Nations", *Statistical Science*, 58-68.

Randers, J (2012) *2052: A Global Forecast for the Next Forty Years*, White River, VT.

Ravenhill, J. (2007) "In search of the missing middle", *Review of International Political Economy*, 15, 1, 18-29.

Ravillion, M (2010) "A Reply to Reddy and Pogge" in S. Anand, P. Segal and J.E. Stiglitz (eds) *Debates on the Measurement of Global Poverty*, Oxford, 86-101.

Ravallion, M. (2010). *Mashup Indices of Development*. The World Bank Research Policy Paper 5432, Washington DC.

Ravallion, M. (2014) *An Exploration Of The International Comparison Program's New Global Economic Landscape* National Bureau of Economic Research Working Paper, 20338, Cambridge, Ma.

Ravallion, M. (2012) "Troubling Tradeoffs in the Human Development Index", *Journal of Development Economics*, 99, 2, 201-209.

Ravallion, M., Chen, S. and Sangraula, P. (2009). "Dollar a Day Revisited", *The World Bank Economic Review*, 23, 2, 163-184.

Ravallion, M., Datt, G. and Walle, D. (1991) "Quantifying Absolute Poverty in the Developing World", *Review of Income and Wealth*, 37, 4, 345-361.

Reddy, S. G. and Pogge, T. (2010) "How not to Count the Poor" in S. Anand, P. Segal and J.E. Stiglitz (eds) *Debates on the Measurement of Global Poverty*, Oxford, 42-85.

Reich, P.R.(1992) *The Work of Nations*, New York.

Reinhart, C.M. and Rogoff, K.S. (2009) *This Time is Different. Eight Centuries of Financial Folly*, Princeton NJ

Robbins, M (2012) "The missing millions of Kibera. Africa's Propaganda Trail, part I of V", *The Guardian*, 1.8.2012

Rodin, J. (2011) "Fertility intentions and risk management: Exploring the fertility decline in Eastern Europe during transition", *Ambio*, 40, 2, 221-230.

Rodrik, D. (2011) *The Globalization Paradox. Democracy and the Future of the World Economy*, New York/London.

Rognlie, M. (2014) A note on Piketty and diminishing returns to capital. http:// www. mit. edu/~ mrognlie/piketty_diminishing_returns. pdf.

Rohrschneider, R. and Dalton, R.J. (2002) "A Global Network? Transnational Cooperation among Environmental Groups", *The Journal of Politics*, 64, 02, 510-533.

Roodman, D. (2007) "The Anarchy of Numbers: Aid, Development, and Cross-Country Empirics", *The World Bank Economic Review*, 21, 2, 255-277.

Roodman, D. (2014) *Straightening the Measuring stick: A 14-PointPlan for Reforming the Definition of Official Development Assistance (ODA)*, Centre for Global Development Working paper 044, Washington DC.

Roodman, D. (2014) "A Replication of "Counting Chickens When They Hatch" (Economic Journal 2012)", *Public Finance Review*, 43, 2, 256-281.

Rooy, P. de and Plantinga S. (1991) *Op zoek naar volmaaktheid : H.M. Bernelot Moens en het mysterie van afkomst en toekomst*, Houten.

Rosenberg, M. (1956) "Misanthropy and Political Ideology", *American Sociological Review*, 21, Dec., 690-695.

Rosenberg, R., Gaul, S., Ford, W. and Tomilova, O. (2013) *Microcredit Interest Rates and their Determinants, 2004-2011*, CGAP, World Bank, Washington DC.

Round, R. (2001) *Presentation on "Controlling Casino Capital"*, World Social Forum, Porto Allegre, 25-30.1.2001

Rubin, J., & Tal, B. (2008) "Will soaring transport costs reverse globalization" *CIBC World Markets*, 4-7.

Sahlén, M. and Furth, S (2014) "Piketty is misleading about the Swedish case", *Timbro*, 7.11.2014.

Saunders, P. (2010) *Beware False Prophets. Equality, the Good Society and The Spirit Level*, London.

Schendelen, M.P.C.M. van (1984) *Consociationalism, pillarization and conflict-management in the Low Countries*, Meppel.

Schenk, C.R. (1994) *Britain and the Sterling Area. From Devaluation to Convertibility in the 1950s*, London.

Schenk, C.R. (1998) "The Origins of the Eurodollar Market in London: 1955–1963", *Explorations in Economic History*, 35, 2, 221-238.

Schlesinger, S.C. (2003). *Act of Creation: The Founding of the United Nations*, Cambridge Ma.

Schmitter, P.C. (2004) "Neo-neo-functionalism?" in A. Wiener and T. Diez, eds. *European Integration Theory*, Oxford.

Schneider, F. and Enste, D. (2000) "Shadow Economies Around the World Size, Causes, and Consequences", *Journal of Economic Literature*, 38, 1, 77-114.

Schneider, F. and Williams, C.C. (2013) *The Shadow Economy*, London.

Schweller, R.L.and Priess, D. (1997) "A Tale of Two Realisms: Expanding the Institutions Debate", *Mershon International Studies Review*, 41, 1, 1-32.

Schwenger, D. Straub, T. and Borzillo, S. (2013) *Competition and Strategy of Non-Governmental organizations*, Paper presented at 4th EMES International research Conference on Social Enterprise

Semenas, V. (2014) "Ethnic Diversity and Social Capital at the Community Level: Effects and Implications for Policymakers", *Student Pulse*, 6(04).

Sen, A. (1970) *Collective Choice and Social Welfare*, San Francisco, Ca.

Sen, A. (1980). *Equality of what?* The Tanner lectures on human values, 1, 353-369.

Sen, A. (1981) *Poverty and Famines: An Essay on Entitlement and Deprivation*, Oxford.

Sen, A. (1985) *Commodities and Capabilities*, Amsterdam.

Sen, A (1999) *Development as Freedom*, Oxford.

Seth, A. and Ragab, A. (2012). *Macroeconomic Vulnerability in Developing Countries: Approaches and Issues*, IPC-IP Working Paper No 94, Brasilia, DF.

Shahine, S.H. (2011) "Youth and the revolution in Egypt", *Anthropology Today*, 27, 2, 1-3.

Sharma, K.B., Khandelwal, G.R. and Rathod, M.G. (2014) "Information Technology, Economy and Banking Sector" *IBMRD's Journal of Management & Research*, 3, 1, 116-124.

Sharma, P.; Basudeb, G-K and Dilli R.K. (2014) *Nepal Human Development Report 2014*, Kathmandu.

Shawki, N. (2011) "Organizational structure and strength and transnational campaign outcomes: a comparison of two transnational advocacy networks", *Global Networks*, 11, 1, 97-117.

Shushan, D. and Marcoux, C. (2011) "The rise (and decline?) of Arab aid: generosity and allocation in the oil era". *World Development*, 39, 11, 1969-1980.

Sikka, P. and Willmott, H. (2010). "The dark side of transfer pricing: Its role in tax avoidance and wealth retentiveness", *Critical Perspectives on Accounting*, 21(4), 342-356.

Singer M.M, Carlin, R.E. and Love, G.J. (2014) "Corruption in the Americas" in Elizabeth J. Zechmeister (ed.) *The Political Culture of Democracy in the Americas, 2014: Democratic Governance across 10 Years of the AmericasBarometer*, Nashville, Te.

Skully, D.W.(2001) "Liberalizing tariff-rate quotas", ERS/USDA *Agricultural Policy Reform in the WTO—The Road Ahead. Market and Trade*, Washington DC, 59-67.

Smith, A. (1776/2014) *The Wealth of Nations* (Reprinted in Shine Classics, 2014)

Smith, C. (1991) *The Emergence of Liberation Theology: Radical Religion and Social Movement Theory*, Chicago.

Snorrason, S.T. (2012) *Asymmetric economic integration: Size characteristics of economies, trade costs and welfare*, Berlin.

Snowdon, C. (2010) *The Spirit Level Delusion: Fact-Checking the Left's New Theory of Everything*, London.

Statistics South Africa (2012) *Census 2011*, Pretoria http://www.statssa.gov.za/publications/P03014/P030142011.pdf

Solomon, R. and Burnett, K (2014) *Pitcairn Island Economic Review*, January 2014

Stiglitz, J.E. (2000) "Capital Market Liberalization, Economic Growth, and Instability" ,*World Development*, 28, 6, 1075-1086.

Stiglitz, J.E. (2013), *The Price of Inequality. How Today's Divided Society Endangers Our Future,* New York.

Stonham, P. (1996) "Whatever happened at Barings? Part two: Unauthorised trading and the failure of controls", *European Management Journal* 14, 3, 269-278.

Strange, S. (1970) "International economics and international relations: a case of mutual neglect", *International Affairs* 46, 2, 304 - 315.

Strange, S. (1988) *States and Markets,* London.

Studenski, P. (1958), *The Income of Nations*, New York UP.

Sturgis, P. and Smith, P. (2010) "Assessing the Validity of Generalized Trust Questions: What Kind of Trust are we Measuring?", *International Journal of Public Opinion Research*, 22, 1, 74-92.

Stuvel, G. (1989) *The Index-number Problem and its Solution*, London.

Sutton, P. (2011) "The Concept of Small States in the International Economy", *The Round Table: Commonwealth Journal of International Affairs*, 100, 413, 141-153.

Sy, A. (2015) "Are African countries rebasing GDP in 2014 finding evidence of structural transformation?", Brookings, Africa in Focus, Blog 3.3.2015

Tabellini, G. (2008) "The Scope of Cooperation: values and incentives", *Quarterly Journal of Economics*, 123, 3, 905–50.

Tanzi, V. (1998). *Corruption Around the World: Causes, Consequences, Scope, and Cures*. IMF Working Paper, wp/98/63, New York.

Taylor, P.J. (2012) "Historical World City Networks" in B. Derudder, M. Hoyler, P.J. Taylor and F. Witlox (eds) *International Handbook of Globalization and World Cities*, Cheltenham, 9-21

Taylor, P.J., Ni, P., Derudder, B., Hoyler M., Huang, J., Witlox, F. (2011 ) *Global Urban Analysis: A Survey of Cities in Globalization*, London, Washington.

Teh, R. and Piermartini, R. (2005) *Demystifying Modelling Methods for Trade Policy*. WTO Discussion Paper No. 10, Geneva.

Temin, P. (1976) *Did Monetary Forces Cause the Great Depression?*, New York

Thomas, M.A. (2010) "What do the Worldwide Governance Indicators Measure?", *European Journal of Development Research*, 22, 1, 31-54.

Toye, R. (2003) "Developing Multilateralism: The Havana Charter and the Fight for the International Trade Organization, 1947–1948", *The International History Review*, 25, 2, 282-305.

Tremblay, M (2012) *The Health Systems of Small and Island States: Issues Overview*, Cincinnati.

Tweede Kamer der Staten-Generaal 2014-2015 (TKSW), 21 501-03Begrotingsraad, Lijst van vragen en antwoorden vastgesteld 11 november 2014.

Ugur, M. (2013) "Corruption's Direct Effects on Per-Capita Income Growth: A Meta-Analysis", *Journal of Economic Surveys*, 2013, 1-13.

UNDP (2015) *Human Development Report 2015: Work for Human Development*, New York.

UNDP (2013) *Human Development Report: Explanatory note on 2013 HDR composite indices: Nepal*, New York.

UNDP (2010) *Human Development Report: The Real Wealth of Nations: Pathways to Human Development*, New York.

UNDP (2011) *Human Development Report 2010*, New York.

UNHCR (2015) *Mid–year Trends, June 1950*, Geneva.

United Nations (2013) *The Millennium Development Goals Report*, New York.

UNSD United Nations Statistical Division (nd) *Review of Country Practices on rebasing and linking National Accounts series*, New York.

United Nations, Department of Economic and Social Affairs (2008). *World Economic and Social Survey. Overcoming Economic Insecurity*, New York.

UN, ESA, Population Division (2004) *World Population to 2300*, New York

UNCTAD, *World Investment Report*, Geneva.

Uslaner, E. M. (2008) "Where You Stand Depends Upon Where Your Grandparents Sat The Inheritability of Generalized Trust", *Public Opinion Quarterly*, 72, 4, 725-740.

Ulander, E.M. (2010) "Trust, Diversity and segregation" ,*Ethnicities*, 10, 4, 415-434.

Uslaner E.M. and Brown, M. (2005) "Inequality, Trust and Civic Engagement", *American Political Research*, 33, 6, 868-894.


Vanoli, A. (2005) *A History of National Accounting*, Amsterdam.

Veenendaal, W.P. and Corbett, J. (2015) "Why Small States Offer Important Answers to Large Questions", *Comparative Political Studies*, 48, 4, 527-549.

Vernon, R. (1974) "The location of economic activity" in J. H. Dunning (ed.) *Economic Analysis and the Multinational Enterprise*, London.

Vitali, S., Glattfelder, J.B. and Battiston, S (2011) "The Network of Global Corporate Control", *PloS one*, 6, 10, e25995.

Vujakovoc, P. (2009) *How to Measure Globalisation? A New Globalisation Index (NGI)* Österreichisches Institut für Wirtschaftsforschung Working Paper, 343/2009, Vienna.


Waever, O (1998) "The Sociology of a Not So International Discipline: American and European Developments in International Relations", *International Organization*, 52, 4, 687-727.

Waller, L (2006) *Irregular Migration to South Africa During the First Ten Years of Democracy*, Southern African Migration Project, Migration Policy Brief No. 19, Waterloon On, Canada.

Wang, L. and Gordon, P. (2011) "Trust and Institutions: A Multilevel Analysis", *The Journal of Socio-Economics*, 40, 5, 583–593.

Ward, M. (1975) "Dependent Development – problems of economic planning in small developing countries" in P. Selwyn (ed.), *Development Policy in Small Countries*, London, 115-133.

Watson, N., Younis, M. and Spratt, S. (2013) "What Next For the BRICS Bank?", *IDS, Rapid Response Briefing*, Issue 3, Brighton.

Wendt, A. (1992) "Anarchy is What States Make of It: the Social Construction of Power Politics", in *International Organization*, 46, 2, 391-425.

Whyte, M.K., Feng, W. and Cai, Y. (2015) "Challenging Myths About China's One-Child Policy", *The China Journal*, 74, 144-159.

Wilkinson, R. and Pickett, K. (2010) *The Spirit Level: Why Equality is Better for Everyone*, Harmondsworth.

Williams, A. and Siddique, A. (2008) "The use (and abuse) of governance indicators in economics: a review", *Economics of Governance*, 9, 2, 131-175.

Williams, M.C. (2004) "Why ideas matter in international relations: Hans Morgenthau, classical realism, and the moral construction of power politics", *International Organization*, 58, 4, 633-665.

Williamson, O. E. (2000) "The New Institutional Economics: Taking Stock, Looking Ahead", *Journal of Economic Literature*, 38, 3, 595-613.

Witte, E. and Van Velthoven, H. (1999) *Language and Politics: The Belgian case study in a historical perspective*, Amsterdam.

WFE (2014a) *2013 WFE Market Highlights* (28.1.2013) Paris.

WFE/IOMA (2014) *Derivatives Market Survey 2013*, Paris.

Woldendorp, J and Keman, H. (2007) "The Polder Model Reviewed: Dutch Corporatism 1965-2000", *Economic and Industrial Democracy*, 28, 3, 317-347.

Wolf, M. (2014) *The Shifts and the Shocks. What we've learned – and still have to learn – from the financial crisis*, New York.

Woods, N. (2008) "Whose aid? Whose influence? China, emerging donors and the silent revolution in development assistance", *International Affairs*, 84, 6, 1205-1221.

Woolcock, M. (2001) "The Place of Social Capital in Understanding Social and Economic Outcomes", *Canadian Journal of Policy Research*, 2, 1, 11-17.

Woolcock, M. (2010) "The Rise and Routinization of Social Capital, 1988-2008", Annual Review of Political Science, 13, 469-487.

World Bank (1989) *Sub-Saharan Africa. From Crisis to Sustainable Growth*, Washington DC

World Bank (1998) *Assessing aid: what works, what doesn't, and why.* Washington, DC

World Bank (2014) *Purchasing Power Parities and Real Expenditures of World Economies Summary of Results and Findings of the 2011 International Comparison Program*, Washington, DC

World Bank (2015) *Purchasing Power Parities and the Real Size of World Economies. A Comprehensive Report of the 2011 International Comparison Program*, Washington DC.

World Health Organization (2011). *Global Health and Ageing*, Geneva

WTO (2013) *International Trade Statistics 2012*, Geneva

Wright S. (2003) *Language Policy and Language Planning: from Nationalism to Globalisation*, Basingstoke.

Wu, H.X. (2000) "China's GDP level and growth performance: alternative estimates and the implications", *Review of Income and Wealth*, 46, 4, 475-499.

Zanden, J-L. van, Joerg, B., Marco, M.D.E., Auke, R. and Marcel, T. (eds.) (2014). *How Was Life? Global Well-being since 1820: Global Well-being since 1820*. Paris.

Zeiler, T.W. (1999) *Free Trade, Free World: The Advent of GATT,* Chapel Hill, NC.

Zhu, W.X., Lu, L. and Hesketh, T. (2009) "China's excess males, sex selective abortion, and one child policy: analysis of data from 2005 national intercensus survey", *British Medical Journal*, 338.

Ziliak, S.T. and McCloskey, D.N. (2004) "Size matters: the standard error of regressions in the American Economic Review", *Journal of Socio-Economics*, 33, 527-546.

Zmerli, S. and Newton, K. (2008) "Social Trust and Attitudes toward Democracy", *Public Opinion Quarterly*, 72, 4, 706-724.

## Online Sources

Recordings of Carmen Segarra
http://www.thisamericanlife.org/radio-archives/episode/536/the-secret-recordings-of-carmen-segarra#play

## Databases

ASEP/JDS Database
http://www.jdsurvey.net/jds/jdsurveyAnalisis.jsp?ES_COL=131&Idioma=I&SeccionCol=02
BIS Statistics
https://www.bis.org/statistics/
Brookings, Global Cities Database
http://www.brookings.edu/about/projects/global-cities
Eurobarometer
http://www.gesis.org/eurobarometer-data-service/data-access/
Gallup-Religiosity
http://www.gallup.com/poll/142727/religiosity-highest-world-poorest-nations.aspx
KOF index database
http://globalization.kof.ethz.ch/
OECD-WTO database

http://www.oecd.org/sti/ind/measuringtradeinvalue-addedanoecd-wtojointinitiative.htm

UN, DESA, Population Division, Database

http://esa.un.org/unpd/wpp/Excel-Data/population.htm

OECD, DAC Database

http://www.oecd.org/dac/stats/data.htm

UNCTAD data on FDI

http://unctad.org/en/Pages/Statistics.aspx

UNDP, DESA, Population Division, World Population Prospects. The 2015 Revision.

Http://eas.un.org/undp/wpp/DataQuery/

UNDP, Human Development Report

http://hdr.undp.org/en/data

World Bank Database, WGI

http://data.worldbank.org/data-catalog/worldwide-governance-indicators

World Bank Database, Gini

http://data.worldbank.org/indicator/SI.POV.GINI

World bank Group. Trading Across Borders

http://www.doingbusiness.org/data/exploretopics/trading-across-borders

WVS Database

http://www.worldvaluessurvey.org/WVSDocumentationWV6.jsp

# Index